Last Run of the Whisperer

A STORY OF A SOLDIER OF THE CONNECTICUT LINE

Calvin J. Boal

WestBow Press books may be ordered through booksellers or by contacting:

WestBow Press
A Division of Thomas Nelson
1663 Liberty Drive
Bloomington, IN 47403
www.westbowpress.com
1 (866) 928-1240

ISBN: 978-1-4497-1203-7 (sc)
ISBN: 978-1-4497-1202-0 (hc)
ISBN: 978-1-4497-1204-4 (e)

Library of Congress Control Number: 2011901252

Printed in the United States of America.

WestBow Press rev. date: 1/31/2014

DEDICATION

To all those who fought and sacrificed, beyond what will ever be known to bring this country into existence: to them belongs the glory and honor.

This book is also dedicated to the history of my family, the Fowlers, particularly Katherine Elizabeth Fowler Boal; my mother and father, Katherine Boal Nearing and Gene Nearing; and my family, Phyllis Reed Nearing, my daughters, Elizabeth Nearing, Rachel Nearing, Abigail Nearing and Brittany Nearing.

In Memory of:
Gene Richard Nearing

Born, June 17, 1929
Died, May 15, 2010

Special thanks to my longtime friend, for his time,
and imparting his knowledge to me,

Father Mark Cunningham
Saint Francis de Sales Roman Catholic Church
Herkimer, NY

Contents

FORWARD

The origins of this book can be traced back to the late 1970's and early 1980's when my grandmother, Katherine Elizabeth "Betty" Fowler Boal showed me documents that had been produced by her sister, Marian Fowler Moxley, regarding the beginnings of the genealogy of the Fowler family. Although the Fowler Family was the main branch of the genealogy tree, it contains numerous families that make up many smaller family branches on the genealogy chart. Years later, when I had the opportunity to spend extensive amounts of time gathering information from several internet sites regarding the Fowlers, I discovered many of these related families. Years later, after I had shown a genuine interest in my family history, and as my grandmother was drawing ever so close to the time of her passing, that she provided and entrusted me with the documents and books regarding the family tree of the Fowlers.

Additionally, two books had been written dating back to the seventh century, regarding the Fowlers and related families, which aided greatly in developing the genealogy information and confirming much of the information that was gathered through the internet.

The first of these two books was *The History of the Fowlers*, published in 1950, which chronicles the Fowler family back to the seventh century. Henry I, surnamed the Fowler, is believed to have been born about the year 876 A.D. The Franks and Saxons chose him King in 919, on the advice of King Conrad I. He died in 936. Henry the Fowler united the Franks and Saxons into what is now modern Germany. Some of his descendants were such renowned fighters, that the King of France offered them Normandy to live in if they would fight his battles. Later, some of these Fowler descendants helped William the Conqueror gain the throne of England. The Fowlers in England, accompanied by numerous bands of retainers and followers, went to England about a hundred years before the destruction of the Heptarch that resulted in the union of the kingdoms of England into one, under Egbert. The Fowlers settled in Sussex and according to this old chronicle, the Fowler family had never failed to have a representative member from the eighth century until the present time of writing. Documented in this book, *The History of the Fowlers*, are the names of a number of individuals whom the reader would undoubtedly recognize as historically significant. These individuals during their time helped shape the face of many countries, as well as countless names of men and women who, in their own way are responsible for this book. For it is through one of these countless undistinguished names, who fought for his country in the American Revolution, that this book is based upon.

The two of note, that we will mention here, are Sir Richard Fowler, who traveled during one of the Crusades with King Richard, The Lion Heart, King of England to the Holy Land and George Washington. The Fowler family was of great antiquity before the reign of King Richard I, when in that warlike prince's expedition to the Holy Land, Richard Fowler of Foxley, in the County of Bucks, served as a commanding officer in one of the holy crusades, circa 1190. Richard Fowler maintained at his own expense a certain number of British bowmen, all his own tenants to serve likewise in the crusade. At the siege of Ptolomais, also called Acon, the Muslims attempted to surprise the Christian camp with a night attack. Richard Fowler through his extraordinary care and vigilance happily prevented the Muslim attack. King Richard, his royal master, therefore in honor of such eminent service, knighted him in the field and caused his crest, which was the hand and lure, to be changed to the vigilant owl.

A second account related that an owl disturbed Richard Fowler in the night. Investigating, he found a sentry had been silently slain near the tent of the king. Richard Fowler aroused the camp in time to save the life of the king and to meet the surprise attack of the enemy.

The name had thus been carried down for countless generations to today and was the maiden name of my grandmother, Katherine Elizabeth Fowler Boal.

The other name that we will mention, as noted above, is George Washington. Farmer, soldier, patriot, Commander of the Continental army, first President of the United States and further described as the "Father of our Nation."

Although it is obvious that George Washington does not bear the name

Fowler, he is in fact, the descendent of the Fowlers. William Fowler (b. 1523) married Alice Stevens and bore several children; one is Alice Fowler (b. 1565). Alice Fowler married October 3, 1585 Robert Ball. Robert Ball and Alice Fowler had Richard Ball (b. 1586). Richard Ball had one son, Colonel William Ball, who married Hannah Atheral July 2, 1638 and had Colonel Joseph Ball (b. 1649). Colonel Joseph Ball married in 1707 Mary Johnson. Joseph Ball and Mary Johnson had a daughter named Mary Ball (b. 1708). Mary Ball married in 1731 Augustine Washington, and these were the mother and father of George Washington.

The second book of note and which helped confirm genealogy information, dates, places and names is *A Memoir of the Forebears and Descendants of Henry L. Fowler and Emma L. Minkler*, published in 1987. Again, this book provided invaluable information in completing the detailed information in the genealogical papers.

That there are, in addition to the two individuals noted above in the genealogical information of the Fowlers and related families, a large number of documented relatives who fought in the numerous wars that this land has seen since the Europeans began immigrating to it. These wars in the New England area included King Philip's War, the Pequot War, Queen Anne's War and the numerous French and Indian wars from the early 1700's to 1755. In 1755, George Washington, in a glen in western Pennsylvania, by having his Virginia militiamen and Indian allies' fire upon French emissary, Ensign Joseph de Jumonville and his soldiers, started what is commonly referred to as "The French and Indian War," which was waged on the North American continent from 1755 to 1763. After this war's conclusion a period of discontent began to develop between the American colonies and England, the motherland. This book will focus on the exploits, triumphs, losses, defeats and eventually contented life of one of these men who fought in the American Revolution.

As part of my genealogical work, I sent several inquiries to the National Archives in Washington, D.C., regarding the records of these individuals who fought in the American Revolution. I was impressed upon reviewing the record of one William Waterman, who in 1832 petitioned the United Stated Congress for monies due him for said service. That he survived his numerous battles, wounds and capture are nothing short of remarkable. That his story is just one of the countless stories of the soldiers who fought in the Continental army, as well as the militias, who comprised the backbone of the colonial army and the cause, cannot be understated.

For countless books detailing similar actions of the American soldier could be told, but this book deals with this one man who dedicated himself above family, and loved ones to help forge what would become the United States of America.

Fowler genealogy to G. Washington

William Fowler of Stonehouse, England (b. 1523) married Alice Stevens and had a daughter Alice Fowler (b. 1565).

Alice Fowler (b. 1565) married Robert Ball October 3, 1585. Their son, Richard Ball (b. 1586) came to Virginia on the *George* in 1617.

Richard Ball had one son, Colonel William Ball.

Colonel William Ball married in London, July 2, 1638, Hannah Atheral and had Colonel Joseph Ball (b. 1649).

Colonel Joseph Ball married in 1707, Mary Johnson and had Mary Ball (b. 1708).

Mary Ball (b. 1708) married in 1731, Augustine Washington and had George Washington (b. 1732).

- CHAPTER 1 -

"The Encounter"

Summer 1772

The deciduous forests of the North American continent were, as always, an imposing and at times, a fearful place to be. It is indisputable that various natives and tribes had inhabited these very forests for countless generations. These natives, or Indians, as they came to be called by most of the white newcomers, had mastered these forests, and thus learned to live within, and even prosper in them. This was difficult for most of the newcomers to begin to understand. For these newcomers, the whites, these forests were foreboding, even a mystery, and became what seemed to be an inexhaustible resource to be exploited for the ever-growing appetite of a new nation, as well as the mother nations in Europe. Equally indisputable is the fact that these various groups of natives had for generations, and at various periods of time in their histories, been at war with each other in attempts to gain and claim lands, as well as captives who were added into the conquering tribe. The savagery with which these natives and tribes waged war on each other was unknown to the white newcomers, and thus was both repulsive and incomprehensible, leading the whites to now call these natives, savages. Similarly, it should be noted that as the two races had ever-increasing contact with each other, that conflict inevitably began between the races. Each engaged in equally barbaric practices of death and torture upon the other, leading to generations of warfare, so that each race would invariably never trust the other. This warfare would continue until one race had, in effect, conquered the other.

It is here that we now find our travelers in the northern reaches of what was then one of the frontiers of North America. It is several years after the conclusion of one of the many wars between the natives of the country and the white newcomers, as to who would be masters of this land.

We had traveled all that morning and part of that afternoon on horseback in what was a bright, clear day, as when the trees parted sufficiently, I could see the clear blue sky. The trail we were traveling down, which was barely a path wide enough for a man or his animal to traverse without bumping into trees on either side, ran next to a large, clear stream. We were almost to the spot where the stream emptied into the Connecticut River when the Calkin brothers, Joshua and Hiram, who were in front of me, stopped. All was quiet, and I looked around nervously, wondering what would cause my Da, who was leading our group, to stop so suddenly on a rise overlooking the river. Da was at the head our group, followed by the Calkin brothers, with me in the middle. John Edgerington followed me, with Eli and Master Bingham bringing up the rear. After a minute of nervous waiting, Master Bingham passed me on foot as he walked in a crouching manner, with his gun at the ready, telling each man in line he passed to dismount, to remain where he was and not to make a sound. As I dismounted, I looked around nervously. I wanted to check my powder, as I glanced down at my flash pan. I nuzzled my horse to keep him quiet and waited for word.

It was a few minutes later when Master Bingham came back, leading horses and pack animals, followed by the Calkin brothers. He motioned for me to follow, as well as John Edgerington and Eli, as we passed them. We moved silently down the trail to a glade about a quarter-mile back. I could see the strain on Master Bingham's face, as I began to realize that serious matters were afoot. Once in the glade, Master Bingham spoke in low tones, making no pretense of the seriousness of the moment.

"Hiram, you are to stay with the horses. If shooting starts, remain here with the horses, and wait for Eli to come to you. The rest of you leave everything here, except your shot and powder, and follow me at 20 pace intervals," he said.

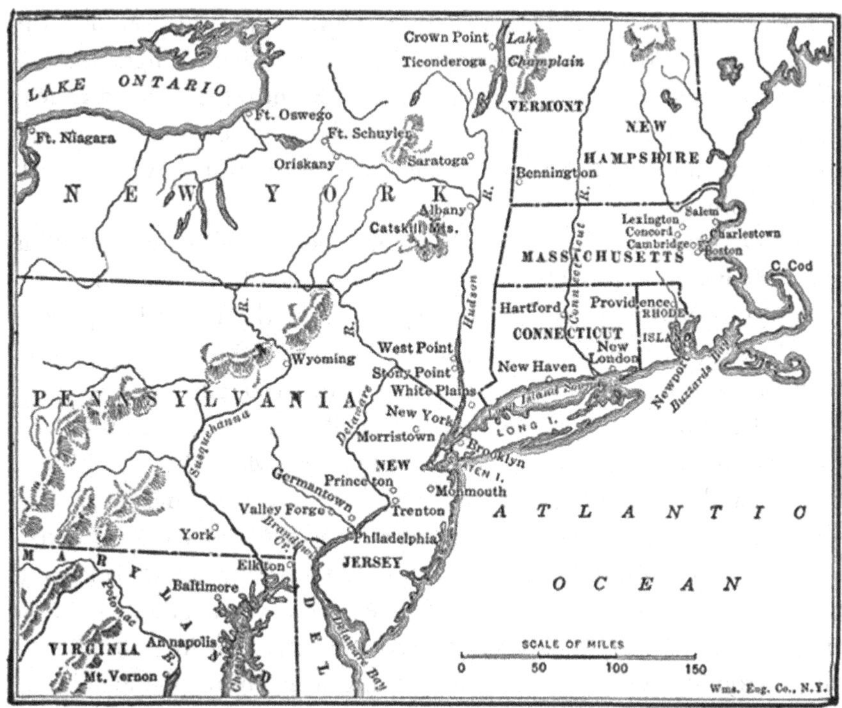

I felt myself begin to tense up as I looked around at the others, as I could see the concern on their faces now. I imagined I looked the same. Master Bingham led out, and we all followed as he had said, without a word. As we retraced our steps, and came up over the rise as it turned to the right, I could see my father bent over the trail studying something. Master Bingham motioned for us to wait where we were as he met with father again. I was the first in line, and could hear the two talking in low tones. I had chills going up my spine as I looked around. I then looked down at my flash pan again. When was the last time I had really checked it? Was there powder there, and was it dry? I couldn't remember. Father motioned for us to move forward. As we gathered around where father and Master Bingham were, father appeared as serious as I ever saw him, as his face was drained of color, looking a strange shade of gray.

Father spoke to all of us in low tones. "We've cut a trail of Injuns here and they appear to be moving fast, with a couple of horses. It looks to John," this was Master Bingham's name, "and me that it is a party of Huron warriors. Why they are here or what they are doing I can't say, but it can't be good," said Da. "Bingham is going to go back up, their trail, while I'll go down the trail to see what they are about. If there is any shooting, go back to Hiram, get the horses and pack animals, circle around to the west a mile or two and come down to the river below us. Bingham and I will do the same, and we'll meet up there. In the meantime," Da directed, "go back down our trail twenty yards. Spread out on either side, with five paces between you, and for God's sake, don't say anything. We'll be back in a few minutes."

As Da turned to go, Master Bingham spoke to all of us under his breath, "Check your powder, but by God, don't go off half cocked."

Da and Master Bingham disappeared into the forest in opposite directions like they were ghosts, and without a sound from either. As we made our way back to the area Da suggested, I thought about the trail we cut. I couldn't see anything that indicated men had crossed that way. There was hardly a depression in the forest ground where they had passed. How Da and Master Bingham could tell about how many men, as well as horses had passed, in the few minutes they were there was a mystery to me.

The wait for Da and Master Bingham to return seemed to be forever, as mere minutes seemed to be hours. While they were gone, I did as Master Bingham suggested and checked, then double-checked my powder. As I looked around I could hear myself breathing, as my heart pounded in my chest. I thought if there were any Indians near, they'd know right where I was. I looked for the others hiding in the bushes with me, on either side of the trail. I could see the strain we were all under, along and their nervous looks in every direction.

I had been coming to the Green Mountains with my Da for three years. We would come for a month of hunting to supply our family with meat for the winter. We would also gather furs to ship to Boston, which we would sell to the tanner, who would, in return, give us the money we needed to purchase supplies for the farm. Each spring after the crops were in, Da and I, along with several other leading families from the town of Norwich, Connecticut colony, traveled to this valley in the Green Mountains, and by Da's own words, it was, "The most beautiful place I have ever seen." I had to agree, although at the time I had not seen near the amount of country that Da had.

I don't know how many times Da came to this place, but I heard him and Master Bingham, as well as others who had fought with Da, talk many a night after dinner about this valley. As we sat around the fire, as they smoked tobacco, or drank rum, they would recount tales from years earlier during the French and Indian War, when they were in a company of rangers in Rogers Rangers. Da always said they had come across the valley after running from Indians, by their own accounts, days after the great St. Francis Raid. The valley had a stream that ran through it that was the clearest I had ever seen. The high mountain valley was wide and lush with thick vegetation and bountiful game. Da would tell me that a day's march to the west was a stone fort, larger by far, than any other fort in all of the English colonies. To the north, two days' journey was the land of the French, along with their despised Indian allies, the Abenaki, Ottawa, Huron, and many other tribes. Da said those lands were the battlegrounds where the English and French had fought much of the war, which at great cost in both men and supplies, was eventually won by the English.

There were seven of us on this trip. I was the youngest, as I had turned fifteen years old this past spring. Our group consisted of Da and me, the Calkin brothers, Joshua and Hiram, who were in their early twenties, John Edgerington, and Master Bingham along with his son, Eli. Eli Bingham, who was my best friend, being older than I was by a year and a half. He was tall and thin for his age, as I was of average size in every respect. This trip was the best I had been on, with warm days and cool nights. The game we hunted was bountiful. We had hunted each day for deer and bear, along with running a line of traps to gather the beaver from the valley streams.

The first week had seen us almost reach our fill, as the amount of meat and furs gathered would almost fill our pack animals. The second week was spent shooting game if we thought we needed it, but more time was spent exploring up the valley. The nights were filled with smoking the meat, preparing the hides for the return trip, and listening to Da and Master Bingham tell stories of the war. Their stories were so real and believable that the hair on the back of my neck would stand on end. At times, I found myself staring out into the dark night, wondering if these same savages that Da had fought were watching us right now, waiting for their chance to spring upon us, and sink their tomahawks in our brains. They would scalp us as a trophy of their conquest to show off to their warriors and family in a distant Indian village. Then they would leave our dead bodies for the wolves to tear apart, with our bones bleaching white in the sun.

As Da and Mr. Bingham talked, they would stare into the fire, with a faraway look that took them back to those desperate and bloody days. Da never said as much, but I knew that he and Master Bingham had lost a number of good friends during the bloody conflict, and that Da felt lucky to be alive. There was more than one night I found myself unable to sleep after listening to tales of warring parties of rangers or Indians doing their worst to each other in the lands just over the mountains from where I lay. I would stare late into the night as I lay in my bedding, looking up at the countless stars, with the cool mountain breezes blowing on my face. Often I could hear a lonely wolf calling to the moon, on a distant mountain. I would eventually drift off to sleep, waking the next morning to our mountain paradise, to my favorite smell of fresh meat being cooked over the fire. Master Bingham was a most excellent cook.

The trip was always arduous, beginning with the planning and packing, which usually consumed parts of the months leading up to the trip. Once the date of departure was set, nothing could move the date, as all had to be made ready. Supplies of food were gathered, and horses and pack animals assembled. Equipment would be checked and doubled checked. Our weapons, ball and powder, gathered and stored to protect them from the weather. Da would always say the most important thing was to be able to keep the powder dry, no matter what else happened. Our route of travel was planned that led west by north from Norwich to the town of Hartford. From Hartford we followed the paths and roads along the Connecticut River, north into Massachusetts colony, past Springfield and Deerfield, and still farther north into the Green Mountains.

All of the first week was spent getting to the Green Mountains and our valley, staying at night along the river outside of the small villages or towns we passed. As we traveled it was always in single file on our horses with the pack animals trailing behind on tethers, with at least 20 paces between each of us in case of attack. No one spoke unless Da or Master Bingham spoke first. Da and Master Bingham always insisted on this, saying you never knew when Injuns or robbers were afoot. I think it made them feel safer after all the raids they had been on with the rangers. It had become their second nature. When Da and Master Bingham came to the ruins of old Fort Number Four, they knew to leave the river and head northwest into the Green Mountains. It was here, from the west and north that a large, clear stream emptied into the Connecticut River.

The remains of Fort Number Four, from the French and Indian War, had become their rescue from the infamous ranger's raid on the Saint Francis Indian village in 1760. This was the infamous raid that destroyed the Indian village that was the launching point of the French and Indians for many raids into the English colonies of New Hampshire, Massachusetts, Connecticut and New York. It had been hailed by many as the greatest victory of the rangers during the war. It also was the most costly; as it had almost destroyed the Rangers during their escape back to the colonies.

The ranger's route for the attack was to travel the length of Lake Champlain from the fort at Crown Point, by whale boat to its northern reaches, then to march across the great swamp, and finally down the Saint Francis River to the village of the same name. The rangers learned during their march, that their boats in Missisquoi Bay at the northern end of Lake Champlain had been discovered by French scouts, causing the unit of rangers' great distress.

Alerted to this information by Mohican Indians left to guard his boats, Major Rogers was forced to change the return route of travel. Major Rogers determined to return by way of the Saint Francis River, then southeast, overland to Lake Memphremagog. Once across Lake Memphremagog, the rangers would cross the Green Mountains at their northern reaches, to the Connecticut River. Major Rogers and the rangers would then travel down the Connecticut River to Fort Wentworth, located at the mouth of the Upper Ammonoosuc River, and safety. During the retreat, Da and Master Bingham spoke many times of the hardships endured by the rangers. Of constant harassing and attacks by patrols of French regulars, Indians and Coeur de Bois, or the bush loppers, who were the French equal to the rangers.

That Major Rogers agonized over the decision to split the ranger force to elude the enemy once across Lake Memphremagog, in an effort to have as many rangers as possible reach Fort Wentworth. Of the rangers food supplies being exhausted. That many rangers resorted to eating tree bark and roots to survive. Many rangers saw their comrades captured, and then tortured and killed at the hands of Abenaki, Ottawa, and Huron warriors. They were massacred without mercy. Then the Indians chopped off the heads of dead rangers and kicked the heads like balls in an act of a twisted kid's game.

When surviving rangers arrived at Fort Wentworth, at the confluence of the Connecticut and Upper Ammonoosuc Rivers, they found it abandoned and in disrepair. The surviving rangers still faced the possibility of capture, torture and death at the hands of their ever pursuing enemies. Major Rogers continued down the Connecticut River with a hand full of rangers to Fort Number Four. Once there, Major Rogers sent supplies back up the river to Fort Wentworth to save what remained of the starving men of his command.

When Da and Master Bingham spoke of the raid and retreat to Fort Number Four; it still brought tears to their eyes. Their voices would trail off as they remembered more than a handful of men that were their friends, who met their tortured fate and death in such a horrific manner. Da did state for a fact that over two hundred Indians and French were killed in the attack on St Francis. Da never spoke of the rangers' losses, but I've heard of numbers ranging from a hand full of dead and wounded, to over one hundred of the roughly two hundred and twenty rangers, along with their Indian allies, never returned. Based upon what Da and Master Bingham recounted of the battle, followed by the forced march to Forts Wentworth and Number Four, I always felt the actual losses by the rangers had to be closer to the higher number, than the lower one.

The two weeks in the valley came to an end all too soon. Eli and I spent our days hunting and exploring up the valley further than we had ever gone before. They were days that I would always remember, and they were memories that drew me to the valley in my later years. At camp at night, around the fires, Eli and I would tell Da, Master Bingham, as well as the others about how far we traveled into the mountain valley. Recounting, that we had reached the summit of a mountain that seemed to be the highest, and as far as the eye could see, where mountains in every direction.

Finally, with enough meat and furs to load down our pack animals, it was time to depart the valley and retrace our route home. The good mood everyone had expressed this morning over breakfast, had suddenly changed to one of deep concern, as our progress toward home was suddenly halted by what Da discovered ahead on our trail.

Suddenly, as ghostly as Da and Master Bingham disappeared, they reappeared. First Da reappeared, and a few moments later, Master Bingham. They came through the woods and down our trail walking hunched over, guns at the ready, looking right and left, for any sign that our presence had been betrayed to our unseen enemy. When we were all gathered together, save Hiram Calkin, who remained with the animals, Da asked Master Bingham what he had learned. Master Bingham was as serious as a man on the gallows about to be hanged when he related what he had learned.

"The trail goes on for a quarter-mile before it disappears into the forest," he began. "It appears they were moving fast and not worried about leaving sign." As Master Bingham continued he looked over his left shoulder. "They came by early this morning. I'd say eight or nine in the party," he concluded.

"It is as I thought," Da picked up the conversation. "The Injuns aren't, but a mile ahead, along the river waiting I would reckon."

"Waiting for what?" whispered John Edgerington in response.

"Someone must be coming down the river," stated Da. "As I headed down the trail, I could smell smoke, midday meal likely. I saw three Hurons wade the river to an island yonder. I reckon it's an ambush. Those Injuns figure whoever it is coming down the river will take the wide channel between this side and the island. When they get in between them, they'll open up," Da concluded.

"How many you figure?" asked Master Bingham.

"I figure you're about right, John, maybe eight or nine. They don't know we're here, and they aren't looking behind them for us either. There must be another hunting party coming down river, around the bend still I'm thinking," Da stated in a whisper.

"What do you propose Will?" asked John Edgerington.

Da looked around the group slowly. Master Bingham was the only other one here that had fought Indians, or had ever fired a gun in anger at another man. He was the only one Da knew he could count on. Da knew what to do and laid out a plan.

First, Eli Bingham was to go to Hiram Calkin with the horses and start circling about a mile out in the woods to the west, eventually turning south by east, and heading downstream and towards the river. Once they came to the river, they were to cross, and wait on the east side for us. Da, Master Bingham, Joshua Calkin, John Edgerington, along with myself were to circle to the north behind the remaining Indians on the west side of the river. Da's plan was for us to spring our attack on the Indians, before they did the same on the poor souls coming down river. Once we had fired two shots, Da would take Joshua Calkin with him, circle again to the north to make contact with the party of hunters coming down stream.

At the same time, Master Bingham would lead John Edgerington and me in a circle to the south, crossing the river, to find Hiram Calkin and Eli Bingham. Da proposed that once he made contact with the hunting party, they'd make their way to the east side of the river, and then meet up with us down stream. Before we left, we checked our guns again. Da looked at each one of us with a look of assurance. Da lingered as his gaze reached me, and it was as if he knew I wasn't sure everything would be all right. Everyone knew not to speak unless spoken to, and then only in the lowest of tones.

We traveled for twenty minutes, at the most painfully slow pace, in single file through the woods, until Da stopped suddenly. We were on a small rise about 50 yards from the river's edge. From this spot, we could see up the river to the bend, and also into the forest in front of us to the river's edge. If there were Indians in front of us, I couldn't tell. Da spread us out in a line, along the top of the rise, about ten paces apart. Master Bingham anchored our right side followed by John Edgerington. I was in the middle. To my left was Joshua Calkin, with Da still farther to the left of him. As Da came by, he spoke to each of us about our final instructions. As he came up behind me, he put his hand on my shoulder. He only did that when he wanted me to pay particular attention.

"Will," he whispered, "when I see the hunters in their canoes come around the bend, I'm going to start to ease forward, about twenty yards. When you see Joshua move you do the same, and move from tree to tree, real slow. I figure the Injuns are just inside the tree line among the thickets along the river. When the canoes are a couple hundred yards upstream from us, I am going to open up. You do the same whether you see anything or not. Fire two shots and leave with Bingham," he said. I couldn't speak if I wanted to in response. My mouth was dry as a desert. He squeezed my shoulder and was gone.

I knew I was a better than average shot, and I had hunted with Da for years, but I had never shot at another man before, Injun or not. My heart raced and I felt hot. I could feel the sweat building under my tricorn hat and my hands were clammy. As I waited by a tree, I could not believe that there were Indians in front of me. Everything seemed most peaceful as the warm sun shone through the upper reaches of the trees, as the birds were chirping with a light breeze that rustled the leaves. As I waited, I saw the first canoe come around the bend. Then a second canoe came into view, and third in succession. There must be seven or eight men in those canoes, heading to Deerfield or Hartford to sell their furs. I waited as they approached from upstream ever so slowly. They mostly appeared to be floating with the current, although I could see the paddles from time to time gleam from the sun, as they were dipped into the river to pull a stroke.

It appeared that they would take the wider channel toward our side of the river. The Indians had set a perfect ambush. I couldn't see Indians in front of me or on the island, just a hundred yards away, but sure as the sun rose this morning, Da said they were there. I saw Joshua Calkin begin to move cautiously forward, and I did the same. I moved from tree to tree for about twenty yards, as quietly as I could. Looking to my right, I saw John Edgerington doing the same. With each step, I made sure that I wasn't stepping on a dry twig or branch. Surely, the sound of the snap of a twig would carry to the Indians in front of us, thus alerting them of our presence. I was now kneeling, and leaning against one of the giants of this forest, a large oak tree some six feet around, that stretched one hundred feet toward the sky. Its canopy provided shade from the overhead sun for thirty feet in every direction. As I looked back upstream, the canoes were much closer now, as I could see the white men in them. They appeared to be wearing buckskins, with their canoes loaded with furs. Were the Hurons bent on killing the white men, or stealing their furs? We would never know.

The first shot startled me so, that I almost jumped up from the tree I was leaning against. The next thing I knew I had fired my first shot at my unseen foe, and was trying to reload. My hand was shaking so, that as I removed the cap from my powder horn and tried to pour the proper amount into the end of my gun, I spilled more than I was able to get into my gun. I wanted to look around but couldn't. I was afraid I might see a war painted Indian approaching me to sink his tomahawk in my brains. Or that John Edgerington and Master Bingham had already fired their second shot, and were leaving without me. I put a ball in the end of my gun with some wadding and rammed it home. With my gun finally loaded the second time, I powdered my flash pan, cocked my hammer, and put the gun to my shoulder. As I looked up, I fired my second shot, at my still unseen enemy.

I looked to my right to see if John Edgerington was still there. He was looking my way as if to say, "Hurry up, let's go." I crouched down and made my way to him. Then together, we headed to where we knew Master Bingham would be. As we approached Master Bingham, he made eye contact with us and turned to go without saying a word. Running in a crouch, we made our way initially deeper into the forest, and then began bending to our left. As we ran up a small gully, I could still hear shots being fired behind us in the area we had just left, where Da and Joshua Calkin would still be.

As I followed John Edgerington through the woods, I would catch a glimpse of Master Bingham. He seemed confident and assured of what he was doing as he led us, to what I hoped was a river crossing and safety. As we moved, I also took notice that Master Bingham was reloading his rifle. First, he moved his powder horn to his mouth to remove the cap with his teeth, and poured an amount in the rifle. Replacing the cap to the powder horn, he just let it fall to his side. Immediately his hand reached in his possible bag, pulling out some wadding and a ball. Placing the ball and wadding in the end of his rifle, he reached for his ramrod and was ramming it home as we continued our run for the river. I thought to myself that it must have taken him years of practice to accomplish such a maneuver while at almost a full run. Something he mastered with the rangers, I concluded in my mind. I knew I couldn't attempt such a reload of my rifle. It seemed we had been running much longer than was necessary, when finally, Master Bingham slowed his pace. A few minutes later we were at the river. As we crouched along the bank in a thicket to conceal our presence, Master Bingham knew exactly what to do.

"I'll wait and cover your crossing from here," he said. "Once you are across, I'll begin coming myself. For God's sake, keep your powder dry and reload as soon as you reach the other side. If something should happen to me, find Hiram and Eli, and then head for Deerfield. Don't worry about your Dad and Joshua, if they're alive, they'll find you," he stated in a hushed whisper.

As I turned to enter the river, Master Bingham turned to face the woods in a defensive position in a thicket next to a rather large log, to detect any approach of our still unseen foe. The river crossing proved uneventful. The water was only waist high at the deepest point, and we held our guns and powder well above our heads to prevent any chance of them getting wet. Once across, Master Bingham wasted little time before entering the river and reaching us on the east side. Since our initial shots, and those that followed as we were running through the forest, I hadn't heard anything. I didn't know exactly what I had expected to hear, but as I hid on the east side of the river, waiting on Master Bingham, I thought we'd hear additional shots or war cries of Indians. Nothing came.

Once across the river, Master Bingham checked his rifle to make sure his powder was dry. With that done, he looked at John Edgerington and me, asking, "Are you two alright?"

"I'm a little scared, sir," I replied sheepishly, as I looked down.

"Good," he answered in a low tone, "you should be, and you John, are you alright?" he asked, directing his attention to John Edgerington.

"I'm fine, sir," John responded.

"Alright then, make sure your reloads are good and your powder is dry, and we'll head downstream to find Eli and Hiram. Don't make a sound unless I talk to you first and keep your distance," he stated as he turned to go.

With that, we were off, heading downstream, running in a low half crouch again to avoid detection by any enemy in the area, I supposed. We moved at a slow steady pace for the space of half an hour, when without warning Master Bingham and John Edgerington stopped. I rested on one knee near some small shrubs, with my gun to the ready, with my finger outside of the trigger guard, and waited. After a minute of silent waiting, Master Bingham whistled lowly, twice, waited a few seconds and repeated the whistle. The reply was one whistle. Master Bingham stood to his feet and walked ahead. About thirty feet away, in a small clearing where Eli and Hiram with our horses and pack animals.

After a short greeting by all, Master Bingham suggested we move south along the river for the space of another half-hour, before we made camp. We moved silently through the woods again. We started out walking instead of the steady, slow run this time, each mulling over in his mind the events of the afternoon. Finally, we reached an open area where a small creek emptied into the river from the east. There was ample feed for the animals, and cover for us in the surrounding thickets. As we began to make camp, my thoughts were with Da and Joshua Calkin. I wondered if they were alive. It had been several hours now since we had come across the Indian trail, and had broken their ambush. As darkness began to close in on us, I realized that I hadn't eaten since we broke our morning camp many hours earlier, and Master Bingham had a stew cooking over a small fire.

It was a restless night of sleep. I tossed and turned all night, waking to the slightest sounds. Not knowing where my father was, or whether he was alive or not, was too much for me. I was up before the sun, only to find Master Bingham sitting against a log keeping watch. I sat beside him, and asked him if he had been up all night.

"Not all night," he replied, "but most of it."

I wanted to ask him about my father, but said nothing. It was as though he was reading my thoughts when he spoke.

"Your pa will be alright, you know. We were in much tighter spots than this little scrap with Rogers and his rangers, more times than I can count. You wait and, see, he'll be here," he said confidently.

I just sat there as the eastern sky began to show the signs of the coming sun, and the new day. I didn't know what to say. I wish I were as confident that my Da would return, as Master Bingham seemed. I waited quietly for what seemed an eternity, and then I went to the fire pit to see if there were any embers to start a fire for breakfast. There was something about a full stomach in the morning. As we were cleaning up afterwards, a call came from up the river.

"Hello the camp?" the voice called.

"It's Da," I said, and began a sprint for the river's edge followed by the rest of the camp. Coming around the last bend, just up the river were three canoes. Da was sitting in the middle of the lead one, among the furs. As the canoes pulled up along the edge of the river by our camp, Da sprang out of the boat. I never saw Da grin so much as when he saw me. Da and the men were ashore in a few minutes. There were handshakes, accompanied by slaps on the backs of everyone all around. We all sat around talking for some time as Da and the new men recounted what happened after Master Bingham, John Edgerington, and I had left the rise of land overlooking the river. Da told me later, when we were alone, that he didn't know what he'd tell ma, if something had happened to me.

I was mesmerized by the story Da related regarding the events. Da said that as with all plans, things didn't go exactly as expected. Da said he saw an Injun moving through the woods, a little to the right of his position. Da said he had to shoot earlier than he wanted to, but that he was sure he had hit the Injun. What the Injun was doing Da couldn't say, but he thought the Injun might be moving to get a better advantage to shoot on the unsuspecting white men. Da said that after the initial shooting, he could hear the remaining Injuns moving northwest through the woods in an effort to make their escape.

Da checked the area of where he had seen the Injun he shot at, and found a blood trail leading off to the northwest, and had followed it a short distance. Da thought the Injun would survive his wound. After that, Da and Joshua Calkin had made their way to the river's edge, and hailed the white men in the canoes, who were making a hasty retreat to the east side of the river. Da and Joshua later crossed the river, and met up with the men they had helped save. Once Da and Joshua explained the circumstances of the shooting across the river, and the ambush the Injuns had in store for the men, Da and Joshua were welcomed by the men as their saviors, at least for that day. Da and Joshua, along with their newfound friends had traveled the rest of the day until sundown. They had made their camp a couple of miles above us. At sun up they headed down river to find us.

Da had introduced the men to us as two families from Hartford Township, who like us had a valley up the Connecticut River where they hunted and trapped furs for their families. Da introduced this party of hunters as Ashbel Fox and his two sons, Ashbel the younger, and John; along with Moses Peake, with his three sons, Asa, Josiah, and Ezekiel. Lifelong friends were immediately made due to our skirmish, and I began to understand the bond that existed between my Da and Master Bingham, from their years of such battles during the French and Indian War. Come hell or high water, it was a bond that could not be broken by war or blood. As it turned out, Da, Master Bingham and Master Fox had briefly known each other during the French and Indian War, as Master Fox had served for a short time in a different unit with Rogers Rangers, and had been on the St. Francis Raid. Finally, before we began breakfast, Da asked all to bend their knee as he gave thanks to our great God, Jehovah, for His protection being upon us the previous day. All seemed right in the world for me.

Following breakfast, both parties agreed to travel together down the Connecticut River, for mutual protection. Our party remained close to the riverbank as we went, and the Fox and Peake party moved slowly down the river in their canoes, always keeping closer to the east side where the river permitted. At Deerfield, one of Peake's sons had mentioned the attempted Injun ambush at a local tavern, and our rescue. Word of the event spread like wildfire throughout the Connecticut and Massachusetts colonies. It took several days of uneventful travel past Deerfield and Springfield in the Massachusetts colony, to reach the town of Hartford, and our departure to Norwich. There were handshakes and hugs for our friends as we parted ways.

"Godspeed to you all," was Master Fox's farewell to us.

As we headed down the trail that led southeast toward Norwich, I looked back over my shoulder as we entered the woods, and to my surprise the Fox party was all still there, watching us go. I waved my last goodbye as we disappeared into the woods.

The following March, the post rider between Boston and New York brought news that the regulars had fired on a mob of Boston citizens who had cornered a patrol of British regulars. The Boston citizens had been taunting and threatening the soldiers. Da was deeply disturbed by the news, and the elders of the town met to discuss the events in Boston. This was the first time I heard of the dark clouds that were gathering between the Crown and her colonies.

- CHAPTER 2 -

"Home and Unrest"

1773

The year following our encounter with the Indians was quiet and as peaceful as any I had ever known. Life around the farm and Norwich seemed to go on as normal. By early spring we had tilled the soil, and our crops were planted. I attended the local schoolhouse, which doubled for the meetinghouse on the Sabbath. Each Sunday, Pastor Gallagher would bring forth the Lord's Word to us, and like all of my family, I believed firmly in the Christian faith. I believed that there was a Creator, a God, Jehovah, as Pastor Gallagher called Him, who made all, and loved all mankind. I gave my heart and my life to my God one Sunday after church, with Pastor Gallagher leading my conversion and commitment.

Although I was only an average student at my studies, I continued to grow and learn about farming and our religion. Who could have foreseen the dark events just over the horizon that would shake our world, and my family to its very foundation?

There were many short hunting trips with Da to the neighboring woods and mountains. Almost all were successful, as Da and I would return home to mother, my younger brother, John, and Rachel, my sister, with game to eat. During these hunting trips, I talked with Da about teaching me the things he had learned as a ranger during the French and Indian War. I had told Da about that day when we had shot at the Indians along the Connecticut River, and how Master Bingham could reload while running. I told Da that I wanted to learn all that he knew about how to read sign.

Da showed me how to march through the woods when you traveled with a large group of rangers, as well as the best places to make camp. I asked Da how to set an ambush, and how to retreat from an engagement. Most important of all, Da showed me how to reload while running through the woods or even while on horseback. I was a fast learner of all Da taught me. After several of our trips to the woods, I could read sign almost as well as Da. I could walk through the woods and not make a noise. I knew where and when to make camp. I knew how to set an ambush, and retreat to a safe location, and most important of all, I could reload my gun while running at almost a full gate, and do it while keeping pace with my Da.

"How did the rangers get their name?" I asked Da one day.

"Will, back in those days, the men who made up the rangers, before they were actually called rangers, would travel from town to town, or from town to fort, making sure the countryside and towns were safe. It was said that these men ranged from place to place, giving them the name 'Rangers'," Da responded. "I guess with the coming of war between England and France and their Indian allies, the name stuck," he added. "I figure Major Rogers liked it and used it for the units under his command during the war. There was a woodsman, Will, and you would have liked Major Rogers. He could read the sign a beaver left on a pond if he had a mind to," Da stated.

"What happened to him, Da?" I inquired.

"Last I heard, son, was that after the war he moved on out west, past the frontier, looking for the route to the Pacific Ocean or some other crazy thing. If it's there, he'll find it," Da concluded.

One day when returning from a late summer trip to the local mountains, Da, stated without breaking stride, "You know all that I know, Will, you'll have to grow on your own from now on," as he kept on walking down the hill.

I ran after Da, and when I caught up to him, I said, "Da, what is it like to shoot a man?"

Da stopped walking and looked at me for what seemed several minutes, but was only a few seconds. "Will," he said as he hesitated, "shooting a man, white or Injun will be the hardest thing you probably will ever do. We are all God's creation, and to take a life is not the same as killing a deer for food. Always remember that, Will, and only kill when and if you have to." Having said that, Da continued to walk home and not another word was said between us on that subject.

The seasons came and went without any further incidents that involved anything to do with Indian raids from the north. Each year we planted our crops in the spring, and each year in the summer we traveled to the valley in the Green Mountains to hunt and trap. I never forgot the summer of '72 when we encountered the Indians, and whenever we passed the area of the ambush, we would stop and look up the river, recounting the events that bound us together. As I look back, I think it was the beginning of my change from boyhood to manhood. Each fall we would harvest our crops, and then set in for the hard winter months.

My youthful impression of our little town of Norwich was that it never seemed to change. A few new families would occasionally move up the Thames River from Boston or Providence. Other than the new homesteads that were started in the countryside outside of town, there was not much else of note that went on, in or around Norwich. Eli Bingham and I were almost always together during our free hours. Our family farm was now located a couple of miles outside of Norwich, along the Quinebaug River, which flowed into the Thames River at Norwich. Our family had moved out to the farm when Da was just a boy, after Norwich had grown too crowded for my grandfather.

We had 50 acres, on which we grew enough crops, along with raising a few cows, and a dozen or two chickens, which provided most of our needs. The Bingham farm was next to ours, being down the road a quarter of a mile, but was much larger. The Bingham's had moved out of Norwich just as my family had, and for similar reasons. Norwich had just grown too large for the Bingham family to live there. Master Bingham farmed over 100 acres and had over 20 cows. As I grew into my teens, I began to realize that the Bingham's had much more than my family and by all standards, were one of the wealthiest families in the area.

Whenever our chores around the farms were done, Eli and I would find each other and go down to the river, spending countless hours exploring, swimming, and fishing, along with boating and catching turtles in the mud flats. It was not unusual that from the time my chores were done until sometime after dark, I was down at the river with Eli. We never noticed how hungry, we were at the end of these days until we got home, and could smell the food left over from the dinner we had missed. Mother and father never seemed to be concerned about our free time at the river. Da knew Eli, and Master Bingham knew me, and knew each was of good stock, and would stay out of most trouble.

Each week, Monday through Saturday, was the same with work on the farm until the chores were done. Sunday was always a day of rest when most families in the area would gather at the town meeting house where Pastor Gallagher would present the Lord's Word. After church we would customarily join with some town families, along with the Bingham's for dinner. While the children usually played games, the grownups would discuss the Pastor's sermon or the latest political news from Boston or Providence. It was during one of these gatherings that I took notice of a girl who was helping to clear some tableware from the Bingham's table, where Pastor Gallagher was seated.

As I looked at her, I realized that I knew her, but hadn't talked to her for several weeks. As I continued my gaze, she somehow seemed different; she looked grown up. I kept noticing to see where she was as the dinner began to end. I thought I'd make my way over to her, to see if I could escort her home. Just as I began to go over to where she was, Eli came running over to me. He excitedly exclaimed that one of the Birchard boys had the biggest snapping turtle he had ever seen trapped down on the mud flats by the river, stating that I had to come see it. "Eli," I said in a bewildered state, "I'm busy right now with something."

"With what?" exclaimed Eli!

"I want to go talk to that girl over there," I stated.

"With who?" Eli responded, as he looked over to where I was pointing. "To Diane Gallagher, whatever for?" Eli shouted. "Come on down to the river," and with that Eli was off and running, without me, to the river's edge.

As I made my way over to where Diane was, my heart began to pound. I slowed down as I walked over, and thought to myself, why is my heart pounding? I didn't understand what exactly was going on. As I walked up to her all I could say was, "Hi."

"Hi to you, Will Waterman, whatever do you want?" Diane stated flatly and without emotion.

I didn't know what to say to that. I was at a loss for words, as I wasn't sure why I noticed that Diane had changed. "I guess I was just noticing you," I stammered, "and, and I was wondering if I could walk you home after the dinner?"

"Walk me home?" she questioned. "You haven't talked to me for a month of Sundays, Will Waterman, and besides, I heard Eli Bingham tell you about that big snapper down at the river. You best be going along with him," Diane concluded.

I wasn't sure what to say now, as I wondered how she was able to hear that Eli had told me about that snapping turtle. "I was just trying to be nice and I noticed how nice you look today and all, and thought I could walk you home," I blurted out. "Besides, I've seen lots of snappers down at the river."

Diane looked at me for a moment as she continued to clean up, like I wasn't even there, "Well, if you want to really walk me home, you'd have to ask my father if it would be okay," she said.

"Your father," I responded as I swallowed hard.

"Yes' em," she said as she turned and walked away to continue her work.

I looked around to see Pastor Gallagher talking with my father, Master Bingham and Master Calkin. What was I to do? As I approached the group of men, I could see that they were having a heated conversation about the British levying of more taxes on the colonies. My heart was racing again and I wasn't sure why. The levying of new taxes was always a heated subject with Da. Each time Da's brother, my Uncle Jeremiah, docked his boat at the mouth of the Thames River, at the small fishing town of New London, Da received more news from Boston, Providence, New York, and sometimes Philadelphia about the growing unrest around the colonies regarding the British taxes.

Now was not the time to interrupt the group of men. I knew from several conversations Da had had with men in our town that he was against the taxes levied on the colonies. He was also against the growing sentiment of several prominent families in town, as well as Boston, of going against the Crown, and openly talking of war with England. Da and Master Bingham would argue, even if war with England were justified, that the colonies would never defeat the most powerful army, and navy in the world.

Da would always go back to the French and Indian War, and what he saw there of the British might. Da said that once England brought her might to bear on the French, despite some early defeats, the outcome of the war would never be in doubt. Besides, Da would argue, the colonies can't agree on their own issues, let alone to fight the most powerful army in the world, and expect to win. I stayed in the background as the men continued their conversation and argument for another half-hour. I looked over to where Diane was working from time to time, and I caught her glancing at me. Finally, the group of men began to break-up, and I saw my chance. As Pastor Gallagher was walking over to his wife, where she was sitting with a group of towns' women, I caught up with him before he reached her.

"Pastor," I said, with a crack in my voice.

"Yes, Will, what is it?" Pastor Gallagher inquired as he continued to walk toward the group of women.

My heart was beating like it would jump out of my chest. "I, I," I stammered, as I thought, why was I so nervous? My head was racing now. As I gathered my thoughts, we walked up to the group of women, who stopped talking as we approached. "I was wondering if I could walk Diane home today, after the meal." I blurted out as all of the women gawked at me. I could feel my face turning a deep beet red. Pastor Gallagher turned, looked me straight in my eyes, and then he looked over my shoulder to where Diane was still working.

Pastor Gallagher then looked back at me and said, "Well, Will, I guess it would be okay for today, but when you get to our house I'd like to have a word with you."

"Yes, sir," I replied, as I turned, and walked away with all of the women staring at me. I had never felt so uncomfortable in my life.

I walked home that day with Diane. We walked about 20 feet behind Pastor and Mrs. Gallagher. Occasionally, Pastor would look over his shoulder at us, as if to say "Is everything okay?" I didn't know what to say to Diane exactly. We mostly talked about the dinner that day, and some of the politics the men had been talking about. I didn't really think we would fight the British, I told her. She said her father thought we would. Before I knew it, we were at their house. Pastor Gallagher was waiting for us at the door. Diane excused herself with a short curtsy, and then disappeared inside with only a glance in my direction.

I was nervous again, like when I asked Pastor Gallagher to walk Diane home. My heart was beating fast again. I didn't have a chance to say much. Pastor Gallagher just started talking. "Will," he said, "I've known your father and family as long as I've known any family in this community, or any other. I have a great respect for your father and your family. I expect that you'll want to be courting Diane from now on," he said, as he looked me square in the face.

"Yes, sir," I responded awkwardly.

"Well, then, I expect you'll be sitting with her and her mother next Sunday at church," he added, and with that he shook my hand and he turned to enter his house. Just before entering the house, he stopped and turned to me and said, "You'd best call on a regular basis, she doesn't like much to be stood up," he informed me as he entered their home. I was left standing outside wondering what actually had happened. As I walked the two miles home, I thought about Diane's brown hair and brown eyes. I went over in my mind what happened that day, and I realized I was well on my way to falling in love with Diane Gallagher.

Word of the Boston Tea Party reached Norwich just before Christmas 1773. Da said the tea belonged to the British East India Company. As he described it, this was a powerful group of investors, blessed by the British government, to trade on behalf of the British government with parties in India and the Far East. Da stated that a fortune, well over a million pounds, of tea had been destroyed in Boston Harbor. He said the British would make somebody pay for it.

The meetings with the town elders grew more numerous as news of the events in Boston, and the other colonies reached our town. What was of note was that Da asked me, if I wanted to attend the meeting to be held at Durkee's Tavern that night, to discuss the latest news. I was hesitant, mainly because I didn't know what to expect, but decided to attend upon Da's urging that I would find it of interest. I had heard that a number of communities throughout the northern colonies had formed committees, to discuss the British levies and taxes on the colonies.

Da and I saddled our horses, and left our house just after dinner. I noticed that there was a particular cold bite to the air this December night, with a light snow falling. As we rode the two miles to Durkee's Tavern, Da told me to say nothing, and to stay in the background. I noticed when we arrived in town that there were an unusual number of men around. When we reached Durkee's Tavern, we walked upstairs to the tavern's second floor meeting room. It was a large rectangular room, with several tables and chairs throughout. Even with numerous candles being lit on the walls and tables, it was dimly lit, as it was hard to make out the men on the far side of the room. Most of the men from each household in and around town were there. I noticed one or two other boys my age among the men. As we entered, Master Durkee welcomed Da to the meeting, "Welcome, Will Waterman, now that everyone is here, I call this meeting to order," he stated loudly. I estimated that there were forty-five or fifty men packed into the room, with several who had come from the outlying towns several miles away.

Master Backus was first to speak, "I expect in light of the recent developments in Boston, this group will finally decide to declare their intentions to be loyal to the colonies, and fight the British when the fight comes, and come it will, mark my words."

Immediately Master Jones shot back, "Those who fight the Crown will be the first traitors to die!" And with that a myriad of voices broke into shouts asserting why their side was right, as fists were clenched and raised in the air in anger. Da and I just stood there looking at the men shouting at each other, with angry voices and clenched fists. After several minutes of this mayhem of shouting insults, Master Durkee once again called the meeting to order, by pounding the butt end of his pistol on the table at the head of the room. As Master Durkee looked around the room his eyes settled on Da, who was still in the back of the room.

"Master Waterman," Master Durkee shouted out, "give us your words of wisdom regarding the situation in Boston, as you understand it, and if war comes, what think you of it?"

The murmuring about the room drew quiet and all heads turned to the back corner of the room. Da looked around for a few seconds, took two steps forward and, as he always did before he spoke, cleared his voice.

"All of us," Da began, "are farmers, millers, smiths or bear one trade or another. If you go to war, with the Crown or against her, who will tend your farms or gather your crops or who will grist the mill, or shoe our horses, or tend our flocks? We are not soldiers, nor can we presume to be professional soldiers in the pay of the Crown. If what a number of you say is true, that war is to come, what do you suggest we would do? Are we to fight our brothers from England and our brothers here in the colonies as well, and for what?"

Before Da could continue, Master Hyde yelled out from the front of the room, "We fight against tyranny, and against unjust taxation from a king three thousand miles away, who places a yoke of burden upon his subjects that stifles us, even unto death. I would rather die fighting to be free of a tyrannical king, than to quietly die the death of a burdened ox, by unjust taxes." Several voices rose in "hear, hear," in assent of what Master Hyde said.

When all was quiet again Da continued, "Aye, to say that the attitude of the Crown towards her colonies seems to be unjust goes without saying. But, a number of you fought with me in the French and Indian War, as it is now called, and we have seen the strength that the Crown can bring to bear upon her adversaries, not only by land, but by sea. If we engaged the Crown in a land war here in the colonies, how long would it be before her naval forces will strangle us from the outside world? Let me ask each of you here," Da continued, "how is it that the colonies will fight this war, when, like the men in this room, we cannot agree on whether to fight with the Crown or against? Let me ask each of you here, are you willing to look down the barrel of your gun and see your neighbor, cousin or brother at the other end of it? Let me ask you, how many of you men have aimed a gun at another man, let alone shot or killed one?" All had grown strangely silent as Da had spoken this. He looked about the room and then continued, "As most of you know, my brother Jeremiah sails a schooner out of Providence, and the reports we get from him are more disturbing than the letters the post riders bring from Boston, or New York. Both sides, the Crown on one and the Sons of Liberty in Boston on the other, are gathering and planning for war. With all that is in me, I want not this war! For there will be those in this very room, who will not see it to its end. The Lord as my witness, I do not believe the colonies can prevail against the Crown, and as for me, I will not fight against my King to whom I swore an oath during the French and Indian War." And with that Da was done, as the room once again erupted into a roar of voices each pronouncing his position as right.

Da and I stayed motionless for some time in the back of the room until the fervor died away. Finally, Master Durkee made a motion to call out the militia for training and drills, in the event that hostilities between the Crown and colonies broke out. The motion was seconded, and once again the shouts for and against the Crown broke out. Those who sided with the Crown or were neutral began to file out of the tavern, while those in agreement with the colonies remained to plan the militia training.

All in the room knew that Master Durkee had himself organized the local Sons of Liberty, and had been involved in several incidents to thwart the Crown's tax collector from collecting several of the new taxes imposed on the colonies. Several men had stated that the Sons of Liberty in Boston, New York and even Philadelphia held Master Durkee in high esteem. There was even a story Da told me about Master Durkee. He said that Master Durkee had led a group of men, most of them from Norwich and the surrounding towns, against the Crown's tax collector. That this group of men rode down one of the Crown's tax collectors, threatening him with death if he didn't resign. Resign he eventually did, after he was imprisoned and threatened with hanging. The raid became known as the raid of Durkee's Irregulars.

While Da and I rode home, Da was unusually quiet. I could tell the events of the evening troubled him deeply. As we approached our house, Da stopped and looked at me directing, "Will, say nothing of tonight's meeting to anyone. Your Uncle Jeremiah will be in Providence by next spring; I believe it's time that you go to sea with him for a while, and have a different experience."

Winter quickly turned to spring and the time of my departure drew near. I spoke with Diane several times before I left, and on Sunday during the church meeting I could tell she was upset. During the sermon's closing, Pastor Gallagher included in his prayer, the resolution of the trouble between the Crown and the colonies, as well as the safe travel for those who were to depart that week. When he mentioned it, Diane took my hand and squeezed it, and I could feel her hand shaking.

The following morning, Da and I were in the barn saddling our horses and getting our supplies together. Da said it was a two-day ride to Providence. It had been several years since I had been there, and I looked forward to the trip, although I was anxious about the unknown, for I had been on my uncle's ship several times, I had never gone to sea.

As Da and I left the barn, we stopped at the front of our house to say goodbye to Ma, and my brother and sister. Ma cried as she hugged me and told me to be safe. "Don't worry Ma," Da said, "I'll see that Jeremiah takes care of him." And with that, we turned and began to walk our horses to the end of our property. We could see a wagon slowly approaching with two people on it. As they drew closer, I could see it was Pastor Gallagher and Diane. I could see that Diane had been crying. As they reined in the horses, Da and Pastor Gallagher shook hands, and wished us Godspeed on our trip. I went over to Diane's side.

"It'll be alright, I'll be back in a month or so, I promise," I said as I tried to console her.

"You'd better be, Will Waterman, I love you," Diane stated as she kissed me, and then pulled her apron up to her face to wipe the tears away. Pastor Gallagher looked at me and said, "Be safe, son, Godspeed to you." Da and I turned and headed down the post road to Providence. I wouldn't return for two months.

- CHAPTER 3 -

"On Board the Whisperer"

1774

It took Da and me two days to travel the post road between Norwich and Providence. The first day was, by far, the longest part of the ride, as Da had stated that he wanted to reach Waterman's Tavern by nightfall.

"Waterman's Tavern, Da?" I inquired.

"There's a tavern just outside of a small town called Scituate in Rhode Island colony," he began. "I discovered it several years ago during one of my trips to visit my brother in Providence. The owner is a man from the old country, and from the many conversations I've had with him, we found out we are distant cousins from the area of Belfast, County Down, Ireland," he concluded.

True to his word, just outside the small town of Scituate, we walked our horse's right up to the sign hanging over the front door that read, *Waterman's Tavern, James Waterman, Proprietor*, with a painted picture of a mug of rum and a plate of food.

"Let's just take our horses around back, to bed them for the night," Da suggested. That completed, Da walked around to the front door and entered. Once inside, it was dark and smoky, and it took my eyes several moments to adjust to the dimly lit tavern. Once they did, I saw an old man hunched over with both his elbows resting on the bar. He looked up at us from behind the tavern bar as we entered. He had red hair, a red beard, and a round face that seemed unusually red. He also was the roundest man I had ever seen, who had no waist, and it was hard to see if there was a neck between his head and shoulders.

When the proprietor behind the bar finally got a good look at Da, he stood up and called out "Ah, Will Waterman, it has been too long." Moving out from behind the bar with a gallon jug of rum in his hand, he walked over to our table and stated, "Sit, sit, my old friend, what brings you to my humble tavern on this fine evening?"

"Master Waterman, let me introduce you to my oldest son, Will Waterman the junior," Da stated.

Looking at me the old man stated, "A fine looking young man indeed, sir."

"We are on our way to Providence, as young Will here is going to sea with his uncle for a couple of months," Da replied.

"Then a meal and a bed for the night and on the morrow, you will be well rested to resume your travels," the old man called as he turned, and disappeared through a door, presumably leading to the tavern kitchen. Several minutes later, after Da and I had engaged in quiet conversation, the old man returned from the kitchen with two large bowls of stew and a plate of bread, along with a small block of cheese.

"Enjoy, and we'll talk later," the old man stated, returning to the bar, to serve the other patrons in the establishment. When we had finished our meal, the old man returned to join us. Many of the other patrons had already left the tavern for the night, with only a couple of men sitting in the far corner, out of earshot.

"William," he began looking at Da, "what do you make of all of this trouble in Boston, with the British?"

"I am not sure what to make of it, but that is why I am taking young Will here, to his uncle," Da replied. "I'm hoping by the time he returns from sea, much of this trouble with the British will have blown over."

"A sound decision, a sound decision indeed, William," the old man agreed. "Heed your father, boy," he said, looking at me, "if this turns into war, it will be an ugly affair."

Da and Master Waterman talked for another half an hour about the British in Boston. We then made our excuses; going upstairs to the room provided by Master Waterman. We were soon fast asleep.

The morning came early, and I found that Da had been up for some time already, and was downstairs. I found him sitting at a table talking with Master Waterman. We had a quick breakfast, then Da stated the horses were saddled, and ready for us to mount. We departed shortly after this, continuing down the post road to Providence.

We arrived early in the afternoon, boarding our horses at the livery just down the wharf from where Uncle Jeremiah usually docked the *Whisperer*. We walked the short distance down the wharf, where we found Uncle Jeremiah barking orders to crewmembers aboard the *Whisperer*.

As I was to find out, she was a two-mast schooner that carried almost sixty tons. When Uncle Jeremiah saw us standing on the dock watching the loading of cargo onto his ship, he yelled for us to come aboard. "Welcome, brother, and young Will, it's good to have you aboard," he greeted.

I could see his white teeth through his thick beard. He was a stout man, who outweighed me by a hundred pounds, although he was only an inch taller than my 5 feet 9 inches. "So, young Will wants to go to sea does he? Well, I'll take good care of him brother, you can be rest assured of that," he added.

I thought my father and my uncle were entirely different people who happened to come from the same family. Da was tall and thin, and always wanted to be a farmer, in addition to being a God-fearing man. While Uncle Jeremiah was much shorter than Da, with a large round stomach and thick dark brown hair, who always wanted to go to sea. Uncle Jeremiah never married, for he said his love was the sea. We had dinner on board the ship that night in the captain's cabin, which was a small dark room that was much too crowded with the three of us in it. That night Da and I slept on the main deck under the starlight, with the sounds of Providence and the harbor all around us.

The next morning, after a quick breakfast, Da left Providence and headed back to Norwich. Da's instructions were simple to us; "Will, obey your uncle, and Jeremiah, take care of my son," he turned and left. As I watched him go, I felt a lump in my throat grow, as I had never been away from home before and certainly never to sea. I knew I would miss him, not knowing when I would see him again.

Shortly after Da left, Uncle Jeremiah began barking out orders. Since I didn't know anything about ships or the sea, he told me to stay by his side until we were underway. He said my education would begin in earnest then. There was a crew of five besides myself, Uncle Jeremiah and the cook. My berth was below deck with the other hands. Uncle Jeremiah informed me, that we sailed with the next morning's tide, and needed to complete the loading of the cargo, as well as the supplies, before nightfall.

It was long after dark when the loading of the ship was actually completed, as Uncle Jeremiah called all hands to dinner and rest. I ate again with Uncle Jeremiah in his cabin, which afforded a little more room for the two of us. During dinner that consisted of a mutton stew, Uncle Jeremiah began to give me the lay of the land. First, he said, "Don't call me 'Uncle Jeremiah' any longer. The calling of a captain other than 'Captain' or 'Sir' aboard his ship is not permitted. The crew is good, hard working men, and they'll expect you to pull your weight, as do I. Second, I'll have you work with one or two members of the crew only. If you work with all of them, you'll only get overburdened with how each man does the same job just a bit different from the others," the captain said.

"I understand, sir," I replied.

"Now, Will, where do you suppose we are off to?" he asked.

"Uncle, I, I mean, sir, not having been to sea before, I don't even know where we can go," I answered honestly.

"That's a right fair answer, Will," he stated. "What would you say if I told you that first we sail for Boston, then for Bermuda? From there we sail to Charlestown, Philadelphia and then back home," the captain informed me.

"How long will that take us, sir?" I asked, as I had only ever heard of a couple of the places he named and did not know where they actually were.

"With a fair wind and no trouble, I'm planning on close to two months," he said as he stroked his beard. Then, as he leaned toward me he added, "If it's a foul wind or we run into a pirate, then we'll have to make a run for whatever safe harbor is near at hand. Then plan on two and a half to three. Don't worry, Will, I'll get you home again, safe. Now let's go meet the crew."

"Yes, sir," I mustered as my answer. "Uncle," I asked, "what made you name your ship the *Whisperer*?"

"Will, no one's asked me that in a long time, and it's a darn right good question. I call her the *Whisperer*, because she'll make a good sail on a whisper of a wind, and out sail any ship with whatever wind there is, as long as we've got the weather gauge in our favor, you'll see."

"What's the weather gauge, sir?" I inquired.

"The wind in our favor son, the wind in our favor," Uncle Jeremiah replied with a slap on my back and a chuckle under his breath, at my ignorance I supposed.

My uncle led the way out of his cabin, then down the passageway to the crew area, which was more cramped than his cabin with five crewmembers and a cook. I was a shy boy by nature, and meeting the crew aboard this ship was intimidating, especially once I saw them. They all appeared to be sea hardened hands, all with deep tans and each being much older than me. No one got up when we entered the crew's area, although all acknowledged the captain by bringing a closed hand to their foreheads. The captain introduced the first mate as Jennings, a man with blonde hair, blue eyes and a big nose who eyed me warily. The rest of the crew was Billings, Jones, Hotaling and Edwards."

"This is Will Waterman, your new mate," the captain said.

The cook was an old man of about sixty, whose name was Sean, who was gray and bald, and who always walked hunched over so that his height of five-feet-five inches was now no higher than five feet. He was the only one who really acknowledged me with a slight smile. With the introductions complete, the captain turned to leave, calling out over his shoulder, "Mr. Jennings, show the boy, his berth, and he'll take the first watch with you in the morning, we sail with the morning tide." With that the captain was gone, and I was left standing before a crew I knew nothing about.

"How old are you boy?" Jennings called out.

"I just turned seventeen this past spring, sir," I stated.

"Aboard a ship of this size, only the captain is called, sir, boy," he responded coldly. "I take it you've not been to sea before, boy," Jennings continued.

"No, this is my first time to sea," I answered.

"Alright then, your berth is in the corner. We're up at six bells in the forenoon watch. Sean, the cook, strikes one bell when it's time to eat. If you're not on watch, you'll be here right away or you'll miss the food. You heard the captain; we sail with the morning tide, so get some sleep if you can. I'll wake you at six bells," Jennings concluded flatly.

I unhooked my berth that was all of a sheet with a hook at each end that connected to rings hanging from a beam in the ceiling. As I climbed into my berth to try to get some sleep, I wondered what I had gotten myself into.

Sleep was hard to come by that night, as the crewmembers played cards and drank rum late into the night. When sleep did come, it was a restless sleep, and I was awakened by Jennings, who was shaking me violently, all the while yelling at me to get out of my berth, as it was six bells.

I hit the floor still dressed from the night before, following Jennings up on deck. It was so dark below deck, that when I came on deck I had to shield my eyes until they were adjusted to the morning light.

As I looked around, Captain Waterman was standing next to the helm barking orders. "Set the sails, Mr. Jennings," the captain called. "I don't want to lose this tide and off shore breeze. We need to clear Brenton Point by midday. Mr. Jennings, get aloft there with the boy and set the mainsail, show him his duty." The captain then took hold of the helm. The lines were cast off and we gently became free of the wharf that held us. Several minutes later, all sails were set. We were sailing down Narragansett Bay, heading for the open sea.

With all sail set, Mr. Jennings stated, "I'll give you the run down on her and by the end of the week you should remember all. We have a deck length of ninety-eight feet and to the bowsprit she's one hundred and thirty-seven feet. The gross tonnage is sixty tons, displacement tonnage is almost one hundred tons, the beam is twenty-four feet and the draft is eight feet nine inches. The mast height is ninety-five feet and the sail area is five thousand nine hundred and sixteen feet," Jennings stated. "The sails are the jib, which we have three, the fore staysail, the fore gaff-topsail, the foresail, the main gaff-topsail, and the mainsail."

As we got into the open water of the bay, the waves became choppier. I began to feel somewhat unsteady from a sensation that was new to my mind and body. The farther we went, the worse I felt. Before long I found myself at the side of the ship, regurgitating what was left in my stomach of my evening meal. Billings, who was on deck, saw my dilemma and came over to my side.

"I figured you'd get sea sick today, boy, but I thought you'd wait until we were out of the bay, and into open water before it would happen. You are a landlubber aren't ye, boy," he said with a laugh as he slapped me on my back. "I guess this means you don't want breakfast, eh, boy?" he asked over his shoulder as he walked away.

"How long does it last?" I called back in between bouts of sickness.

"Depends on the person," he said as he disappeared below decks for his meal, "a week or two, on and off, probably."

Several hours later we passed the island of Rhode Island itself, and the small town of Newport. There were many sailing and fishing vessels to be seen in the harbor as we passed. Uncle Jeremiah came over to me as I looked over the side at the small town at the water's edge on the island. He pointed out to me, the two frigates flying the Union Jack. I had never seen the English flag before.

"A prettier little town with a deep water port you won't find in all the colonies, Will," he stated. "If I weren't so well established in Providence,

I'd have a mind to move my operation and home port to that harbor," he added.

"What advantage does it have, sir?" I inquired.

"It is nearer to the open sea, by far than Providence," Captain Waterman replied. "Mark my words, Will, if war comes, there will be battles over which army has control over that harbor," he concluded.

I remained at the side rail and watched the small town slowly slip past our view. It was under an hour later when we passed Brenton Point, and into the open ocean. As we entered the open ocean, it seemed to me that the Atlantic Ocean stretched on forever before us. I found it to be an intimidating sight.

That night after the evening meal, I spent an hour in the captain's cabin with my uncle, while the hands had another night of cards and rum.

"Come over to my table, Will," he said, "and I'll show you where we are, as well as where we are going."

He pulled out a map from a pile of rolled up maps on the edge of his desk, unrolling it out for me to see.

"I haven't done my calculations yet today, but I figure we are about right here," as he pointed to a location on the map. "And here is Boston. We'll be there in a few days, but first we have to weather these shoals here off the cape." As he pointed to some lines on the map off of a crooked arm of land that jutted out into the ocean. "Them's the worst shoals in all the Americas, and we'll sail well clear of them for sure," he said with a serious look. "More ships have gone down in them shoals, than a man can count."

"But uncle, how do you know where we are, and what are these things on the map here?" I asked.

"Well, Will, navigating takes some time to get used to, but I take a rope with a number of knots on it spaced out evenly, with a board attached at the end. We throw the wood end over board, counting how many knots go out for an amount of time, say 30 seconds. That would be your rate of travel, let's say seven knots. Then during the day, I take several readings with an instrument known as the sextant, which gives me the declination of the sun in the sky, which will tell me the time of day. Combining the two together will give me roughly how far we have traveled, in addition, where to place our location on the chart. Do you understand, Will?" he finally said.

I looked bewildered and I knew it, so I looked at him and said, "No, sir."

"Look here," he began and he started out again to try to explain everything to me, and it all just seemed to run together. I didn't understand any of it. He looked at me again and said, "On the morrow, when we are running under a smooth sail, and Mr. Jennings can set you free from your duties, come to the poop deck. I'll begin your education on navigation. The markings on the map here, you asked about, are the islands of Martha's Vineyard, and Nantucket. We'll pass 'em on the morrow. It's time for my rest now, Will. I'm going to take one walk around deck to make sure all is well, and turn in for the night, as should you."

And with that, I knew our evening was over. I went down the passage to the crew's berth and crawled into my berth. I slept a little better than the night before.

The next day during the forenoon watch, Mr. Jennings declared that all sails were set. I was now free to meet with the captain regarding my next course of learning. I found the captain on the poop deck overlooking the ship with Mr. Hotaling at the helm. Billings, Edwards and Jones had gone below deck to rest. Here, the captain took me under his wing, and began to try to teach me about navigation again.

In two days' time, as we approached Boston from the east, I had learned more about sailing a ship than I had ever imagined I would know. Finally, as land was sighted, I climbed the ratlines to the lookout. Off in the distance was a gray mass on the horizon. Boston was in sight. When we were about a mile out, I heard what I thought was thunder. When I asked the captain about it, "No, Will," he said. "That is Castle Island in the outer harbor, announcing to the harbor master, and the British, that a ship is approaching. Listen, Will," the captain continued, "when we get into the harbor and are docked, there undoubtedly will be a large number of British soldiers about. By all means, stay well clear of them. With the latest problems between the Crown and certain people in Boston, the regulars will be on high alert."

"I've never seen a British soldier," I replied, "but I will certainly keep to myself."

As we entered the harbor, we passed Castle Island on the port side of the ship, and from atop of the fort located on the island, I saw the flag of England. Once past Castle Island and fully in the harbor, the captain began to call out orders.

"All hands, all hands to wear ship," he shouted.

Immediately, everyone was in motion. I followed Jennings up the ratlines to the rigging, and began to pull in the sails. The orders continued until the ship was without sail, being dead in the water, when the captain finally shouted, "Drop anchor!"

Finally, we all relaxed, looking over the rail at the town of Boston. It was the biggest city I had ever seen. I had really only been to Hartford, and Providence outside of Norwich. As I looked out, I saw two boats approaching the *Whisperer.* Each boat had several rowers. An officer, who was wearing a scarlet uniform, distinguished the larger of the two boats. A gentleman, who had the appearance of an official about him, accompanied the officer. As they approached the *Whisperer*, the boats heaved to, as the official next to the officer shouted to our ship, "What ship and were out of?"

The captain shouted back, "*Whisperer*, out of Providence."

The official cupped his hands over his mouth again and shouted, "What cargo?"

Captain Waterman replied in like manner, "Lumber, furs and grain!"

The official replied, "Come aboard."

With that, the boat containing the official and officer pulled alongside the *Whisperer.* Once on board, the captain greeted the official and the officer, welcoming them on board. "Captain Waterman, at your service gentleman, shall we go below and look at the manifest," the captain said with a sweep of his arm toward the hatchway that led below deck.

The official was the only one who responded. "I'm Harbor Master Warren. This is Lieutenant Hargrove of the 60th foot of the Royal Marines, at your service," introducing himself, in addition to the officer with him. "Please lead on, Captain," he stated.

The captain, along with the harbor master began to move to the stairs that lead to below decks and the hold, but the lieutenant held his position, looking at everyone on deck with a wary eye. After several moments of hesitation, the lieutenant moved to follow the captain below deck. After what seemed an eternity, all three men returned on deck. The harbor master and the captain shook hands, and smiled with a seamen's familiarity, while the lieutenant, scolding the captain stated coldly, "Keep your men in check."

With that, both men were over the side and in their boat. Lines were thrown to the second boat, known as a tender. The *Whisperer* was then pulled to a dock that jutted out several hundred yards into the harbor, which I was to learn, was Long Wharf. As soon as we were tied to the wharf, laborers on the dock immediately began swinging arms to unload our cargo. The captain oversaw the beginning of the unloading of his ship, which would take the rest of the day. The only other observation of note was that every few feet along the wharf; a scarlet clad soldier was standing at attention, with his musket at his side, its bayonet gleaming in the sun.

Finally, with the unloading of his cargo well in hand, the captain said in a tired voice, "All hands below deck, to my cabin if you please."

There was hardly room for all of to squeeze into the small captain's cabin, as all had to stand. The captain looked at each of us in the dimly candle lit room, and then looked down to his desk with the numerous charts on it. "We will be taking on a load of wood on the morrow, bound for Bermuda," he began. "Each of you is at liberty for the next few hours. But mark my words, that lieutenant who came aboard earlier is the son of a jackass, and has already threatened me that any actions deemed by him, or any of his subordinates that are untoward the Crown will be dealt with swiftly, if not unjustly. Things ashore are worse than I thought they could be, but with the ruining of over a million pounds of East India tea in Boston Harbor, the lobsters are in a dangerous mood. You are forewarned and I sail with the afternoon tide for Bermuda, with or without you. Mr. Billings, you have the first watch. That is all."

With the meeting over, we all began to shuffle out of the captain's cabin and onto the deck. There were looks all around, but not a word was said. I waited on deck looking down the wharf at the town of Boston, watching all of the people moving about. It seemed like an anthill that had been stirred up. Suddenly, I realized that the captain was standing at my elbow.

"Come ashore with me, Will, I have business to attend to," he said flatly.

"Yes, sir," I replied. We were down the plank and on solid ground for the first time in several days. When I got to the wharf, I almost fell. The difference between land legs and sea legs became very apparent to me. As I stumbled to get my feet under me, Uncle Jeremiah was already walking down the wharf, several steps ahead of me. The wharf was crowded with workers, soldiers, carts, horses, and cargo being loaded and unloaded from any number of ships that were tied up along it. Uncle Jeremiah and I had to weave our way to the beginning of the wharf. Here, Uncle Jeremiah stopped in front of a building, and then walked inside. That he had been here before was obvious. I followed him, as he stopped at a counter and began talking to the man behind it, who was familiar with him. Uncle Jeremiah then turned to me, and stated, "Will, wait outside and if you would, count the number of warships in the harbor. They'll be the ones with three masts with the English flag flying on the jack staff. I'll be out presently."

"Yes, sir," I replied as I walked outside to the edge of the wharf, looking over the harbor. As I looked about, I thought to myself, "What is a jack staff?" but knew better than to ask right then. As I looked over the harbor, I began to realize that there seemed to be a significant number of warships in port. As I was counting, I was knocked to the ground from behind. As I looked up, I found a rather large, angry looking soldier staring down at me.

"Watch out where ye stand, boy, or next time I'll push ye into the ocean," he barked with a snarl, as he marched off with several other soldiers in tow, on an apparent mission.

I got up, checking myself for damage. After several minutes of counting ships, I was finished and waited for my uncle to return.

Finally, Uncle Jeremiah along with the man who was behind the counter exited the building.

"The loading of your ship will begin first thing in the morning, Captain, and I believe the silversmith has the item ready for you," the man stated, as he held out his hand to Uncle Jeremiah.

"Thank you, sir," said Uncle Jeremiah taking his hand and shaking it warmly, "I will see him presently, and will dine with him tonight. I'll sail with the afternoon tide on the morrow, sir."

His business completed, Uncle Jeremiah turned and began walking up the street into town. I followed close at hand. After several minutes, Uncle Jeremiah stopped at a shop and began to look in the window. It was a shoe shop and I wondered what Uncle Jeremiah was doing. After a moment, he asked me how many warships I counted in the harbor.

"Sixteen," I answered.

"Good," he said, continuing on. As we walked, I was overwhelmed with the many smells, along with the large numbers of people walking about. I took particular notice that it seemed that on every street corner was stationed a British soldier. Several minutes later, the captain stopped at a house, knocking on the door. After a moment, the door opened a crack by a young lady and Uncle Jeremiah stated, "Miss, is Master Revere at home?"

"Indeed he is, sir. Who is calling?" she inquired.

"Inform Master Revere that Captain Waterman, accompanied by his nephew await his reception, and wish to obtain an order placed several weeks ago."

"Please, wait a moment, sir," she stated as she closed the door and was gone.

Momentarily, the door reopened, and the young lady stepped aside with a curtsy as she said, "Master Revere is in the dining room, and is expecting you, sir."

We entered the house and met its master who was seated at his dinner table. He stood up upon our entering the dimly lit room, and welcomed Uncle Jeremiah with a friendly handshake and smile. Uncle Jeremiah turned to me and said, "Sir, let me introduce to you my nephew, William Waterman, Jr., of Norwich, Connecticut colony."

"I am pleased to make your acquaintance, young man, as you are most welcome in my house," he added, "please be seated, dinner is about to be served."

Dinner was shortly served, during which Uncle Jeremiah and Master Revere engaged in conversation, which at the time meant little to me. Finally, Uncle Jeremiah pushed himself from the table and stated, "As always, sir, dining with you has been most enjoyable. I believe our last bit of business is in order and I'll be on my way. As we speak, my ship is being unloaded of its cargo. I take on a cargo of wood bound for Bermuda, which will be completed on the morrow. I'll sail with the afternoon tide," Uncle Jeremiah concluded.

"Yes, of course, sir," and Master Revere turned to a desk behind him in the dining room. Opening the roll top, he produced a wax sealed envelope, which he handed to my uncle. "Godspeed to you, sir, and give Benjamin my regards," he stated.

"I will, sir, and a good evening to you, sir," replied Uncle Jeremiah.

We departed Master Revere's house and began to retrace our path to Long Wharf. A short distance down the street, Uncle Jeremiah turned to me, handing me the envelope. "Will," he said, "place this inside your shirt and return it to me once we board the ship. If we are stopped, say nothing of its existence to anyone."

"Yes, sir," I said as I wondered about its contents.

Our return to Long Wharf and the ship was uneventful, other than the groups of British soldiers we passed along the way, none of which challenged our passing. Upon our arrival at the *Whisperer*, Uncle Jeremiah inquired of the dock laborer, who seemed to be in charge of the unloading of cargo, how things faired. The worker informed Uncle Jeremiah that all was on schedule, with the unloading of the cargo. Uncle Jeremiah seemed to be satisfied with this answer. Boarding the ship, Uncle Jeremiah went directly to his cabin, followed by myself. Once inside, he closed the door, and asked for the envelope.

"I am sorry to have burdened you with this, Will, but once we are to sea, I will explain all," he said. "Get your rest and I'll see you in the morning."

Six bells came early, as preparations were made to get underway, even though we would not sail until the afternoon tide. The crew seemed to be in good spirits, as their conversation centered on the pub they had visited, the good-looking wench who had served them, along with the rounds of rum which were consumed by all. The day passed quickly with our preparations and the loading of our wood cargo. Within short order, two tenders had rowed up to the side of the *Whisperer*, this time without the harbor master or the disagreeable lieutenant among them. We untied from Long Wharf as tow ropes were attached to the tenders. After half an hour of rowing and maneuvering out into the harbor, we pulled in our tow ropes. The captain barked orders to set the mainsail. We slowly sailed out of Boston Harbor. I had no idea how long it would be until I'd see Boston again. Once we were out to sea and under full sail, the captain ordered me below to his cabin.

The captain was looking at a chart and did not look up when I entered.

"You asked for me, sir," I stated as I entered.

"Yes, Will, it is more than a week's sail to Bermuda, which is an island located here in the middle of the ocean," he said as he pointed to the center of the chart, "I wanted to discuss a matter with you."

I remained silent, waiting for him to continue. "Will, have you ever heard of a group of men called the Sons of Liberty?"

I hesitated, thinking back to the meeting at Durkee's Tavern in Norwich the previous winter. "Yes, I have, sir. I recently attended a meeting with father, where one of the founders of the Connecticut Sons of Liberty was there," I said and added. "Perhaps you have heard of him, his name is Mr. John Durkee and I think they call him Captain Durkee. I believe he is an important man in the cause of the colonies."

"I know of him," Captain Waterman stated, "but I've never had the privilege of meeting him. Although, Will, I believe your father fought with him during the French and Indian War, as a member of Rogers' Rangers."

"Da never mentioned that to me," I said, thinking back to the meeting.

"Will," the captain continued, "your father, my brother, is a good, hardworking, honest and God-fearing man. But I fear I am on the opposite side of the fight that is brewing regarding the course the colonies are on. The Sons of Liberty are a group of men from around the colonies, which started in Boston, who openly want the colonies to separate from England and become a nation, by force if need be. Mr. Revere, with whom we had dinner with last night, is one of those men. Your father is strongly against their ideals and sides with the British. I fear if it comes to a fight, your father will side with the British.

The envelope entrusted to me last night by Mr. Revere contains important information regarding the movement of British warships and troops in Boston, as well as the greater New England area. I am to deliver this letter to a man in Philadelphia who supports our sentiments. I am charged never to open the envelopes I deliver. That way, if I am someday captured as a spy, or patriot if you will, I will not know the details of the information contained therein. By my not knowing the exact contents of the document, the operations of the Sons of Liberty are isolated from discovery, although they would discover whom I delivered the information too. Doubtless though, the information contained in the envelope would cost the lives of many men, as well as the bearer. It was wrong of me last night to give you the envelope. If something had happened, clearly your life would have been in danger. In fact, all of our lives are in danger, if the contents of that envelope are discovered aboard this ship. You and I are the only ones who know of its presence on board this ship. The rest of the crew knows nothing, and so it must remain. Go about your work and we'll say nothing more about it."

I was dismissed, and sent to go about my business of learning more of the ship. After a week's sail out of Boston, Master Jennings told me that we should sight Bermuda within the next day or so. In the entire expansive ocean, I could not see how an island could be located so far from anything else. Suddenly, Master Jones, who was on the lookout in the rigging shouted, "Sail ho!"

"Where away!" shouted the captain.

"Two points off the port beam, sir!" yelled Jones in response.

Immediately, the captain had a piece to his eye, as he was looking intently over the horizon at the ship sighted by Jones. After several moments, the captain slammed the piece closed as he shouted to Jones, "Let me know if she changes course, if you please!"

I couldn't see the ship, but from the actions of Jones and the captain, it was out there, unseen by me, just over the horizon.

"Aye, sir," Jones said in reply.

"Will, come here," the captain ordered.

"Sir," I said as I met him at the stern rail of the ship in the corner.

"It appears to be a British warship bearing right down on us. If we're boarded say nothing, even if you are spoken to, Will, do you understand," the captain stated. "In all likelihood, they want to inspect our cargo, but they may want to press some of our crew into service. Say nothing. I'll do all of the talking, is that understood?"

"Yes," I replied and then added, "couldn't we outrun them, sir?"

"That we could, Will, easily, but then they'd think we were hiding something and if caught, they'd tear the *Whisperer* apart until they found it. No, it's best if they continue down on us, and that we heave to and be boarded. It is like as not, they'll not find what they think they are looking for," Captain Waterman concluded.

Within a half-hour a sail was on the horizon. Within the hour, the whole ship could be seen. "Master Jones," the captain shouted, "have they changed course?"

"No, sir, they are running down on us. I think they want us to heave to, sir!" shouted Jones. "Yes, sir, I can see a puff of smoke from the bow chasers, they're trying to put a shot across our bow!" Jones shouted.

"Did you see a splash, Jones?" the captain shouted back.

"No, Captain!" yelled Jones.

I didn't know what all this meant, but I knew it could not be good. As I watched the approaching ship, I suddenly saw a puff of smoke from the bow of the ship. A moment later about a hundred yards ahead of our port bow a splash was seen in the ocean.

Captain Waterman immediately shouted, "All hands, all hands, up the rigging, shorten sail, we'll heave to, Mr. Jennings!"

All hands scrambled up the ratlines and shortened sail. The ship heaved to and we were like a cork bobbing in a tub. Within a half an hour the British warship was along our port side, about a hundred yards out. Immediately, a boat was lowered from the warship, as a number of seamen followed by several scarlet clad soldiers were seen to go over the side, and into the boat. Jones, who remained in the lookout, shouted down to the captain, "At least twenty coming to board us, Captain, and it looks like they mean business; they fixed bayonets once they got in the boat!"

The captain only cleared his throat at this revelation and remained steadfast in watching the approaching boat. When only a few yards off, the boat turned and ran parallel with our ship. The officer in the stern of the boat stood up as he ordered, "Move from the port side while we board your ship!" The captain didn't say a word, but motioned with his hand for all of us to move to the starboard side. Within a minute, British soldiers were coming over the side. Once they were on deck, their muskets were charged to the ready with bayonets gleaming in the sun, menacingly pointed at us. Lastly an officer from the British warship, clad in a royal blue uniform, came over the side and onto the deck. He looked around briefly. Finding the captain, he made his way to the stern of the ship.

"What ship is this, what port have you sailed from, what cargo do you carry, and where are you bound?" the naval officer demanded as his eyes met the captain's.

Captain Waterman for his part did all in his power to keep his composure. "Sir," he began, "this is the good ship *Whisperer*, home port Providence, recently departed Boston with forty-five tons of wood, bound for his Majesty's colony on the Island of Bermuda."

All was quiet for a moment as the naval officer mulled over in his mind, the information which Captain Waterman had provided, as he surveyed the deck. "I am Captain Buckham of His Majesty's ship *Wales*," he finally stated firmly. "We have intercepted several ships recently in these waters, meeting with ships of foreign powers, taking on arms, presumably for the rebels in the colonies. Do you carry any arms on this ship, Captain?" he demanded.

"We are only a merchant ship, sir, bent on delivering goods for profit," the captain replied, adding, "nothing more."

"We will see, Captain, we will see. Order your men to the stern here." the naval officer demanded.

We all complied with the order of our captain. When all were at the stern of the ship, the naval officer ordered half of the soldiers to the stern, presumably to hold us in that area. Immediately, the other half of marines, without a word being said, began to scramble below decks presumably to search the cargo hold, the crew's berth, along with the captain's cabin for weapons or other contraband.

Captain Waterman stepped forward to the naval officer and stated, "Sir, I do protest…," but before he could continue his protest, the naval officer pulled a pistol from his waistband and in one fast calculated motion, struck Captain Waterman on the right side of his head. The captain fell to the deck in a heap. He lay motionless for a few moments with blood streaming from a gash on his head. The naval officer yelled to the marines, "Charge bayonets!" With one movement, the marines brought their guns to the ready, each pointing his bayonet at us. Slowly, Captain Waterman got to his feet, holding a kerchief to the side of his head to stem the flow of blood.

Presently, a marine returned from below deck, reporting to the naval officer that no weapons were found and that all seemed to be in order. One marine presented to the British captain the bill of laden regarding our cargo, which the officer looked over thoroughly for several moments. "All seems to be in order here, Captain, but there is one more matter to deal with," the officer stated. "My ship finds herself short of crew due to a recent outbreak of the pox," he said. "I will need to press some of your crew." As the officer went down the line of us, he looked each of us over and asked about our years of experience at sea. When he came to me, it seemed as if he held my small frame with disdain. "And you, boy," he demanded, "what is your experience at sea and name the ships you've seen duty on."

I was exceedingly nervous and even though the captain had told me not to speak, I blurted out, "This is my first time to sea and the only ship I have sailed on, sir."

The British officer looked at me with even more disdain as he grabbed me by the shoulders and arms. Satisfied that I was not what he wanted, he looked at Jones and Hotaling and said, "You and you are pressed into service on His Majesty's ship."

The marines began to scramble over the side and into their boat with Jones and Hotaling in tow. There wasn't even a "pardon me" or a "by your leave." By the time they had returned to their ship, Captain Waterman had the remaining crew setting sail, and we were under way again. I thought to myself that my first two encounters with the British military had not gone well.

That evening I found the captain in his cabin tending to his wound. The gash on the side of his head was about three inches long and deep. "Head wounds," he said, "always bleed worse than they are." I helped my uncle dress his wound and when completed, he asked me to sit down. "Will," he continued, "now you see the tyranny and the power of the British navy, and the unjust practices they subject us to, on land as well as on the seas. A search of our cargo without warrant, along with the pressing of crew without issue," said Captain Jeremiah with disdain. "Now we are short of crew ourselves for the rest of our sail." I didn't say anything, but from what I had seen in Boston, coupled with the treatment of my uncle and his crew on the high sea, I had developed my own ill feelings towards the British military.

The rest of the sail to Bermuda and then onto Charlestown was uneventful. The first thing I now noticed at each port we entered, was the number of British warships at anchor in the harbors, along with the large number of soldiers in each city. At each port our ship was unloaded of her cargo and loaded with new goods bound for the next port. We carried sugarcane from Bermuda to Charlestown. At Charlestown, our cargo hold was loaded with tobacco bound for the city of Philadelphia.

When we were at sail and I had time to myself, I would look out at the endless ocean in front of me. I longed to be home with my family and Diane in Norwich. I couldn't wait to be back and tell them of my adventures. The sunrises and sunsets at sea were beyond description, with a huge orange ball appearing above or slipping below the waves on the horizon. At night I would find the North Star. I would wonder to myself if anyone back home were looking at the same stars, imagining where I was. At times like these I would say a prayer for my family and friends, that God would bless them and keep them.

The captain was unusually quiet for the rest of the trip. Only when we approached the mouth of the river on which Philadelphia was located, did his spirits rise. We waited several hours for the evening tide to come in and rode it up the river several miles, aided by a light wind, until we were within a half-mile of the city. It seemed to me that Philadelphia was all that Boston was and perhaps more. A boat met us at anchor. We were then towed to the dock for the unloading of our cargo. The captain called me to the stern of the ship and said, "Will, do you remember where the envelope that Mr. Revere provided me, is located in my cabin?" he asked.

"I do, sir," I replied.

"Good, son, go and get it and bring it to me," he stated. I was back in a moment. Without looking at the envelope or me the captain turned to leave the ship, stating as he departed, "Mr. Jennings, the ship is yours. I shall return later this evening. The order of the watch on the ship is your responsibility, sir." And with that we were down the plank and on solid ground.

The captain walked at a brisk pace and I was hard pressed to keep up. Clearly, he was on a mission and wanted to be somewhere quickly. Presently, after ten minutes of walking, he stopped, peering in the window of a printing shop. It appeared that no one was there as Uncle Jeremiah walked in the shop and up to the counter. Presently, an older looking man who was bald, but otherwise had long straggly hair, came to the counter from the back room and looked over the glasses on his nose at my uncle.

"Captain Waterman," he said in recognition, "it is good to see you again, sir. What brings you to my shop today?"

"Master Franklin, it is with great pleasure, sir, that I see you again. I have here, sir, a correspondence from a most distinguished gentleman in New England, who is interested in your opinion on matters contained herein. I believe the distinguished gentlemen in your group will find it most interesting. It has been with great distress and peril to my ship, my crew, and even myself that I deliver it to you, sir."

Once again we were invited to dine. After introductions by my uncle of Mr. Franklin and me, we were escorted to the dining room. The conversation between my uncle and Mr. Franklin centered on the events in Boston, as well as other cities in the colonies along the American coast.

Mr. Franklin, pulling a piece of paper from the desk behind his dinner seat, asked my uncle "How long have you been at sea, Captain?"

"Almost two months, Benjamin, why?" my uncle replied.

"Then you haven't heard of this," Mr. Franklin stated, handing my uncle the piece of paper.

Taking it, my uncle took several minutes to read the document over thoroughly before placing it on the table. Hesitating a moment, my uncle finally stated, "Quartering of soldiers in residences in Boston is intolerable."

"Yes," Mr. Franklin began, "but it is probably seen as retribution to the residents for the Tea Party, and as a way of controlling the populace of Boston. We have even received reports that the British may plan to quarter soldiers in any city that begins to show signs of serious unrest." Uncle Jeremiah could only shake his head in disbelief.

Mr. Franklin turned the conversation to people who couldn't be trusted, speaking in low tones as he leaned across the table to get closer to my uncle. He spoke as if even then, there may be someone listening whom he couldn't trust, although we were the only three in the room. He spoke of others who may even be spies, who were believed to be passing information to the British in Philadelphia.

Finally, with dinner complete and the conversation ended, my uncle pushed his chair away from the table stating, "I sail with the morning tide and I wish you Godspeed, sir."

Mr. Franklin took my uncle's hand and stated, "When we meet again, sir, we may no longer be under this oppressive rule."

"God willing, sir," my uncle replied. He turned and exited the warm comforts of the printer's shop and residence. When we reached the ship, the captain appeared to be extremely tired from the journey. He went directly to his cabin for the night. We did sail for Providence on the morning tide and with a week of fair winds, we were within sight of Brenton Point, and the opening of Narragansett Bay. We docked that night. In the morning the captain called the remaining crew to his cabin and we were paid off. I never had so much money that was my own. I had almost twenty pounds sterling in my pocket. Uncle Jeremiah directed me to a stable down the street where he had a horse boarded, which he said I was welcome to. "Just tell the stable hand, you're my nephew, and if he has any questions, to come see me," he said. I thanked my uncle for all he had done and headed for the stable. Norwich and home were only a two day ride away, and I had so much to tell everyone. I missed my family and Diane.

In the years to come, I would remember my time on board the *Whisperer*, Uncle Jeremiah and all that I had seen and learned.

- CHAPTER 4 -

"Boston and the Regulars"

1775

Spring 1775 was busy with the planting of the season's crops. The problems and tension between the Crown and colonies only seemed to grow with the passing of time. There were meetings, followed by more meetings in Durkee's Tavern, as tempers between the men in town seemed to be coming to a boil. A small representation of all of the colonies I supposed. As it turned out, tensions between the Crown and the colonies would soon boil over.

The post rider rode by our house and to Norwich with the thunder of a thousand hooves on April 20, 1775. He was waving his hat and shouting something about a fight. Da and I stepped out of the barn as we heard him riding by and yelling. Da slowly turned and went back to what we had been doing, which was shoeing one of our horses. After another hour of work, he finally put down his tools, took off his apron, and stated as he walked out of the barn, "Let's go see what happened, Will." He knew I was on pins and needles, as I could hardly contain myself for finding out the news.

We rode our horses to town and as we approached Durkee's Tavern, we could see that a large group of men had gathered. The people we passed in town were all talking about a battle outside of Boston. A notice had been placed on the tavern signboard, as everyone who was in town, and had heard the post rider shouting, came to the tavern to read the news. There was already a large group of men gathered outside Durkee's Tavern, talking with great excitement. As we approached the group, Eli Bingham broke out of the crowd, and he came running over to me, "Will," he shouted, "have you heard!"

"Have I heard what, Eli?" I responded.

"It's happened! The British marched out of Boston to secure stores of ball and powder reportedly being hidden in the towns of Lexington and Concord. The militia was called out. They met on the Lexington Green and they fired on each other! It's started!" he shouted as he ran off down the street in his excitement. I stood there in shock for several moments. In the following days and weeks, the full details of the battle became known. Someone had placed two lanterns in the tower of the old North Church, which was followed by midnight rides by Mr. Revere, Mr. Dawes and Mr. Prescott, to warn the local populace of British regular leaving Boston. I wondered secretly, if this was the same Mr. Revere I had met the year before with my Uncle Jeremiah in Boston. It had to be. How much did my uncle really know, and he never told me.

The information described a small group of militiamen standing before a column of British regulars, on the Lexington Green and being fired upon. The commander of the British troops ordered the militia to lay down their arms and no one could really say who fired first. There were numbers of dead and wounded on both sides. As the regulars returned to Boston, the gathering numbers of militiamen from the surrounding towns and countryside harassed them until they were within the safety of Boston itself. The word was that before the British reached Boston, they were soundly whipped.

I continued to be on pins and needles for days, waiting to hear the latest news. One evening after dinner, Da was sitting enjoying his pipe. As I was about to excuse myself from the table, Da cleared his throat, as he stated to me, "Will, we've got things to talk about."

"Yes, Da," I answered.

"I know that ever since you sailed with your Uncle Jeremiah last year aboard his ship, you've not held the Crown in much esteem," he began.

I said nothing, but looked at my father as he continued. "With this latest problem in the Massachusetts colony, with dead on both sides, I am interested to know what you are thinking, son?" he asked.

I was ready to burst to tell him what was really in my heart, but I held my tongue to gather my thoughts. Finally, I said, "Da, it seems to me that this fight has been coming on for years. I have had some contact with the British regulars, in Boston last year when I was aboard Uncle Jeremiah's ship, as well as with the British navy while at sea. If I experienced just a small amount of how they have treated the rest of the colonies for years, I am surprised this hasn't happened earlier," I replied. As I continued I looked at Da and said, "I know you are against fighting the Crown, Da, and I understand your reasons, but the French and Indian War was years ago. I have to tell you that it is in my heart to fight the British, if this fight is to continue."

All was quiet for several moments and I knew that mother, who was in the kitchen, was listening. Finally Da spoke up, "You are right, Will, I am against fighting the Crown. I also don't want you to join the militia or going to Boston to join any fighting there."

"But, Da!" I shouted, as I almost jumped out of my chair, "how can you say as much, when you know they have treated us with utter contempt, and continue to do so!"

"Will!" Da said strongly, as he raised his voice, "this is not our fight, and I don't want you in it!"

"Da!" I shouted in reply, "you are wrong, and you don't understand!" I stormed out of the house. As I walked down the road, I didn't know where I was going. I had to clear my head. How could there be fighting and I not go? How could it be that Da doesn't understand? I was just walking and before I knew it I was at Eli's house. I knocked on the door. I didn't even realize that Master Bingham was at the door standing for a moment before he said, "Yes, Will, what can I do for you?"

"Is, is Eli home?" I stammered.

"I believe you'll find him in the barn doing his evening chores, Will," he responded.

"Thank you, sir," I replied. I ran around the Bingham house to the barn. As I opened the barn door and entered, I found Eli cleaning out several stalls where the horses were kept.

"Eli?" I asked as I entered.

"Here, Will," I heard him reply.

"Eli, I've got to talk to you," I said as I approached. "I've just had an argument with my father. He has forbidden me to train with the militia, or go to Boston to join the fight."

"I'm not surprised, Will," Eli answered, "I had the same conversation with my father last night. I expected your father was of the same mind."

"What are we to do, Eli?" I responded.

"Well," Eli began, "right now I'm not doing anything. But if this really is a war, I plan on joining it if it continues. If there is any more fighting in Boston, I think I'm going."

"I think I'll go with you, Eli, when the time comes," I replied.

The next few weeks passed without much news from Boston or anywhere else in the colonies. The colonial militias had set up a ring around Boston itself, a sort of siege of the city. I spent my days working in the fields, or with Eli and Diane, when time allowed. It was turning out to be a hot spring.

Mid-May brought word that a force under two commanders, Benedict Arnold and Ethan Allen, leading Allen's Green Mountain Boys, had taken Fort Ticonderoga without a shot being fired. The fort being taken in the early morning hours, with the entire garrison surprised. Da could only shake his head. He had recounted many stories from the French and Indian War, of sorties by Rogers' Rangers from that very fort, which had been so successful against the Indians to the north in Canada.

On June 20, 1775, the post rider came riding hard into town again. This time he seemed much more ragged. I was in town with Da delivering some milk to the local mercantile. He had important news to give, but instead of riding right off, he went into Durkee's Tavern for food and a drink. The crowd in the tavern drew near him as he sat down. Word was spread throughout the town that the post rider was at the tavern. Master Durkee himself was the first to speak up.

"What news have ye, Mr. Brown," he demanded, "out of Boston?"

"What news ye say, Durkee?" Mr. Brown hesitated as he took a deep drink of ale. "I have news of a tremendous battle, on Charlestown, on Breed's Hill." As he paused to gather his thoughts, a mummer went out from those gathered to hear the details.

"On the night of the 16th, the colonial militias decided to fortify Bunker Hill in Charlestown," he started. "But as I understand it, the night being so dark with a new moon, they got confused about which hill they were on. They went one hill too far, and ended up fortifying Breed's Hill. By the time the sun rose on the 17th, the British discovered the fortifications, but by then they were almost finished. Several of the British warships in the harbor opened fire on the colonials, but with little effect."

"What of the fighting!" One of the men shouted from the back.

"As I understand it," Brown continued, as he put down his mug after taking a large gulp, "the British landed boat after boat of regulars from Boston, along with many cannons. After they had gathered in sufficient numbers, they began their assault on our fortified positions early in the afternoon. I was told, mind you I didn't see it, that the redcoats marched up the hill several times under heavy fire from the colonials. The hill leading up to the fortifications was covered with the red coat dead and wounded by the battle's end, including many officers."

As Mr. Brown paused to take another long drink of ale, several men implored him to continue.

"Well," Brown continued as he placed his mug on the table, "late in the day after several assaults, the regulars finally made it to the top of Breed's Hill and the fortifications, but only after the colonials' powder gave out. The rear guard left behind by the colonials to cover the general retreat paid a heavy toll. The redcoats, as I understand it, showed no mercy, bayoneting many. Angry from their losses, they were, I suppose. Most of Charlestown was burned to the ground by the British during the fighting, to root out the colonial militia snipers," Brown concluded shaking his head.

Finally, Durkee shouted out from behind the bar with some disappointment, "Then it was a British victory!"

Brown looked over his shoulder at Durkee and with a stern face replied, "The British may have taken the hill and held the ground in the end, but the cost they paid was too high to consider it a victory for them. The siege of Boston is unbroken, with supplies reaching the British from the sea only. Word is that the colonies are sending a Virginian, by the name of Washington, to lead the militia's siege of Boston. Nobody knows much about him," Brown stated flatly. Brown made his way to the door. He got on his horse, and slowly trotted out of town without saying anything else.

When Mr. Brown had departed, all was abuzz again in the tavern, as the men made their way to the door to go tell their family, friends and neighbors of the news of the battle of Bunker Hill. The news spread like wildfire, and within several minutes, all in town had heard of the battle. Within days, all of the cities and towns in the colonies had heard the news. It was really a war.

I walked out with Eli, and I think we were both shocked at the news. I told Da I would walk home with Eli. Da said that would be fine as he had business with the blacksmith, and he would be home later. As we walked home not much was said between us.

"Eli," I finally said, "I need to talk to you about this whole thing. Can we meet later tonight down at the river, by the fishing hole to talk about this?"

"Sure," Eli responded.

That night not much was said at the dinner table. I could tell by the somber mood of my father, as well as mother, that the news had hit them hard. I knew enough not to say anything to Da about my feelings, or what

I thought or wanted to do. After dinner was over and the chores completed, I asked Da if I could go fishing with Eli. He agreed, but told me not to be out after dark. As I walked down to the river with my fishing rod in hand, I could only think of all that the post rider had said. That there had been a real battle between the British regulars and colonial militias, with untold dead and wounded on both sides. The British held the field, but suffered heavy losses. The siege around Boston was unbroken. I wanted to enlist, but what would Da say? As I approached the river, Eli was already there with his line in the water.

"Hey, Eli," I greeted as I sat down, "are they biting tonight?"

"Not much," Eli responded. "I wasn't really trying to catch anything. I was thinking more about what the post rider said today."

"Are you still thinking about enlisting?" I asked.

"Well, I'm thinking about it, are you?" Eli inquired.

"Yeah, I am, but I don't know how to tell my Da or Diane," I replied.

"Will, I heard several men in town talk about going to Plainfield in the next week or so to join up. Word is that Durkee is going to be a colonel in the Connecticut militia. He will be leading our men to Boston to help with the siege," Eli said. "He has already left for Plainfield. He left word with the Sons of Liberty to ask for him at headquarters in Plainfield, as we'll all form a unit," Eli stated. "Several men have already left for there, Will," Eli added.

"Eli, don't go without me," I replied. "I've got to talk to my Da first before we go, even if he doesn't understand. We'll leave by the end of the week," I concluded.

The conversation didn't go well with my father. I didn't expect it to, really, but I hoped that we could come to an understanding. He raised his voice, as did I. Finally, mother spoke, and the conversation became more civil. "Will," Da implored, "do you know of the hardships a soldier faces, and I don't mean by just facing the enemy?" he asked. I didn't say anything as Da continued. "There will be a lack of food, lack of ammunition, lack of clothing, along with diseases, in addition to facing the British army," he stated flatly. "What if you are wounded or captured?" Da added. "You'll likely die of your wounds, and surely die if you are sent to a British prison."

"Da, I understand what you are saying, and you are probably right about most of this, but my mind is made up, I have decided to go," I said. "I'll pack my things and be gone in the morning," I said with finality. As I walked upstairs to pack my meager belongings, I could hear my mother crying in the kitchen.

That night after packing, I saddled my horse, Chester, riding him to Diane's house. Things went there as they had at my house. Diane didn't understand why I had to go. She said that there were others, who could do the fighting, if it had to be done. "What about us, Will Waterman?" she finally implored. "Am I to wait to hear of you being wounded or killed on some far away battlefield?"

"I'll be back, Diane," I insisted. "Everything will be alright, you'll see."

"Will, I don't want you to go and I don't know if I can take the waiting, or worrying, not knowing if you are okay or not," she insisted.

"Diane, I will be back for you, you'll see," I stated. "I'll write to you while I'm gone. Besides, maybe this war won't last that long anyway."

We hugged, and kissed as we said our goodbyes. I then rode home, wondering when I would return home again.

In the morning, after a restless night, I found Eli outside of our house waiting for me on his horse. He had a bag packed that contained food, along with warm clothing, a canteen, and a blanket roll, his musket, powder horn and ball. That was all he needed, he said. I was ready to go. As I brought my horse out from the barn, and around to the front of our house, I found Da and Mother, along with John and Rachel. Ma was crying again. Pastor Gallagher and Diane arrived shortly in their buckboard, as we were saying our goodbyes.

Pastor Gallagher was the first to speak. "Will, let's pray together before you and Eli go." I didn't say anything as Pastor Gallagher began to pray, "In the name of our Lord and Savior, Jesus, the Christ, we pray for Will and Eli, that as they depart to go and fight in a cause they feel is just and right, that you, oh Lord, will go with them. Father, we pray that you will guide their steps and that your hand of protection will be on them. We pray that they will return home again, safely to us, Lord, in your name we pray, Amen," Pastor Gallagher concluded.

"Will, remember all that I've taught you, and trust your instincts," Da instructed. "Write your Ma, and come home when you can. Now give your mother a kiss before you go," he said. I hugged and kissed my Ma. As I turned to go, Da stopped me, giving me a hug. I looked away, not wanting him to see my emotions, and mounted my horse. Diane came and held my hand briefly as I sat in the saddle looking down at her.

"I'll be back, you'll see," I said as I reined my horse. Eli and I headed down the road. As we left, I looked back over my shoulder. I could see several people moving about our house, and that Diane was watching me go.

- CHAPTER 5 -

"Enlistment and the Siege of Boston"

1775

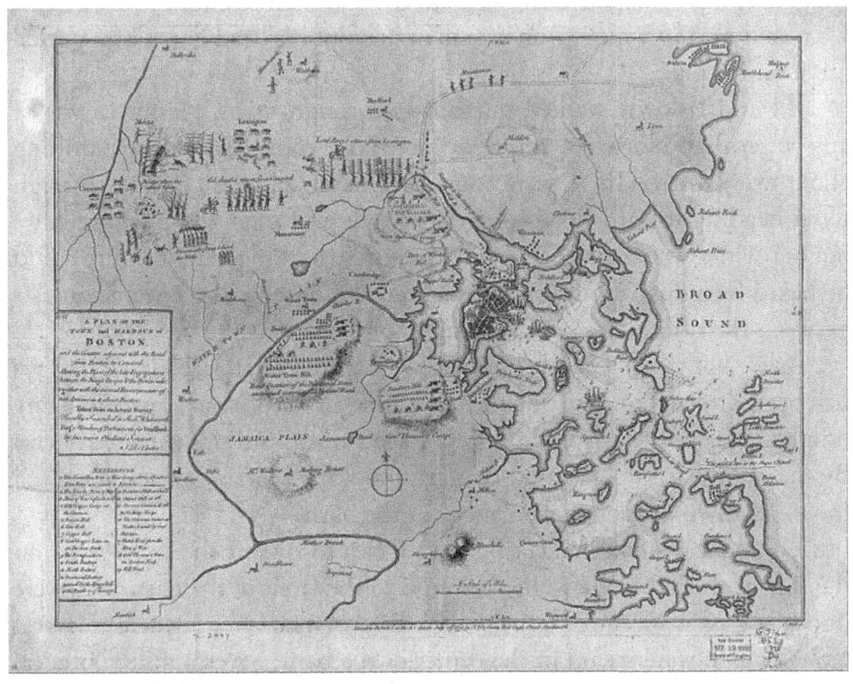

Eli and I made our way the 15 miles or so to Plainfield without incident. Along the way we came upon any numbers of groups of men from around the Connecticut colony who'd heard of the enlistment. There were men from New London, New Haven, Hartford, Storrs, New Britain, Manchester and numerous other towns throughout the colony that I had never heard of. Some of them were men who had been traveling for days to get to Plainfield. As we approached the outskirts of the town, there were tent camps popping up everywhere, with more and more men coming into the area all the time. It seemed to be an almost controlled chaos of men moving to and fro. Finally, Eli asked a man who was sitting outside his tent on a barrel, smoking his pipe, "Can you tell us where we need to go to enlist around here?"

The man slowly looked up at the two riders before him and said, "Where you boys from?"

"We're from Norwich, there about," Eli stated, as I just sat on my horse listening to the exchange.

"I'm from the Woodstock Valley myself. Been here two days," he said. "Name's Joshua Woods. Now if you want to enlist you boys need to ride right to the other side of town, where you'll see a big red barn. That's what they're calling headquarters. You go in there and ask around, you'll be told what to do." As we moved on, the man just put his head down and puffed more on his pipe.

Eli and I slowly walked our horses through town. Plainfield wasn't any larger than Norwich. Yet, there were large numbers of people milling about everywhere. There were wagon trains of supplies coming through town heading toward Boston. Another group of men was pushing cows out of town toward one of the many pastures that ringed it. Gunfire could be heard from just about every direction. Presumably these were contests between the militiamen, each trying to prove he was the best shot.

As we got to the far side of town, we found the large red barn that we had been directed to. Outside the barn, men could be seen engaged in any number of activities, as the officers of the various militias directed them. By the main barn doors stood two gruff looking sentries, which observed the militiamen as they moved about at the barn.

Eli and I dismounted, tying our horses to one of the horse rails on the side of the barn. We walked around to the front of the barn, and were unchallenged as we entered. Inside were lines of men standing before several tables, which were set up in the center of the barn. Several militia officers sat at each table with open books before them. Behind them stood several additional officers who were looking at each recruit as they approached the tables. The ages of the men in the barn ranged from old men, who appeared too old to hold a gun and fight, to boys who seemed younger than Eli and me. We got in the end of the line nearest to us, standing there for a moment. Finally, Eli whispered in my ear, "What are they doing up there?"

"I'm not sure, but I think they are asking each man to make his mark, or sign his name." I said.

Suddenly, from the corner of the barn to our right, I heard my name called out, "Waterman, Will Waterman!" the man called.

I looked over and recognized Master Durkee. Eli and I broke out of the line, walking over. Master Durkee greeted us warmly as he shook both of our hands.

"I'm glad to see you and Eli here," he said. "Did your father come, Will?" he asked.

"I'm afraid not, sir," I replied.

"I was afraid he'd not come," Master Durkee stated dejectedly. "Still, loyal to the Crown is he, to the end?" he asked.

"It is something like that," I replied.

"Well, here's the long and short of it for now," Master Durkee began. "Don't wait in line here to sign up. I've already got a list of those I think are coming from Norwich, or the surrounding towns. I check them off as they show up." As he continued, he looked around, "Our unit is gathering to the east of the barn, in the field with the spring house in it. I'll see you there later," he said as he began to walk towards an officer, who was calling his name from the other side of the barn. "There is a sergeant out back with tents," Master Durkee directed as he continued to walk over to the man hailing him.

Behind the barn, a gruff looking sergeant threw a tent to us off of a wagon.

Eli and I gathered our horses; belongings and new tent, and then headed to the field Master Durkee had directed us to. When we got there we found about fifty men pitching tents in the field. Many of these men we recognized as men from Norwich, or from one of the nearby towns. A sergeant there was trying to keep order, by directing the militiamen where each tent should be pitched. The sergeant was lining the tents up in a straight-line grid and square.

That night, the men in the pasture each sat around their campfires cooking dinner. Each was telling another where they were from, and why they had come to enlist, to fight the British. After the evening meal, Eli and I tended our horses, settling in for our night's sleep. It was a restless night, sleeping in the tents. The many sounds from around Plainfield of men drinking, firing their guns, as well as the many animals roaming about, went on far into the night. When morning came, both Eli and I were almost as tired as the night before. After a fresh wash at the springhouse followed by some food, along with hot coffee, we both felt much better. Eli and I recognized many faces of the men, as being from Norwich. The

Calkin brothers, Joshua and Hiram, were here, as was John Edgerington, Mr. Smith, John Allyn, Samuel Hyde and his brother William, and several other men of prominent families from Norwich. In all there were over fifty men and boys from Norwich or the surrounding towns, now under the command of Colonel Durkee. A number of them were also counted as members of the Sons of Liberty from town.

Shortly before nine, several officers were seen riding up to our camp, among them was Master Durkee. Our men were all called together, as it was Master Durkee, who spoke to the small group of militiamen gathered. "My name is Colonel Durkee and this is Captain Fitch," he began as he went down the line of officers who had arrived with him. All of the men from Norwich, as well as the surrounding communities already knew both Durkee and Fitch, but the order of the military dictated that they are properly and formally introduced. When he had finished the introductions, Colonel Durkee began telling us what to expect in the next few days.

"All of you have either made your mark or were signed up to serve eight months in the 4th Connecticut Regiment, the Rhode Island Brigade," he stated. "On the morrow, be ready to march to Boston by nine in the morning," he instructed. "You will gather in the field, half a mile to the north on the post road outside of town. There will be many other companies, or groups of militia gathered there, so listen to Captain Fitch's instructions, and that of your assigned sergeant. The rest of this morning, along with a good part of the afternoon will be spent on drills, as well as to assess each of you as to your shooting and riding skills. All of you have been entered into the book of enlisted men that have signed up for eight months service in the Connecticut militia," he repeated. "Good day to you men," Colonel Durkee added. Then turning to Captain Fitch he continued, "I leave them in your hands. Do your duty, sir." With that Colonel Durkee wheeled his horse, riding off, followed by a number of junior officers with him.

Captain Fitch remained with the hard-nosed sergeant who had provided us our tents the previous day, who was introduced as Sergeant Hartshorn.

Captain Fitch went down a whole list of rules and regulations that were to be followed. It included everything from how to set up camp, to saluting officers, the chain of command, marching, when to get up, when to go to sleep, and what times each meal would be served. The morning's drill seemed never to end, until finally, Sergeant Hartshorn said we were dismissed for a half-hour for lunch.

The afternoon went much quicker. First, was some marching again, followed by lining up in two rows, to complete shooting and reloading drills. Firing in volleys followed this. After that came individual firing at targets at varying distances up to several hundred yards. Eli and I were distinguished as two of the best shots in the unit. When that was completed, those of us who had horses were ordered to saddle them, then to return to our encampment area. Our riding skills were evaluated, as the horses were thoroughly looked over by the officers.

The next day, all were up early. By eight in the morning, camp was broken, as all was made ready for the march to Boston. Shortly before nine, Sergeant Hartshorn formed us up in marching order, with all of our baggage being stored in the company wagon. Our unit was marched to the gathering area outside of Plainfield. In a field just north of town, about 500 men from several companies were gathered along with supply wagons, horses and livestock. The Order of March was provided to each unit by the company commander and by ten, the leading elements of the column headed down the Post Road to Boston, an hour late. Our unit was assigned to the back third of the column, and it was almost quarter to eleven before our unit was ordered in-line to begin our march. At the end of the column of marching men was the wagon train, followed by the livestock, which is where Eli's and my horse were relegated to.

After several hours of marching, we were halted for lunch, which consisted of some bread and cheese. A rider rode up and down the line informing each unit that we were about half way to Providence. The march was shortly resumed, and by six that evening we were on the outskirts of Providence. Our unit pitched camp in a cow field of a local farmer along with the rest of our column.

The following day, camp was broken at six in the morning. Our entire unit was on the march by eight. Our march was similar to the previous day, with the exception that we marched much longer to reach the outskirts of Boston that night. As we approached the area we were increasingly met along the road by sentries, or mounted patrols of men who challenged our unit commanders as to the nature of our unit, and which colony we were from. Upon learning we were a unit from the Connecticut colony, our unit commanders were told to follow the Post Road to Roxbury, where further orders would be given. After another half-hour march, our unit was directed to a farm just to the south of the town of Roxbury, a small farming community outside of Boston. Here our 500 man unit was directed again into a farmer's field to pitch camp. Each individual unit of about 50 men was directed to set up camp in a square formation with the unit commanders in the center. Our wagon train and supplies were sent to the south of the encampment, as the livestock and horses were sent to a field yet farther south.

That evening after supper, each unit's commanders held a meeting with their men. Captain Fitch and Sergeant Hartshorn stood in front of their tents at the center of our encampment as our unit gathered around. "Men," Captain Fitch began, "on the morrow our unit will be sent up to the line. From this position we will watch the British in Boston. I don't anticipate any immediate action, but always have your gun loaded when on the line, and be ready at all times to be called to action when in the rear area. When you are not on the line, you all will be called upon to perform other duties. These duties will include sentry duty, picket duty, foraging for food and supplies, or as messengers. Each morning, Sergeant Hartshorn will give each of you your duty for the day. Perform it without question. That is all till the morrow." With that, the men began to mill about and head back to their tents for the night. As Eli and I began to make our way to our tent, Sergeant Hartshorn called after us.

"Waterman, Bingham," he called. "Come with me to Captain Fitch's tent, he has a matter to discuss with you." Following Sergeant Hartshorn, we entered the captain's tent, removing our tri-corns and saluted. Captain Fitch sat at a small desk in the middle of his tent. On the far side was one cot, and the entire tent was dimly lit by three candles.

As Captain Fitch looked up from his desk, he said, "Relax boys. You have distinguished yourselves as not only the two best riders of our unit, but of the entire regiment. Colonel Durkee and I knew about you before we left Norwich for Plainfield. As Colonel Durkee is familiar with you boys from Norwich, he has personally requested you two as dispatch riders and scouts for the regiment. Each morning, report to Sergeant Hartshorn for orders, and unless otherwise directed by Sergeant Hartshorn, you will then report to Colonel Durkee's tent at the center of the encampment for dispatches, or scout duties. Is this understood?"

"Yes, sir" Eli and I replied in unison, as we stood at attention.

"Don't let me down. You're dismissed," Captain Fitch said as he looked down at the papers on his desk.

As Eli and I walked back to our tent, we were filled with excitement that we'd have more chance of action in our new duties as dispatch riders and scouts for Colonel Durkee. The next day was a dark, dreary day with low-lying clouds and occasional rain. Our unit was mustered at eight that morning, as Sergeant Hartshorn marched us the remaining half-mile to the entrenchments, which weren't more than a small ditch along a rise of land outside of Boston. There were men from several militias working to enlarge the trench in depth, as well as length. Off to the right of our line, on a hill some half-mile distant, more men could be seen working feverishly in the same occupation as the men in front of us were.

As I looked down the hill, I could make out many familiar sights from my voyage the previous year on my uncle's ship, *Whisperer*. From this vantage point, in front of our position, I could see the neck of land connecting Boston with the mainland. Beyond that I could see long wharf, where we had docked, and all of Boston Harbor, which was full of British warships, as well as numerous cargo ships. Off to our right, beyond Dorchester Heights was Castle Island. From this position, I could see the British flag flying over several buildings in Boston along the harbor front, as well as on Castle Island. British soldiers in their scarlet uniforms could be seen moving about all parts of Boston itself. Most of the British seemed to be engaged, like us, with the building of fortifications.

Sergeant Hartshorn restated our duties at the front lines. Our unit would take turns with the other militias in our area, with the building of our entrenchment, and holding the line outside of Roxbury. Additionally, we would man the entrenchments on four-hour shifts each day, reporting any movement of the regulars to the officer of the watch. Already, we were instructed not to fire our weapons unless the British left Boston in force, either over the neck of land connecting Boston to the mainland in front of us, or by boats in the harbor. Sergeant Hartshorn informed us that the only ball and powder available at this time was what each man had brought with him, and until sufficient stores of ball and powder were obtained, firing on the enemy would be kept to a minimum. When not on front line duty, the men were to remain in the encampment area and would be assigned to picket, or other duties as needed.

And so, our first few days turned into a few weeks. Most of the men in our unit were busy while on duty at the front with extending the entrenchment lines, or improving those already completed. The first signs of discontentment among the men in the militias, and the individual units began to show quickly. There were militia units from all over New England, each with individual commanders who thought they knew what was best for the army. There was never enough food for all of the men. The quartermasters, in an effort to locate additional stores of food, was forced to send patrols out, to search the surrounding countryside, and towns continually.

The men complained of the lack of training, and due to the boredom that soon enveloped the entire army, men resorted to drinking, and thus fighting to occupy their time, when they were not on duty.

There were also squabbles between generals who were in charge of the three main units of the army. To the north of Boston, General Lee commanded the left wing of the army. To the west of Boston, the middle wing of the army was commanded by General Putnam, and to the south of Boston, the right wing of the army, was commanded by General Ward.

It was to the last of the generals mentioned that Colonel Durkee reported regarding the activities of our regiment. Although General Putnam was from Connecticut, and he was in command of most of the Connecticut regiments, we found our unit, the 4th Connecticut under the command of General Ward and the Rhode Island Brigade. It was rumored throughout the army that the Continental Congress was going to assign one man to lead this disorganized menagerie of militias, and make them into a fighting force.

If the British had known at this time the extent of the disarray of the American forces facing them, they surely would have marched out of Boston enforce, and routed our entire army. The men who had survived the battle of Bunker Hill said that the British, even though they took the field, were still smarting from that engagement. This, along with the beating they took during their retreat from Lexington and Concord, convinced everyone that the regulars would not leave Boston.

Two weeks after our arrival, word spread like wild fire that the commander from Virginia colony had arrived. Rumors immediately began to swirl about this new commander. That he was a veteran of the French and Indian War, like my own father, was indisputable, although he only saw action in the south. It was rumored that he was responsible for the actual beginning of the French and Indian War, but no one could say why. He immediately began reorganizing the various militias and commanders, as the ragtag groups of militias from the northern colonies, finally began to resemble an army. His name was General George Washington, and his mere presence changed the outlook of the war. By late summer our ranks swelled to between fifteen to eighteen thousand men. This would be one of the highest counts for the American army during the war.

And so the summer months began to wear on. Eli and I were mainly engaged with the delivering of dispatches between the commanding officers. Once Colonel Durkee had provided us with dispatches for General Ward, General Ward would then use us for dispatches for the other generals farther along the line. It would not be unusual for both of us to make several trips a day to the other generals, and due to the lateness of the hour when our duties were completed; we would sleep in the encampment of whatever unit was near to us.

In addition to overhearing the generals complain of the shortages of just about everything needed to fight a war, they also complained about having to submit their units to the authority of commanders from other colonies. Additionally, we also learned about what the men from other units, and the colonies were complaining about. Mostly the lack of food, along with ball and powder were the biggest complaints, but later as the summer waned, and fall began to make its appearance, most men began to complain of the lack of warmer clothing and winter quarters. When the first frosts covered the ground, almost all complained that they needed to be home for the fall harvest.

Shortly after the arrival of General Washington, word reached our lines from one of the many spies in Boston, that the British had plans to send a force to secure Dorchester Heights, and fortify it. From this position, the British would be able to hold the high ground and protect their forces in Boston, as well as their ships in Boston Harbor. With this knowledge, Washington ordered the army to begin fortifications on Dorchester Heights, before the British did the same. When British General Gates learned of the works the Americans were building on Dorchester Heights, he hesitated for several days, making it too late to attack the position without facing another Bunker Hill.

Following the Dorchester Heights fortification, General Washington immediately began the fortifying of Cobble Hill and Plowed Hill to the west and north of Boston. The American noose around Boston was getting uncomfortably tight for the British.

During the course of the summer months on several occasions, each side would make occasional forays toward the other's lines to determine the enemy's strength in that area, or to attempt so secure outlying supplies. With the British only able to receive supplies by sea, their forays out of Boston became more frequent. Word continually reached the American lines that in Boston, food was terribly short. The citizens and British regulars alike were beginning to resort to eating dogs, and even rats. Word was received that the regulars would soon be eating the remaining horses.

In late August, Eli and I found ourselves riding dispatches between the camps of General Putnam in the center of our lines and General Ward on the right. We were in the area of the town of Brookline, crossing the Muddy River. We could see a commotion at the entrenchment of the Massachusetts militia in front of us. Almost immediately, sporadic gunfire came from the earthworks. Eli and I instinctively began riding toward the sound of the firing. As we approached the earth works, it became apparent that the regulars were coming out of their defensive position, at the neck to Boston, on a foraging raid. As they came out, they formed up, concentrating a heavy fire on the Massachusetts position, as smaller groups of men with wagons, or on horses made for the few barns still standing between the lines.

"They must be desperate for food if they are still looking in those barns," I said to no one in particular. The sergeant at the right of the Massachusetts line formed up one of the militia units and moved out of the earthworks, to begin an advance on the regulars. Farther behind the earthworks, a lieutenant was forming a squad of dragoons, or mounted soldiers. Eli and I began moving toward these men. As we drew near we could hear the lieutenant in command instructing his men.

"As soon as the militia engages the regulars in the open, we'll ride to engage the regulars at the barn nearest to our position," he said as his horse nervously moved from side to side, as it sensed the coming fight. "Remember," he said as he continued, "the goal is to take some alive for intelligence purposes, so don't kill them all, if you don't have to. This comes directly from General Washington, he wants some alive. Is that understood," he said as he looked around at his men. There was a spattering of "yes, sirs" under the breath of any number of the twenty-five or so dragoons who were gathered. They instinctively looked past their commander at the developing engagement, anticipating the danger they were about to ride into, as they listened to the lieutenant. "We'll be within range of their cannons down there, so be quick about it," said the lieutenant as he wheeled his horse to prepare for the charge. I quickly rode up to the officer as he drew his saber from its scabbard.

"Sir," I said as I rode up, "can you use two extra men for the attack?" The lieutenant glanced in our direction for a brief moment and as he looked back toward the advancing militia on the regulars, stated "You're not mounted infantry."

"No, sir, we're dispatch riders and scouts, but we're the best shots you'll ever see and we can ride as well as any of the men you've got here," I stated emphatically. "Besides, the more men you have during the attack, the better chances of getting a prisoner for General Washington," I added, trying to think of anything that would convince the lieutenant to allow us to join in the engagement.

"Move to the rear and when we attack, keep with us," the lieutenant said without looking at us. "When their artillery engages, we'll only have a few minutes to get a prisoner before they blow us to pieces."

"Yes, sir," we said almost in unison, as we reined our horses and moved to back of the group of dragoons. Several of the horses were moving about with nervousness as they could sense the impending excitement and danger. Our horses began moving about, and I patted my horse's neck to calm him. Most of the dragoons had drawn their sabers, and a few had a pistol in their hands. I realized this was my second real engagement with an enemy, and my mouth became uncomfortably dry. I looked at Eli and as he looked back, I realized that he looked as scared as I felt. Eli and I only had our rifles and suddenly I felt we were in over our heads and inadequately armed. I quickly thought back to the encounter with the Huron Indians on the Connecticut River back in '72. I suddenly felt sick to my stomach. "Was my gun loaded?" I thought as I looked down at the flint and flash pan. Of course it was. I never left camp without checking them, I thought to myself. Everything began to slow down. I looked to my left and from the entrenchment; the Massachusetts men were firing on the regulars marching out on the field. Before us and to our left, the sergeant had formed his unit of militia and they were marching toward the regulars. From the British fortifications at the neck to Boston, I could see sporadic gunfire and, behind the lines, the British artillery was being moved into position.

Suddenly, without notice, the lieutenant along with the front group of dragoons moved forward, and all was in motion. We left the Massachusetts earth works in a gap between the lines, and were moving down the hill toward the flats. As we raced toward the group of regulars at the barns on the flats, I realized the white puffs of smoke coming from their guns meant that they were firing at us. I thought their fire was ineffective, until I saw a dragoon in the front of our group slump in his saddle, and then fall to the ground, dropping his saber as he fell. As I looked to the left, the Massachusetts unit was fully engaged with the regulars who had formed up in front of the Massachusetts lines. Both were pouring close range musket fire into each other's lines, as men from both sides could be seen falling to the ground.

From the British defensive works at the neck to Boston, a heavy fire was concentrated in our direction as we bore down on the regulars at the barn. Suddenly, with a crash of horses, we were among the regulars at the barn who were about our equal in numbers. The regulars on foot defended themselves with their muskets, as the horse mounted regulars engaged the dragoons with sabers and pistols. Gunfire seemed to be everywhere, and as I rode into the enemy, I lost contact with Eli. Several dragoons and regulars already lay on the ground wounded as I whirled my horse around looking for a British regular to attack. I saw the lieutenant in a close attack with two regulars on horses. He was doing all he could do to defend himself. I reined my horse to hold him steady, and instinctively drew my rifle to my shoulder, firing at the regular making his way to the back of the lieutenant, to strike him from behind. My rifle jumped in my hands, and as the smoke cleared, I saw the regular slumped in the saddle, riding off. With one of his adversaries wounded, and out of the fight, the lieutenant was more than a match for the remaining regular, as his saber flashed through the air.

I immediately turned my horse in a circle to check my back, when I saw Eli chasing a regular on a horse behind a barn. Reloading as I turned my horse, I sensed danger was approaching, as I saw a flash of red out of the corner of my right eye. Reining my horse to the right, I found a regular on foot advancing toward me with bayonet charged. I spurred my horse in the direction of the regular, forcing my twelve hundred pound animal to slam into him, knocking him to the ground, rendering him defenseless. As he lay there unresponsive, I jumped from my horse to secure his hands with some leather.

Suddenly, all around the barn began to explode with a deafening sound as the British artillery was engaged, and began to find the range. A shell exploded about 50 feet from me, and I felt a burning sensation on my right arm. As I put my left hand to my arm and pulled it away, my hand was covered with blood. Suddenly, the lieutenant was waving his sword over his head, trying to regroup his men. I found Eli at my side and together, we hoisted the still unconscious British soldier over my saddle. Most of the regulars at the barns had already begun their retreat. Those who weren't were either the dead and wounded on the battlefield, or were prisoners.

Eli and I reined our horses, and as a scattered group, we accompanied the dragoons back to the Massachusetts lines. We left several dragoons dead on the field. I looked over toward the Massachusetts unit that had engaged the regulars on the flat. They also left several of their number dead on the field, with the wounded being helped toward our lines. We left many of the regulars' dead, as well as the wounded on the field of battle. As we approached our lines, I realized that besides the regular Eli and I were bringing back as a prisoner, there were two other prisoners being escorted at gun point by the dragoons. Once through the break in the Massachusetts entrenchment, a rider approached who had on a smart uniform that I hadn't seen before among the New England militias.

"You men take your prisoner to the commanding general's headquarters past Brookline," he commanded Eli and me. As he wheeled his horse he shouted to the dragoons as they came back through the line. "You dragoons bring your prisoners to headquarters, and show these scouts where to go." And with that he spurred his horse and was off. Our prisoner was coming to his senses and I slid him off my horse to the ground, as Eli was riding up with a spare mount. Eli had the prisoner mount the horse he provided. Eli then tied the prisoner's hands in front of him and to the saddle's pommel. Eli and I fell in behind the dragoons as they headed down the road toward Brookline, as I held the reins of the prisoner's horse.

"Is that your blood, Will?" Eli asked me as he rode alongside me, looking at my right shoulder.

"It is only a scratch," I replied. "A shell exploded near me and a piece of it must have grazed my arm. We'll tend to it back at the line," I said as we rode on.

The lieutenant who led the charge was seen riding up behind us. As he approached, he reined in his horse and said, "I must thank you two for volunteering your services in our skirmish. I believe I owe you a great debt, sir, for wasn't it you who shot one of my assailants during the heat of the battle?"

"I only did what was needed, sir," I replied. "Besides, it was the least I could do for you allowing us to participate in the skirmish."

"I am Lieutenant Chamberlain," he said. "Who am I addressing?"

"This is Eli Bingham and I am Will Waterman. We hail from Norwich, Connecticut colony," I said. Looking at the lieutenant, I continued, "We are from Captain Fitch's Company, under Colonel Durkee's 4th Connecticut Regiment, Rhode Island Brigade, assigned to General Ward's wing of the army. We mostly ride dispatch and scouting missions for Colonel Durkee between the different commands of the army, sir."

"If you get a chance, stop by the Massachusetts's line by the Muddy River. You know where we're at, I want to thank you properly," replied the lieutenant. He reined his horse, as he headed back to his lines.

Eli and I followed the dragoons to the area of General Washington's headquarters. We crossed the Muddy River and into the town of Brookline, where we took the Brookline Cambridge Road north. After another half-mile of riding, we turned off the road into a field occupied by a number of tents. Flying over one particular tent was a flag that looked very similar to the British Union Jack, but with a series of alternating red and white stripes. As I looked at it, one of the dragoons stated over his shoulder to me, "That's the Grand Union flag, and General Washington's headquarters. That's where we're heading."

As we approached the headquarters tent, the officer in the blue uniform whom we had seen at the Massachusetts's line, and who had ordered us to bring the prisoners to headquarters, reappeared. He addressed several sentries nearby, directing them to take control of our prisoners. As we were about to turn and leave we heard a voice from inside the tent call out.

"Alex, are those the men from the engagement earlier?" the voice resounded.

"Yes, General," the officer in front of us replied.

"Bring them in," the voice commanded.

The man in front of us who was addressed as Alex directed us to tie our horses to the rails nearby, as he waited for us by the entrance of the large tent. As we approached on foot, he pulled the tent flap open and as we began to enter he stated to us, "Remove your hats."

As Eli and I entered, removing our tri-corns, the large tent almost seemed like a home. It was large enough to be sectioned off into several areas. In the center was the largest room with a large table with numerous documents on it, as well as maps, along with several candlesticks with each holding numerous candles. Several men in uniforms were at the table looking over several maps. Suddenly, I realized that Colonel Durkee, along with General Ward were among them. As we approached the table, the man in the center slowly looked up.

"Are these the men of which we spoke, Colonel?" he said.

"Yes, General," Colonel Durkee replied, "these are the dispatch riders and scouts of whom I spoke earlier."

"Gentleman," the general continued, "it was a bold move to attach yourselves to the troop of dragoons who were the main body of attack in this morning's action. Colonel Durkee did not overstate your expertise as riders, as well as in the use of your rifles. From our vantage point, you certainly distinguished yourselves in today's action. The operation this morning was strictly a prisoner snatch, and it worked almost to perfection, not counting the dead and wounded. I anticipate a need in the future for men of your nature, excellent horsemen and marksmen, who will be of service to me. May I count on your services?" the general asked.

"Yes, sir," we replied.

The general looked past us to the officer who had escorted us into the tent. "Lieutenant Colonel Hamilton, my aide-de-camp, will provide you men with some rum," the general stated, as he lowered his head to look at the maps on the table again.

Eli and I both stated, "Yes, sir," as we turned, following the aide-de-camp from the tent. Around the side and down the hill a short distance we were taken to a quartermaster's office.

"Sergeant Murphy!" Lieutenant Colonel Hamilton yelled as we entered the storehouse. A scruffy looking older man appeared from the back room of the building.

"The general says these men are due a ration of rum, and all the powder and shot they need, see to it, and perhaps a bandage for this scout's arm," Lieutenant Colonel Hamilton said as he turned to us with a smile on his face. "Gentlemen, I believe the general will be in contact with you as needed. Until then, resume your duties. It has been my pleasure to be of service," Lieutenant Colonel Hamilton stated as he departed the quartermaster's office. The quartermaster obliged us with a full ration of rum, as well as with new stores of powder and shot, followed by a bandage for my arm. We were content to return to our unit along the Roxbury lines.

The summer wore on with occasional raids, and excessive boredom on both sides. As summer waned to fall, our ranks began to show signs of significant thinning. It seemed that every night, men from all units were slipping past the sentries, and deserting to return to their families.

Our unit was down to half strength, with many units throughout the rest of the army being down to less than half strength. The remnants of several units had to be combined to make up one full unit. More time was spent on the line due to our reduction in numbers.

Many men left due to the lack of food, clothing, or because of disenchantment as to the real cause for which we were fighting. With the onset of fall, the harvest drew near, and large numbers of men simply slipped away from the army to return home to harvest their crops before the winter set in, and to take care of their families. Eli and I felt no such need to leave the army for those reasons, although food was always in short supply, and we were in desperate need of winter clothing and quarters.

During the late fall season, our unit was assigned to longer, and more frequent duties on the line watching the enemy. Surely, the British in Boston was suffering more than we were, we thought. An occasional supply ship slipped into Boston Harbor, but certainly they were so infrequent, that the British generally were as under supplied as we were.

We had occasionally sent letters by way of the post rider to home when we could afford it. Occasionally, we would receive news from home, which always lifted our spirits, along with giving us a different perspective from the front. Our parents missed us and Da always seemed to want us home, although he never came out and said so. I knew he didn't approve of us supporting the cause against the British. I wrote Diane when I could, and she always wrote back. Usually she asked when we'd be home and how things were going or if was I being safe. With the army getting dangerously low of men, I didn't know if or when we'd get home. One day Sergeant Hartshorn called Eli off the line.

"You've got a post with the quartermaster," the sergeant barked, "be back within the hour."

I was still on the line when Eli returned. He came walking up to me as I was looking over our entrenchment at the British lines and Boston. Things had been relatively quiet for weeks, with neither side venturing out to engage each other. Each seemed content to let the siege linger on. Eli looked forlorn and anxious, as he walked up to my position.

"What is it, Eli?" I said as he sat down.

Eli looked at me a moment before he spoke. "My Ma says my Dad is really sick. She says I'm needed home. I don't know what to do, Will. I'm committed to the cause, but you know as well as I do, this siege will go on with or without me. And with Dad being sick now and winter coming on...," Eli hesitated as he thought, "I think it's time I go home."

"Eli," I said, "how will you get away from the lines?"

"I don't know, maybe I'll go on a scout to the west of Putnam's lines and keep going. I'll circle way to the west and then south. I'll be home in a few days," he said.

And so it was one day, in late October, that as Eli and I were riding dispatches from General Ward to General Lee on the north wing of the army, that Eli and I parted ways outside the town of Cambridge. We shook hands for what seemed a long time. As I looked in Eli's eyes, I could see that he was torn about leaving the army. I handed Eli a letter to my folks, along with one for Diane. He said he'd be sure to deliver them. He knew I understood about going home to tend to his father and the farm. As I turned to go, I shouted over my shoulder, "Tell my Ma and Da I'm okay, and tell Diane I miss her." I spurred my horse to a trot as I called back, "Take care, Eli Bingham, I'll see you soon."

With that Eli went down the west Post Road out of Cambridge and toward home.

Winter set in and in November, word circulated through the remaining troops that General Washington had sent Colonel Knox to the west to secure the guns at Fort Ticonderoga, with hopes of ending the siege. Colonel Durkee came to me and said that I would have been one of the men picked to go, except with Eli being gone, along with my enlistment being up in January, he wasn't sure I would return. I told him that I was thinking about what to do. That I wasn't sure I'd reenlist, and that he made a good decision in not sending me. Although, when I heard that Colonel Knox and his men were going to Fort Ticonderoga, I envied them. I knew that was one of the forts where Da and the rangers were based during the French and Indian War, and I would have been anxious to be at the fort.

As winter set in, the months of December and January were spent trying to stay warm. The New England winter buffeted both the British and American armies. The colonial soldiers from the south suffered particularly, as they were not used to such severe conditions of winter in the north. With a shortage of food, winter clothing and winter quarters, survival was the order of each day for both armies.

It was around Christmas time that I received letters from home. I was on the line, as Sergeant Hartshorn was seen riding up on his horse, which looked like she was suffering greatly under his weight. He handed me two letters, one from Ma and Da, along with one from Diane. I opened the letter from Diane first. She was hoping to see me for Christmas, but understood my being away. She said that Eli, who had made it home safely, had explained to her my duties as scout and dispatch rider, which normally kept us out of harm's way. But, apparently Eli had told her of our attack with the dragoons on the British at the flats, outside of the neck leading to Boston, and of my slight wound. She was well, as were her parents. With the coming of good weather, she expected to see me.

I opened the letter from Ma and Da. It was in my Ma's handwriting. She expressed concern for me, and desired me to be home. All was well with my family, but Da didn't understand why I was still there. Ma said Da thought that when the British forced its way out of Boston, that they would chase the colonial army all the way to the colony of Virginia and destroy it. Ma said that Mr. Bingham was still ill, but recovering. It was expected that by spring he would be well.

By the middle of January, with the siege at the point of breaking, word was received that Colonel Knox, along with his men and cannons, were only a few days travel from reaching our lines from Fort Ticonderoga. With this news in hand, Colonel Durkee called our unit together to address the men who remained. Most of whom were due to leave the army at the end of January, when their enlistment was up.

"Men," he began, "many months ago, we all enlisted to fight in the colonial army against King and country; because we all believed we are just and right in our cause. It has been many months, and we all have endured hardships and dangers. Yet, we few still remain, and now word has been received that Colonel Knox was successful in securing the cannons from Fort Ticonderoga. He and his men, along with the guns will be here in a few days' time. Many of you and indeed many of the officers standing here before you will be free to go, to return to our homes at the end of this month, when our enlistments expire. The commander of this army, General Washington himself has asked me, to ask each of you, to sign a two month extension on this enlistment, just to see the army through the siege. I know you are all cold and hungry, as am I, but I ask each of you, to stay and see the army through, to stay the course a little longer. Who will come and stay with me."

Many men grumbled and turned away, determined to go home at the end of their enlistment. I stood there not moving for several moments. I was thinking of home, of Diane and Eli. Oh, how I wanted to be there. Suddenly, I realized someone was standing next to me. It was Sergeant Hartshorn. He was looking at me.

"Well, Will," said the sergeant, "what do you think you'll do?"

"I'm thinking I want to go home, Sergeant, but I'll be staying on, at least until spring, and planting time. I'll give it a little longer," I stated. Many men left and went home when their enlistments were up. From all accounts, the army was under half strength from its height of eighteen thousand men only a few months earlier, and the warmer weather.

Upon reenlisting, I found out I was no longer to be in Colonel Durkee's Regiment. The next day, Sergeant Hartshorn ordered me to report to Captain Fitch for further orders. Due to the low numbers of soldiers reenlisting, I was assigned to Captain Gordon's 6th Company, in Colonel Douglas' 1st Connecticut Regiment of the Connecticut troops under General Putnam, and the center of the army. Captain Fitch said that Colonel Durkee's staff was being attached to General Washington's staff for the duration of the siege.

The train of cannons arrived a few days later, which raised all of our spirits in hopes that the cannons would be a means to end the siege. They were stored behind our lines, while plans were formulated for their use. In early March, Colonel Douglas gave me dispatches, ordering me to deliver them to General Lee at the north arm of the army. The orders were that General Lee was to begin a general bombardment of Boston and the British positions on the night of March 2nd, from Cobble and Plowed Hills. With the beginning of the bombardment, I returned to Cambridge and my unit.

Colonel Douglas then ordered my unit to Dorchester Heights, with orders to build a defensive work, and to place the cannons from Fort Ticonderoga at that position. We worked throughout the night and with the diversionary bombardment across the harbor from the Cobble and Plowed Hill batteries, the British were not the wiser to our activities. With the morning came the realization to the British that their position in Boston, along with their ships in the harbor was untenable. We all knew that we had forced the British hand. They had two choices. Attack our position on Dorchester Heights, to destroy the cannons, and occupy the high ground, or evacuate Boston. Rumors swirled that the attacks would come any day. Day after day passed, but the expected attack by the British failed to materialize. If only the British had known that we lacked both the powder and shot to bombard Boston, from Dorchester Heights.

Finally, on March 17th, the British began to evacuate Boston. The siege of Boston was nearing its end. It took the British over a week to gather their soldiers, cannons and equipment together to depart Boston in their warships.

As the last ship sailed out of Boston Harbor and over the horizon, the American army began to be marched across the neck, and into the city. We were marched to Boston Common, and from there you could see our positions that ringed the hills around Boston, and how dominating they were. With the British gone for now, and spring coming in April, many units in the army were disbanded, and sent home. After all, Congress reasoned, it could not support such a large standing army without an enemy to fight for the moment. At least that was what we were told. So, after ten months of service to my country during the siege of Boston, and with little fanfare, I was paid off, and my unit under Colonel Douglas was disbanded. All those left said their farewells as we packed our baggage for our individual trips home. Colonel Douglas thanked me for my services personally, informing me that in the future, if the fighting continued, he would welcome me back into any unit he commanded. He said he could always use a good scout. He shook my hand, wishing me well, and I was no longer a private in the colonial army.

- CHAPTER 6 -

"Filling the Connecticut Levies - The Battle for Long Island"

1776

My journey home from the siege of Boston was uneventful. To occupy my ride, I went over in my mind all of the things I had seen and done during the siege. Along the way I encountered a large number of men like myself, soldiers who had enlisted to join the army to fight for the cause, and were dismissed with perhaps a thank you and a long ride ahead of them to reach home. I was one of the lucky ones, as Norwich was only a long two-day ride away. Late on the second day, I arrived at our farm outside of Norwich. It was dark when I arrived, and I thought no one at the house would notice a lone rider slowly making his way to the barn at that hour. I was tired and my horse was more so. As I began to dismount and my foot hit the ground, the back door of the house opened, and my mother came running out.

"Will!" She shouted as she realized I was really home. She was hugging and kissing me so, that I could hardly get my breath. Soon my brother, John, and sister, Rachel, were there all hugging me, and asking me questions.

"Ma," I finally said, "I've got to take care of my horse."

"John will do that," Ma replied, "come inside and see your father."

As I turned to go inside, John took the reins of my horse and I walked inside with my arms around my mother and sister. As we entered our house, Da was at the table enjoying a pipe, with a warm fire crackling and glowing in the fireplace. He looked up as we entered, and I saw his reassuring smile cross his face. He stood to greet me and as I approached him, he opened his arms wide, giving me a hug.

"Sit down, sit down," Ma said, "I'll get you something to eat, and you must be starved from your journey. Why didn't you get word to us you were coming, Will?" she said over her shoulder as she left the room.

"I was only mustered out of the army a few days ago, Ma," I replied. "By the time I could write a letter, and get it posted with the quartermaster, I'd be home already." I said as I sat down with Da at the table.

I could hear Ma in the kitchen working to get some food together for me, as there was the familiar clanging of pots and pans. John returned from putting the horse in the stable, sitting next to Rachel at the other end of the table. Da looked at me and asked, "How did you fare, Will, at Boston?" Before I could answer, Da continued, "When Eli returned, we thought you wouldn't be far behind. He told us so much about what was happening there. The whole town came out to hear what he had to say. Pastor Gallagher even had him say a few words at church before the sermon. Seems you and Eli are famous in these parts now, along with the rest of the men from Norwich who were with you."

Ma returned from the kitchen with a plate of supper and some fresh milk. It all looked so good compared to the rations we were on at the siege. I said a quick prayer and began to eat.

"Slow down," Ma said, "or you'll make yourself sick. Does Diane know you're here?" Ma asked as I gulped food. "She'll want to see you."

"No, Ma," I said, "I came right home. I'll see her tomorrow. I'm just tired and hungry."

"We'll have none of that Will Waterman," Ma said, "she'll be mad as a hornet if she finds out you're here, and you didn't go see her." Ma thought about it another minute and stated, "You're right, Will, tomorrow will be soon enough to see her. You should get your rest tonight."

Rachel finally spoke up and said, "Will, tell us about the war."

As I looked up from my food, and was about to answer her, Da cleared his throat, speaking up and stating, "Rachel, let your brother have a night's rest. There will be plenty of time on the morrow to hear about the war."

I went back to my food, and before I knew it Pastor Gallagher, followed by Diane, was coming in the front door. Pastor Gallagher gave me a hug, and shook my hand so hard and long, that I thought it might fall off. Diane gave me a hug and a kiss on my cheek, as I took hold of her hand. I had forgotten how she felt, and how soft she was. I now realized how much I truly missed her.

"How did you know I was home?" I asked, surprised to see them.

"Will, when a returning soldier comes home, somehow the word gets out," Pastor Gallagher stated confidently.

Suddenly, Eli burst through the front door, almost knocking over my brother John, and Pastor Gallagher trying to get to me. He had a grin from ear to ear on his face, and he seemed taller to me than I remembered.

"Will!" he shouted as he grabbed my shoulders, pushing Diane out of the way, "you're back and okay? I knew you would be," he said. "I was telling everyone what a hero you are, and how all the commanders wanted you to be their scout and dispatch rider." Before I could say anything, Eli just started in with telling about our one major engagement of the siege. "And how about that battle we were in, where you wounded that one British officer, and saved the dragoons lieutenant from getting killed for certain. What was the lieutenant's name? Show everyone where you were wounded!" Eli had continued with great excitement in his voice.

I could see that at least my Da was uncomfortable about the talk of the war. Diane and my mother were beginning to cry.

"Eli," I spoke up, "there will be plenty of time to talk about the war.

I'm just glad to be home with my family and friends. We'll talk about the war on the morrow. I'm really tired," I stated.

"That's right," my mother said as she wiped her eyes with her apron. "Will needs his sleep, and you can come by on the morrow, Eli," she continued as she escorted him to the door. Pastor Gallagher made their apologies as soon as Eli was out the door, as he and Diane began to leave also. I walked with Diane to the door, holding her soft hand. There were still tears in her eyes, as I squeezed her hand.

"It wasn't like Eli said," I told her in an effort to get her to stop crying. "I'll tell you everything tomorrow. I just need to get some rest."

"I understand, Will," she said as she let go of my hand, following her father out the door.

Pastor Gallagher shouted over his shoulder as he headed down the street, "We'll have you over tomorrow for dinner, Will, you can tell us all about it then."

Ma closed the door, and ushered both John and Rachel upstairs to their rooms for bedtime. I sat down with Da again at the table, and neither of us said much for a few minutes. Da and I stayed up another hour talking about what happened in Boston. He never came out and said it, but from his facial expressions, as I went over some of the events of the siege, I could tell it went against what he believed. Finally, we both were very tired, and we said our good nights. I kissed my mother on the forehead, and gave Da a hug. All he said was "It's good to have you back, son." I turned and went upstairs to the room that I shared with John. As I lay down to go to sleep, I knew Da and I would have to talk more about the war.

The next morning I slept in, finally awakening around nine in the morning. Breakfast was already over, although the smell of breakfast still filled the air. Da had had John and Rachel working out in the barn doing chores for several hours already. Word had spread quickly through town that I was home. Individuals and families throughout the town, that I had grown up with, and even some families that I didn't know, that were new in town, stopped by our farm during the next few days and weeks to say hello, and to see how I was faring. I told and retold the accounts of my activities at the siege of Boston, until it seemed everyone who wanted to know, knew my stories better than I did. It was really overwhelming at first, and even grew to become somewhat of an annoyance. I was somewhat of a quiet and reserved individual, and all of the attention was unwarranted. Or at least, that was how I felt. What about all of the other soldiers who served in and around Boston, just like me, many of whom were from Norwich or the surrounding area also? Some of whom were wounded and even killed that no one was talking about.

I also knew that all this attention made Da feel uneasy, with his stance on the war. I also found out who the people were in town that supported the Crown in this war. Most of them just ignored me if I walked by, or saw them at some town activity, or at our church service. Some though, would give me an unwelcoming look or glance over their shoulder as I walked past them.

It wasn't until I was walking past Durkee's Tavern one afternoon, about a week after I had returned when I realized how divided the town was about the war. There were two men standing outside the door to the tavern looking at the notes left on the town board. I had seen them around town, but didn't know them. As I walked past on my way to the Gallagher's house, one of the men sneered over his shoulder, grumbling something about a "dirty rebel." I continued on not realizing he was directing the insult at me. When I arrived at the Gallagher's house, and was seated at their table with Pastor Gallagher, waiting for Diane to come down stairs, I asked Pastor Gallagher about the men.

"As I passed the tavern on my way here, there were two men standing outside, that I didn't recognize," I said. "As I passed, I believe one of them said something about a dirty rebel."

"It's one of the unfortunate side effects of this war, Will," Pastor Gallagher began. "Some of the new people in town are firmly on the side of the Crown, like your father. Most of the town's people are on the side of the colonials. Some of the people supporting the Crown have begun calling the people who support the colonies, rebels or Whigs. While some of the people supporting the colonies are calling the people who support the Crown, loyalists or Tories. I fear that the longer this war goes on, the worse things will get all around the colonies," Pastor Gallagher said as he looked down at his hands.

"Where do you stand, sir?" I inquired.

"Will, that is a hard question to answer," Pastor Gallagher began. "My heart is with the colonies for this is where I was born, and have lived my entire life. But I understand both sides, and the issues in this fight. As a minister of our Lord's Word, and a follower of the Christian faith, I must minister to the needs of those on both sides and so, I will not choose sides or fight," he concluded looking at me.

"I understand, sir," I said as Diane came downstairs. "Sir, may I take

Diane over to our farm, one of our horses had a foal, and I'd like to show her. I'll have her back after lunch," I said.

"Of course, Will," the Pastor said, as I stood with Diane, and we left their house. I was unusually quiet as we rode the two miles to my house. Finally, Diane spoke up, "What's bothering you, Will?" she asked.

"I don't know really. I guess I'm thinking about this war, and if I'm on the right side or not," I stated. As we continued to ride, I was also thinking to myself that I was spending a lot more time with Diane. The world was changing, I thought, but was it for the better.

All was quiet for the next few weeks as I settled down to work on the farm with my family, and with Da. I saw Diane every day that allowed, and had dinner with her and her family several times a week. I saw Eli, but only once or twice a week now. He was busy with the Bingham farm, and with his father still recovering from what Doctor Post said was pneumonia, it took up most of his time.

Then in the middle of May, a rider came to town that would change my world yet again. He posted a note on the board outside of Durkee's Tavern and continued on. It was a notice to all patriots of the Connecticut colony, and was signed by General Washington himself, ordering the colony to levy two brigades for eight months service in the colonial army. Men from each town were to muster together, and make their way to Hartford to be formed into companies, regiments, and then into brigades. Each town's men were to be gathered by week's end, to be in Hartford by the middle of next week.

I had a sick feeling in my stomach, as I knew I would sign up, but what would Da and Diane say. My head was spinning as I made my way home, after I heard the news about the levy. I sat at the table until I heard the door open, followed by the all too familiar clomp, clomp, clomp, of my father's boots on our wood floor as he came toward the dining room. He looked at me, and I at him, and he just said, "Let's talk, Will," as he turned to go back outside with me in tow. We walked out to the barn where John and Rachel were doing the afternoon milking of our cows.

"You're finished with your chores for now, children, go inside and help your mother with dinner." Da stated. They left us, and the barn seemed eerily silent even with the cows there, as I waited for my Da to speak.

"Will," he began, "I've heard that another notice was posted on the board at Durkee's Tavern today. Do you plan on enlisting and filling the Connecticut levy?"

"I do, Da," I said in a low voice without lifting my head.

"You know my feelings about this war, and what I think about you fighting against the Crown," he began. "There is more that needs to be said now. While you were gone fighting at the siege of Boston, I had correspondence from the British army. The Crown has offered me a commission in the British army as a lieutenant in the Queen's Rangers, organized by Captain Rogers for the upcoming fight. I plan on taking that commission, Will, and it pains me to think that you are on the other side, perhaps, within the sights of my own gun. Do you understand, Will, I'm asking you not to go?" he pleaded. "It is folly to fight the Crown and think you can win," he implored. "I know. I've been there, and I've seen the power and strength of not only the British army, but their navy too. Tell me, son, that you won't go this time," he said, as I looked up at him to find a tear trickling down his face.

"I'm sorry Da, but as you feel about the Crown, I feel about the colonies," I stated. "I've shed blood, and had my bloodshed. I'll not change now, Da."

Nothing was said for several minutes. Finally, Da stirred, and put his hand on my shoulder as he walked by without saying a word. Now I had to go talk to Diane.

As I arrived in town and was riding toward her house still trying to figure out what to say to her, I saw her at the front of her house tending some flowers. Diane had already heard about the levy, too. As we met, neither of us said anything at first. My silence must have confirmed in her mind that I was going to sign up again.

"So you've heard about the levy?" she asked finally.

"Yes, I did. I was just talking to my Da about it," I replied as I tried to think about what to say next.

"And you've decided to sign up again, haven't you, Will?" she asked with a note of anger in her voice.

"It's not that easy, Diane," I implored.

"And what about us," she retorted with a definite note of anger in her voice and tears welling up in her eyes. "What if you are hurt or killed on some far off battlefield? What am I to do, William Waterman? Wait here in this little town of Norwich for word from some soldier, I don't know, or a post from some officer that you are not coming back to me?" Her voice was now strained and tears were flowing down her face.

I could only hold her, as I told her I'd be back. The next week went by quickly as I had to gather together the supplies, as well as clothing I might need. Eight months would put us into winter again, and I didn't want to get caught in a winter campaign without proper clothing this time. I also met with Eli a couple of times. He had decided that he couldn't leave right now with his father still on the mend from being sick all winter. He told me he'd be there later on when his father had his strength back.

On May 8, 1776, I said my goodbyes, and met a group of thirty five men from Norwich, who had gathered just on the west side of town to travel together to Hartford. I only felt bad about leaving Diane, and it felt eerily strange not to be accompanied by Eli. Among those who were in this group of men were Jonathon Pease, John Edgerington, the Fuller brothers, Samuel and John, Sean Leffingwell, and William Bradford. Most of the other men were from surrounding communities, and I didn't know them well, although I'd seen all around town from time to time.

As we approached Hartford, it reminded me very much of the previous year when Eli and I had gone to Plainfield to enlist. Men were riding in from all over the colony, and as we approached the town, we saw that tents were springing up everywhere, only on a much larger scale. We found the enlistment tent, and all made their mark or signed their name, as we were mustered into Captain Dixon's Company, Colonel Sage's Regiment, General Wadsworth's Brigade, under Major General Joseph Spencer's Division. Sergeant Major John Cole inquired of each man his experience. Most had been at Bunker Hill, the siege of Boston, or had had performed some duty in that area. When I told Sergeant Major Cole of my experience as a dispatch rider for Colonel Durkee, he told me to report to Captain Dixon.

I reported to Captain Dixon as ordered, who inquired as to any experience I had. I explained to him my duties, and experience from the siege of Boston the previous year. He said it was good to know, and that he'd pass the information up the chain of command to Colonel Sage. There wasn't much time for settling in, as the next morning, the men that were in camp were formed into units, then companies and were marched about for several hours.

The first day was spent in drill and training. This training went on for several days. Then on the night of May 15th, orders were passed to make ready to depart for the city of New York in the morning. Rumors began to spread that General Washington had already passed by to the south along the coast with the main army from Boston. Word was that he had left a brigade in Boston to defend against the British returning there. The big rumor was that General Howe had already sailed from Halifax, Canada, with the British army for the very city we were to occupy.

As I lay on the ground in my tent that night, I thought back to my conversation with Da in the barn, when he pleaded with me not to enlist again. He said something about the upcoming fight. Had he already known that Howe had sailed from Halifax, and that Washington was even then marching an army from Boston to New York, with the intent to intercept it? I kept saying in my mind that night as I fell asleep, that he must have known.

The next morning we were marched down the Connecticut River to New Haven, where we caught up with the trailing elements of Washington's army, and the rear guard. Several more days of marching by day and training in the evenings brought us just outside of Greenwich, Connecticut colony. It was a small, sleepy town on the coast, with a post road between New York and Bridgeport. That night, Captain Dixon called together the company, and gave us instruction on the coming day's march.

On the morrow, our column would lead out at nine in the morning. We would be in the colony of New York by noon. That night we were to encamp across the Harlem River from Manhattan Island. The following day, we were to cross the Harlem River onto Manhattan Island. From there, most of the army would cross the East River to Brooklyn, while the remainder of the army would immediately begin fortifying lower Manhattan Island against attack, or invasion from the British. This is when I first heard the army addressed as the Continental army, that is, as Captain Dixon explained it to us, "If we were called up to fight anywhere on the North American continent, we would go." Upon dismissing the company, Captain Dixon requested my presence. Upon meeting him outside of the mess tent, I accompanied Captain Dixon to Colonel Sage's tent.

As we approached Colonel Sage's tent, Captain Dixon ordered me to remain outside. I could hear Captain Dixon speaking in low tones in the tent, but could not overhear the conversation. Finally, Captain Dixon called out, "Private Waterman, front and center."

I entered the tent, removing my tri-corn, and stood at attention in front of Captain Dixon and Colonel Sage. Colonel Sage returned my salute as he said, "At ease, Private." And then he continued, "I have had occasion to speak with Colonel Durkee of you, and your activities during the siege of Boston. He speaks highly of you and your friend, ah....,"

"Eli Bingham, sir," I said as Colonel Sage searched his memory for Eli's name.

"Yes, Eli Bingham, is he with the army now?" Colonel Sage inquired.

"No, sir, his father has been in poor health, which required Eli to remain at home to tend the farm and his family," I answered.

"That is too bad. It seems the army could use another good man," the colonel replied. "The reason you have been called here before me is that based upon the information that Colonel Durkee has supplied about you, it indicates that you are one of the most experienced men in Captain Dixon's Company. Therefore, you are going to be placed in command of a twenty man rifle unit, attached to an artillery unit. You will train your men to provide long-range rifle support to the artillery unit to which you are assigned. Which means, if the artillery unit is to come under direct attack by dragoons or infantry, you are to provide firing cover until the threat is eliminated, or the artillery unit is evacuated from the field of battle, or the unit is captured or destroyed. Captain Dixon will give you more specifics as to your orders in the next few days. Is that understood?" Colonel Sage asked. As he looked back down at his desk and papers he was reviewing, he stated without looking up, "Choose your men wisely."

"Yes, sir," I stated as I saluted.

"You are dismissed. Return to your duties," the colonel replied.

"Oh, by the way, Private Waterman, you are now Corporal Waterman," he added.

As I walked back to my unit I thought of who was in it, and whom to select. I was thinking that I would have liked Eli to be with me now. I felt comfortable selecting the men I knew from town. These were Jonathon Pease, Thomas Birchard, John Edgerington, the Fuller brothers, Samuel and John, Sean Leffingwell, and William Bradford. For the rest of the men, I went to Captain Dixon, stating to him that I didn't know the other men in our unit too well, and requested that he select them. Most of the men he selected to complete our unit were from Hartford.

The following days went as planned, as the entire army entered Manhattan Island without incident. The army crossed over the Harlem River on the King's Bridge and the flood of men, animals and supply wagons seemed to overwhelm the residents of the island. As we moved south, different units were detached from the main body of the army, and were given orders to fortify and protect certain key areas of the island, in the event that the main British attack didn't occur in Brooklyn, as believed would happen.

I noticed almost immediately that the island of Manhattan was covered with areas of impressive high hills and lower areas of creeks, marshlands and bogs. The highest land was at the north end of the island, in the area of King's Bridge, where we crossed onto the island. The center of the island was dominated by smaller hills and valleys. There were only a couple of main roads that ran the length of the island, the largest being Bloomingdale Road. As the army continued south, down the island, the land was dotted by various farms, apple orchards and crops. It wasn't until we reached the southernmost point of Manhattan that we encountered New York City, which consisted of many buildings and streets, compressed into the lower part of the island.

As we reached lower Manhattan, the main body of the army immediately began to gather all of the boats in the area to be used as transports to ferry men and supplies across the East River to Brooklyn. This took several days' time to complete.

My twenty man unit was assigned to an artillery unit already assigned to Nutten Island, in New York Harbor.

From lower Manhattan, we could see the island, and the activity already occurring there. It appeared that the artillery unit had several days' head start on us with the building of the defensive works on the island. The island appeared to be about a half-mile south of the tip of Manhattan, and considerably closer to the Brooklyn shore. Boats were constantly ferrying supplies to the island, and it was on one of these boats that we obtained passage. Within the hour, we found ourselves on Nutten Island, a one hundred and seventy acre island in New York Harbor.

Upon our arrival, a Sergeant Cunningham directed us to the commanding officer, who in turn was directing the placement of the arriving supplies. I instructed my men to remain near the wharf while I went to present myself to the officer in command. Approaching him, I saluted, as he looked my way.

"Corporal Waterman of Captain Dixon's Company, Colonel Sage's Regiment, Lieutenant General Wadsworth's Brigade, and Major General Joseph Spencer's Division, of the Connecticut militia, assigned to the Continental army, reporting for duty. I have a twenty man rifle unit assigned under orders of Colonel Sage, to provide your artillery company with rifle support in the upcoming engagement, sir," I said as the commander returned my salute.

"Your men are a welcome sight, Corporal," he said and continued, "I am Captain Doughty of the 2nd Artillery Division, under command of Colonel John Lamb, assigned to the Continental army, under orders to protect the main army's flank in Brooklyn. We can expect a smart action here, and will need to build our defensive works. Corporal, report to Sergeant Cunningham, as he will have your men assist in the construction of the defensive works, or fort, if you will."

"Sir," I stated as I again saluted the captain and returned to my men and the sergeant who had directed me to the captain upon our arrival on the island. The sergeant directed us to the area designated to make camp, and within a couple of hours we were helping the 2nd Artillery Division with the defensive works on the island. The north end of the island held the high ground and thus the defensive works and fort were placed there with the rest of the island being used for the encampment of the artillery unit, my rifle unit, as well as the storing of supplies. May soon turned to June and the army settled into building and reinforcing the defensive works, which consisted of a small star fort with supporting trenches and abatis. With our works complete on Nutten Island, I was again used from time to time to run dispatches on Manhattan Island and on occasion, across the East River to Brooklyn, to the various wings of the army.

During late June, a strange thing happened one day as I was speaking with Sergeant Cunningham, while on duty in our works on Nutten Island. Several ships appeared on the horizon that proved to be British warships. They began disembarking men, and supplies onto Staten Island, a large island to our south, being much closer to the shore of New Jersey colony. First, there were only a handful of ships, but as the days and weeks went by, the British fleet that occupied the lower end of New York Harbor seemed more like a forest of trees, being too numerous to count. The British warships I now saw in the harbor far outnumbered the British warships I had counted in Boston Harbor the previous year during the siege of Boston. I heard rumors spread that over four hundred ships were now at anchor.

Although new recruits were enlisted every day to swell our ranks, it was believed that we were badly outnumbered by the British army that occupied Staten Island. Most officers said by as many as two to one, and without a navy of our own, we were seriously hampered by the fact that the British navy could land a force anywhere they chose to.

To counter the constant threat of the British navy, General Washington sent a division to Fort Washington, at Harlem Heights at the northern end of Manhattan Island. He then ordered three divisions to the fortifications of Fort George at the southern end of Manhattan Island, and placed a division on Long Island at Brooklyn Heights. This latter location was to be the site of an upcoming engagement that would cost General Washington and the Continental army, New York City and nearly the entire army.

By the middle of August, General Nathanial Greene, who was the commander of the division of the Continental army in Brooklyn, fell seriously ill and command of his division fell to Major General Putnam. The fortifications of Brooklyn Heights stretched from the Gowanus Marsh in the south, to Wallabach Bay on the north.

On the morning of August 22nd, General Howe moved several warships of the British navy from lower New York Harbor to the upper harbor. At the same time, numerous transport vessels were seen moving between Staten Island and Long Island, in southern Brooklyn. With British ships moving up the harbor toward our position, and that of the batteries of Fort George, on lower Manhattan, as well as the movement of troops, a general alarm was given, and the entire Continental army was placed on alert. Even so, there was nothing we could do to prevent the movement of the British troops to Brooklyn.

Within an hour of their movement, the British frigates were well within range of our batteries on Nutten Island, and those at Fort George. Soon, a general bombardment began between the two opposing forces. The bombardment lasted most of the day without either side inflicting much damage. By the day's end, General Howe had landed a significant force in Brooklyn. To counter General Howe's move, Major General Putnam moved his forces from Brooklyn Heights to guard the passes that ran through the low hills that were the main feature of the landscape in the middle of Brooklyn.

Major General William Alexander, or Lord Sterling; for Alexander claimed an Irish title of Lord Sterling, held the Gowanus Road Pass on the right. Major General John Sullivan held the Flatbush Pass, which was at the center of the American lines, while Major General Putnam held the Bedford Pass on the left of the lines.

For several days, General Howe sporadically engaged the American forces at the Flatbush and Bedford Passes. From our position on Nutten Island, we could see, through the smoke of battle, the movement of red coated masses of men as they attacked and probed the American lines.

Then on the night of August 26th, undetected by the American forces, General Howe force marched ten thousand men through the Jamaica Pass. This pass was located to the left of the American lines, and farther east than Major General Putnam's position at the Bedford Pass. A general engagement began on the morning of the twenty-seventh by the remainder of Howe's army against Sullivan and Putnam's positions at Flatbush and Bedford Passes. Shortly after the engagement began, it was learned from the Americans that ten thousand British regulars were marching down the Jamaica Pass Road in the American rear.

The American forces at the Flatbush and Bedford Passes, realizing that they were badly outnumbered, and about to be flanked, fled their positions in great disorder to the relative safety of the defensive works of Brooklyn Heights. This left Major General William Alexander, and his men exposed between two British forces on the American right.

From our position on Nutten Island we could see it all. The feinted attacks at the American lines, held Alexander's forces in place, all the while, the British column came marching down the Jamaica Pass Road towards their rear. Captain Doughty began barking orders, and our batteries on Nutten Island came to life. We fired to provide some retreating cover for Sullivan and Putnam, and to provide support for the now desperately isolated Alexander forces. The guns from Brooklyn Heights also joined the battle, as General Washington himself took command, by leading reinforcements from lower Manhattan to Brooklyn Heights. If General Howe's men crushed Major General Alexander's men and took Brooklyn Heights, the entire army would be in jeopardy. As Howe's ten thousand men continued marching down the Jamaica Pass Road, the commander of the British left attacked the Gowanus Pass, thus holding Alexander's men in place, and preventing their retreat.

It became increasingly apparent that Alexander and his men were in serious trouble. As he attempted to engage, in an orderly retreat to Brooklyn Heights, a unit of about four hundred men repeatedly assaulted the British regulars who were trying to take Gowanus Pass. How many times they charged the British I cannot remember. Was it four, five, no..., at least six assaults were made and their bravery was unmatched. In the end Alexander's unit was almost entirely destroyed, with the survivors being captured by the British. It was clear these men voluntarily sacrificed themselves to save the army. As I watched this all play out before me, I nearly forgot that our guns had laid down a continual bombardment for the last few hours, which also played a small role in saving the army. But I never forgot the sacrifice made by those brave men that day.

With the main engagement of the day over, General Washington prepared for the assault on Brooklyn Heights by General Howe and the British army before him. But the attack never came, as General Howe began building entrenchments from which to attack Brooklyn Heights. Rain and bad weather slowed the British efforts for several days. With time to think and reorganize the remnants of his army, on the night of August 29th, under the cover of a heavy fog, General Washington evacuated his army from Brooklyn Heights to Manhattan Island. With the evacuation of Brooklyn Heights, our position on Nutten Island became untenable with the British navy anchored in New York Harbor, and the British army now in control of Long Island. Thus, on August 30th, we were ordered off Nutten Island, and took up new positions with the batteries at the southern tip of Manhattan Island, at Fort George.

- CHAPTER 7 -

"Battles of Manhattan Island, Harlem Heights, White Plains and the Dangerous Wound"

1776

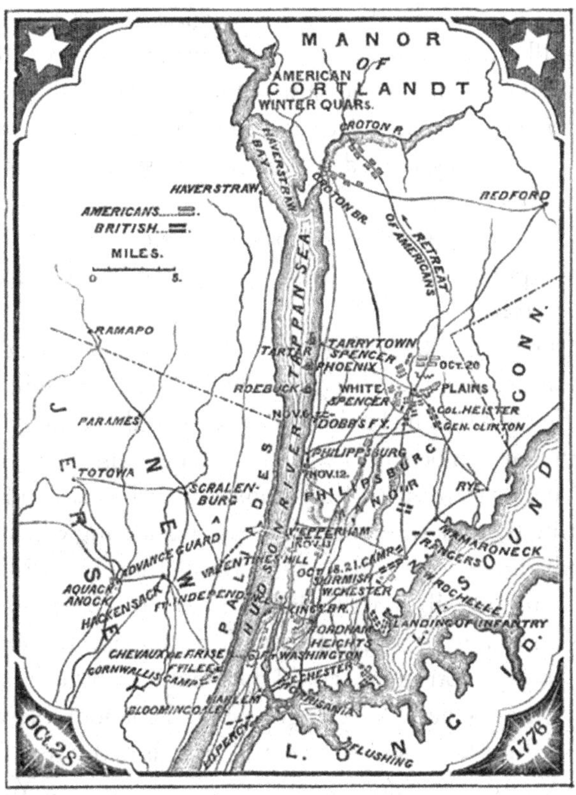

With the main army now on the island of Manhattan, work began immediately to improve the battery at the lower end of the island. This area was now called Fort George. Additional work was also carried on at the fortifications at Fort Washington, at Harlem Heights at the north end of the island.

Additional defensive works were being constructed along the East River facing Brooklyn, as well as the Hudson River facing the New Jersey colony. All of the next few days were consumed with the reinforcing of the fortifications along Manhattan. With time to take stock of our forces, including the missing, it was learned that we were without more than one thousand men, most of them lost from Major General Alexander's Brigade. Of the thousand men killed and missing, over one third of those men were from the brave unit that shattered themselves against the British advance, to save our army.

Late on September 5th, as we watched the British on Long Island from our battery position at Fort George, Captain Doughty was seen walking the ramparts. Occasionally, he put his spyglass to his eye, to view the British fleet still anchored in the southern portion of New York Harbor, near Staten Island, while at the same time inspecting the labors of the British army across the East River in Brooklyn, less than a mile distant. From our position, they looked like a lot of busy little red coated ants, constantly in motion. But we knew these little red ants had a sting to them. As Captain Doughty approached my position, I stood smartly to attention.

"Relax Corporal," he said as he approached, "has there been any activity of note today?"

"No, sir," I replied as we both gazed over our fortifications at the army of red ants constantly in motion. "Captain," I inquired, "why didn't the British press the attack when they had us bottled up at Brooklyn Heights, last week?"

"Will," the captain began, "I've had several meetings with the colonels and major generals from several divisions this past week, and not only is everyone asking that question, but we're also wondering why Howe hasn't pressed his advantage against us here on Manhattan Island? Over half of our army is scattered all over this island right now. If the British chose to, they could sail any number of their ships up the Hudson River and outflank us. There is nothing we could do about it. Most of the officers are of the opinion that General Washington should abandon New York City, and pull us off this island before the entire army is destroyed. But is seems that General Washington has decided not to give up New York, without a fight, at least for now.

Also, most of the officers think that as the army stands presently, it is not a fighting force that can match the British army. That we need some serious training and drilling is obvious. But in addition to that, we are in need of just about everything, from food and clothing, to weapons, in addition to powder and shot. As it stands, we are still just a ragtag army consisting of many different units from around the colonies, all of us more or less thrown together to make up this army."

After standing there in silence for several moments after the captain had said all this, I finally spoke up.

"Captain," I began, "did you see that unit from Major General Alexander's Brigade that kept throwing themselves at the enemy attacking the Gowanus Pass?"

"Yes, I saw them," Captain Doughty replied.

"What unit was that, and did any of them survive the battle, sir?" I asked.

As Captain Doughty stared out over the river towards Brooklyn with a faraway stare, and without looking at me, he stated, "That was a Maryland unit of four hundred highly trained riflemen. I believe that less than twenty-five returned to the heights. The rest, well the rest laid out there in a common, unmarked grave, we saw the British dig two days ago, and a few were captured, and will spend the rest of the war in a British prison, if they live. The sad fate they suffered was partly due to Major General Alexander's own order to burn a bridge, which spanned the Gowanus Creek earlier that day. Otherwise, some of those men could have saved themselves. I heard tell that when General Washington himself saw their sacrifice that he stated, "Good God, what brave fellows I must this day lose! I dare say that none of us, who saw what the Maryland Four Hundred sacrificed that day, could ever forget the bravery and resolve of our men."[1]

"The Maryland Four Hundred," I repeated, "I will never forget."

"Will," the captain continued, "I dare say that there will be many more days like that, as well as sacrifices similar to those before this war is over."

Another week passed without a move by either army. It seemed as if both were content to watch each other, although we were jittery thinking we could be outflanked at any time on Manhattan Island. During this time, I rode several days as a dispatch rider for Colonel Sage, who was in command of our position under Major General Spencer, whose division was spread all over southern Manhattan. Most of my dispatch riding took me to the northern end of the island to Fort Washington. This fort, having been strategically built on the heights at the northern end of Manhattan Island, was well fortified against any assault by land or sea.

Then, on September 13th, a day that broke with a bright blue sky, with not a cloud to be seen, the British attack began. As I was returning from

1 "Maryland 400' helped turn the Revolution's early tide." http://www.somednews.com/stories/053106/entefea173542_32080.shtml

Fort Washington to Fort George to report to Colonel Sage, I saw a sight that stopped me dead in my tracks, as I reined in my horse. I had decided to take a secondary road off the Bloomingdale Road, one that would take me by the highest hill in the southern half of the island, Murray Hill, which was named for the Murray farm that occupied the area. From there, I could see up, as well as down the East River. I first took notice of Blackwell's Island, a large, thin island that ran several miles in the middle of the East River. Blackwell's farm and orchards could be seen from my vantage point on Murray's Hill.

I then turned my gaze to the shoreline of Brooklyn, across the East River and as I moved down the shoreline I realized the British were beginning to cross the river enforce. There, across the East River from my position overlooking Kipp's Bay, were several hundred British redcoats boarding transport boats, beginning to cross the East River into Manhattan. The American brigades, under the command of Colonel Douglas at the Kipp's Bay fortifications, were already abandoning their position without a fight. Just down the road from me was a post at the intersection of the Bloomingdale Road.

I spurred my horse into action. As I approached the post I yelled out, "The British are crossing the river enforce, ride north and give the alarm to Fort Washington, I'll go to Fort George. Give the alarm to everyone!" I shouted as I rode off. All the way down the island to whomever I saw, I gave the alarm.

As I approached Fort George, all was in a stir as the alarm had already been given there. I reined my horse up in front of the headquarters, and saw Colonel Sage coming out of his tent.

"Colonel," I said breathlessly, "I've just seen perhaps a thousand redcoats beginning to cross the East River at Kipp's Bay, enforce, sir." "Corporal," Colonel Sage replied, "Spencer has already heard and has ordered the division to immediately retreat north to Fort Washington. There is no time to gather the artillery. Ride to the battery at the point of the island and tell Captain Doughty to spike the guns, and make as orderly and hasty retreat up the island to Fort Washington. Is that understood?"

As I remounted my horse, I replied, "Sir!" as I wheeled my horse and was off at a gallop to the battery, at Fort George at the end of the island. As I approached, all was in a stir, as word of the impending disaster had not reached them.

"Corporal Waterman," Captain Doughty called out, "what news? What is going on?"

"Captain, the British are crossing the East River enforce about half way up the island. Spencer has ordered a retreat to Fort Washington, and to spike the guns and leave them, sir!" I yelled.

As the men in the immediate area heard this, all was in disarray as men began yelling and running everywhere.

"Without a fight?" Captain Doughty said in disbelief. Then, after a few moments thought, he began barking out orders to the sergeants near him. All was in motion at once as men began gathering what they could. The cannons were spiked, as the powder and shot were thrown over the side of the ramparts and into New York Harbor.

The retreat, if that was what it could be called, was more like a mass confusion of men in motion. Men, wagons and horses all streamed north out of Fort George and New York City, up the few roads in Manhattan that ran the length of the island, some thirteen miles, to Fort Washington. As men on foot began to tire, they threw everything of weight off of them, from their packs, to their canteens and food bags. Some even discarded their weapons. From the wagons, invaluable stores of food and ammunition were thrown by the wayside so that tired men could ride in them.

As this ragtag group approached Fort Washington, most of the army was told to continue north and cross the King's Bridge, across the Harlem River and into the Bronx. There was already a division stationed at Fort Washington. Our brigade, under the command of Lieutenant General Wadsworth, consisting mostly of Connecticut militia, was ordered to remain at Fort Washington. The rest of the day we watched as the remnants of various haggard units straggled past our position.

Finally, as the day began to wane, the rear guard was seen riding into sight. It consisted of about two hundred dragoons. The officer in charge stopped to report to the officer at the gate of Fort Washington. We could see that they talked for several minutes and the dragoon officer was very animated as he wheeled his horse several times, and continued to point down the road on which he had so recently ridden. Finally, as his column of dragoons began to ride out of sight, he spurred his mount and followed them north to the King's Bridge and safety.

The column of dragoons was not out of sight for more than five minutes when far down the road to our south, a redcoated column appeared. All became eerily silent in Fort Washington. It wasn't long before every man there, could not only see the approaching British column, but could also hear the sounds of the fifes and drums, as they led the column north to the impending fight.

Suddenly, I found Captain Doughty standing next to me. "They are an impressive sight, are they not?" he said, as he smiled at me with a grin.

"Yes, they are," I replied softly.

"Don't worry," he said, "there won't be a fight tonight, but on the morrow, I fear we'll have to deal with General Howe and his British regulars, as they'll be knocking at our door."

The rest of the evening and late into the night, all was in motion in and around Fort Washington, as everything was made ready. For all were certain that with the morning light, the British would indeed be at our door.

A rumor spread that night that Mrs. Murray, at Murray's Farm on Murray's Hill, slowed the advance of the British army by offering the officer's tea. While the British officers were so engaged, and their army's advance stopped, most of our army was able to slip past the enemy on the Bloomingdale Road to the relative safety of Fort Washington, or across the Kings Bridge and into the Bronx.

With the morning light, all was as expected as the British drew up before us in battle lines. The morning light also showed that the British had been busy during the night, as several batteries of artillery were arrayed before Fort Washington, and within range of reaching not only the outer works of the fort, but reaching the inner fortifications as well.

Most of Brigadier General Wadsworth's units were assigned to provide support to the existing artillery units within Fort Washington. My twenty man rifle unit, remained detailed to provide support to Captain Doughty and his artillery unit. We found ourselves, waiting for the commencement of hostilities from the ramparts of Fort Washington.

That morning brought no new change in either our position, or that of the British. It appeared that General Howe was content with having his army face ours, without causing injury to either. It was believed that General Howe was shying away from assaulting our fortified position, as the British were believed to still be smarting from the costly victory at Bunker Hill, in 1775.

General Washington had other ideas. With the lack of movement of the British army at Fort Washington and the Harlem Heights, Washington sent a force of New England Rangers numbering around one hundred and twenty men, under the command of Captain Thomas Knowlton, forward to scout out the enemy positions. Captain Knowlton's force left the safety of the heights and went down onto the plateau to the immediate south of the heights.

Sporadic firing broke out when Captain Knowlton's Rangers ran into the pickets of the British light infantry. More British troops came up in support of the pickets, and the outnumbered New England Rangers were forced to begin a hasty retreat. Seeing the rangers in retreat, Washington sent a force to reinforce them in an effort to draw the British further out onto the plateau. The ruse worked as desired. As the resistance of the reinforced New England unit stiffened, the British pressed their attack, moving further out on the plateau. At the same time Washington sent another force under Major Leitch in a flanking maneuver around the British right, which was hidden by the many small hills and orchards, in an effort to cut the British units off from their reinforcements. As Major Leitch's units moved around the British right, they encountered skirmishers from other British units. A sporadic fire broke out between Major Leitch's men and the British skirmishers.

On hearing the firing to their left and then their rear, the British light infantry realized that they were in jeopardy of being cut off by the American flanking movement, and broke off their attack. Washington sent more men up to the front to press the attack on the light infantry, as Howe realized that his men were in peril of receiving serious casualties. After several hours of firing, the British retreated to more secure ground, as still more British reinforcements moved up.

At day's end, news came that, however small, it was clearly a victory for our forces, as we held the field after the British retreat. Our units spent the day watching and listening to the firing from various locations in front of our fortified positions, as the sounds of gunfire and rising smoke marked the locations of the heaviest fighting. Our losses were light, and our exuberance around our campfires that night with a small victory over the British army was cut short, when news was received that among our few killed in action that day, was both Captain Knowlton and Major Leitch.

On the night of September 20th, sentries on the bluffs of Harlem Heights reported that the sky over New York City was aglow with a red light. That night and most of the following day, a quarter of New York City burned. General Howe, fearing a rebel ruse and attack, denied repeated requests by the citizenry of New York City to help in fighting the fire. Later, General Washington stated that he thought some patriot had been overzealous in denying the British winter quarters.

Several days later most of the army was moved across the King's Bridge and into the Bronx. Colonel Robert Magaw was left in command at Fort Washington with three thousand men.

For the next month, our forces moved north of the Bronx, fortifying positions as we went, leaving strongly armed fortifications along our lines of communication. In the middle of October, word was received that General Howe and the British army were again on the move. A force disembarked from Kipp's Bay on Manhattan, landing on Throg's Neck. A unit of Pennsylvania riflemen, under the command of Colonel Edward Hand held the only bridge off of Throg's Neck. When they were reinforced, the British army departed Throg's Neck on their transports. They landed next at Pell's Point a few miles away and moved inland. Word came that a brigade under the command of Colonel John Glover, with a force of 750 men, engaged General Howe's men at the town of Eastchester. Although badly outnumbered, Glover's men made a good showing and inflicted more casualties on the British than they received, before the British continued their move up the coast.

General Washington mirrored the British army's movement by marching the main body of the American forces up the Bronx River. It was rumored that Washington wanted another fight with Howe.

Several days later, word came by a rider that another engagement had occurred. This time, a Delaware regiment under the command of Colonel John Haslet met a regiment of the Queen's Rangers, under the command of Captain Robert Rogers at the town of Mamaroneck. Again, the Americans had a good showing. When I heard the name of Captain Robert Rogers, I could only wonder if my Da was in that regiment fighting against the very army I was in. I thought back to the days before I left for Hartford to fill the Connecticut levy. Da had said he had been offered a commission in the Queen's Rangers, and he seemed to know that the next battleground was going to be New York. Robert Rogers was also the name of the commander of Rogers' Rangers during the French and Indian War. A name that was familiar to me, as Da had often spoken of Major Rogers when he would tell me the stories from that war. That night, as I lay on my cot in my tent, thoughts of my Da ran through my head. Was he really only a few miles away in the opposing army's camp? Had he actually fought in the engagement at Mamaroneck? Was he wounded or even killed? How could it be that we opposed each other in such a fight?

The next morning the main body of the army moved again, this time to a town called White Plains. For the next week fortifications were hastily made, in anticipation of the coming fight. On October 27th, with the approach of the British army, our outlying units and pickets began to have sporadic contact, and exchanged fire with the leading elements of the British army. After a day of skirmishes, everyone knew that tomorrow would be the day of the next general engagement. There seemed to be a renewed sense of urgency to complete the defensive works, and everyone went about their business with new energy, if not with more earnest resolve.

Our main position was to the south of the town of White Plains. On our left was the division of Major General Heath. Major General Putnam held the center. On the west side of the Bronx River on Chatterton's Hill, were Colonel Spencer's Division and Colonel McDougall with four thousand men. To the north of town were General Washington and the reserve units. My rifle unit was located about a hundred yards behind the main defensive works on Chatterton's Hill.

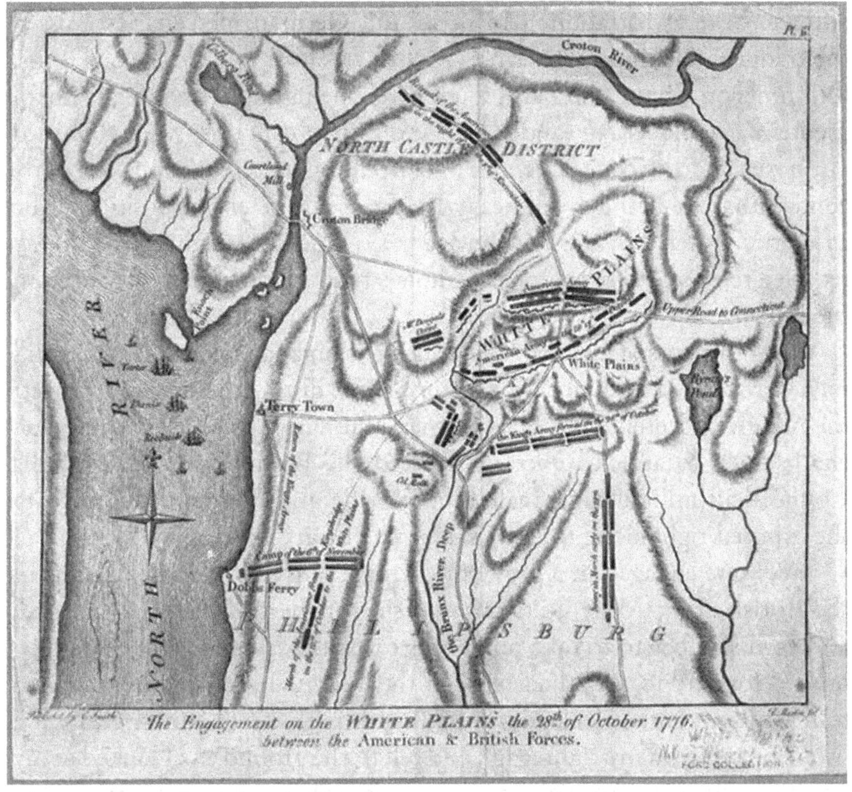

The Engagement on the WHITE PLAINS the 28th of October 1776. between the American & British Forces.

That night the camp was busy late into the night, with everyone trying to complete the many details that could be thought of in preparation for the coming battle. Even when the camp finally settled down for the night to rest, no one actually slept. It was a night of unrest and uneasiness before the coming fight. I could not help but wonder if the British soldiers felt the same uneasiness the night before a battle.

The following day, all were up before the sun in the cool autumn morning. There was no need to be awakened by the morning drum rolls. All was made ready and all were in place long before the British advance on our positions began. The British formed their lines before us, but hesitated for what seemed hours before they advanced to begin their attack. When the attack did come, it was on our center and was strongly made, but our forces were equal to the task as heavy casualties were inflicted on the attacking units. The British also laid down a heavy bombardment from their artillery units at our center, but our positions held well.

Unknown to us during this attack, just down the Bronx River from the main attack, the British had constructed a bridge, crossing the Bronx River enforce. Several battalions of British and German mercenaries crossed the bridge, attacking Chatterton's Hill in an effort to dislodge our units. Our units on Chatterton's Hill fought well, being supported by the fire of Lieutenant Colonel Alexander Hamilton's two cannons, we maintained our positions. The engagement in and around Chatterton's Hill was hotly contested as we laid down a heavy fire from our defensive positions. The casualties' suffered by the British were heavy, and it wasn't until the British received reinforcements of foot and horse, that we were finally forced from the hill.

The remnants of Colonel Spencer's Division and Colonel McDougall's men were pushed through Washington's camp during their retreat, and left the American center under Major General Putnam, as well as Washington's camp, open to attack. Once we crossed the Bronx River, most of the Connecticut militia units, including my rifle unit, were ordered to cover the exposed right along the east side of the Bronx River.

We were engaged in a heavy fire across the river with several units of the British army. More units on each side of the river became engaged, and each side began to take numerous casualties. As men fell, more men pushed forward to take their place in the line. As I was ordering my men to reload for another volley into the British ranks across the river, I felt a severe burning on my right thigh and fell to the ground. As I looked at my leg, it felt like I had been kicked by a horse, as blood ran down my leg. As I grabbed at my leg and wound, the realization set in that a British soldier had hit his mark and his ball was deep in my upper right thigh. Suddenly, Samuel Fuller was at my side lifting me from the ground.

"Will," he questioned, "are you badly hurt?"

"I don't know how bad it is, Sam, but it burns like a branding iron right now. Help me to the rear," I pleaded.

With the help of Sam and leaning heavily on his shoulder, we made our way to Washington's camp, well behind the engagement.

"Will, I'll come for you when this engagement is over," Sam said as he laid me against a wagon wheel, returning to the line.

"Take charge of the men and keep them firing!" I yelled after him as he ran to the sound of the firing, not knowing if he even heard me.

I lay there for several moments against the wagon wheel listening to the sounds of battle. From the river, the firing continued and seemed to be the heaviest. From our fortifications, the firing continued, but only scattered now. It wasn't long before men on foot began streaming by me. I pushed myself up holding on the wagon wheel, and using my rifle as support. None of the men seemed to be too concerned about their movement from the line.

As a group of men approached me, I yelled to them, "What news from the front lines?"

A burly redhead with a slight wound on his forehead, left the group and came over to me. "Word is that our right gave out on us," he said as he looked down at my leg. "We've been ordered to begin a retreat north to the Croton River, and a place called Castle Hill to regroup. Best you get yourself on one of the wagons coming and get to the hospital," he said as he left to catch up with his group of friends. As he left, I looked toward our front lines, and could see more men coming. As the stream of men began to pass me, I saw a wagon with wounded approaching. I made my way, half stumbling and using my rife as support, through the men toward the wagon. As I approached, the Teamster driver pulled up short.

"You best get on the back, soldier," he said, looking down at me, "the whole army will be coming down this road soon. You don't want to be left behind."

Grimacing as I hobbled to the rear of the wagon, I muttered under my breath, "Yes, sir."

As I reached the back of the wagon, the tailgate was down and I could see somewhere around twenty soldiers with various wounds, some sitting and some lying down in the wagon. A passing soldier gave me a hand up into the wagon, and handed me my rifle as I settled in. The teamster gave a shout as I heard the slap of the reins on the backs of the horses as the team pulled, and the wagon lurched forward. Several of the wounded men groaned as the wagon began to move down the road. I tore my shirt and tried to cover my wound in an effort to stem the flow of blood. As we headed north out of Washington's camp, I could see a stream of men coming out of White Plains. The firing off to the west along the Bronx River was beginning to die down. As we passed men walking along the road, most had their heads down as they trudged the five miles to Castle Hill. Most looked downcast, and somewhat broken. I could not help thinking that this was not much of an army, and it looked like a broken one now. It took several hours to reach Castle Hill, over what must have been the worst road in New York colony. Each time our wagon hit a rut or one of the numerous bumps in the road, several of the wounded would groan. Some of the wounded were now unconscious, and could have been dead as far as I could tell.

When we arrived at Castle Hill, our wagon was directed to a field that held several large tents and numerous wagons, as large numbers of wounded men lay out on blankets around the field. As our team of horses came to stop, I slid off the wagon and hopped around on my left leg, looking where I should go. Several orderlies and nurses came over, and began to help the wounded off the wagon. One, taking my right arm and putting it over his shoulder, helped me several yards to a blood stained, but empty blanket. As he helped me lay down, he said to me, "You'll probably be here several hours before they get to you. Try to rest as best you can." He pulled my bandage down as I grimaced to look at my wound. With that, he went off toward the wagon to remove more wounded. The men lying on either side of me didn't move or make a sound, and I thought them to be dead. I could hear the moans of the other wounded around me as I lay there staring up at the sky. The night was now quickly approaching. Just before dark, an orderly came by to cover me with a blanket, and looked at my wound. "They should get to you by morning," he said as he began checking the soldiers around me. Wounded men from the front had been streaming in all afternoon and into the evening. This would be the same for two more days.

As night drew nigh, I felt extremely tired despite the constant pain and throbbing of my wound. I can only think that I passed out, as I found myself the next morning being prodded by an orderly.

"You alive, son?" he was saying to me as he poked me with a stick.

As I came out of my sleep, his face came into view right above me. "I, I'm still here," I said.

"Good, we'll be taking you to see the doctor soon," he replied as he looked around.

A second orderly came up and the two of them lifted me to my feet and helped me into the nearest tent. Inside the tent was several tables with men laying on them with doctors and nurses hovering over them. I was assisted to the nearest empty table. I was lifted on the table and was told the doctor would be right with me.

Several minutes later, an older man who had gray hair and a bushy mustache that covered his entire upper lip came over, accompanied by a nurse. He instructed the nurse to tear away my pants past the wound and to clean it, while he rummaged through his bag of doctoring instruments. He was mumbling to himself about where he had placed a certain tool when he stood up, holding a long metal probe that looked like half a ramrod to a rifle, stating, "Here it is."

As he turned to me, he looked at me and asked me, "What's your name young man?"

"Will Waterman, sir," I replied as I looked at the long metal probe in his hand.

"Well, Will Waterman, I'm Doctor Morehouse, and I'll be treating your wound shortly," he said as he looked at his assistant. "Give him something to bite on Miss Woodson, if you please."

Immediately, the nurse pulled a six-inch piece of wood from her pocket and stuck it in my mouth, and then she grabbed my shoulders.

"Hold still, young man," Doctor Morehouse said as he took the probe and began to insert it into the hole in my leg. The pain increased the deeper he inserted the probe, as I bit as hard as I could on the wood as tears were streaming down my cheeks.

As he removed the probe, Doctor Morehouse looked at me as I relaxed from the pain I was in. "I am afraid young man, that the bullet has adhered itself right to your bone, although the bone doesn't seem to be broken. I would try to remove the bullet, but fear I will be unsuccessful. If your leg had broken from the impact of the bullet, I would not have any reservations about cutting into your leg to remove the bullet. As it is, if I can't pull the bullet free, we will have to leave it where it is and hope it heals. Infection will be your biggest worry then," he finished as he turned around and began to rummage in his bag of tools again. Turning around he pulled out a pair of tweezers that were about nine inches long. I tensed up immediately as he prepared to push the tweezers into the hole in my leg, as the nurse again grabbed my shoulders to hold me still. The tweezers were larger than the probe, and the pain was more excruciating than the insertion of the probe. I groaned deeply as he moved the tweezers in my leg, as he tried to free the bullet from the bone and my leg. Sweat beads began to form on my forehead and my leg began to quiver uncontrollably.

Finally, after several moments of trying to remove the bullet without success, Doctor Morehouse removed the tweezers from my leg. I fell back on the table, covered with sweat and totally exhausted from the few moments of torture.

Dr. Morehouse cleaned his tools and leaned over my face. "Young man, it is as I suspected," he began. "The bullet has fused itself to the bone and rather than risk your life by cutting open your leg to try to get it out, we'll leave it be to see if your leg heals," he said. "Do you understand?" he asked.

I could only shake my head as my eyes were still closed, and my breathing was just now beginning to return to normal.

"Miss Woodson will dress your wound, and I'll check on you later," he said as he turned to move onto the next patient. "Mind you, the wound may never heal at all, but may keep oozing blood and pus from time to time," he said over his shoulder as he left me.

As I lay there, I began to wonder how I got myself into this mess, as the nurse began to apply a fresh dressing on my leg. As she finished, she swung my legs around to sit me up and helped me off the table.

"We'll dress your leg each day and if it starts bleeding or oozing pus, remove the bandage to let it drain. Then come to the hospital for a new dressing," she said as the two orderlies came and took me by each shoulder, helping me outside to my blanket.

Two days later, with the army in retreat to Peekskill, I was placed in a wagon of a train comprised of twenty-five wagons, used to move the wounded with the army. At Peekskill, Washington and most of the army crossed to the west side of the Hudson River. The remainder of the army, mostly the New England Regiments, under Major General Putnam was dispersed to the New York Highlands to defend against British movements. I was placed in a separate wagon train moving troops to Connecticut, which was returning the wounded to points closer to home. We received news each day from dispatch riders, as our column moved east.

Howe hadn't followed Washington north as first reported, but had turned south, cutting off Fort Washington from support and supply. After a short battle, Fort Washington fell, with its entire garrison being captured.

For his part, Washington moved the remainder of his army south into New Jersey colony. Howe crossed the Hudson River shortly after taking Fort Washington and surprised General Greene and his entire garrison at Fort Lee. General Greene and his garrison escaped only moments before the fort was surrounded, thus saving part of Washington's army, but leaving behind precious supplies of cannons, powder, shot and food that the army desperately needed.

Most of the men in our column were from the Connecticut colony or the Boston area. We were all dispirited on our journey back to our homes, and tired from our efforts against the British. It seemed to all, that no matter how well we fought, that we didn't have the experience, training or understanding of how to fight the British army. I could only think back to what Da had told me months earlier, that the Americans could not defeat a professional, well trained army, like the British.

And so it was, late on a dark, cold and windy November night, what remained of our column, only three wagons now and twenty men, slowly made our way down the main street in a small quiet town in Connecticut. Finally, they pulled up in front of an old farmhouse outside of town. I was home.

- CHAPTER 8 -

"Rest and Home Again"

Winter 1776 – 77

It almost seemed impossible to be home. The familiar surroundings of home quickly returned to me, as Mother, John and Rachel all welcomed me and made me feel at home. Missing, though, was Da. Mother sat with me to explain that Da, at the urging of Captain Rogers himself, had left only a week after I had to fill the Connecticut levy, to join Captain Rogers and the Queens Rangers attached to General Howe's army. I was shocked and it took several days to get over the disbelief that Da was fighting with the British army.

So much had happened during the months I was away, especially, the last few months with the engagements with the British army on Long Island, at Harlem Heights, and finally at White Plains. Everyone loyal to the American cause wanted to hear from someone who was there, what it was really like, and what actually happened. Post riders had come by on a regular schedule, bringing news of the war, but actually hearing it from a soldier seemed to interest everyone. No one else from our unit had made it home yet, as no one was injured enough to be pulled from the line of duty, and sent home to recover from their wounds.

I spent most of the first several weeks at home resting. By the time I arrived home in late November, I was extremely weak from the loss of blood, along with the infection that had set in. The only doctor in Norwich was Dr. John Post, who lived just down the main road from Durkee's Tavern. When Dr. Post saw my leg the day after I arrived home, it was apparent that he was extremely distressed over the amount of blood and pus still flowing from the wound.

He was the kind of doctor that you could never tell what he was thinking, as the most he said while examining someone might be an occasional grunt and snort that would not lead anyone to what was on his mind. So, I was subjected to a more thorough second examination of my wound. He went into the back room, for what he didn't say. As he came back to the examination room, he had in his hand a long metal probe, similar to the one that Dr. Morehouse had inserted into my wound, at the field hospital at Castle Hill. My mother came with me to the exam, as it was hard for me to put any weight on my leg without experiencing face twisting pain. As Dr. Post approached me with the long probe in his hands, my mother let out a loud gasp, as she realized that the good doctor intended to insert the instrument into my wound. Dr. Post hesitated for a moment to take into account the concern of my mother.

"Mrs. Waterman, you may find this to be of some discomfort, but not as much as young Will here. You may, if you wish, leave the room for a few moments, as I need to do a thorough exam of this wound, if I am to ascertain to what extent the infection has spread," Dr. Post stated flatly.

"I will remain with my son, Doctor," mother said, trying to show an unwavering fortitude. "You may continue with your examination."

My mother grabbed my hand to give me comfort, but it was really more for her pain than for mine. As the doctor slowly inserted the probe into my wound, try as I may to hide the pain, my mother saw the excruciating discomfort I was in, causing her all the more. I wouldn't find out until years later, when I had my own children, how hard it is for a parent to endure seeing their children in pain.

And so it was, as Dr. Post inserted the probe deep into my wound that the pain grew increasingly more intense the farther the probe went. My mother saw my growing discomfort as my face reflected my pain. What seemed to be an eternity came to an end as Dr. Post removed the probe, laying it aside.

"Well, young William, it is well that your mother brought you to me as soon as she did. If this wound was left to fester on its own, surely the infection would take your life," he stated coldly.

"Oh dear God, is it that bad Doctor?" My mother blurted out.

"That bad and all the worse, my good lady," he said. "Look here, ma'am," he began pointing to my exposed leg above the wound. "Do you not see the reddish pink condition of the leg in this area?"

"Yes, I see it," my mother said with a concerned look.

"If this infection is allowed to continue unchecked, it will spread above his waist and into his general blood stream, killing him, certain!" the doctor stated emphatically, and then continued. "As it is, I will give the wound a good cleaning and some fresh bandages. I recall, ma'am, that there is a good stand of pine trees just down the road from your house?" he inquired.

"Yes, there are sufficient stands of pines just up the river from our farm, Doctor," my mother stated.

"The pine needle is a most excellent source of vitamin c," the doctor replied. "Does young William not have a younger brother who is still in the house?" the doctor inquired.

"Yes, young John, and even his sister, Rachel, are still at home," my mother answered.

"This is good," the doctor went on. "Have them gather as many pine needles off of the trees as they can place in a bushel barrel every day. Boil water, while placing two hands full of pine needles in the water and let it stand for oh..., five minutes or so. Give him as much of this drink as the boy can stand every day for the next month," the doctor flatly stated. "Oh, yes, and remember to bring him to me every other day, so I can check the progress of this nasty infection ma'am."

The doctor seemed to be done as he turned away from us. And then as if he remembered something suddenly, he began, "Mrs. Waterman, keep him off of that leg for the next month. I have here in my back room," and he disappeared as if he thought he wasn't talking to anyone, only to appear with a long piece of wood, with a rest running six inches on the top and a second about half way down sticking out the side. As he returned he was still talking as if he never left. "This thing which I'm sure you've never seen before is called a crutch. Its purpose is to aid a person with an injured leg to walk. Make sure young Will, if he has to move about your house, uses this and doesn't put any weight on this leg. Is that understood, young man?" the doctor questioned, as he looked at me from his bushy eyebrows.

"Yes, I understand, doctor," I replied. And as I continued, I asked, "Doctor, how long do you think it will be until I recover from this wound, sir?"

"Tell me, young man, what the field surgeon who first examined this wound, said to you about it, and how long ago did this happen?" he asked.

"I was wounded, sir, on the 28th of October, while we were engaged with the British army in a heated battle at a small town in the colony of

New York called White Plains," I began. "The field surgeon was a Doctor Morehouse, and I believe he said that he thought the ball had fused itself to my bone. Rather than to cause more injury to my leg, he said that it should be left where it was to see if my leg would heal, with the bullet in it. He also said that if it had shattered my thigh bone, it would have been better, because he would be able to remove the bullet and rest my leg at the same time," I concluded.

"The good Doctor Morehouse was correct," Doctor Post stated, and then continued, "did he say anything else about the wound?"

I looked at Doctor Post and stated flatly, "He said it may never heal at all."

"Doctor Morehouse told you right, Will," the doctor replied. "In fact, Will, sometime many years from now, this very wound, if it does not heal, may take your life."

My mother was taken aback at all that was said, turning white as a ghost. Doctor Post noticed her condition, and helped her sit down in a chair in the corner of his examination room. The doctor re-bandaged the wound after giving it a thorough cleaning, restated his instructions to my mother about staying off the leg, along with coming to see him every other day until further instructed.

As we started home in our wagon, I stated to my mother, "Please don't tell Eli or Diane how bad it is, Mother."

She looked at me with a concerned look and said, "Will, I won't say anything for now, but you shouldn't keep it from them, and will have to tell them eventually."

"I know, Ma, but I'll tell them my own way and when it's time," I informed her.

I spent the next month laid up in bed trying to keep my leg still and getting it to heal. I saw Doctor Post on a regular basis as he had suggested, and after the first two weeks, he said he finally began to see improvement in the leg. After a month, he said I was on my way to recovery, and that I could walk about on it until I felt fatigued or until it began to bleed or ooze pus again.

Diane came to see me every day and stayed at our house for most of the day. While she was there, she would help mother with house chores and cooking, which mother was grateful for. With Da and me both being gone for so long, and with John still being a little too young to do all of the farm work, a lot of our chores fell on mother. I had noticed that she looked very tired one day. Diane would ask me about the war, and I was reluctant to tell her about all of it. It just wouldn't come out. How could I tell her about all that I had seen and done? How could I tell her of the battle of Long Island, and the Maryland unit that sacrificed its self so that the army could escape? Or would I really recall the retreat up Manhattan to Harlem Heights and Fort Washington in disarray, although the Harlem Heights engagement was clearly a victory for us? I told her what I could about White Plains and how I was wounded. She was always concerned for me and didn't want me to return to the army. I told her I wasn't sure what I'd do in the future, always staying noncommittal.

Eli was always Eli, and whenever he was finished with his chores on the Bingham farm, he came over to our house to talk. Usually, he came for dinner and if Diane had to go home early, he would come back after I had escorted her home in our wagon. He wanted me to tell him about the war. It was easier for me to open up to him, in part, because he was with me at Boston, and knew what went on in an army camp and in battle. Eli was fascinated by what I told him and when he heard about the Maryland unit, he couldn't believe that Washington hadn't sent other units to help them. I tried to tell him that it was impossible by the time Washington took command, to do anything to help them. I told Eli about Harlem Heights, along with the battle at White Plains and how I was wounded. Eli could only shake his head that I had been wounded in battle.

"Eli," I asked, "how many men did we see kill during the siege of Boston?"

"I don't know," he replied quietly under his breath.

"Maybe a hundred?" I asked. Continuing I stated, "I saw many times that killed on Long Island and as many at White Plains, not counting the British losses."

"What are you saying, Will?" he asked.

"I'm saying what my father said a long time ago, at Durkee's Tavern before this war broke out," I responded. "That this war would be fought here, and that some of the men standing in that upper room at Durkee's Tavern, would not come home. I never thought I'd be wounded, Eli," I said as my voice trailed off.

"We'll make it, Will. You'll see," Eli said as his face brightened.

"I don't know, Eli," I said. "My Da is out there fighting for the British, and I may have been fighting against him at White Plains. I believe a unit that he may be in, was engaged in a fight only a few miles away from White Plains, only a few days before I was wounded," I said. "What if he doesn't come home? What if I have shot at him or him at me? I have to think about it, Eli, if I'm going back or not."

"You'll see, Will," Eli began. "In the spring when you're feeling better and all healed up, we'll go back together. My father is better now, and once the crops are planted, we can go back. We'll whip those redcoats like we did at Boston," he stated with conviction.

"Eli, the British army we saw leave Boston with their tails between their legs was not the same army that landed in New York. For the better part of a month, they whipped us at every turn. We couldn't match them," I said.

Eli was more optimistic about the war than I would ever be, but then again, right now the only war he had seen, we had been the victors.

News from the war came with every post or dispatch rider. By the end of November, the British army had pushed Washington and the American army from Hackensack, to Newark. Then the British army had pushed and harassed the American army from Newark to Spanktown; from Spanktown to New Brunswick; from New Brunswick to Trenton and across the Delaware River from New Jersey and into the colony of Pennsylvania. To make matters worse, the post riders brought news that the enlistment's of many of the men were up and thousands returned to their homes. What was equally of note was that the desertions outnumbered the loss of the men who didn't reenlist. By the end of December 1776, as we were at home, making preparations for Christmas, General Washington was left with the remnants of an army that consisted of only a few thousand men. Hardly the army that had a few months earlier, in New York colony swelled to around twenty thousand.

A wagon came by with soldiers in it who were gathering stores for the army. Besides food, which was always a need for a standing army, the soldiers said they could use any spare winter clothing that was available. They stated that what remained of Washington's army was facing the British army and winter, in summer uniforms. Things were at a critical stage for the army.

Mother often talked about Da. She never let her feelings be known about how she felt about the war, or what side she thought was right, if either side was right. She told me that she received a couple of letters from Da when he left to join the British army. She said he was deeply troubled that I was fighting for the Americans. He had expressed concerns that one day he may be in an engagement with my unit. She said his letters were posted from somewhere around New York. She was now concerned that she hadn't received a letter for some weeks. She felt that if he was well, and the army was in winter quarters, he would write. I tried to reassure her that he may be busy with special duties or on detail somewhere that prevented his writing. She pretended to understand and not to be too concerned, but I knew deep down she was concerned about his health and whereabouts.

Christmas came and went, as did the New Year without news from Da. I had spent a lot of time with Diane and her family during this time, as I was up and about on my leg. I saw Doctor Post once a week now and he was encouraged by my improvement, but always cautioned me not to do too much.

Two weeks after Christmas, when we were experiencing the coldest winter weather of the year, the post rider from Boston brought news of an American victory in Trenton, New Jersey colony. The town was abuzz about the news and those who supported the colonies were at Durkee's Tavern reading the posted accounts of the engagement with great excitement. Those who supported the Crown grumbled that when spring came, things would be different, as they felt the British army would corner, and finally crush the American army and end this rebellion.

Eli and I read the account together at Durkee's Tavern. All of the details were still unknown, but the account read that General Washington and what remained of his army crossed the Delaware River from Pennsylvania into New Jersey on Christmas Day, at a crossing called McKonkey's Ferry. In all, the account read that three crossings had been planned, but two commanders failed in their missions. Brigadier General James Ewing, with seven hundred men was to cross the Delaware River at the Trenton Ferry, and hold the bridge across the Assunpink River. At the same time Lieutenant Colonel John Cadwalader was to cross the Delaware River with his column near Bristol, and attack the Hessian garrison at Bordentown, and hold the garrison there. Both of these attacks eventually failed. General Washington, for his part, crossed the Delaware River as planned. He split his forces in two, and marched the nine miles down to Trenton. General Greene commanded the left, and traveled down the Pennington Road, while General Sullivan commanded the right, traveling down the River Road. The account stated that the American forces arrived at the town of Trenton, New Jersey colony just before eight o'clock in the morning. The post further read that the Hessian troops garrisoned at Trenton, were the same forces engaged at Chatterton's Hill during the battle of White Plains. "Eli," I commented, "that was one of the units I was engaged with at White Plains. Maybe it was one of those Hessians who wounded me and not a British soldier."

"We'll never know, I guess," Eli said. "Come on, let's read on," as we both continued to read the account.

It said that the Hessians tried a bayonet charge to break the American attack, but were beaten back by General Knox, as his artillery units commanded the town, while Major General Mercer laid down a heavy fire on the Hessians from their left flank. The Hessians had withdrawn from the town where their commander, a Colonel Rall was mortally wounded. There, the remaining Hessian troops surrendered. The account went on to say that a number of the Hessian troops did escape the American attack and retreated to the British lines. In all, it recounted what was a major victory for the American army, renewing the belief that the war could be won, or at least could continue.

It was learned that General Howe had dispatched General Cornwallis to crush Washington's army if he chose to fight, or if not, to keep him bottled up in Pennsylvania until spring, when the entire British army would hunt down Washington and his army to destroy it.

Apparently, General Washington had other ideas. A week passed and another post rider came with news of another American victory. Eli and I read the post outside of Durkee's Tavern with great excitement. General Washington had not waited for the British to come find him. This time, while a small portion of his army distracted Cornwallis at Trenton, General Washington moved his army north toward Princeton. There in two separate engagements, Washington's army drove one division of the British army from the field and into retreat toward Trenton. Then, General Washington concentrated on the regiment of British soldiers defending Princeton. Lieutenant Colonel Alexander Hamilton fired his artillery into a stone fortified building, causing the British to surrender. In all, the Americans came out of the engagements with fewer than thirty killed in action, and about the same number of wounded and missing. The British lost more in killed, wounded and missing, with over 200 captured at Princeton alone. As Eli and I read this account, we were more excited than ever about rejoining the army in the spring.

"Eli," I said, "I am going to reenlist in the spring if my leg continues to heal and the colony calls for another levy." As I looked away from the post outside of Durkee's Tavern, I looked at Eli asking, "What are you going to do?"

Eli looked at me, and with a big smile on his face stated, "With the two of us in the American army, how could we possibly lose?"

We slapped each other on the back and walked home, each of us caught up in our own thoughts of battle and glory.

If only Diane was as happy about my ideas of reenlisting. I was at her house the following Sunday after church services having dinner with her family when the subject was brought up by her father.

"So, Will," he began, "what are your plans for the coming spring?"

I wasn't sure if he was asking me about the war, or about the planting season. Not sure which he was asking about, I hesitated in thought before I answered and stated, "Well, hopefully we'll have an early spring to get the crops in, sir."

"Then you don't plan on enlisting if the colony calls for another levy?" he asked.

"Well, sir," I began, "I have read the posts on Durkee's Tavern the last couple of weeks. It appears that General Washington, and his army has some fight left in them, since we were pushed out of New York colony. If my leg continues to heal, as Dr. Post believes it will, and if the colony calls for another levy, then I do believe I'll reenlist."

Diane was in the kitchen with her mother doing the dinner dishes and afternoon chores. Apparently, they had been listening intently to the conversation I was having with the Pastor, and when I mentioned that I planned to reenlist, a collective gasp was heard to come out of the kitchen, as both the Pastor and I looked in that direction.

The Pastor looked back at me and asked, "What of your mother and family, and you still haven't had word from your father, have you?"

"Well, if we get the fields planted, my brother and sister are old enough to take care of most of the rest of the chores, and as far as my Da is concerned, we expect to hear from him any time now. I'm sure he's okay and is only on a detail that prevents him from getting a note posted to us," I said trying to convince myself that everything was okay.

As Diane came out of the kitchen, Pastor said we'd talk more about it later on. The rest of the afternoon was generally quiet as we all talked about the happenings in and around Norwich. As I decided to return home early in the evening, Diane walked me to the door, grabbing my hand as we went outside.

"Will," she began as she looked up at me. I knew what she was going to say before she said it. I didn't have an answer for her that would give her comfort. "Do you really plan on enlisting in the army in the spring?" Before I could answer she continued on as a tear streamed down her cheek, "Haven't you done enough for this cause with Boston, and then being wounded in New York? Why would you go again?" she pleaded.

"I can't explain it to you Diane, but I have to go," I said quietly.

Everything was quiet for what seemed several minutes. Finally, Diane said she had to go and slipped inside the door without saying goodbye, or that she would see me later. I didn't know what to do. If I went to fight again, would I lose the young lady I loved to a cause that may be destroyed in the end? What was I to do?

Another week went by without any war news. In late January, my mother received a letter posted in New York from my Uncle Jeremiah. She read it out loud to us around the dinner table. It read that while in New York City on business and delivering a cargo of goods to port there, he had cause to go to the army hospital. Why he had cause to go there he didn't say, but while there; he had found my father in hospital suffering from a wound received sometime during the battles in and around the New York colony the previous fall. Uncle Jeremiah wrote that Da had received a flesh wound to his left arm, that in and of itself was not too serious, but that an infection had set in that had almost killed Da. As it was, Da had been in hospital for the better part of the last few months, and was now well enough to travel. Uncle Jeremiah requested me to meet him in Providence at the end of January to get Da and return him home.

My mother was visibly upset at the news of my father. She sat at the dinner table holding the crumpled letter from Uncle Jeremiah, as tears streamed down her face. The weight of not knowing where Da was or what had happened to him for all this time came pouring out. We tried to comfort mother the best we could, and in the end, all we could do was help her upstairs, and into bed. There, she cried for a while longer before falling asleep. Before I left her and before sleep came on I told her I'd leave for Providence on the morrow, to bring Da home. When she was finally asleep, I quietly slipped out of her room and went out to the barn. My brother, John, met me there and together we made sure that the horses, along with the tack, and as well as the wagon, were all prepared for the morning trip to Providence.

Sleep was hard to come by and the morning broke sunny and cold. A light snow had fallen during the night and covered everything with a fluffy coating. John was up early to help me hitch the team, and Rachel was busy in the kitchen making breakfast, as mother was still too shaken by the news of Da to do much. When the team was ready to go, John and I went in and had breakfast. John said he wanted to go with me, but I told him it was best he stay at home to help mother until she was feeling better. Rachel packed a bag of food for me and brought down a blanket to cover myself with, as the winter was still hard upon us, being late January.

Finally, it was time to go and I kissed mother on her forehead, and told her I'd be back with Da, in a few days.

"Will," she said, "there is some money in the empty flour jar in the kitchen on the counter over the cooking fire. Take what you need," she said as she went on, "you'll need to stay overnight going to and coming back from Providence, and it is much too cold to sleep outside."

"Yes, ma'am," I replied as I knew not to argue with her regarding what little money we had, finding the jar in the kitchen contained a little over a pound and a half.

I went out to the barn, and placed my food on the floor of the buckboard between my feet. The horses stomped on the ground as they sensed we were going on a long journey. Their breath was like steam coming out of their nostrils in the cold January air. With a smart slap of the reins on their backs, they lurched forward and pulled out onto the road. I was so busy with my preparations, that I hadn't had a chance to tell Eli or Diane of the news. I thought Eli would have to forego knowing, but I had to stop at the Gallagher's house, and tell Diane that I was going to Providence to get Da.

As I pulled the horses up in front of the Gallagher house, the Pastor opened the door.

"Going somewhere this morning, Will?" he asked.

"We received a post late yesterday from my Uncle Jeremiah that my Da was wounded in one of the battles around New York colony," I said. "Seems he was in hospital in New York City for some time, and that is why we didn't hear from him," I stated. "I'm going to Providence to fetch him, and bring him home, sir," I said. "Is Diane home, I'd like to tell her what is happening', if I may?"

The Pastor shook his head as he looked down the street. "I'm sorry, Will, but Diane and her mother left early this morning' to run some errands and I don't know exactly where they've gone," he said.

"Will you tell her where I've gone when you see her for me, sir?" I asked.

"I will and we'll be praying for your father and your safe return, Will, and Godspeed to you," he said.

"Thank you, sir," I said as I slapped the horses with the reins to get them moving. I had a long, cold journey ahead of me to Providence.

My trip to Providence was uneventful other than staying overnight at Waterman's Tavern at Scituate, Rhode Island on the way there. Master Waterman treated me well, as I explained to him that I was traveling to

Providence to get my Da, who had been severely wounded during the battles around New York colony. He was more than accommodating to me, and provided ample food and rum, as well as a bed for the night.

I made good time as the horses were fresh, and they pulled easily along the road. It was all of a two-day trip by wagon and by the time I sighted the harbor in Providence, it was nigh on dark of the second day. The horses were tired now and needed a good rest, as they hadn't been worked much since the harvest was brought in.

As the horses slowly pulled along the harbor front, I looked for my uncle's ship. It was hard to see with all of the masts and rigging of the several ships in port. Finally, I saw the familiar shape of the good ship *Whisperer.* I reined in the horses alongside the ship and just looked. I was tired and very cold. As I sat there watching the activity on the ship, I noticed there was a lot of ice in the harbor. It always seemed colder along the waterfront. There were several hands at work hoisting the cargo out of the hold and swinging it to the dockworkers next to the ship.

"Master Will!" someone shouted from the ship. As I looked up, I saw Billings smiling at me from over the rail. He disappeared and returned with my uncle who began to bark orders.

"Master Billings," he shouted, "get down there and relieve Master Will of those reins, he looks half frozen."

With that said, Master Billings swung off the ship using one of the tackle ropes on a yardarm, and was down to the dock next to me before I realized what he had done.

I slowly stepped off the wagon, as I was stiff and cold from my two-day ride. As I stomped my feet to get the feeling back in them and the blood flowing, Billings grabbed my hand and started shaking it. As he continued shaking it, Uncle Jeremiah yelled at Billings, "Be off with you, Billings, and let my nephew come on board and get warm."

Billings finally let go of my hand and climbed up on the wagon, slapped the horses with the reins, and headed down the street to the livery. As I walked up the gangplank, I saw Jennings looking down into the hold directing the hands there with the loading of the next cargo net of materials to be hoisted out, to be placed ashore. He gave me a friendly smile as he saw me, and returned to his work.

Uncle Jeremiah shook my hand as we walked to the door that led to the captain's room. He was saying it was good to see me, and that he wasn't sure the post would get to me in time. As we entered the dark cabin, it took my eyes a moment to adjust to the fading evening light. With only one candle lit in the corner, I could only see that there was a form in the captain's bunk, but couldn't make out who it was, until I drew closer.

I finally could recognize Da in the dim corner, lifting himself up on his good arm, as he saw me approach. He was still gray from his recovery from his wound, with his left arm still wrapped up and in a sling.

"Will, it is so good to see you," he said as he struggled to get up.

"Da, don't get up," I answered as I approached the side of the bunk.

"Ah, you're right, Will, I am still too weak to be up and about much yet," he stated as he lay back down on his right arm to rest.

"I'll excuse myself, as I need to see to the unloading of my cargo, and let you two get reacquainted," Uncle Jeremiah spoke up as he made an excuse to leave us to talk in the cabin.

I pulled up a stool that Uncle Jeremiah had next to the small table that he kept his charts on, and sat next to Da in the bunk. He put his head back on the pillow, as he closed his eyes and said, "I didn't think I'd ever see you or anyone in our family again, Will."

"Da," I inquired, "what happened to you?"

"I was assigned to Captain Rogers from my old unit during the French and Indian War, but Rogers calls them the Queen's Rangers now," he began, as his eyes closed, and he recounted his time with the British army. "As we pushed your army up Manhattan Island, our unit broke off from the main armies thrust and we were ferried up the sound of Long Island and landed at the town of Mamaroneck. Our landing was uneventful, and we were ordered inland to make contact with the enemy units that might be in the area. There was an inexperienced British lieutenant commanding the lead element, and despite repeated warnings and urgings of the officers and senior rangers with him, he went headlong up the road, ignoring all the signs that the enemy was enforce in the area."

Da paused a moment and took a few deep breaths as he ordered his thoughts before he continued his account. While he was thus in thought, I couldn't help but think that every time he mentioned the enemy, he was talking about me.

Finally, he resumed his story. "I was in a unit of rangers two or three removed from the lead element. They were caught in an ambush that was so cleverly devised that even the rangers in the lead unit didn't see it coming, until it was too late. The second ranger unit moved up immediately and spread out to the right to see if they could flank the attacking soldiers, without any effect. My unit came up to support the lead unit that was ambushed, and we were engaged in a heavy fight for the better part of two hours. Most of the lead unit was killed or wounded. My unit lost over half our company before the enemy finally left the field after inflicting severe casualties on us. Near the end of the engagement, a soldier, I never saw shot me in my left arm. I don't know who trained those colonials, but they gave better than we ever expected or wanted." Again, there was a long pause as Da thought about what happened and what he wanted to say next.

I was looking down at my feet as I sat on my stool next to his bunk, and thinking about how grateful I was that it wasn't my unit engaged in that fight and how lucky we were to be together, when he began again.

"I was placed on a wagon train of wounded and sick that traveled down the coast, then crossed onto Manhattan Island a few days later. We were moved down to the southern end of Manhattan Island where a hospital was set up, in one of the old hotels. There I remained between heaven and earth, until I finally came to my senses some weeks after being wounded.

It was by chance that your Uncle Jeremiah had a sick hand on board his ship that needed medical attention. It was in the hospital that he saw me being treated for my wound, and overheard the doctor talking about removing my arm, as it had not by then, and is still not properly healed. Jeremiah stepped in and that night under the cover of darkness, returned to the hospital, removing me to his vessel, which was anchored in New York Harbor. Once Jeremiah's ship cleared customs, and we were out of New York Harbor, it was several days of clear sailing to Providence and home. Of course, just before we departed New York City, Jeremiah posted a letter to your mother regarding my condition, requesting you come get me, to bring me home. I don't know if the hospital missed me, or listed me among the dead, otherwise the British will consider me a deserter."

Da had concluded his story and still being weak from his wound, he closed his eyes, and a few minutes later, fell asleep. I quietly made my way on deck, and observed the unloading of cargo from the hold of the ship. That night I had a quiet dinner with Uncle Jeremiah, as Da was still fast asleep. Uncle Jeremiah related his version of the story of finding Da gravely ill in hospital. He was determined, once he overheard the doctors talking about removing Da's arm, to remove him to his ship and to safety. Uncle Jeremiah talked late into the night about the war and the different opinions he heard at each port that he visited while shipping goods with the *Whisperer*. Most people, he stated, in the cities along the coast were solidly for the rebels, as it was these cities that felt the impact of the British tariffs and oppression, the most. Uncle Jeremiah felt that it was the people who lived in communities inland who were mostly noncommittal due to their lack of contact with the British. Other than the inspection of his cargo and crew, along with the steep tariffs he had to pay at each port, Uncle Jeremiah stated that the British had left him alone for the most part.

We talked late into the night about the war and Uncle Jeremiah talked about becoming a privateer.

"I don't understand what a privateer is, Uncle," I said as he began eating from the plate of food just brought in by the cook, a young boy I didn't recognize.

As the boy left the captain's cabin with Uncle Jeremiah watching him intently, until he was sure the boy was out of earshot, Uncle Jeremiah explained.

"Will, a privateer is a ship which gets papers, orders if you will, from a government that is at war, to attack merchant ships supplying the enemy, and to capture those supplies. The supplies are then to be shipped to any port supporting said government, at which time we are compensated for the supplies," he said looking at me. "There is much more profit in it than shipping cargo's around the Atlantic, and it provides invaluable supplies to the colonies."

"You mean you will be fighting for the colonials, Uncle?" I asked.

"Aye, Will, and with pleasure, if I can profit from it and cause the bloody British discomfort in the process," Uncle Jeremiah said. "But, Will, it can be a dangerous and bloody business," he cautioned. "If we are caught in such an enterprise by any British warship, we will be lucky to live through it. Most likely we will be killed outright, and if not, we certainly will spend the rest of our days in a stinking British prison hulk somewhere, probably in New York Harbor," he concluded as he took a large gulp of grog.

We ate the rest our meals mostly in silence. When the cabin boy came for our plates, and had cleared the cabin and departed, I said, "I'd like to go make my regards to the crew for a few minutes, but before I do, I have something to tell you and need your advice."

"Go on, Will," Uncle Jeremiah replied.

"I don't know how to tell Da," I related as I looked over at my still sleeping father. "That I was with the American army in New York colony during the very battles Da spoke about, although I was not engaged in the battle where he was wounded, and I have myself just recovered enough from my own wound, to come fetch Da home."

"Will, tell your father when the time seems right," he began. "I think you'll find him a changed man, now that he's seen a different side of the

British army than the one he knew during the last war, against the French and their Indian allies."

All was silent for a few moments, and then Uncle Jeremiah finally stated, "Will, why don't you go see Jennings, Billings and Edwards? They'll be glad to see you and they can introduce you to the rest of the crew."

I made my way below deck just past the main cargo hold area to the crew quarters. There I found Jennings, Billings and Edwards in their customary card games when not on duty. They were happy to see me as we were reacquainted again and they introduced me to the new hands. There was the cabin boy, Johnny, whom they picked up in Philadelphia; as the previous cook, the old man, Sean, had died at sea, and was relegated to a watery grave.

In addition to Jennings, Billings and Edwards, Uncle Jeremiah had taken on three new hands after the pressing of Hotaling and Jones off the island of Bermuda, three years earlier. There was Jeff Garden who was a middle-aged man that was bald and had a great fuzzy beard. He had much sea experience as he hailed from Portsmouth, New Hampshire, and had spent the last twenty years at sea. Garden planned to retire to his family farm near Concord in the next few years. Then there were Ian McKiernay and Matthew Boyle, both Irishman from the old country, whom Uncle Jeremiah took on in Boston. Ian had fiery red hair, with a quick smile and was the friendlier of the two, while Boyle had blonde hair, who, when he looked at you, it seemed as if he were looking through you, with cold, even icy, blue eyes. I found out quickly that no-one in the crew's berth had any regard for the British oppressors, and all had stories of British brutality leading up to the war, and at the various ports of call since the war began. We talked long into the night, and it was well after midnight when Uncle Jeremiah came to the crew's berth to scold us, directing us settle in for the night.

"We've a busy day ahead of us on the morrow, and young Master Will has to begin his journey home with his father," Uncle Jeremiah stated as he made his way back to his cabin.

I spent the night below deck with the crew, and as usual had a restless night in a hammock that Billings and Edwards set up for me in a dark corner.

When morning came, I found that I was the last out of the crew's berth, as I was assured that the crew was up before the sun, making preparations to sail, by getting the remaining cargo ashore, and finishing the storing of the new cargo in the hold.

I went and saw Da in the captain's cabin, and he looked somewhat better than the day before as he had had a good night's rest. He was gathering what few belongings he had, which consisted of a change of clothes, a knife, powder horn and his rifle, which were in the corner.

"Will, I'll be ready in a moment. Why don't you go see about the team, and wagon, as I'll be on deck shortly," he said not looking up at me.

I could tell he wanted to be to himself, and so I went on deck to be with Uncle Jeremiah.

"Will," Uncle Jeremiah began as we made our way to the railing of the ship and the area of the gangplank. "Let's walk together, as we go get your team and wagon from the livery," he stated. As we walked down the gangplank, Uncle Jeremiah yelled back to Jennings, "Help Master Waterman with getting off the ship, and make sure the hands are to their tasks," he said and continued, "I want to be away with the next tide." As we walked down the dock toward the livery Uncle Jeremiah spoke his mind. "What are your plans once you get your father home, Will?" he asked.

"I am not sure, sir," I said. "There has been talk of a new levy in Connecticut for regular troops in the Continental army," I stated. "I may reenlist again, sir," I added.

"Your father may have something to say about that, Will," Uncle Jeremiah replied, "but keep this in mind. I do plan on becoming a privateer and I expect to have my papers near the end of this voyage, as I will be making a stop in Philadelphia. There is money to be made, Will, and this war won't go on forever. When the war is over, you'll need some money to make a new start of it, I expect," he stated as we arrived at the livery.

Uncle Jeremiah, being familiar with the premises and the owner, instinctively walked into an adjoining room. As he did so he yelled out, "Master Thomas, are you about, sir. We are here for a team of horses and wagon."

From the back room came the response, "Aye, aye, Captain, all is ready for you around the corner," said an old man appearing wearing a furrier's apron and smoking a pipe. "Follow me," he said as he led the way outside and around the corner from the door of the livery. There, standing patiently was our horses, already harnessed to the wagon, awaiting our trip home.

Uncle Jeremiah paid the livery charges, and we rode on the wagon the short distance back to the ship. On the way, Uncle Jeremiah warned me not to mention anything about becoming a privateer to my father, and that if I needed to get in contact with him in the future, to get word to Master Thomas at the very livery we had just left. Da was waiting on the dock for us, as we pulled up. Uncle Jeremiah spoke in a low tone to me to be on guard, as rumor had it that the British planned to attack Providence in the future.

I helped Da into the seat of the wagon and placed his belongings on the floor of the wagon behind us. As I turned around I found the entire crew of the *Whisperer* before me. There was great affection between myself and Jennings, Billings and Edwards, and it seemed that the new hands had a respect for me. Uncle Jeremiah gave me a hug reminding me to keep in contact through the livery. I climbed onto the seat of the wagon and slapped the horses and yelled "get on!" The wagon lurched forward as the horses put their weight into the harnesses.

We traveled most of the day without saying much, only stopping to eat and to rest the horses, and provide them with some grain and water. We saw an occasional traveler along our route, and greetings were shared in passing. It was well after dark when we slowly made our way into the small town of Scituate along the post road.

The Waterman Tavern was the only place in town to stay, and we found ourselves fortunate to find a room for the night. Master Waterman was glad to see Da as well as me, and stated that the dinner hour was well past, but he'd have his niece warm some stew and bring a drink for us. I left Da at the table by the fire and went out to tend the horses. Around back was a stable for the horses with ample hay. Leaving the horses watered and fed, I entered the inn as a young girl of perhaps fifteen was bringing dinner from the kitchen. She placed two large bowls of stew before us and a mug of rum for each of us. We said our thanks to God for our food and began to eat, as our rations for the day had been meager. We spoke in low tones over our food, and then Master Waterman returned and sat with us. He had a long look on his face as he could see that Da was still suffering from his wounds inflicted in battle. Da explained to Master Waterman what had happened at the battle around New York with the British army. At the end, Master Waterman stated, "It's just as well that you stay out of the war for good, William. This war has divided the colonies, and it will be hard to recover from it," he said making his excuses and going about tending his other patrons.

"Will," Da said as he took the last swig of rum from his mug, "tell me what happened with you when you went to Hartford to fill the levy." I hesitated several moments before I began, as I knew not where to begin. I related being marched to New York colony and being on Nutten Island when the British invaded Long Island. I explained of our narrow escape, and retreat up Manhattan Island to Fort Washington followed by the subsequent battle there. I then related to Da that the main army moved north through the Bronx to White Plains, as we mirrored the advance of the British army along the coast. Then I told Da of the battle at White Plains, along with being wounded during the battle. I explained to Da how I received treatment, and was sent home with the other wounded with a supply train of wagons headed for Boston. Da seemed genuinely concerned when I made mention of my wound to him. I told Da how worried Mother had been, with not receiving word from Da for so long a period of time, but that she understood once she found out that he was wounded and in hospital.

The only thing Da said when I finished was that it seemed that our units had not faced each other in the numerous engagements in and around the New York colony, and he was thankful for that.

Master Waterman came over and provided us with another mug of rum. For the remainder of the night, which consisted of the consumption of the second mug of rum, Da and I talked about home and folks around Norwich. With the completion of our rum, Da stated he was tired. We made our way up the stairs to our shared bedroom. Da slept on the bed, as I took up my sleeping on the floor.

Morning came much too early, as the sun broke through our window. I left Da asleep as I went to hitch up the team to the wagon, and made ready for the day. When I returned to our room, I found Da out of bed and getting ready for the day. I helped Da down stairs. After a quick morning meal, we paid Master Waterman for our lodging and food, and made our way to our waiting team. It took the remainder of the day to get to Norwich, as the weather was cold, but relatively normal for the time of year, with occasional light snow falling. As we came into Norwich, it was again after dark and the horses knew the way now. They slowly meandered up the main street through town.

"I never thought I'd see home again," Da stated as we passed Durkee's Tavern.

I looked at Da and could see a single tear streaming down his cheek as the light from inside the tavern reflected off of his face.

Mother must have heard the horses and wagon pull up outside of our house. I had stepped off the wagon and was helping Da down as the door opened. Mother, John and Rachel came streaming out. Mother was crying before she got to Da and John and Rachel were excited to see their father. Mother hurried Da inside to warm him by the fire, and to get him some food, as John and Rachel followed. I slowly led the team around to the barn and tended them for the night. I seemed to move more slowly than normal, as I was cold and stiff from the two-day journey from Providence. Once inside, I had a bit to eat as did Da and we warmed ourselves by the fire before making our excuses, and going to bed. We were both tired.

The following weeks went by quickly as late winter turned to spring. Da and I shared our trips to Doctor Post's office together as he treated our wounds. Da's wound healed much better under the care of Doctor Post and I continued to improve, although if I exerted my leg too much with work around the farm, it had a tendency to break open and ooze blood and pus. Doctor Post stated that this was due to the ball still being in my leg and that this was likely to continue to happen for some time to come. My time was spent between helping Da on the farm, with Diane and her family, and occasionally with Eli.

Finally, spring was full upon us and the fields were plowed and most of the crops were planted. We were enjoying a warm spring evening after planting a field of corn, when a troop of ten Continental dragoons, in their smart blue uniforms, rode slowly past our house, into town and stopped at Durkee's Tavern.

- CHAPTER 9 -

"Duty on the Hudson"

1777

It was early spring when the Continental dragoons were in town. They were here only a few days, but they called several meetings at Durkee's Tavern to draw recruits to fill the new Connecticut levy. Undoubtedly, Colonel Durkee played an all-important role in having the Continental dragoons come to Norwich for the purpose of recruiting to fill the new levy.

A Sergeant Jackson was in charge, and he was the one who always spoke, and he sent his troopers to the outlying villages to bring in more men. Each day there were twenty or thirty men milling about town, and particularly in the area of Durkee's Tavern, where Sergeant Jackson gave the call for men to sign up and fill the levy. He wanted men to sign or make their mark, and that by the 25th of April, they'd be in Hartford to officially fill the levy. Sergeant Jackson and his men were in town for a short time, but it seemed he had the commitment of over a hundred men, at least twenty of whom were from Norwich alone. As always, Eli was excited about going back to war, and almost every day he would ask me what I intended to do. I had not said anything to Da or Diane about my plans, and for their part, they had not asked. I suppose that both Da and Diane were hoping that I was not going back to the army, as their and my silence at times, was deafening.

It all boiled over about a week before I was to leave for Hartford. It was Sunday afternoon, after our church service, and Pastor Gallagher had invited my family over for an afternoon dinner. Of course Da was more than willing to accept, as he was feeling much better, being almost completely recovered from his wound. The Gallagher's had killed two fatted chickens and Mrs. Gallagher made stew with all of the fixings. The invitation was unexpected and mother for her part, was unprepared, but managed to bring a couple of loaves of bread, along with a carrot salad. All was going well with the parents were engaged in a quiet conversation about the war. Diane and I were engaged in our own conversation about the warmer weather. Suddenly, my brother John blurted out, in response to something that Da and Pastor Gallagher were talking about, "Will plans on signing up again, to fill the new Connecticut levy." He looked from face to face as everyone stared at him, and then he said in his own defense, "Well, that is what Eli Bingham told me."

Suddenly, all eyes turned to me. I felt so small, as if the stares were looking right through me. I looked from Mother to Da, to Diane and finally to Pastor Gallagher. No one spoke.

Finally, I said, "I'm sorry, I planned on telling each of you in my own way."

Nothing was said, as the room remained eerily silent. I turned slowly making my way to the door, as it creak unusually loudly as I opened it and stepped outside. No one said anything, and no one tried to stop me. The next several days, and even into the next week were filled with unusual tension between my family, Diane and myself. I had Eli to thank for all of this trouble. It was true, that I had planned to sign up for the new Connecticut levy, but I wanted to tell everyone in my own way, especially Diane. I knew most of all, she wouldn't understand.

No one spoke to me that night, or the following morning for that matter. After breakfast, and after the milking was done, Da came back to the barn.

"Will," he began, "I know you've thought this through, or I wouldn't believe you'd be going back, but you should have talked to your mother and me about this before John said something."

"Da," I started in an effort to begin to explain, but before I could go any further, he raised his hand in a motion for me to stop.

"Son," he continued after a moment, "I've done a lot of thinking since I joined the Crown's cause, and was wounded in New York. The British army, the men in it, and especially the men leading it, are not the men with whom I fought and bled with in the late war against the French and their Indian allies," he said. "I now know it was a mistake for me to go, and fight with them against our cause. But if you go again, Will, and are hurt or killed, it will crush your mother and especially Diane," he warned. "You should have at least said something to us before Eli had time to say anything to your brother," he said, hesitating as if he were finished.

"I had intended on saying something soon to you and mother, and Diane early this week," I replied in a low voice.

"I think now I understand better why you have to go, Will, but think of this before you leave," he said with a sigh as he paused. "Replacing one corrupt government with one you don't know, which may be equally as bad or worse, is not necessarily, the right thing to do, nor may waging war be the right way to go about it. Go and talk to Diane, and I'll go and talk to your mother, and try to calm her nerves about all this," he said and he turned to go. "Will," he added, "there is a price to be paid for all this. Will the cost be too dear in the end?" As he walked away, he added over his shoulder, "John and I will do your chores the rest of the morning, we'll be expecting you back after lunch."

I did the dead man's ride on my way over to Diane's to try to explain to her why I was going back. On the way I had time go over in my mind what Da had said. It kept sticking in my mind that he had said "our cause" and that it was a "mistake" for him to go, and fight with the British. Was he now on the side of the colonies? I wasn't sure. What about what he said about replacing one bad government with another. What if he was right and that the government that replaces the British is worse or becomes worse than the one we have now. My mind was going through all these things and before I knew it, I was standing before the Gallagher's door. I stood there for a moment and was about to knock when the door suddenly opened. There was Diane looking at me with those icy brown eyes, looking right through me.

"Yes," she said as she stood in the doorway, not allowing me to enter.

"I thought we might talk," I replied.

"Well, you might have thought of that a while ago, Will Waterman," was her short and angry response.

I knew I was in for it now. She seemed as mad as I had ever known her to be.

"Can we go for a walk?" I asked. She slowly closed the door, and began walking down the street towards the bridge that crossed the Thames River past Durkee's Tavern. Nothing was said until we got to the bridge, and Diane stopped about a third of the way on the bridge. She stood looking down at the water as it slowly flowed past us. I stood next to her, and from here I could see to where the river turned a little to the north, then east and out of view.

"I was going to tell you, Diane, I really was," I began. "I didn't want you to hear it the way you did and I'm sorry for that," I said.

Diane didn't say anything for the longest time, so I thought I'd begin to explain to her about the war. As I was about to begin, she finally broke the silence.

"My father says that you have your convictions, and that I must somehow try to understand and come to grips with them," she said, as she stared up the river at nothing in particular. "But I have my convictions too, Will Waterman, and I don't understand this war, and I don't want to grow old waiting for you to return. Or worse yet, that you may not return and die in a field in a town I've never heard of," she complained.

I didn't say anything to this, and as I thought about what she said. I was going over my thoughts on how to answer her, when she began again.

"If you go again, Will, I don't know if I'll be here when or if you get back," she declared. "You know, Will Waterman, you aren't the only young man who's spoken to my father about courtin' me," she stated coldly. Finished with what she had to say, she turned, to walk off the bridge back toward Durkee's Tavern. As she turned to go, I could see that tears had made streaks down her cheek, as she had been crying the whole time she'd been speaking to me.

I didn't know what to do or say as we walked back toward her house. When we pasted Durkee's Tavern, Diane continued on to the right, toward her house. I walked a few steps behind her. When she got to her house, she opened, and then closed the door behind her without saying anything. I untied my horse from the rail and began my long ride home.

The next week passed by quickly. On Sunday my family went to church as usual. When we got to church, I found Diane sitting in the front pew, at the end with her mother sitting next to her, situated so that I couldn't sit with her. I could only wonder about how planned that was. My family sat in a pew in the middle of the church, and on the opposite side from Diane. This was the first Sunday since I had spoken to Pastor Gallagher about courting Diane that I had not sat with her when I was home. For his part, Pastor Gallagher spoke on loving your fellow man, no matter their circumstances, or who they were, and mentioned at the end of his sermon that this war would not go on forever. I noticed that while he spoke, he never looked in my direction.

As the service was dismissed, I looked for Diane, only to notice that she stayed near the front of the church, talking to Jonathon Reynolds, a young man a few years older than me. He had not been around Norwich much the last few years as he was apprenticed to be a blacksmith in Boston, and spent most of his time there. It was rumored around Norwich that his family supported the British, although they never came right out and said so.

I turned and walked out of the church, and slowly began to walk home. I could hear my father's words ringing in my head on whether the cost was going to be worth it, and were we going to replace one bad government with another.

I spent the rest of Sunday afternoon checking my horse tack to make sure all was ready for the trip in the morning. I packed what clothing I thought I would need, cleaned my rifle, and checked my powder and ball to make sure all was ready. I placed several flints in my possible bag, to ensure that I had enough. When all was complete, it was starting to get dark. I decided to go to Eli's house to see if he was ready. Eli had spent his day much like I had, and we agreed to meet at the bridge at eight in the morning to begin our trip to Hartford.

I spent a restless night thinking about leaving. Morning came early, and after a quick breakfast of eggs, bacon and milk, I was ready to depart. I loaded Chester up with my belongings. He looked over his shoulder at me as if to say "What is all this about?" I walked around to the house to say my goodbyes to my family. Mother cried, as Da shook my hand, looking me square in the face and instructed, "Take care, and be sure to post us a letter when you can." With that he slapped Chester's rump and I slowly made my way to Durkee's Tavern. When I got to the tavern, Eli was already there. As I approached Eli, he was all excited about the trip and almost yelled at me, "This is going to be great, Will, we'll show those lobsters, just like we did at Boston."

I reined in my horse, and looked about at the others who had gathered in the area. There must have been about 50 men with their horses all gathered in the area of Durkee's Tavern. A lot of them, I didn't recognize, but there were a number of men gathered from the families in Norwich that I had grown up with. There was Samuel Fuller, who had helped me at the battle of White Plains, when I was wounded along with his brother John. I saw the Calkin brothers Joshua and Hiram, as well as John Edgerington and William Bradford, again. We waited around for another fifteen minutes for stragglers to arrive. I looked around several times, and although Diane's house was just down the road, I didn't see her or any movement in the house.

Finally, Colonel Durkee was seen riding up with Captain Fitch from the south. They reined their horses in front of the tavern. Colonel Durkee made a few comments about our travel for the day, and the cause for which we were fighting. I really didn't hear anything he said, as I was thinking about Diane. Finally, I realized that most of the men on their horses had already followed Colonel Durkee across the bridge heading west out of town.

"Come on, Eli," was all I said as I passed Eli and his horse onto the bridge without stopping. Eli reined his horse to follow, and we were on our way to Hartford. Eli must have known I was in a foul mood, as nothing was said between us for the longest time. When we had traveled for about an hour, Colonel Durkee called a halt, as we had stopped by a creek to water and feed our horses.

"Eli, you shouldn't have said anything until I had a chance to talk to my parents, and Diane," I finally said.

"I'm sorry, Will, I was so excited about going, that I couldn't help myself," Eli replied.

"Next time, if there is a next time," I said, "make sure I've had time to talk to my family first."

Eli didn't reply, and I knew I couldn't stay mad at him, for deep down inside I was as excited as he was about going back to war. The rest of our trip to Hartford was uneventful. As we approached the town, it was much the same as when we had approached Plainfield two years before. Tent towns were popping up everywhere and it seemed as if men were streaming in from all over the Connecticut colony. As we were approaching the edge of town, our column stopped. Since Eli and I were at the back, we couldn't see exactly what was happening. After a few moments, we began again and it wasn't long before we saw Colonel Durkee rein in along the road, speaking to everyone in our group as they passed. As we approached, he looked at Eli and me to inform us, "Captain Fitch has information on where we are to set camp for the night. Follow the column, set up camp, and we'll get more organized on the morrow."

The next day, Colonel Durkee called our unit together, and gave us instruction regarding the uniforms we were to wear. "As you know," he began, "Durkee's Irregulars have historically worn a distinctive brown uniform. In keeping with that tradition, our uniforms are as follows: those who can afford them will wear a brown double-breasted coat with red collars and cuffs. Trousers and breeches will be brown if available, but white is also acceptable," he stated. "We will try to have gray woolen stockings for everyone, and sergeants will be distinguished by a red cloth epaulet on the right shoulder and corporals will be distinguished by a green one," he concluded briefly. He looked around for a moment and then added, "To distinguish the Connecticut line of the Continental army from the rest of the Continental army, this will be our uniform unless the Commander-in-Chief so directs. You are dismissed," he stated.

Rumors persisted on where we were going. Some said back to Boston in case the British returned there. Others said above New York to keep the British bottled up there like we had done in Boston, and yet others said we were going down south to fight in Virginia. No one really knew, and I told Eli as much.

Several days later General Putnam arrived, and a general assembly of all able bodied men was called. Several thousand men crowded the town square to hear what he had to say. He spoke in terms of loyalty and liberty, stating that as part of the Connecticut levy to the Continental army, we were under orders to support the main army under General Washington, and we're committed to fight anywhere on the North American continent. That being said, General Putnam stated he had received general orders from the Commander-in-Chief, General Washington, to march the Connecticut line of the Continental army to specified parts of New York above New York City, thus preventing the British army from leaving New York by land. General Putnam stated we would march within the week, and we were summarily dismissed. As the general assembly broke up, the noise was almost deafening as everyone spoke to his fellow soldier about our orders.

True to his word, within the week and only after two weeks of encampment in Hartford, the army was ordered into formation, and we were marched to the New York colony. The army itself stretched for several miles, as the wagon and supply trains that followed were several miles longer still. It took hours for the entire army to get moving and hours for the entire army to arrive at camp at night.

It took several days' march from Hartford to reach Waterbury, Connecticut colony. Along the way we picked up several more units of volunteers. From Waterbury it took several more days' march to reach Danbury, Connecticut colony. Captain Fitch informed us at camp one night at Danbury, that we were just a few miles from the New York frontier, and within a week's march, we would be in the New York Highlands.

We crossed the New York frontier after a few more days' march, and found ourselves in the highlands on the east side of the Hudson River, forty miles above New York City.

Our division, under General Putnam, was detailed to the east side of the Hudson River. General Putnam located his headquarters in the small town of Peekskill, New York. Putnam had three brigades under his command; each comprised of four companies. The various companies were dispersed throughout the countryside to perform various guard duties, and to occupy the countryside. One company was sent down to Verplanck's Point, opposite Stony Point, to guard the eastern side of the King's Ferry. The rest of the companies set up various picket and guard posts along the various roads eastward for several miles. Our company under Colonel Durkee, were detailed to provide security for Fort Independence on the east bank of the Hudson River, about a mile northwest of Putnam's headquarters at Peekskill.

For the most part everything was quiet in this sector of the war for the time being. There was the occasional foraging by either army for supplies into each other's area of operations, which resulted in several skirmishes, but there were no major engagements.

It was late spring in the New York Highlands, and other than being in New York, both Eli and I figured we could have been in the Green Mountains, on one of our hunting trips with our families. The mountains were exploding with green color, and the valley with the Hudson River running through it was a beautiful valley. For now, it was hard to believe we were at war.

Across the Hudson River, and a couple miles north of our position at Fort Independence, General Clinton and his brother James were in charge of two forts that guarded the highlands where the Hudson River narrowed down from being over a mile wide to less than half a mile. These two forts were Forts Clinton and Montgomery. Additionally, a chain and boat barriers stretched the length of the Hudson River at these two forts to prevent the British from gaining access to the interior of New York colony, by way of the Hudson River which was navigable for another seventy miles north to Albany.

Several miles north of these two forts were two additional forts, being West Point on the west side of the river and Fort Constitution on an island in the middle of the river.

A few weeks after our arrival at the New York Highlands, Colonel Durkee and Captain Fitch had Eli and I accompany them to General Putnam's Headquarters at Peekskill. We passed a number of checkpoints on our short ride to Peekskill, and the sentries we encountered recognized both Colonel Durkee and Captain Fitch. We moved through the checkpoints unchallenged. Upon arriving at Peekskill, Colonel Durkee proceeded directly to General Putnam's headquarters. As we dismounted, we tied our horses to the rails outside the building, which was a two-story sandstone house. Colonel Durkee directed us to remain outside as he and Captain Fitch entered General Putnam's headquarters.

As Eli and I waited by our horses, I remarked to Eli that there seemed to be a lot of activity in town.

"It looks like there are officers here from every company," Eli replied.

"General Putnam must have to know what is happening where every company is detailed, and I heard that the New York units on the west side of the river report to him, too," I stated.

"Well the burden of command can't be easy, Will," Eli replied.

We stood there without talking for several minutes, watching men and wagons passing in each direction. Suddenly, Captain Fitch appeared directing us to follow him into the building. Removing our tri-corn hats, we followed Captain Fitch. There were sentries inside each door, with activity going on everywhere in the building. I noticed several rooms off the main hallway as we entered, and proceeded further into the building. The building appeared much larger on the inside with several large rooms.

We entered the second room down the hall on the right, and upon entering we encountered several high-ranking officers from several companies. All were engaged with Major General Putnam in serious conversation over a map of New York on a large table in the center of the room.

Captain Fitch came to attention as did we, and saluted as Colonel Durkee, whom we found in the room, addressed General Putnam.

"General, sir," he began, "Corporal Waterman and Private Bingham reporting as ordered, sir." Still holding our salutes until the general acknowledged them, we waited for the general to look up from the map on the table. After a moment, when General Putnam had concluded his comments to his commanders, he addressed Colonel Durkee.

"Colonel," he said, returning our salutes as he looked from Colonel Durkee to Eli and me. "Are these the two men of whom we spoke earlier?"

"They are, General," was Colonel Durkee's reply as the general looked at us. Colonel Durkee added, "You may recall, General, that at the siege of Boston, these two were instrumental in both duties as dispatch riders and scouts, and I may add General, that they both distinguished themselves in at least one engagement during that siege."

Again, General Putnam looked in our direction as if to size us up for whatever duties he may have for us. Addressing the other officers in the room, General Putnam, excused them, and when the room was cleared, other than for Colonel Durkee, Captain Fitch, Eli and myself, he called us to the table.

"Gentlemen," he began, "we have received some troubling intelligence that the British mean to move on New York from three directions, and to drive a stake in the heart of our cause by splitting the New England colonies, from the colonies to the south. To accomplish this, they intend to send three armies at New York," he stated. "Look here," he said as he pointed at the map. "We believe that they will send one army south out of Canada and down Lake Champlain to attack Albany from the north. We believe a second army out of Canada will traverse into Lake Ontario here, from the St. Lawrence River and attack this fort, Fort Stanwix. Once that fort is reduced, that army will continue on down the Mohawk River Valley to attack Albany from the west. Right now our concern in this whole affair is that General Clinton, in New York City, will come out to attack our forts in the Hudson Valley. If he is successful in his efforts, he will take his army north to meet the other two British armies in Albany, thus, in effect splitting the colonies, and possibly destroying our cause." General Putnam paused, as he looked up from the map, and particularly at Eli and me.

"Colonel Durkee tells me that you two are the two best riders, and shots he has," he stated. "You've both got the experience as scouts and dispatch riders. This is what I need from the two of you over the next few weeks. We want you to ride dispatches for the various commanders at these forts here," the general said, pointing to Forts Clinton, Montgomery, West Point, Constitution and Independence. "You will travel a circular route from fort to fort. First, crossing here at Kings Ferry, and then traveling up the west side of the Hudson River to Forts Clinton and Montgomery," he said as he began to write a note. "From there you will travel up to the fortifications at West Point and Fort Constitution. Then cross the river at the ferry just above Fort Constitution at the narrows, coming down the east side of the river to Fort Independence and Peekskill.

Your mission on the surface is to deliver dispatches to the commanders at the various forts and posts you visit. The mission that I charge you with, in addition to delivering dispatches is to interact with whatever populace you come in contact with, and to glean whatever information you can, in regards to the British movements out of New York against us. Rest assured gentlemen, your mission is a dangerous one, as there are as many Tories in these hills as there are patriots. If you are discovered or captured, you must not divulge, to your death, the existence of information of this army, and that we know the British must come out of New York City to attack us. Is that understood?" he said, looking up from the note he had just finished.

"Yes, sir, it is," I said to the general.

"This note will give you safe passage past any outpost or sentry you may encounter during your mission," he said. "But be certain of this men, if this note is discovered on you by the enemy," the general paused as he wrote a short note which was a duplicate, one copy for me and another for Eli. As he looked up from his writing, handing a note to Eli and me he stated, "It is certain death. Is that understood?"

"It is understood, sir," I said, looking at Eli.

"You will report to Colonel Durkee or me only, you are dismissed," he said.

Colonel Durkee, Captain Fitch, along with Eli and I saluted the general and upon his returned salute, we left the room, and the headquarters of General Putnam.

On our ride back to Fort Independence, Colonel Durkee advised us that we'd begin our new assignment the next day. He cautioned us to be careful with our intelligence gathering as the general, in Colonel Durkee's opinion, grossly understated the dangers we may encounter from those loyal to the Crown in the area.

The next day Eli and I began our duties of riding dispatches for the various officers. We rode into Peekskill and were given a brown dispatch bag containing dispatches by General Putnam himself, who never looked up from his desk to provide them to us. He just said to deliver it to General Clinton at Fort Clinton on the west side of the river.

We rode down to Verplanck's Point, crossing at the King's Ferry to Stony Point on the west side of the river. From there we rode up the west side of the river for a mile or so. Here the road bore off to the left, traversing through a narrow gorge pass along the side of the Dunderberg Mountain. The gorge was the steepest that Eli or I had ever seen as there were sharp rock outcrops on either side of the narrow road reaching to a height of fifty or sixty feet. Where it was possible, trees grew on the rocky outcrops dimming the light of even the brightest day. As we came out of the gorge, we came to a small town at the intersection of three roads.

Here, at Doodletown, a garrison of fifty men was detailed to hold the intersection of the road. A sergeant and three men challenged us at this intersection, as both Eli and I produced our passes signed by General Putnam. The sergeant looked at the notes, then at us, and back at the notes. In a gruff voice he stated "Proceed," and watched as Eli and I reined our horses to continue up the road toward Fort Clinton. It took all of the morning to make the ride from Peekskill to Fort Clinton.

At Fort Clinton we were challenged several times as we encountered each level of defensive positions until we were at the center of the fortifications of an, as yet, unfinished fort. Fort Clinton was on the south side of the shore where the Popolopen Creek entered the Hudson River. On the north side of the creek was the unfinished second fort, Fort Montgomery. A young looking sergeant took us to a tent within Fort Clinton and saluted the commander, General Clinton. "Dispatch riders from General Putnam, sir," he said.

"Yes, yes," the general said, "bring them in."

As Eli and I entered the tent, we removed our tri-corns, and saluted the general, who returned our salute.

"Corporal Waterman and Private Bingham, reporting as ordered by General Putnam, bearing dispatches for you, sir," I said, opening my dispatch bag, and handing them to the general. The general took them, and opened the first dispatch, reading it quickly. Handing us new dispatches, General Clinton sent us farther up the river to the fortifications at West Point. West Point was an even farther ride from Fort Clinton, than the ride from Peekskill to Fort Clinton. The river continued to narrow as we traversed the road between a steep mountain and the river.

West Point proved to be a much larger area of fortifications and was, in fact, several forts ringing a rocky outcrop at a point where the river narrowed to under a half-mile, with an island in the middle of the river. Only the river passage between West Point and the island was navigable by ships the size that the British would bring up river. Thus, the commanders at West Point were building artillery fortifications on Constitution Island as well. All was busy in the area of West Point, as it seemed that every soldier was engrossed in completing the area fortifications. This fact didn't keep Eli and me from being challenged by many sentries as we traveled the roads to the inner fortifications. There we met a very young looking sergeant of the 2nd Artillery Division. The sergeant led us to the innermost and highest fortifications of West Point that was commanded by Colonel John Lamb. Upon our presentation by the sergeant to Colonel Lamb, we provided our dispatches from General Clinton. Upon reading them, Colonel Lamb looked up and asked, "When did your day begin, gentlemen?"

"We began early this morning with dispatches from General Putnam in Peekskill, sir, arriving here before dark," Eli replied.

"A long day indeed, eh?" The colonel replied, and without waiting for Eli or me to reply he stated, "Sergeant Willoughby, will see to your needs and that of your horses for tonight. In the morning, I'll have dispatches for you to deliver to General Knox at New Windsor."

"Sir, may I ask, is Captain Doughty with your unit, as I served with him on Nutten Island during the battle of Long Island?" I inquired.

"Corporal," the colonel replied, "you have been in good company, as Captain Doughty is one of my finest officers. He has been detailed to an island again, as he is responsible for the defensive fortifications on Constitution Island. I will send for him, and will have him here in the morning, along with your dispatches."

"Yes, sir," we said as we were led outside by Sergeant Willoughby. We spent the night with a unit of the 2nd Artillery Division at the innermost works. They were generous in sharing their meager rations of pork and beans with us, all washed down with some old grog. As darkness fell on our position, on the rocky hill overlooking the river we could see the lights of the camp fires on Constitution Island, as well as several fires on both sides of the river, both to the north and south. Presumably the fires of units detailed up and down the river at points where boats or ferries were located. Eli and I found ourselves sound asleep long before most of the soldiers, who stayed up talking around their campfires.

In the morning, Sergeant Willoughby found us and escorted us to the tent of Colonel Lamb. Upon our arrival we found the colonel engrossed in a morning meal with several other officers, including Captain Doughty.

"Gentlemen," Colonel Lamb began as the officers looked at us, with Captain Doughty standing to welcome me, "join us for a morning meal of bacon and eggs, along with the worst coffee the army has to offer."

We took seats at one end of the table, and were content with our breakfast, when Colonel Lamb asked Captain Doughty to relate the story he had begun just before we entered.

"Well, sir, as I was telling you before the corporal and private entered, I had the good fortune of serving with Corporal Waterman during the battle of Long Island and Harlem Heights," Captain Doughty began. "We were on Nutten Island in New York Harbor when the British began their attack on Long Island. To begin the engagement, the British sent several frigates up the harbor from Staten Island, and our batteries engaged in a long range duel with the British warships. The corporal here not only assisted us in defending the island, but while in charge of a twenty man rifle unit, provided covering fire when the British ship got too close. I swear by the great Jehovah, that I saw the corporal himself shoot several British marines from the fighting tops at such a great distance that I didn't think it possible to shoot a man so far away," the captain concluded.

"Is this an accurate account, Corporal?" inquired the colonel.

"Well, sir, it is true that the captain engaged the British frigates and that my rifle unit did provide covering fire, but as to me shooting any marines from the fighting tops, it was most certainly one of my other men and not me," I stated.

"What did I tell you, Colonel," Captain Doughty spoke up, "a top scout, a dispatch rider, as well as being a crack shot that is too humble to take advantage of his skills. I believe we need to promote such a man," the captain added.

"It is not all as Captain Doughty states, sir, I assure you," I replied. "The real heroes of that battle were the Maryland unit that sacrificed themselves, so that the main body of the army could make it to the safety of Brooklyn Heights, and then to Manhattan. The Maryland Four Hundred, those were the heroes. God as my witness, they are all dead now so that we can live," I stated as my voice trailed off.

"Yes, Corporal," there have been hundreds, if not thousands of others similar to your Maryland Four Hundred, who have sacrificed themselves for our cause. Before this war is over, there will be many more Maryland Four Hundred's," Colonel Lamb interjected.

The rest of the meal was spent in conversation on the war, and what the officers thought General Washington would do next. Finally, after a filling breakfast, Colonel Lamb provided us with dispatches and correspondence for General Knox, who had his headquarters in New Windsor, several miles to the north. Captain Doughty offered his regards and told us to stop at Constitution Island whenever we passed the area.

It took us the rest of the morning to reach New Windsor, where some snippy low-level lieutenant would not let us deliver our communications to General Knox directly, but took them from us outside his headquarters, and delivered them to the general.

While leaving town, we saw a small tavern named the Highland Tavern, and decided to get something to eat before we headed south to Fort Independence. The maid at the tavern was a particularly attractive young lady with long curly black hair and brown eyes. The manner in which she carried herself reminded me much of my own Diane, if not in her total outward appearance. She immediately took a shine to Eli, and it was almost amusing to watch them interact. Finally, after our meal was finished and I could not take any more of Eli's and this maid's flirtations, I pushed Eli out the door, assuring both him and the maid, that on our next ride north to New Windsor, we'd be sure to stop at the old tavern. And so, later that evening we arrived at Fort Independence on our tired horses.

The following day, Colonel Durkee sent an orderly to find us, ordering us to report in the afternoon watch, and to give details of our activities. We reported the events of our dispatch riding to Colonel Durkee, who was satisfied with our efforts, and wasn't surprised that we gathered no intelligence regarding any movements of the enemy in New York colony. Colonel Durkee did give a little chuckle, with a smirk on his face when I told him of Eli's maid at the tavern outside of New Windsor. Eli's face turned a deep red as he was embarrassed by the attention.

"What was the young maid's name, Eli?" Colonel Durkee asked.

"Her name was Rebecca, and I will speak no more of it," Eli stated flatly, embarrassed by the attention drawn to him.

Spring quietly turned to summer, and Eli and I continued to be deeply entrenched in our dispatch duties. In fact, we rarely spent more than a couple nights a week with our unit at Fort Independence. Then, during early August, Colonel Durkee stated that we were needed urgently at General Putnam's headquarters to deliver dispatches. Upon our arrival, we were ushered into the general's office, where he was in a heated conversation with several junior officers.

As we entered, the general was overheard stating..., "Word arrived that the British under General Burgoyne have eight thousand men and are moving south out of Canada. Additionally, General St. Leger has another army of one thousand regulars, Tories and Indians moving east down the Mohawk Valley on Fort Stanwix, and then on to Albany. Clinton may come out of New York at any time. To make matters worse, Washington is making rumblings that he needs more men." Looking up, he saw Eli and me, "Ah, Waterman and Bingham, good, good, these dispatches are of the utmost importance, and may hold the key to victory in the north. Deliver them with all speed, and then return for further orders as soon as you can," he said, pushing several sealed orders for us across his desk. "Get the last one to General Knox as soon as you can, Godspeed gentlemen," he stated as he turned his attention back to his desk, giving additional orders to his subordinates.

Eli and I wasted little time heading south to the ferry at Verplanck's Point. Once across the river we headed up the river road to where it left the river and entered the woods at the pass at Dunderberg Mountain. Once we entered the pass, we stopped to water our horses at a small brook. While thus engaged, I felt an eerie sensation that I hadn't felt since our ambush of the Indians back in '72 along the Connecticut River in the Green Mountains. It was as if we were being followed. I felt that we were being watched, even hunted.

"Eli, do you feel that?" I asked.

"Feel what, Will?" Eli replied.

"It's as if we are being followed or something. It feels like the ambush back in the Green Mountains," I said.

"It does seem strangely quiet, Will," Eli agreed.

"Let's just move on slowly and quietly and see what happens," I said. "Have you checked your powder, Eli?"

"A little while ago," Eli answered. "When we entered the pass."

"Good," I responded as we moved out.

We hadn't gone a hundred yards when the woods came to life. Above us on the rocks, several men could be heard scurrying through the woods at us. Eli and I spurred our horses at the same time. Shots began to ring out above us, from the rocky ledges, but none seemed to come close. Suddenly, as I looked around, I caught a glimpse of a group of men on horses coming up behind us at a great speed.

"Eli!" I yelled, as I unslung my rifle from my shoulder, pointing behind us. Eli's eyes went wide when he saw the ten men on horses trying to ride us down. As I looked back, I could see several puffs of smoke come from their guns as they attempted to bring us down, but to no effect. I leveled my rifle as we rode our horses as fast as we could, and squeezed the trigger. The lead man slumped in the saddle, trying to hold on to the horse's neck and mane before he slid to the ground, run over by the horses following him. I eased up alongside of Eli as I reloaded my rifle on the run, and waited for Eli to shoot. He squeezed off his shot, but none of the pursuing men seemed affected by it. Several puffs of smoke from our pursuers' guns followed by the whine of bullets past us only spurred us on all the more. We ran the mile through the pass at breakneck speed. As we emerged out the other side, we could see the detail of men at Doodletown coming to life as they heard the shots, and could now see our pursuers close behind. As we had been riding dispatch through this area for the last several months, the men immediately recognized Eli and me, as well as our dilemma, and began firing at our pursuers. Once we were within a hundred yards of Doodletown, our pursuers broke off their attempt to ride us down, as a general engagement ensued between the Doodletown detachment and our antagonists. The distance was too great and although each side fired several volleys, no one was wounded in the exchanges. The enemy broke off their attack, slowly riding back toward the Dunderberg Mountain pass, and disappeared into the woods from whence they came.

We rode hard to Fort Clinton and delivered our first dispatches to General Clinton, relating the information about the ambush we narrowly escaped at Dunderberg Mountain pass.

"Undoubtedly a group of Tories scouting out our positions, and as well as our strengths and weaknesses for my long lost cousin, General Clinton in New York City," General Clinton stated.

I had never put the association together, that of our General Clinton and the British General Clinton in New York City were related, until I had heard our General Clinton mutter this under his breath.

"You must have a long ride ahead of you today, men, so I won't keep you," the general said as he read his dispatch. Eli and I rode to West Point that day, delivering our next dispatches to Colonel Lamb, who was of the same opinion of the men who ambushed us earlier in the day. As he read his dispatch, he stated to no one in particular, that General Washington was calling for more men. Colonel Lamb didn't think his units would be there to see the British move north out of New York City. We then rode hard to New Windsor and arrived there long after dark. We found General Knox at his headquarters pouring over maps. As he read the dispatches, he looked from them to his maps.

"Do you two riders know what is in these dispatches?" he asked us.

"We don't read the dispatches, sir," I replied, "but from what we've heard spoken of today, I think we have a good idea what is contained in them."

"That's fair enough, young man," the general countered. "It seems the British have finally begun to move south out of Canada, and are also moving east down the Mohawk River Valley. The only question now to be answered here is when General Clinton will move north against us out of New York City. To top it off, General Washington is in dire need of men, as well as supplies. It looks like he is going to order at least part of this army south to Pennsylvania to help him," General Knox concluded.

Eli and I hadn't counted on part of the army being ordered south, looking at each other, as General Knox went back to his maps. Looking up again after a few moments he stated, "I imagine you two are tired, get some rest. I'll have return dispatches to General Putnam for you in the morning, you're dismissed."

Eli and I found sleep quickly that night, as morning came early in General Knox's camp. Upon our arrival back at General Knox's headquarters, he was again found looking over his maps as if he had never left. His orderly handed us some sealed dispatches with orders that they were for General Putnam's eyes only. We departed heading slowly south out of New Windsor. Long before we had reached the local tavern, I knew Eli wanted to stop to see the maid, Rebecca, at least for a few minutes. As we sat down to a small meal and a mug of rum, Eli and I were engaged in conversation regarding the British movements. Rebecca overheard us, and once our meal was served, Rebecca pulled up a chair.

"Eli," she began, "I overheard the two of you talking about the British army's up north. My father had business in New York City last week, and learned some important information regarding the upcoming movements of General Clinton. My father's contact told him that when the army coming down the Champlain Valley gets closer to Albany, General Clinton will come out of New York City. This is to hold your army in the highlands here, to keep them from helping the American armies around Albany and out the Mohawk Valley," she stated.

"Has your father told anyone this?" Eli asked Rebecca.

"No one except me, as he knows Tories can be found even here in New Windsor," Rebecca replied.

"How long from now will Clinton move?" Eli asked.

"It depends on the movements of the other armies," Rebecca stated, "but probably no later than October, my father believes, with winter coming on after that."

"Do you know in what strength General Clinton will come?" Eli inquired.

"Not in detail, but my father said with at least a thousand men, with ships besides. My father was told that General Clinton is waiting for reinforcements, too, before he moves north," Rebecca stated.

"Eli," I said, "we need to get this information to General Putnam as soon as we can."

We thanked Rebecca for her information, and loyalty, and Eli said he'd be back as soon as he could. We rode hard the rest of the day to Fort Independence to report this important information to Colonel Durkee, who in turn, continued on with us to Peekskill to assist us in relaying the plans to General Putnam.

General Putnam looked genuinely concerned regarding this information about General Clinton in New York City, as he began barking orders to his officers and orderlies. Looking up, he stated, "That leaves me about two months to finish all of the forts and defensive works between here and West Point. I'm not sure it can be done," he concluded.

Finally, he said, looking at Colonel Durkee, "This coming battle won't be any of your concern, Colonel," he said with a tired voice. "Varnum's Brigade, as well as a New York Division of artillery has been ordered to Philadelphia to be detailed to the Continental army there. It appears that Washington's army is in more dire straits than ours. God be with you and your men, Colonel," General Putnam said adding. "Varnum already has his orders, and I suspect you'll be moving out by week's end."

As we left Putnam's headquarters, my head was spinning. We were ordered south to Philadelphia. I knew I had one thing to do before we left in the next week. I had to see the quartermaster to post a letter to Diane.

- CHAPTER 10 -

"Germantown"

Fall 1977

Our march from New York to the Philadelphia front was uneventful, altogether overtaxing to both man and beast, as we traveled from one country town to another, over the worst country roads I had ever seen. We lost both men and supplies during the three-week long arduous journey. I had to question what shape we'd be in when we arrived to help General Washington, and his already weakened army.

We arrived outside Philadelphia in late September, only to learn of two recent defeats inflicted on Washington's army. The first occurred in early September when we were on the march. It was called the battle of Brandywine, after the creek which the battle was fought around. We heard our losses were around a thousand men killed, wounded and missing, while the British losses were estimated at half that.

After the battle, Washington had moved west and then north to keep some distance between himself and General Howe, the commander of the British army in the area. The loss at the battle of Brandywine cost our cause the city of Philadelphia, as the Continental Congress evacuated the city, and moved west to York, Pennsylvania colony.

The second defeat came in late September and only a few days before we arrived outside of Philadelphia. General Washington had left Major General Wayne along with fifteen hundred men in the area of Paoli's Tavern, to attack and harass Howe's baggage train. Unfortunately for General Wayne and his men, General Howe discovered his whereabouts through captured dispatches, and information supplied by Tory spies.

General Howe dispatched Major General Gray and five thousand men to attack General Wayne and his men. General Gray's men attacked General Wayne and his outnumbered men in the early morning hours of September 21st, with orders for a bayonet attack. Mass confusion entered the camp of General Wayne, as the British attack pushed the sentries into camp. By the time General Wayne had organized his confused men to begin his retreat from the area; General Gray's men had killed fifty men by bayonet, and wounded another hundred. The British losses were a meager handful of men.

When our units arrived, General Washington and his army were outside of Germantown facing the British army there, where General Howe had established his headquarters, while reports filtered into our camp that the Tories of Philadelphia cheered the arrival of the British army.

Major General Varnum's division was held in reserve regarding the anticipated upcoming engagement, while Colonel Durkee ordered me to report to him. Upon reporting, Colonel Durkee informed me that I was detailed with a number of men from our unit to Captain McLane, of the mounted light infantry, assigned to General Washington. Colonel Durkee read from a list, which contained the names of the men that were to be detailed with me. There was Eli Bingham, Nathan Smith, William Bradford, Joseph and Dayton Birchard, Samuel and John Fuller, Allan Reed, Thomas and John Gallagher, cousins of my Diane, John Edgerington, Josiah Adgate, Isaac Backus, John Lathrop and John Allyn.

Captain McLane was General Washington's main eyes and ears as to what the British movements were, and also, as I later found out, was the most extraordinary horseman I would ever see.

Most of the artillery units of the 2nd Artillery Division were diverted to Fort Mercer, at Red Bank on the east side of the Delaware River, or to an island in the middle of the river called Mud Island, where Mud Island Fort was located. Both of these fortified locations were two miles south of Philadelphia, as was the meager American fleet. This is where both Colonel Lamb and my good friend, Captain Doughty, were detailed. Captain Doughty told me before departing with his unit that if we could hold Fort Mercer at Red Bank, along with Mud Island Fort on Mud Island, we could keep the British in Philadelphia from receiving supplies of men and communications from the sea.

General Washington, for his part, observed that General Howe had neither fortified Germantown, nor entrenched his army, which led Washington to believe that General Howe considered an attack by Washington's army to be so remote, as to be discounted. Washington devised a plan for a four pronged attack on General Howe's position in and around Germantown, which necessitated a night march. Washington's plan called for General Armstrong with his artillery on the American right to advance to the Wissahickon Creek, where it emptied into the Schuylkill River, and to attack Howe's left flank. General Green on the American left was to attack Howe's right, while Generals Sullivan and Wayne with the majority of the Continentals, were to attack Howe's center with General Stirling in reserve and support.

Upon reporting to Captain McLane, he stated to me "You and your Connecticut men are most welcome, Corporal Waterman. I have roughly one hundred men under my command, and most of them were recruited by me from the area surrounding Philadelphia. Your Colonel Durkee speaks most highly of you and your men. Your men certainly will be needed in the upcoming engagement." I could only tell the captain that we'd do our best not to let him down. For our part, Captain McLane went on to explain that we were to advance in front of Generals Sullivan and Wayne's men. We were to push the British sentries back to allow Generals Sullivan and Wayne's men unfettered access to the British front lines.

On October 2nd, word was received that the attack would come the next night, and to prepare for an all night march. My unit and I had never prepared for a night march, or attack for that matter, and didn't know what to expect. We spent that day and all of the next preparing, but didn't know exactly how or what to do. Captain McLane came by during the early afternoon of the 3rd, and told us that all we really needed was fresh loads in our rifles and pistols, and to follow his men. Most of his men were armed with sabers or pistols for the attack. Captain McLane told us to get what rest we could, and that by five that evening we would be moving. My men and I spent a restless afternoon in camp, as the commotion in the camp leading up to the pending attack was enough to keep all awake.

At quarter to five, Captain McLane sent a rider for us. We mounted and proceeded to the edge of camp to find Captain McLane with his men waiting. General Sullivan's Continentals were already formed up and ready to march. Far off to our left we could see General Wayne's Continentals forming up. As dusk fell on our camp, the word came to move forward. We were the first to move out, and proceeded down the Skippack Road from Evansburg. Everyone knew that there was to be no unnecessary noise made, and it was surprising how quietly the Continentals moved out.

We marched for several hours without stopping, and before midnight on October 3rd, a halt was called to rest the men and water the horses. Captain McLane, under special order of General Washington, sent riders to the other wings of the army to ensure that the entire army was at the same point of their night march. The march was resumed, and shortly after midnight we passed through the small town of Whitemarsh. At two in the morning, a second halt was called and word was passed to remain on station and rest, but be prepared to move forward for the attack. We dismounted from our horses and let them graze as we waited. I told Eli to gather our men so that I could talk to them. In short order, Eli had our men gathered in a small clearing just past a small brook. As I had the men gather around, I could hardly see their faces by the moonlight.

"Listen, men," I began, "I expect that within the next hour or two, we will be engaged with the enemy. Follow Captain McLane's men, and remember that our primary objective is to push the sentries out of the way for the Continentals to attack the main British forces. Stay with McLane's men and we'll all meet up afterwards, is that understood?" I asked. There was a mumbling of "Yes, sirs," under my men's breath, and from what I could see on their faces, they seemed as nervous as I felt. "Return to your horses and stand by," I stated. As my men broke up and returned to their mounts, in groups of two or three, I called for Eli to remain. "Eli," I said, "do the men seem unusually nervous to you?"

"Will, I think everyone is nervous tonight," Eli replied and then added, "from our men to McLane's to the Continentals."

"Let's not let the men see how nervous we are, and I pray to God everything goes as planned tonight," I said. "Looks like there's a fog coming on now," I added to Eli as we walked back to our horses.

Just before four in the morning, a rider slowly made his way past our position, telling everyone to prepare to move at four, and to pass the word. We mounted our horses forming up behind Captain McLane's men. The Continentals could be heard behind us in the dark forming ranks, as the rattle of guns and equipment made an unmistakable sound. We moved out slowly, shortly before the Continentals. Word was passed that we were only a few miles from Germantown now.

A rider appeared out of the dark, and approached the front of our column. I could see the rider motioning down the road in an excited manner. When he had delivered his message, the rider wheeled his horse, and headed off in the direction of the Continentals. As the rider left, Captain McLane turned his head, stating something to the man behind him. That man, in turn, passed the word to the man next to and behind him. Thus, the word was passed quickly, and the man in front of me turned and said, "British light infantry a quarter-mile down the road, prepare to move." I, in turn repeated the information to each man on either side of me. The nervous men in our unit began to rein their horses.

Suddenly, Captain McLane spurred his horse, and began moving forward at a walk. First, a hundred yards passed in this manner. Then we had gone two hundred yards at a walk. Then, as we reached three hundred yards at a walk, Captain McLane pulled his saber from its scabbard, as did a number of men from his unit, while others pulled out a pistol, and we began to trot.

Suddenly, in the distance I could see a light in front of us. I thought it must be the dying embers of the fires of the British camp. When it seemed we had gone a quarter-mile, and should be upon the enemy, Captain McLane spurred his horse again, and we were at full gallop. Captain McLane's men began to yell just before they crashed full into the camp of the British soldiers. The yells were initially from McLane's men, but as the British soldiers began to pour out of their tents, the yells and screams came from both sides, as the men drew courage from their screams to engage the enemy. There were flashes from pistol and musket fire, along with the flash of light from the campfires off of the swinging sabers, as the men on horses and the soldiers on the ground engaged in a death struggle.

Our initial attack left several British soldiers on the ground dead or wounded. British soldiers were coming out of the tents and darkness to engage our men. Suddenly, a British soldier came out of the darkness, and was right in front of me, thrusting at me with a long bayonet at the end of his musket. I wheeled my horse to my left to avoid his thrust, coming full circle back on to him with the front of my horse hitting him full in his chest sending him sprawling to the ground. The soldier didn't move, knocked unconscious from the blow of a twelve hundred pound horse hitting him. I looked around to see the ebb and flow of men engaged to control the small piece of land we were fighting over.

A British soldier appeared thirty yards in front of me, silhouetted by the campfire, he was standing by, as he was reloading his musket. I raised my rifle to my shoulder, steadying my horse with the reins in my left hand, and as the front site of my rifle leveled on the soldier's body, I pulled the trigger. The shot startled my horse, causing him to spin in a circle, and as I struggled to regain control of my horse, I looked to the spot where the soldier had been standing, and he was gone. I wasn't sure if I had hit him or not. Had I killed him, wounded him or missed all together, I would never know.

I looked around me to see if I was in harm's way of a British soldier's bayonet or shot, as I instinctively began to reload my rifle. It seemed as if we had been engaged with this enemy for a long time, as more British soldiers were pouring in from the darkness into the illuminated camp, to engage our unit. I thought that our initial attack was destined to fail.

As I was about to engage another British soldier with a shot from my rifle, I suddenly found myself engulfed in a wave of men washing forward like a human wave, over the British camp. The Continentals under General Sullivan had arrived, and were sweeping the British from the field before them. Wave after wave of Continentals swarmed by me, and I was amazed at their uniformity as they moved forward into battle. Before a few minutes had passed, I found myself at the back of the front line of battle. As I looked around the sun was beginning to lighten the eastern sky, and dark forms could be distinguished as they walked around what use to be the British forward camp. Many more dark forms were on the ground, many of them moving ever so slightly and moaning from battle wounds and injuries. Several of the dark forms on the ground were not moving at all, and would never move again.

As I moved about the destroyed camp, I looked for any familiar face from the Connecticut men I led into this engagement. To make matters worse, a heavy fog had rolled in as the sun rose, making it even harder to find anyone. I could see burned out tents in front of me, so I made my way closer. The sounds of battle were now moving farther away from us to the east. Also, on either flank, the sounds of battle could now be heard. As I made my way to the burned out tents, several men from Captain McLane's unit passed me, leading British soldiers at gunpoint away from camp. As I continued on toward the tents, I passed many wounded, and some dead of the British camp. I even encounter one man who was from Captain McLane's unit who was dead, shot in his chest. His jacket was covered by a large circular bloodstain that looked darker than it should be. I found Captain McLane in a burned out tent, which had been the quarters of the commander of this forward post for the British army. Captain McLane was issuing orders to several men around him at once, trying to reorganize his men in case they were to be needed again before this day's engagement was over. He saw me after several moments, and called me to draw closer.

"Corporal Waterman," He called out, waving me over with an upraised arm.

"Sir," I replied as I approached the group of men around him.

"It seems your men performed admirably in this morning's action, Corporal," he said. "It would have been much the worse for us if we didn't have you here," he admitted. "As it was, it turned out to be a spirited engagement, more spirited than we anticipated. I believe we lost several men, dead and wounded."

I looked more closely at him because of this comment.

"It seems we've both lost some of our men, and I think you will find at least part of your company over by the creek under a stand of cottonwood trees," he said. "The rest of our men are probably scattered somewhere between here and the battle front to the east, as they were pushed along with the Continentals. Gather what you can of your men, and be ready to move if needed for additional attacks on the enemy. I will be sure to include your activities in my report to General Washington, when this action is over. See to your men, Corporal," he said as he turned his attention to his men at hand.

I reined in my mount and headed in the direction of the creek where Captain McLane indicated I would find what remained of my men. As I made my way over to the creek, I recalled that Captain McLane said I had causalities. I suddenly felt a knot in my stomach as I wondered who it might be.

I found a number of my men as Captain McLane said I would down by a creek just outside of the British camp. Some were standing around looking down at the ground, while several remained on their mounts several feet from those on the ground. As I rode up, I could make out the forms of at least two men who were laid out on the ground. I dismounted and slowly walked past the mounted men, to the men standing by those who lay on the ground. No one said anything as I approached, and the men looked at me with forlorn looks as I drew closer. Lying on the ground with their faces covered by their coats were two men from our company. I pulled back the coats to see Josiah Adgate and Isaac Backus lying dead. Both had what appeared to be gunshot wounds to their chests, and Isaac, it appeared, had several stab wounds to his left leg and arm, presumably from some British soldier who came upon him wounded on the ground. I stood up and looked around at the faces of the men gathered here.

"Put them on horses," I said to no one in particular. As I looked around again, I realized that Eli was not here, as well as several other men. "Where are the other men?" I inquired, again to no one in particular.

"Eli took Dayton Birchard, John Gallagher and John Edgerington to the rear to find the field hospital," Samuel Fuller began. "No one has seen John Lathrop, my brother John or Nathan Smith since the battle began," Samuel added.

"We think that they were caught up with some of Captain McLane's men along with the Continentals, and were pushed forward with the battle," Joshua Calkins added.

"How badly are the injuries to Birchard, Gallagher and Edgerington?" I asked again to no one in particular, but to everyone who could hear me.

Again, it was Samuel Fuller, who answered, "None of their wounds seemed too bad. Dayton had a bayonet wound to his shoulder, Gallagher had a bullet graze his left leg, and Edgerington fell off his horse during the battle, and broke his collar bone, we think."

Looking around at the men, I could see that everyone was already battle weary from their first real engagement, and appeared to be in battle shock. That is, they weren't really sure what had just happened, and what they had been through.

"Wait here for me," I said, looking around at everyone. "I'm going to talk to Captain McLane, to determine if we will be ordered to further details in this engagement. Samuel and Joshua, I want you two to come with me," I said to Samuel Fuller and Joshua Calkins, as these two seemed more engaged in what was happening than many of the others. "We'll return shortly men, wait here for us," I said as we turned to go to the tent where Captain McLane had his headquarters at what remained of the British camp.

As we rode the short distance to the camp, the sounds of the battle that raged to the east of us, a mile distant, seemed to gain in intensity. It seemed that the sound of battle was coming from several places along the battle front, but due to the heavy fog that had settled in, it was impossible to make out what units were engaged.

I found Captain McLane, as before, at what remained of the tent that belonged to the commander of the British units at this camp. He had set up a table along with several chairs, and was talking with several men from his unit as they looked down at a map on the table. I dismounted, informing Samuel and Joshua to wait for me as I walked over to the table. I stood patiently to the side of these men, as Captain McLane was in a serious discussion with them.

"From the reports we have received recently, men," Captain McLane was stating. "This bloody fog is so dense at Germantown that several of the Continental units have become disoriented, and may have fired on each other.

In addition to that, word is that a British unit has fortified itself in a stone house, and is now surrounded, being behind our lines. Several assaults against this house have met with severe loss of life to our men." He continued, "To make matters worse for us, we have lost several men here. Some of our men were swept forward with the Continentals, and we have no idea where they are." Looking up from the map, he looked at the men around the table. As his gaze fell on me, he hesitated for a moment and then continued. "I want each of you here to gather what remains of your units, and then set to task to find and account for your dead, wounded and missing. Regarding your missing, send riders forward to attempt to locate them, and draw them back from the front lines. We are the eyes and ears of this army gentleman, and if we are scattered across this battle front, we can't provide General Washington with needed information as to the developing movements of the British army," he said. "You have your orders, gentlemen, be about them," he concluded. Looking at me again, Captain McLane inquired, "Corporal Waterman, do you have a report, sir?" he asked.

"Sir," I began, "as the result of this morning's engagement, I have two confirmed dead, three wounded and three missing, presumed, sir, like several of your men, pushed forward with the front lines of Continentals. I can count ten men ready and fit for duty, nine actually on hand," I concluded.

Captain McLane said nothing as he looked back down at the map on his table. "I, too, have several dead, wounded and missing men, like you, Corporal. I am afraid there is not much more we can do during this battle with this bloody fog that has hampered all our efforts," he said. Looking up again, he continued, "You and your men performed better than expected, go and mourn your dead, take care of your wounded and find your missing if you can. You are relieved here, Corporal," he stated tiredly.

Saluting and turning, I remounted my horse and looked at Samuel and Joshua. "Joshua," I began, "go to the creek where the men are and make your way back to our camp behind the lines. Find Colonel Durkee and report to him the details of our engagement here, of our dead and wounded. Tell him that Samuel and I will be moving forward to find our missing men and will be back by evening to report to him. Then, find Eli at the field hospital and see how our wounded faired," I concluded, as I wheeled my horse, followed by Samuel, and moved ever so slowly forward in the fog toward the sound of battle.

We found the Skippack Road in the gray, damp fog of this day, continuing down it toward the sound of battle. After an hour of slow forward movement, we encountered the rear of the front of the line, and the battle that was occurring at the stone house that the British had fortified as the Continentals swept past them, hours earlier in the darkness and fog. Even now, with day light full upon us it was hard to see the battlefield due to the dense fog combined with the smoke from the battle. Off to the left, were the commanders and the artillery units, relegated to watching what they could see of the battle due to the fog.

I walked my horse up next to a sergeant who was beside a supply wagon loaded with powder and shot, as Samuel followed close behind me. The sergeant looked up at us, but didn't say anything.

"What happens here, Sergeant," I finally said after several moments of watching fire by our units in the house at the unseen defenders.

"A whole regiment of British light infantry has fortified themselves inside that stone house," he began. "Maxwell's Brigade under General Lord Stirling has been ordered to storm and reduce it, having tried several times and failed," he said.

As I looked down the road I could see a large number of dead and wounded littered about the grounds before the house. Off a hundred yards away, I could see a large number of men gathering again, to attempt to storm the house. Around the house, hiding behind wagons, out buildings, stone fences, trees and other battle debris, I could see men directing their fire into the house, to what effect was unknown.

"Do you know where I would find General Sullivan's men?" I asked the sergeant.

"Somewhere up ahead in the fog," the sergeant answered without taking his eyes off of the battle in front of him. I looked down the road at the house, and I could understand the difficulty in taking it. It was a two and a half story house, from top to bottom, constructed of stone, mortar and brick. On each side of the house and on each floor of the house, were numerous windows that provided protection from the outside fire, but provided a clear field of fire in every direction, to the fields and men before the house.

I was about to move my position to a wagon somewhat closer to the firing, when I heard from the men gathered, a loud chorus, as they began their next assault on the house. It appeared that several hundred men had gathered, and were fully involved in the charge. Their numbers, combined with their resolve, seemed that their efforts to take the fortified house would certainly be successful. As the mass of men moved forward, the firing from the house suddenly intensified. Several men were hit and were seen falling before the mass of men, possibly trampled to death by their fellow soldiers. The mass of men drew to within fifty yards and the firing on both sides became heated. The mass of men continued forward despite their many losses and as they drew near to the house, the true reasons for the many failed attacks on the house became clear. There was only one main door to the house, which had been fortified and was well defended.

Additionally, the large number of windows on the first and second floors provided unobstructed fire into the attacking Continentals. Even when the Continentals reached the front door, the firing was so intense that they could not maintain their foothold for long, before a large number of casualties were taken in both dead and wounded.

As I watched in horror as these men threw themselves at the front door to this stone and brick castle, it reminded me so clearly of the Maryland Four Hundred, who sacrificed so dearly their lives on Long Island to save the army.

Suddenly, a handful of men broke free and stormed up the stairs to the main door. Several were actually seen as to enter the door while their comrades fought desperately with the defenders to maintain their position. Without support they were doomed to fail, as the remainder of the mass of men slowly and begrudgingly began to give ground, taking many of the wounded with them. The attack had, as all the others had, failed. There were many more Continentals who now littered the fields before and around the house, adding to the dead and wounded. Surely they would not attempt another assault on the house. But as I watched the men again gather outside of the range of the soldiers in the house, to my amazement, they were gathering in a formation to bring forth another assault. It would take many minutes for them to gather together the forces sufficient to conduct the next assault. As they did so, it also provided the defenders of the house, time to refortify and reload their weapons for the anticipated attack.

After what seemed to be a half-hour, the attacking units were again massed and formed for an assault. As all watched and waited for the attack, it was interrupted by the arrival from the battle raging to east of us, by Continentals in retreat. At first it was only a trickle of men. But after a few minutes, it became clear that the Continentals were retreating as the numbers grew considerably. It wasn't a panicked retreat with men running for their lives, but a very controlled withdrawal of units from the front. The unit that had been assaulting the house stood down, and they too began to leave the field of battle.

After an hour, the entire Continental army was upon us as we were overwhelmed by men, much like we were earlier that morning during our attack on the British forward camp. The sergeant had long before this ordered his supply wagons to the Skippack Road, and to Evansburg. Likewise, the artillery units had withdrawn lest the advancing British army overrun them.

The sounds of battle had drawn uncomfortably close as the Continentals withdrew and the British advanced. Suddenly, riding two hundred yards to our left, up a rise into a stand of trees beyond, was thirty mounted light infantry from Captain McLane's unit.

"Was that Captain McLane's men?" I said to Samuel without looking at him.

"I think I saw John Lathrop riding in that group, but I can't be sure," Samuel replied.

We spurred our horses and began working our way back among the mass of Continentals. We rode several miles back up the Skippack Road, passing the British forward camp that we had attacked that morning. When we passed it, it was now totally deserted and the only remnants of the battle that occurred there earlier were the weapons left behind, and burned out tents. All of the dead and wounded had been removed.

We rode another mile, and were just outside of the town of Whitemarsh when we came to a large Dutch barn along the road, with numerous horses tethered to the rail fences around it. Upon riding up, we finally found our lost men who were gathered around a warm fire, enjoying a warm mug of rum. We dismounted and walked over to the men gathered at the fire. As we walked up, John Lathrop was the first to speak up.

"Will," he began, "are we glad to see you. We didn't know how to find anyone from our unit again, once we were pushed forward past the camp we attacked. The sergeant here was certain we'd find some of his men back at the British camp, but it was deserted when we got there," he stated handing me and Samuel each a mug of rum. I hadn't thought about it before this, but this was the first nourishment we had had in almost twenty-four hours, and I suddenly felt very hungry and tired.

"Well, I'm just glad we found you men," I began. "After the Continentals swept through the camp and it was secured, we began to gather up the prisoners and count our losses. It wasn't until later that it was realized that you were missing. Captain McLane sent out riders to find most of you, but I guess we are the first to find you," I stated.

"Did we lose anyone, Will?" John Fuller inquired.

I took a deep gulp of rum before I replied, "Yes, we suffered both dead and wounded in the British camp. You were the only men unaccounted for. Captain McLane lost several men, too, and is looking for you men," I stated as I looked at his men gathered around the fire. "Best get back to your camp before dark so he can stop looking for you," I suggested. I looked at my men and stated, "I'll tell you about our losses on the way back. I'm tired and need to report to Captain Fitch and Colonel Durkee," I stated as I turned to go, followed by my men.

We mounted our horses and began a slow ride back to Evansburg, and the camp of Major General Varnum of the Rhode Island Brigade. It would be dark in an hour or so and I wanted to be in camp before then. We rode silently for a while, and as we came to a brook, we stopped to water our tired horses. As Lathorp, John Fuller and Smith dismounted, I decided it was time to relate our losses to them.

"We lost two men today," I began. "After the battle at the camp was over, we learned that Josiah Adgate and Isaac Backus were killed and John Gallagher, Dayton Birchard and John Edgerington were wounded," I stated. "I haven't seen the wounded men, but I believe they all may survive their wounds."

No one said anything for what seemed to be a dreadful amount of time. I could see that John Lathrop was the most affected by the news, as he wiped a tear from his face as it ran down his cheek.

"Who's going to tell their families?" Nathan spoke up.

"I'm not sure how that'll happen, Nathan," I said. "I'll meet with Captain Fitch and Colonel Durkee when we get to camp, to report to them the details of our engagement, and provide a list of our casualties. It may be up to them to notify the families of Josiah and Isaac," I concluded as I remounted my horse and headed toward camp.

When we arrived at camp, I turned my mount over to Samuel Fuller and walked over to the tent that I knew would be Colonel Durkee's. The sentry outside the tent announced my arrival.

"Corporal Waterman, enter!" Colonel Durkee called out.

Upon entering I found Colonel Durkee along with Captain Fitch sitting at a table in the middle of the tent with a map on it. Both Colonel Durkee and Captain Fitch were sipping from glasses what appeared to be some type of Madeira. I saluted, which both officers returned. There was an empty chair at the table and Colonel Durkee offered it to me, which I gladly accepted as the fatigue from the day was now weighing heavily upon me.

"Corporal," Colonel Durkee began, "enjoy a glass of Madeira with us and report your day's activities," he stated as he poured me a glass without waiting for me to answer.

I related the events of the day leading up to the attack on the British forward camp and the rest of the day's activities. I then had to tell him of the casualty report.

"Sir," I said, "I have to report that Josiah Adgate and Isaac Backus were killed during the attack on the British camp, and that John Gallagher, Dayton Birchard and John Edgerington were wounded. They are at the field hospital being treated for their wounds."

"Yes, we know, it's an unfortunate side effect when two armies meet," Colonel Durkee replied. "I received a dispatch from Captain McLane's orderly, some time ago detailing the attack on the camp and its outcome. Those were the first casualties the brigade has suffered and it is the talk of the camp. It seems that you and your men performed admirably though, as Captain McLane speaks highly of you," he stated. "Go and get some rest and return here in the morning," he instructed. "I'll have some letters to post with the quartermaster sergeant in the morning bound for Norwich regarding the casualties. I imagine that you'd probably like to post your own letters to home, so that they don't find out about your exploits in the local newspaper," he said. "If this is any indication of your military career, you are going to be the most famous son of Norwich, Connecticut, sir. You are dismissed," he concluded.

I left Colonel Durkee's tent, to make my way over to our unit's camp. As I walked I felt lightheaded from fatigue, the Madeira and the events of the day. I had to post a letter in the morning. If Diane or my family were to hear about the battle in the paper, they wouldn't like it. I reached my tent, removed my boots, and was asleep before I lay down.

Morning came early, and I seemed to be as tired in the morning as I was when I went to bed. I found most of the men gathered around the cooking fire talking about the previous day's events. Eli was the first one to speak up.

"Will, are we going to have a service for our men?" he inquired. "Everyone is asking about it."

"Yes, we'll have a service in a couple of hours," I said. "I have to meet Colonel Durkee this morning on another matter, and when that is concluded, we'll have our service."

I gulped down a quick cup of coffee, along with some cold bacon, and then made my way over to Colonel Durkee's tent. When I arrived it was as if Captain Fitch and Colonel Durkee had never moved. They were still seated at the table in his tent, and their glasses were still filled with Madeira. The only change was that on the table in front of Colonel Durkee were several letters in a stack tied together with a string.

Colonel Durkee handed me the letters along with two bits, informing me to post whatever letters I was sending, too.

"Sir, if I may ask?" I began.

"Go ahead, Corporal," Colonel Durkee interrupted me.

"The men were wondering about a service today for Josiah and Isaac?" I asked.

"Yes, yes," he replied. "General Varnum has called for the brigade to assembly today at one in the afternoon for a service, followed by the burial of our dead. As I said last night, since these are our first killed in action, and I dare say not our last, he wants to make an impression with the men. This is very important to the general," he concluded.

"I'll let the men know, sir." I replied.

"And Will," Colonel Durkee began. "Make sure you and your men are dressed as smartly as you can under the circumstances. General Varnum wants your unit front and center at the ceremony."

"Sir," I responded as I saluted and turned to do my duty of posting the letters to home. When that was completed I made my way to the field hospital, to find all three of my wounded men in good spirits.

The nurse tending them had already had her fill of them. She said that

John Gallagher with his bandaged leg, and John Edgerington with his left arm in a sling to protect his broken collarbone, could return to camp. Dayton Birchard had to stay another day or two because the doctor wanted to watch for infection in his wound. I asked the nurse if we could at least borrow him for the burial ceremony of our friends, to which she replied with a devilish glint in her eye that, "We could if we returned him before the doctor made his afternoon rounds at three o'clock." I promised we'd have him back, as we all made our way to camp together, although John Gallagher walked with a limp from his bullet wound to his leg.

When we returned to camp, I told the men in my unit to dress as smartly as possible and that after lunch we'd make our way to the other side of camp for the ceremony. Not a lot was said at lunch or after. Everyone just went about preparing their business in their own way to say goodbye to our friends.

The men of General Varnum's Brigade had gathered long before the hour of one o'clock, and no one needed to be reminded by their unit commanders to be prepared, or on time. Men from the four regiments lined the field for the burial service for a quarter-mile. The two Rhode Island Regiments were on one side and the two Connecticut Regiments were on the other, facing each other. Two graves had been dug at the end of the field by a large oak tree. General Varnum and the regimental commanders were beside the gravesite. Next to General Varnum and the commanders were Colonel Durkee and Captain Fitch. My men and I were stationed behind Colonel Durkee and Captain Fitch. Beside General Varnum was the regimental Chaplain, Ebenezer David.

Off in the distance, drums could be heard as the drummers struck their drums once, every other step. The monotone striking of the drums drew ever closer until finally cresting the hill at the far end of the field, they could be seen leading a wagon followed by two soldiers leading two saddled horses. As they entered between the two rows of soldiers, men began to salute as the wagon passed. Finally, the wagon reached the end of the lines and pulled up in front of the graves. I could see the two wooden caskets in the back of the wagon now. Men were detailed to remove them from the wagon and lay them beside the graves. Once this was done the chaplain opened with a prayer. I heard the beginning of the prayer, but after that, all was a blur. I didn't even hear what General Varnum said or the words spoken by the Chaplain afterwards. I could not believe that we were burying two men that I had known since my childhood. Two men I had led into battle, that were now gone. Before I knew it, the service was concluded, as the two caskets were lowered into the ground and covered. I looked around at my men and a dry eye was not to be found among them. Orders were given and the units were dismissed, as all headed back to camp. Barely a word was spoken among the brigade.

The next day, October 6th, I was ordered again to Colonel Durkee's tent. I found Colonel Durkee reviewing several correspondences when I was allowed to enter his tent. Colonel Durkee looked up at me and stated, "Corporal Waterman, have a seat." I sat in a chair opposite the table before the colonel and waited for Colonel Durkee to address me. Finally, he put the first correspondence down and stated, "It seems our battle of Germantown will be recorded as a defeat. Our casualties total more than six hundred dead and wounded, with four hundred still unaccounted for. The estimates of the British casualties are around five hundred. If it wasn't for that bloody fog and some of the units becoming disorientated on the field of battle, and actually firing on each other, I think we would have soundly defeated the British, and perhaps pushed them out of Philadelphia."

I said nothing of all this, going over in my mind the two deaths we sustained from our unit during that battle.

Nothing was said for a moment, and then Colonel Durkee cleared his throat and stated, "I'm sure you found all this information interesting, but the real reason why I called for you is this. The British have pulled back to Philadelphia and General Washington is going to circle the city in a kind of siege warfare, not unlike that at Boston. We now anticipate the main battle will be a mile or two below the city on the Delaware River." Pointing to a map, Colonel Durkee continued, "We hold the forts here on this island, called Mud Island and here on the east side of the Delaware River, at an area called Red Bank. The idea is to hold these forts. By doing so, we can keep the British bottled up and from resupply or communication from the sea. If we can keep them isolated into the winter, they may be forced to evacuate the city. The 2nd Artillery Division under Colonel Lamb has been detailed to these forts for their defense. Our brigade has also received orders to support the defense of these two forts. The 1st and 2nd Rhode Island Regiments are to provide the primary support at each of the forts," he stated. "The 4th and 8th Connecticut Regiments are to be in reserve three miles below Fort Mercer at the Billingsport batteries. I want your rifle unit on Mud Island at Mud Island Fort," he ordered. "Lord knows we are going to be in a fight again, and your unit will best be served, I believe, on that island. The brigade should be moving out in a day or two," Colonel Durkee stated. "Report with your unit on the morrow to Captain

Doughty at Mud Island Fort on Mud Island. Here is your pass signed by General Varnum," he concluded, standing up from behind his table and handing me a piece of paper.

I saluted the colonel and said, "Very good, sir."

- CHAPTER 11 -

"The Defense of Mud Island Fort on Mud Island and Fort Mercer at Red Bank"

October – November 1777

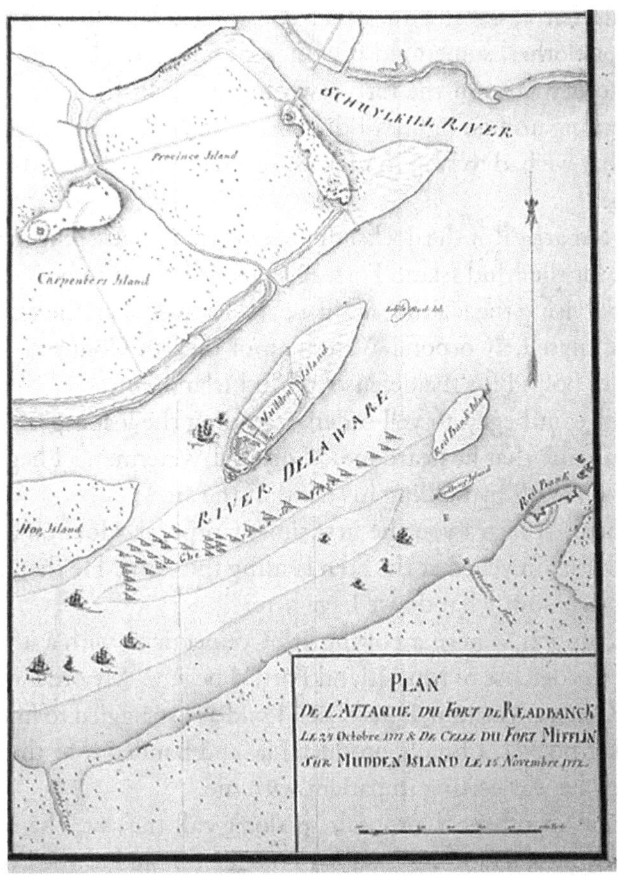

On October 7, I found myself looking over the ramparts of Fort Mercer on the Delaware River at a fort a half-mile distant on an island in the middle of the river. Men could be seen on the island and at the fort, busily at work. Several boats could be seen rowing in each direction, bringing men and supplies to the isolated fort on the island.

An unshavened sergeant came by and sternly said to all within hearing, "The last boats of the day depart the docks in five minutes. If you men from Connecticut plan on being on them, I suggest you get down there," pointing to the docks at the river's edge.

I looked around and my men were all close by, but all were fascinated by the flurry of activity at the riverfront before them and the fort we were bound for. All was being prepared for the coming storm of battle.

I took a deep breath and with the deepest voice I could gather, I yelled, "Men of the 4th Connecticut, let's get down to the docks!" My men gathered all that we came with, which consisted of our guns, powder, shot, a change of clothes, some food provisions, and a few blankets and tents. We made our way from the fort down to the docks through the masses of men coming and going in all directions. Several of us were jostled so roughly, that we had to stop to make sure we had not dropped any of our possessions.

Upon our arrival at the docks, there were three boats being loaded with provisions for the Mud Island Fort. A sergeant seemed to be in charge, as he was supervising the loading of the boats. I approached the sergeant and introduced myself, "Corporal Waterman of the 4th Connecticut, with a unit of rifles bound for the defense of Mud Island Fort."

The sergeant began to yell orders regarding the loading of the boats, and I wasn't sure that he heard me. "Corporal Waterman," I began, as the sergeant cut me off by holding his hand in the air.

He stated, "I heard you the first time, Corporal. Hold on a minute," he said as he again yelled at the men loading the boats. He then turned to me and said, "Now, what do we have here?"

"I'm Corporal Waterman of the 4th Connecticut, with a unit of rifles bound for the defense of Mud Island Fort," I began. "My order of passage, signed by General Varnum, is here, sir," I said as I struggled to find my pass in my jacket pocket. I finally produced it, and handed it to the sergeant, as it seemed he was getting impatient with me.

"I'm not an officer, Corporal, so don't call me, sir," he said as he reviewed my pass. Handing it back to me, he pointed to the boats at the dock and said, "Get your men down to these boats here. It'll be crowded, but you'll be on the island shortly" he concluded.

"Thank you, Sergeant," I replied.

"You may not be thanking me in the near future, Corporal," he said. "I fear that that island is going to seem like hell's fury before this battle is over."

I looked to my men, and they followed me down to the boats. Within a quarter-hour we were loaded onto the already overcrowded boats, as one by one they left the docks. The men that were rowing the boats strained to get them to move under the weight of supplies and men in each. One of the men in the lead boat began to call out a cadence, in a deep Boston Irish accent that somehow seemed familiar to me, and the boats began to move with more ease, and rhythm towards the island. Within a half-hour we were approaching the docks on the east side of Mud Island. As we disembarked the boats, I looked down the river for the first time. Three or four miles distant, I could see a forest of masts from all of the British warships, and support vessels that were in preparation to begin battle with our forces. Eerily, it reminded me of the forest of masts of the ships in New York Harbor leading up to the battle of Long Island.

We soon found out why Mud Island, was indeed called Mud Island. It was such a low lying island with the water of the Delaware River, that most of the time the ground was saturated with water. Wherever you walked, you were walking on what seemed to be a sponge, as with each step, mud would ooze out of the ground underfoot. Mud Island Fort was located at the south end of the island on what was considered the high ground, with the northern two thirds of the island being nothing more than a swampy marsh.

This island and fort were as busy with activity as was Fort Mercer at Red Bank, on the east side of the river. Everyone worked with a purpose. I sent the men to the barracks, while I went to look for the commanding officer to report for duty. At the south end of the fort, where the main batteries were located, I found Captain Doughty of the 2nd Artillery Division, directing the work on the defenses.

When there was a break in the efforts of Captain Doughty, I spoke up as to be heard, "Captain Doughty," I began, "Corporal Waterman, with a unit of rifle from the 4th Connecticut Regiment, reporting for duty."

The captain turned, and as he looked upon me, a smile crossed his face. "Will," he stated, "it is good to see you, although not under these circumstances."

"May I ask as to the condition of the defenses here, sir?" I inquired.

Captain Doughty hesitated for a few moments before he answered. "We are woefully under supplied, undermanned and outgunned," he began. "We have four hundred twenty-five effective men fit for duty. The defenses here are inadequate to stop a determined attack by water, and I fear that if the British build land batteries to our west on Province

Island, we will be in a duel we cannot win. Look down the river there," Captain Doughty said, pointing to the south. "The British have man-of-war, frigates and floating artillery barges, just waiting to assault us." Pointing to the river, he stated, "In the river we have Chevaux-de-Frise there. The British have been systematically trying to remove them from the river. Once they remove enough of them, they'll be able to sail up to this fort, or Fort Mercer, and pound us from the land and the river, thus reducing us to rubble."

"I don't mean to be ignorant, Captain," I stated. "But what are Chevaux-de-Frise?" I asked.

"I'm sorry, Corporal," he replied. "I assume you know all that I know, you seem so adapted to warfare. Chevaux-de-Frise are log boxes about twelve feet square that are loaded with stone to sink them to the bottom of the river. They have large spiked logs sticking out of them that are hidden just below the water line. Any British ship attempting to pass upstream without knowing the location of the Chevaux-de-Frise below the water's surface, risk serious damage, and possibly even sinking. They are an effective tool in keeping the British navy at bay for now." Turning, Captain Doughty looked to the north and said, "Anchored to the north is the American fleet under command of Commodore Hazelwood. They will be a help, but they are just a mishmash of river galleys, floating batteries, and schooners. No real match for the British navy."

Captain Doughty then turned to the west. Pointing to the land less than a half-mile away and much closer to Mud Island Fort than Fort Mercer was, Captain Doughty stated, "A week ago the British built a bridge across the Schuylkill River at Webb's Ferry, just above where it empties into the Delaware River. They have been building batteries on both Province and Carpenter Islands. When they show their heads, we fire on them, but with little effect. And as you can see, on this side of the fort there is only a wood palisade to protect us from any British bombardment. I must be about my duties, Corporal," Captain Doughty stated. "But I think in the next day or two, we may have a use for you and your men. Major Thayer is in overall command here," Captain Doughty said, and in conclusion added, "he is a very able soldier indeed."

The next day was spent with getting acquainted with the defensive works on the island, as well as in the fort, along with helping the engineers to complete the works. Occasionally, during the day, the south or west batteries would come to life as a British warship came within range, or the British on the islands to the west showed themselves. When this happened all work stopped to see what effect we had on the enemy.

During the evening of October 8th, shortly after dark, Captain Doughty ordered the fort to battle ready. Commodore Hazelwood's fleet had been unusually close to Mud Island all day. A rocket was fired from the fort at six in the evening and shortly afterwards, Hazelwood's ships began a bombardment of the British batteries on Province Island. Apparently, they had sailed closer to the island under the cover of darkness. The bombardment lasted for only an hour, but it lifted all of our spirits. Before Captain Doughty retired for the night, he stated to me as he walked by, "You will find tomorrow night even more interesting."

The next day, late in the afternoon, the fort was again on alert as the units not directly detailed to support the batteries on Mud Island, were ordered to the docks on the east side of the island. One hundred twenty soldiers were gathered for the attack, a full one quarter of the men on the island, as were five large transport boats. As on the day before, elements of Commodore Hazelwood's fleet were seen anchored to the north of Mud Island. Captain Doughty addressed the assault units. "Men, tonight, shortly after dark, Commodore Hazelwood will again begin a bombardment. This time it will be on the batteries on Carpenter Island. While this bombardment is engaged with the enemy, you will land on Carpenter Island, and assault the batteries by land. Your objective is to destroy the enemy batteries, and if possible, capture several British soldiers for questioning. Godspeed men," Captain Doughty stated. We all nervously waited for sufficient darkness to descend upon us. Once it had, the boats were loaded, and pushed away from the docks, slipping silently out into the darkness of the Delaware River.

We rounded the southern tip of Mud Island and headed toward Carpenter Island, and the British batteries. When we were half way across the river, Hazelwood's ships began their bombardment. Dirt and debris could be seen flying in the air as we drew closer to the Island. Shortly thereafter, fire and smoke began to rise from the battery. We landed unopposed, and moved inland, spreading out as we approached the batteries. We scaled the abatis unopposed, and were in the batteries before the bewildered British defenders realized that they were not only under attack by bombardment, but by a direct frontal assault as well. The loss of life was minimal as the British soldiers and artillerymen were in disarray from the bombardment. We began to destroy stores of powder, and spiked the cannons. We then receive word that the Hessians were about to counterattack. With several prisoners in tow, we embarked in our boats for Mud Island. We regained the safety of Mud Island and Mud Island Fort without incident. The following morning, the prisoners were transferred to Fort Mercer for questioning.

On October 11th, only two days after we had assaulted the batteries on Carpenter Island, those same batteries, being rebuilt by the British, opened a barrage on Mud Island Fort. Since the west side of the fort was less heavily built, with a wood palisade only, the barrage had a great effect on causing damage to the wood structures.

Thus, the daily bombardment and the duel between the defenders of Mud Island Fort with the batteries on Carpenter and Province Islands, as well as the British navy began. The bombardments each day never caused catastrophic damage, but after a week, the cumulative damage began to tell, as the fort's defenses began to be in disarray. It became impossible to make repairs to all of the battle damage. Added to the daily battle damage was a growing list of casualties, both dead and wounded.

October 12th, was a bright and sunny, yet an unusually cool day. Word arrived from Fort Mercer that a Hessian force of two thousand men was moving to that fort. It was anticipated that an attack would occur as soon as the next day. Coinciding with this, several ships of the British navy were seen moving steadily north with the tide. To help support Forts Mercer and Mud Island, Commodore Hazelwood moved several ships and galleys south, to a position just north of Mud Island.

On this same day, word came that British General Burgoyne had been defeated north of Albany, in New York colony, and a gun salute was fired from both Forts Mercer and Mud Island.

October 22nd, greeted us as a cloudy and windy day. The Hessians had arrived, demanding the surrender of Fort Mercer. The Hessian commander said that if the fort didn't surrender, no quarter would be given. Colonel Greene's reply was that no quarter would be given or expected, as the fort would be defended to the last extremity. Colonel Greene then removed his men from the forts outer defenses, thus concentrating his men within the fort proper. That night the Hessians began their attack. Finding the outer defenses deserted, the Hessians thought the defenders had abandoned the fort, and were in retreat. When the Hessians reached the fort's inner walls and abatis, they found they were not prepared to scale a fort of such height. The defenders fired with both musket and cannon at close range on the Hessians with great effect. Several times the Hessians attempted to gain the inner walls of the fort, but were repulsed each time with great loss. The fallen among the Hessians included their commander, who would die from his wounds.

During the attack by the Hessians, the British sent several warships up the Delaware River to bombard Fort Mercer from the river. Commodore Hazelwood's fleet engaged the British warships, as did the cannons on the east side of Mud Island Fort. The view from Mud Island Fort was nothing short of spectacular, as cannon fire lit up the evening sky from both forts, combined with the ships from both navies. Engaged in a cannon duel, fire and smoke could be seen rising above Fort Mercer late into the night sky.

The battle this night lasted less than an hour and only ended after four hundred Hessians were either killed or wounded. During the night battle, the British warship HMS *Augusta* ran aground, only to be discovered the next morning.

The following day was a dark day with thick clouds covering the landscape. Most of the men from Fort Mercer were engaged in burying the Hessians dead in several mass graves. Those of us in Mud Island Fort were engaged in repairing battle damage that had occurred from the previous night's engagement, as our casualties were limited to some minor injuries.

Around mid-morning the alarm was sounded from Fort Mercer. A quick glance over our ramparts revealed that several British ships of the line, HMS *Eagle, Summerset, Isis, Pearl, and Liverpool*, along with several frigates, and fire ships, had come up to within five hundred yards of the Chevaux-de-Frise from our island stronghold. At the same time several galleys from our squadron moved south and again a general engagement developed between our forts and galleys, and the land batteries on Carpenter and Province Islands and the British navy. As seen by my soldier's eye, the engagement was again spectacular to behold. The river was awash with ships of both navies engaged in battle, with four great fire ships ablaze on the river. Forts Mercer and Mud Island were covered with smoke and fire. To our surprise and distress, we observed British soldiers draw up in battle lines on Carpenter Island; ready to board boats, and storm our fiery fort. We seemed to be the prize in this day's battle. Repeatedly, the British batteries fired hot shot into the palisades, and wood buildings of our fort, setting several on fire.

During this engagement, I noticed Captain Doughty looking intently through his spyglass at the batteries on Carpenter Island. Noticing I was standing next to him, Captain Doughty stated as he handed me the glass, "Look to the flag pole. The British batteries on Carpenter Island, raised a red flag under the Union Jack, to warn our garrison on Mud Island, that if the British troops storm this fort, no quarter would be given!" he shouted to be heard over the firing of our guns.

"They mean to kill us all!" I shouted back as I looked through the glass at the red flag

"Kill us all as a deterrent to future resolved defenses, like here at Mud Island Fort," the captain replied.

Our floating batteries and the southern batteries from our fort began to fire into the still grounded HMS *Augusta* from the previous night's battle. A heavy fire was poured into the ship, which eventually caught fire, causing the magazine to explode. This was the loudest noise I had ever heard, and reportedly the explosion was heard thirty miles away.

To make matters worse for the British fleet, HMS *Merlin* also ran aground during the battle below HMS *Augusta*, and was within range of the Billingsport batteries of General Varnum to the south. General Varnum's batteries fired into her as she shared the same fate as HMS *Augusta*, as she caught fire and exploded. The remainder of the British fleet withdrew to safety below Hogs Island farther to the south. The batteries on Province Island fired on us well into the evening, but the gathered British soldiers never moved to enter the shore boats, to attempt to storm our position, and thus the day's victory remained with us and our island fort.

The twenty-fourth to the thirtieth was a week of relatively warm, fair weather with sunshine. We daily expected a visit from the British soldiers who regularly formed up in battle array on Carpenter Island. Daily the batteries on Province Island kept a constant fire on us at the Mud Island Fort. During this week of constant bombardment, our unit had a most unexpected visitor. I was ordered to what remained of Captain Doughty's quarters. Upon entering the remnants of the officer's quarters, to my surprise, I encountered Colonel Durkee, who was enjoying an afternoon tea with Captain Doughty.

"Sir," I said, as I was startled to see my own colonel at the battered fort.

"Corporal Waterman," Colonel Durkee began, "I am glad to see you still alive, and in good spirits. How do the rest of your men fair?" he asked.

"I am sorry to report that all of our men have received some type of wound, from the constant bombardment we are daily suffering to endure," I stated flatly. "Although, none of our wounds are, to date, life threatening. I'm sure you've seen the casualty lists coming off this island, as the number of dead and wounded mount daily," I added.

"Yes, yes, most distressing," Colonel Durkee said. "General Varnum is daily proud of the men who defend both forts, and resist so stalwartly the constant effects of our enemy to dislodge them."

Clearing his throat, Colonel Durkee further stated, "There is another matter that both of you will find most interesting, I'm sure." Continuing Colonel Durkee began, "As you may recall, before we were detailed here from the Highlands of New York, the British were in the process of orchestrating a three prong attack on the northern reaches of New York. The attacks were both out of Canada, as well as New York City, in an effort to capture Albany, and split the colonies.

You will recall that on the twentieth, word came that the attack down the Champlain Valley by General Burgoyne was defeated north of Albany. To add to that news, the attack down the Mohawk Valley by General St. Leger was defeated at Fort Stanwix. The British siege of that fort fell apart when the colonial militia fought St. Leger's Indian allies to a stalemate in forests to the east.

The most interesting part is that two days after our battle at Germantown, General Clinton did leave New York City, and attacked the New York Highlands with a force of three thousand men. This report reads that, strangely, as it may seem, General Putnam retreated at the sight of the enemy and played no role in defending the highlands. In fact, Forts Clinton, Montgomery, and Constitution all fell with loss of life, leaving the Hudson Valley open for invasion all the way to Albany. It seems General Clinton sent a General Vaughn up the Hudson River Valley with two frigates. General Vaughn sailed all the way to Albany only to learn that General Burgoyne had surrendered the day before. Realizing he couldn't hold Albany without support, General Vaughn sailed back to New York City."

"Did the British realize how close they came to defeating us and splitting the colonies?" I replied. Then I thought of General Putnam and stated, "It seems strange that General Putnam would retreat before the British without a fight."

"Strange indeed," Colonel Durkee agreed. "I'm sure there will be an inquiry."

"What of the defenses at West Point?" Captain Doughty asked.

"Those defenses held and although they couldn't stop the British forces, they remain to this day. They will continue to be our anchor in defending that region," Colonel Durkee stated.

"Now, Will," Colonel Durkee continued, "before I leave this God forsaken island, let's go see the men."

We left Captain Doughty's quarters and made our way over to the northeast corner of the fort, by the northeast docks. Most men when not on duty, rested here, as it afforded the most protection from the constant bombardment from Province Island, and I knew I'd find my men there.

As we rounded the corner of what remained of a storage house, there huddled around an open fire, and consuming part of their daily rations were my ten men of the 4th Connecticut Regiment. Dirty, unshaven, and all in tattered clothes that use to resemble their Connecticut uniforms. All were suffering from the effects of a cold October, and all with bloody bandages covering their numerous wounds, revealing where they had been injured from the flying debris of wood, rock and stone, as the fort was shot out from around them. As they saw us round the corner, they all stood as they recognized Colonel Durkee was with me.

"Stand easy, men," Colonel Durkee said as we approached. He said nothing for a moment as he took in the sorry shape of his men, and the surrounding fort. "I know the suffering is great here," he began. "General Varnum as well as General Washington, indeed the whole army knows of the indefatigable defense of Mud Island Fort and Fort Mercer," he stated. "Indeed the whole army is watching and waiting the outcome of this battle. If we," he paused for a moment and then said, "if you men can hold the British navy and army at bay for another few weeks, we believe that General Howe will be forced to abandon Philadelphia. Without communication and resupply from sea, he will be forced out.

Major Thayer and Captain Doughty have been ordered by General Varnum and Colonel Greene to hold this fort to the last," he stated. "That is how important this fight is. I can see that each of you has received wounds from battle, and indeed need relief," he observed. "The general asks for a few more weeks. God be with you men," Colonel Durkee stated as he headed for the docks, and the boat returning to Fort Mercer. I accompanied him to the docks and in an unusual show of emotion; Colonel Durkee shook my hand and said, "Take care, Will. I don't like leaving you or the others on this island." Colonel Durkee entered the boat, and waved as the boat pushed off from the dock.

I returned to my men who were finishing their meal. No one spoke. The batteries on Province Island were firing at us again.

Friday, October 31st, welcomed us as a sunny day. Word came that the Hessian commander who had led the attack on Fort Mercer on the twenty-second had died. We fired on Province Island, and for our efforts, we received their fire for most of the day. The defensive works of the fort are in tatters again, and several cannons exploded today. They, like the men are worn out.

Saturday, November 1st, greeted us as a cold, windy, and rainy day. We were pounded with a cold rain all day, in addition to the daily bombardment from Province Island. Word came by boat that two pilots would be hung at one o'clock over the river ramparts of Fort Mercer. These two had been the ones who led the British across the Schuylkill River that allowed the enemy to build their batteries on Carpenter and Province Islands. They had been captured trying to cross our picket lines to the north of Philadelphia. We all gathered, and watched as the men were hanged. No one said a word of mercy for them, nor prayed for their souls, as they were the ones responsible, in a large part, for our daily suffering. Colonel Greene at Fort Mercer left their bodies dangling in the air for a week.

From Sunday, November 2nd, through Sunday, November 9th, the weather continued to be cold, and we daily dueled with the batteries on Carpenter and Province Islands. The red flag of no quarter still flew over the batteries on Carpenter Island. General Varnum moved eleven hundred men three miles downriver, for what cause we did not know. Our garrison was much reduced by the dead, wounded and sick men. Eli had developed a deep cough, and seemed to be very ill indeed. A deep fatigue set in as no one could sleep on account of the continuous shelling from Province Island. The nights drew increasingly cold, and the men turned to the hospital due to the inclemency of the weather. A northeast wind blew and raised the water level of the river, and at high tide, the river breached the works and overflowed Mud Island. The water drew two feet deep in Mud Island Fort, as well as what remained of the barracks. The weather was so foul that even the batteries at Province Island stopped firing on us. Mud covered everything the water had covered, and the stench of death and mud was everywhere. Yet we remained on the island.

On Monday, November 10th, the storm of the previous few days abated, as the sun broke through the clouds. We woke this day to discover the enemy had three more batteries on Province Island. These along with the other batteries opened a steady fire on us. We soon realized that the British meant to totally destroy Mud Island Fort before winter set in, otherwise they would have to abandon Philadelphia. The incessant fire all day at the fort finally destroyed all of the palisades on the west side of the fort. The ditches were still filled with mud and water from the northeast storm coupled with the high tides. A captain and lieutenant were killed from the bombardment this day. The garrison was entirely exhausted, and the fort almost reduced.

On Tuesday, November 11th, the weather continued windy, blustery and cold. The enemy continued the around the clock bombardment of Mud Island Fort. Several more of our cannons exploded, killing one and wounding eighteen. All of the wounded were evacuated to Fort Mercer.

Wednesday, November 12th, was a cold, yet sunny day. It began with the batteries on Province Island bombardment, which lasted all day. A Lieutenant Smith was wounded, and this day much of the garrison was evacuated to Fort Mercer.

Thursday, November 13th, was a cold, rainy day. We woke again to a new battery on Province Island that was directed against us. The daily bombardment from Province Island seemed more directed than previous days. We felt secure in that the Chevaux-de-Frise kept the British navy at bay. We were determined to remain on the island, although our fort was almost entirely reduced. That evening, an hour before dark, two British frigates moved up river, and to our dismay, it appeared that they were attempting to pass the Chevaux-de-Frise. What remained of our batteries engaged them with a heavy fire, as did the batteries along the riverfront of Fort Mercer. I directed my men to fire at the British marines on the fighting tops, and we had them cleared in short order. We then shot at any British officer we could make out on the frigates. The broadsides from the frigates reduced much of our docks and the defensive works on the east side of the island and Mud Island Fort. To our surprise, the British frigates sailed past our fort and up the river to Philadelphia, providing invaluable provisions to General Howe's embattled army. As I looked around our battered positions, I realized two of my men were down. Jacob Allyn and Thomas Gallagher were both lying dead, killed by flying debris and splinters of wood. A cannon ball from one of the frigates had hit the defensive work they were behind, completely destroying it.

No one said anything as we gathered their bodies, took them to the hospital, and laid them on the ground. A number of other dead were laid beside them as the evening's battle total was ten killed and seventeen wounded.

On Friday, November 14th, we were greeted with snow. The batteries on Province Island kept up a steady bombardment this day. We exploded several more cannons sustaining several wounded from the explosions. Again, our wounded and dead were evacuated to Fort Mercer. Jacob Allyn and Thomas Gallagher were taken on the second boat. We would see them no more. There seemed to be significant activity by the enemy below Hogs and Tinicut Islands this day.

Saturday, November 15th, was a cold windy day with skies that reminded me of a winter's sky, being dark and gray. At eight o'clock this morning the British began a concentrated attack on Mud Island Fort by both land and river. The bombardment from Province Island was particularly heavy and several ships sailed as close to the fort as the river and Chevaux-deFrise would allow on the southeast side of the fort. Another ship sailed around the protection of Hogs Island, and anchored several yards off the southwest corner of Mud Island, where Mud Island Fort was now particularly exposed.

Major Thayer had Captain Doughty move several guns into position to defend both the southeast and southwest corners of the fort. We poured several shots into these vessels, as my men placed volley after volley at the British marines in the fighting tops. Suddenly, these ships opened up with three or four broadsides of grapeshot. The fire was so intense and constant that for a period of half an hour a man could not expose himself without being killed. Within this half-hour all of the remaining parapets, carriages and platforms for our guns, along with all of our remaining guns themselves were destroyed. Not a gun in the fort was able to return fire. The British then sailed an eighteen gun schooner, HMS *Vigilant*, up to the west side of Mud Island and fired cannon shot into the remnants of the fort for the remainder of the afternoon.

Several galleys from our fleet came to our defense, and fired cannon shot at HMS *Vigilant*, as well as on the batteries on Province Island the remainder of the day. What remained of our garrison was unable to retreat during the day due to the heavy bombardment from the British, and was unwilling to do it that night, as we expected reinforcement.

Surprisingly, however, the British still didn't move to take the fort. Major Thayer ordered a council of war in the midst of the firing just before nightfall. It was determined that it was impossible to defend the fort with such a small force of men and to call for reinforcements from Fort Mercer. If Fort Mercer could not reinforce, it was determined to evacuate Mud Island Fort. During the council of war, a shell fired from HMS *Vigilant* exploded in Mud Island Fort, killing an artillery officer.

A boat was sent from Fort Mercer with word that no reinforcement was coming. Major Thayer determined that, with the fort open at all four walls, and with not a gun inside to return fire, that the defense of the fort, and the river was no longer viable.

Major Thayer ordered the evacuation of the remaining two hundred men, all of whom wore the bandages of one wound or another, as well as the stores that could be taken. My unit remained on the island, along with Major Thayer and Captain Doughty, as well as a remnant of artillery men. In all, twenty-five of us set to the torch, what remained of Mud Island Fort. We arrived at Fort Mercer at twelve o'clock at night. We had defended Mud Island Fort for forty days, while enduring the harshest conditions a defending force could endure, and despite all our efforts, had in the end, lost the fort to our enemy. Our numbers had been reduced by more than half by the time the fort was abandoned, and all those still remaining had suffered wounds.

Sunday, November 16th, broke as a cold windy day. From Fort Mercer we watched as the British landed a small force unopposed at the deserted Mud Island Fort, hauled down our colors, which were left flying over the fort, and ran up the British Union Jack atop the ruined fort. A council of war was held at Fort Mercer and we believed we would be evacuating this fort as well.

On Tuesday, November 18th, word was received that a large force of British regulars was marching on this fort. At ten O'clock at night, orders were given to march. We struck our tents and loaded what provisions we could in the wagons, spiked the guns we could not take with us, and departed Fort Mercer. It was said that although we had lost the fort on Mud Island and abandoned Fort Mercer, we had gained invaluable time to keep the army together, as we marched to winter quarters.

We rejoined the rest of the regiment and General Varnum outside of Haddonfield, New Jersey colony. From there we marched through the town of Moorestown, and continued on to Mount Holly. As a light snow floated to the ground, we spent a cold night by a large barn, where a halt was called. In the morning we were ordered to be ready to march. Most of the regiment drew clothing along with fifty rounds of cartridges. Shortly thereafter, we began our march to winter quarters. We marched north through Trenton and on to McConkey's Ferry. Here we crossed the Delaware River above Philadelphia, Pennsylvania colony. After another day's march, we were back with Washington's army outside of Philadelphia. From here the army marched north and west to our winter quarters, near a small farming village in the Pennsylvania colony, named Valley Forge.

- CHAPTER 12 -

"Dark Days of Valley Forge"

Winter 1778

ON December 19, 1777, the American army, eleven thousand strong, arrived at a small valley twenty-five miles from Philadelphia on the banks of the Schuylkill River, Pennsylvania colony. I'm not sure why this location was chosen for our winter quarters, other than it was apparent that General Washington, along with some of the other officers were very familiar with this area. The distance from Philadelphia provided our army some security from attack by the British, who seemed content to spend the winter in the relative warmth, and safety of Philadelphia. We began to move into our meager winter quarters.

From the time we arrived everyone was busy for the next two weeks building huts, which consisted of a roughly twelve foot by 16-foot structure to house all of the soldiers, and to provide some type of protection from the winter weather. All of the soldiers were so busy building huts for shelter that Christmas came and went without much notice, other than that we received one of our few good meals at Valley Forge. Also, from the day we arrived, and for the next few months the greatest threat to our army was not attack from the British, but starvation, sickness, disease and desertion.

For most, all there was to eat on most days was a food we came to call "fire cakes," which was a dull combination of water and flour baked into a thin crisp pancake. Even as we were building our huts, many of the men went without food for several days, and were seen walking around the camp as walking dead men, with barely enough strength to hold themselves up. For all the lack of food, the army put all of its energy into the building of the huts, and after two weeks, approximately one thousand huts had been completed. Soldiers had scavenged for miles around the Valley Forge area, taking everything that could be used to make a wood structure, in addition to all of the trees that were felled for their wood.

Each hut was to hold twelve soldiers. An officer's hut was built to the rear of the soldiers hut, and although it was the same size as the soldiers hut, it was to house fewer men. Each brigade was also ordered to build a field hospital, which was roughly a fifteen foot by 25-foot structure. A headquarters building was also built for each division. No farmer's fence, barn or wagon was safe when the farmer wasn't there to protect it, when a foraging party of workers came by.

During this time, General Washington himself, refused to sleep indoors until every soldier had a roof over his head. The general set up a tent, and spent his nights there until the huts were completed. Then the general moved into a Fieldstone house at the western end of the camp, and established his headquarters. Many of the other commanders initially quartered themselves in local farmer's homes to stay warm from the bitterly cold winter, only to later relent, even moving into the very huts their men were staying in, to be closer to their men.

When we arrived at Valley Forge, the Rhode Island Brigade, which consisted of four regiments, the 4th Connecticut, 8th Connecticut, 1st Rhode Island and 2nd Rhode Island, had one thousand, twenty-three men fit for duty, out of one thousand, seven hundred fifteen men under orders. Our division was almost seven hundred men under strength. By the end of the December, seven more men had died and four deserted. All of the other regiments, brigades and divisions had the same problem of men becoming ill, and thus not being fit for duty, along with numbers of men who died or deserted. Of an army of over eleven thousand that arrived in Valley Forge on December 19, 1777, far fewer than ten thousand men were fit for duty by January, 1778. Our Rhode Island Brigade was located on the north side of camp along the south shore of the Schuylkill River, where a local ford known as the Flatland Ford, crossed the river. Here, a low-lying island was located in the middle of the river. On the north side of the river was Sullivan's Brigade.

To better cross the river, a bridge was constructed to span the river just east of the ford location. We built a redoubt that overlooked the ford and bridge in the event the British actually ventured out of their winter quarters to attack our camp. Our redoubt became known as redoubt number one, being under the command of the 1st Division.

Redoubt number two was located at the beginning of the eastern defenses, which was the location of the 2nd Division. Redoubt number three was located at the beginning of the high ground that ran through our encampment, north to south. This was where the 3rd Division was located. This high ground was our area of last defense if we were attacked and overrun at our outer defenses by the British. This is also where General Knox put his artillery units when they arrived. Redoubt number four was to our west along the Schuylkill River and much closer to General Washington's Headquarters. This is where the 4th Division was located. Many additional redoubts and defensive works were built along the outer and inner defensive lines to reinforce our winter quarters.

Once we were done building huts, redoubts and defensive positions, I took the time to write to my family and Diane. It was hard finding pen, and ink, or even paper to write on, as every imaginable item was in short supply. I had to borrow all from Captain Fitch. I tried to tell them some of what had happened during the fall months since we had left the New York Highlands, but I had to leave much out. I didn't want to worry my mother, or Diane. I knew Da would be able to read between the lines. I wondered as I wrote, if Da knew how badly it seemed to be going for our army. When I went to post my letters with the quartermaster, Captain Fitch told me to return to General Varnum's Headquarters for orders.

Upon arriving at General Varnum's Headquarters, I waited outside to be allowed to enter, as one of the sentries at the door went inside to announce my arrival. "Corporal Waterman," I heard Colonel Durkee call out from inside the building, "front and center."

Removing my tri-corn, I stepped into the building as the reporting sentry stepped out. It was particularly dark in the building, even in the daylight, as the building didn't have windows. There were only two small candles to light the room. General Varnum was seated at a table and off in the corner was a crudely constructed bed of wood. Colonel Durkee and Captain Fitch stood to the right of the table. I approached the table, and stood at attention the best I could, and saluted the general. He returned my salute and looked at the papers on the table.

"Corporal Waterman," General Varnum stated, "due to your stalwart and indefatigable defense of Mud Island Fort on Mud Island, your commanding officers have put you in for a field promotion from corporal to sergeant. It is my pleasure to do so," he stated. "You are now Sergeant Waterman," he said as he handed me a green epaulet that was to be sewn on my jacket's left shoulder. "See the quartermaster regarding the attachment of your insignia."

"Sir," I responded as I took the epaulet from the general, as he briefly shook my hand.

Colonel Durkee now spoke up and asked, "How do the men in your unit fare now that the huts are completed?"

"Well, sir," I began, "my three wounded men from Germantown seem to be almost completely healed. Also, as you may recall, I lost two more dead at Mud Island Fort, Jacob Allyn and Thomas Gallagher."

Before I could continue, Captain Fitch broke in and stated, "Yes, letters were already posted to their families before we arrived at our winter quarters here."

"And," I added, "Eli Bingham became ill during the defense of Mud Island Fort, and I'd like to take him to the field hospital to be looked at. He has a most distressing cough."

"Yes, yes," Colonel Durkee began, "when we are finished here see to it, Sergeant."

"Right now I think I can count thirteen men fit for duty out of the twenty that I began with when we engaged the enemy at Germantown."

"Colonel Durkee will get several more men detailed to you," General Varnum began as he started writing on a piece of paper in front of him. "As you know, Captain McLane is General Washington's eyes and ears of this army," he instructed. "This is going to be a most difficult winter quarters, I fear. Captain McLane has need of men who can ride and shoot, while keeping one eye on the British, and the other in the fields to locate provisions for this army. You and your men are now, and until otherwise ordered, detailed to Captain McLane's light mounted infantry, to provide security and sustenance to this army," he stated as he handed me the folded piece of paper. "Contained on this paper are your orders, and pass to cross our lines at any time."

"Sir," I stated, as it was apparent that our meeting was concluded.

As I turned to leave, Captain Fitch stated, "Take Bingham to the hospital, and come to my hut before the evening meal."

"Yes, sir," I replied as I departed headquarters.

I walked immediately back to my hut to find several of my men talking just inside the hut door, and Eli lying on his bunk resting.

"Eli, Captain Fitch wants me to take you to the field hospital to get you properly looked at," I said as I helped Eli up on his elbow to get him up on his feet. As he sat there he coughed and hesitated to stand. Eli looked particularly bad today, as his face was gray, while his hands shook as I grabbed his arm below the elbow to help him stand. Samuel Fuller saw me struggling to get Eli to his feet, and came to my aid. Together we got Eli to his feet, and I walked him the hundred yards or so to the field hospital.

As we approached the hospital, it was obvious that the army was in bad shape as on either side of the door, sat men lined up, all sick with one affliction or another. I took Eli right in the door. Once inside, the scene was much worse than could be imagined. The walls were covered with bunks three high and two wide, all full of ailing men whose continuous groans confirmed their suffering. Wherever there was room, men sat on the ground and against the walls. In one corner of the room, where no beds were placed, an examination table was located. There, the doctor was examining the never-ending flow of sick men. He had two ladies with him, but these were not nurses, but the wives or girlfriends of some soldier who followed the army, and were pressed into service assisting the doctor.

There was no modesty as men were stripped almost naked to be examined by the doctor. The doctor himself looked haggard as he certainly had not received much rest himself in days, if not weeks. I made my way to the doctor through the maze of sick men.

"Doctor," I began, "can you look at my friend here?" I pleaded. The doctor didn't even acknowledge my plea as he continued the examination of his current patient.

"Doctor," I began to implore.

"I heard you the first time, soldier," he said without looking up from his current examination. "You have several men ahead of you. Leave him and I'll get to him presently," the doctor stated in a weak tired voice.

"I'll wait," I said as I helped Eli to the nearest space against the wall, and sat him down.

I looked around at the men in the room more closely, and it seemed to me that a number of them would not leave the room alive. Still others looked as if they weren't sick at all, and yet others needed wounds redressed, which indicated to me that they had been engaged at either Germantown or Fort Mercer. I didn't recognize any of them as being at Mud Island Fort with me. Finally, after what seemed to be an hour, the doctor addressed me.

"You there," he stated, "you can bring your friend over."

I helped Eli up, as I put his arm over my shoulder and grabbed his belt around his waist. I half walked, and half carried Eli to the table.

"Now what is the problem here?" the doctor inquired.

"About a week before we left Mud Island Fort on the Delaware River, he developed this cough. He is weak, as well as tired, all the time," I informed the doctor.

"Let me see," the doctor said as he began to look at Eli's face and head. He then moved to his arms and shoulders. Lifting up Eli's shirt, the doctor asked him to take several deep breaths, as he listened through an earpiece he placed to Eli's chest. When he was done with that, he went back to Eli's face. He opened Eli's mouth like he was buying a horse. He made some grunts, then took an instrument out of his bag of tools and hit Eli's knee, which jerked involuntarily forward.

"Well, young man," the doctor said to Eli as he poured a liquid out of a flask and into a cup, handing it to Eli, "take a drink of this," he said. The doctor then rummaged through a bag on the examination table, and pulled out a container of large white pills, pouring three onto Eli's hand.

"Swallow down those pills, and have a seat along the wall, or take a bed if you can find one," the doctor stated. "You'll be staying here a while I imagine."

As Eli began to try to swallow the large pills, I asked the doctor, "What is wrong with him?"

"Well," the doctor began, "how long did you say he has had that cough?"

"Since late October, I think," I answered. "I recall it began sometime when we were at Mud Island Fort. Isn't that so, Eli," I said, looking at him as he nodded his head.

"He has pneumonia, probably from being on that Godforsaken island so long without proper food or clothing," the doctor stated. "And I think he has the beginning signs of scurvy, too. I gave him laudanum for the cough, and those pills have a high dose of vitamins in them. They may help, but at the very least he has to stay here for a week or two, to see if we can get him better," the doctor concluded.

I knew what pneumonia was from people being sick up north during the cold winter months, but laudanum and scurvy I'd never heard of.

"Doctor, what are laudanum and scurvy?" I inquired.

"Laudanum is a strong narcotic drug that will take away any discomfort he is feeling, and help him sleep for a while. Scurvy is a disease derived from the lack of good food that can lead to teeth falling out, finger nails falling off, open skin sores and in the worst cases if untreated, death," the doctor replied flatly.

"Is he that bad?" I asked.

"We'll see," was the doctor's response as he turned to his next patient, as I helped Eli to the wall to rest.

"I'll be back with your blanket," I told Eli, as I had to leave him at the hospital, and go see Captain Fitch.

I informed Captain Fitch of Eli's condition when I reported to him. Captain Fitch said he'd look in on Eli, as he handed me a list of seven new men assigned to my unit. I looked it over as I walked back to my hut. There were Moses Rowley, John Lathrop, William Knowlton, Johannes Minkler, Samuel Abbe, and Thomas Bourne. The men were all from our brigade, and I knew most of them or was familiar with their families from Norwich.

In the morning they were to report to my hut, and as a unit we were to report to Captain McLane by General Washington's Headquarters.

The new men reported to my hut in the morning as expected, and we now had a unit that resembled a fighting squad again. I had my epaulet sown on by the quartermaster, and everyone knew of my promotion. After a brief conversation relating to what our duties would be, I told the men what our equipment would consist of. Each man was to carry his musket or rifle, along with a pistol or two if they could be had, a full powder horn, hunting bag, bullet pouch, a knapsack or haversack for extra clothing; a blanket, a plate, spoon, fork, knife, tumbler and a canteen. I sent several men to the horse corral across the Schuylkill River to gather the needed horses for our unit, while the rest of the men went to their huts to gather the needed equipment for our travel.

The rest of us had a quiet breakfast of water and fire cakes. After breakfast, the men had returned with the horses. We mounted, and then slowly made our way toward Washington's headquarters, to locate Captain McLane's men. We traveled a quarter-mile or so, and as we turned a corner a sentry blocking our path halted us. After a brief discussion, the sentry directed us to the field past General Washington's headquarters. As we passed the sentry, I now realized how close the 1st Division was to Washington's headquarters, as the two-story Fieldstone house appeared in front of us, with a steady stream of smoke emitting from the two chimneys. We rode by in silence, as several officers of high rank were seen entering, or exiting the house, all obviously busy with their own duties.

On the other side of Washington's headquarters, we found the camp of the light infantry, commanded by Captain McLane. We dismounted, and I told the men to wait for me as I walked over to the main tent in camp, to locate Captain McLane. I entered the tent, and announced, "Sergeant Waterman of the 4th Connecticut reporting as ordered," as I removed my recently written orders from my breast pocket, making them ready for inspection by any officer in the tent.

A lieutenant approached me taking the paper out of my hand, and looked at it as he walked over to an officer at the only table in the tent. "Captain," he said, "the squad from the Rhode Island Brigade has arrived," handing my orders to the officer. The officer took them, and looked at them without looking up. Finally, Captain McLane looked up at me from his desk. This was the first I had seen of Captain McLane in some time, and he seemed extremely fatigued as he finally addressed me.

"Sergeant," Captain McLane began, "you and your men are greatly needed for the task before us. Unfortunately, many of the other units from the other brigades that have been assigned to assist us are not able to move due to illness, wounds and lack of equipment and food. Take your men back to your camp, and as tomorrow is New Year's Eve, we will not move out until January 2nd. Be here on the 2nd, at ten in the morning ready to move. You're dismissed. And, Sergeant," Captain McLane added, "it is good to see you again."

"Yes, sir," I said as I reached for my orders, and then exited the tent. I told my men of the situation as we mounted our horses and retraced our route past Washington's headquarters, back to our camp along the Schuylkill River. I told the men to be ready to move on the second, as they dispersed to their respective huts to seek warmth, and to prepare for the New Year.

I reported to Captain Fitch the circumstances of our delay, which he said was understandable considering our relatively recent arrival at Valley Forge. I spent the rest of that day, and the next with Eli at the field hospital. He seemed to be in better spirits, even though I thought he didn't look any better from the previous day. The doctor and ladies tending the wounded and sick, came by several times to look at him. They gave him some more laudanum or pills, but never said anything about whether he was improving or not. New Year's came and went without notice by Eli or me as we both slept on New Year's Eve, and long into the next morning.

I left Eli, and the hospital to report to Captain Fitch. I found him along with Colonel Durkee talking over some papers at the officer's hut, near General Varnum's headquarters. Now that I had the rank of sergeant, the sentry no longer challenged my entry.

"Ah, Sergeant," Captain Fitch said as I entered. "It is not surprising Captain McLane had to delay your departure a few days ago," he confirmed. "We have been reviewing our new monthly strength report for December, and the numbers explain it all."

Colonel Durkee spoke up and said, "We currently have 814 men fit for duty out of our full strength of seventeen hundred men. Most of these men are suffering from various illnesses, with the rest recovering from battle wounds. There is already talk of disbanding several units to send the men home for the winter," he concluded.

"All of the other brigades are showing similar strength reports," Captain Fitch added. "All of the commanders are trying to put units together to keep the army running."

"Sir," I began, "we'll be trying to leave again on the morrow with Captain McLane. While I'm gone will you check in on Eli for me, please?" I implored, trying not to show the emotion I was feeling regarding Eli's situation, and not being there for him.

Captain Fitch spoke up without hesitation, "I will look in on him every day, Sergeant, you can be sure of that."

"Thank you, sir," I said.

I was up early the following morning as I made my preparations to depart on our patrol with Captain McLane. I wanted to make sure I left myself enough time to see Eli before we departed. After a quiet breakfast of water and fire cakes, I made my way over to the field hospital. Eli was awake, but not feeling well. I told him of our detail with Captain McLane, and Eli seemed genuinely envious that he was not going with us. I told him not to worry, and that I'd see him when we returned. I felt by then he would be better, and would be going out on the next patrol with us.

"I will see you in a few weeks," I said, as it was time for me to leave, find my men and report to Captain McLane.

When I arrived at my hut, I found my unit saddled, and waiting for me, all nineteen men. I mounted my horse, Chester, and reined him to the left as we headed to Captain McLane's camp. It was one of the coldest mornings of the winter, with a light snow falling.

Upon reaching Captain McLane's camp, all was busy with activity in preparation for departure. There were many more men here than I had believed were going on this patrol, as I estimated we were well over a hundred men from various brigades in the army. Shortly after ten in the morning, we were called to order, and provided our order of march. My company of men was near the rear of our column, behind a similar unit from the 5th Pennsylvania Regiment.

We left camp, making straight for the British lines at Philadelphia. It was said that Captain McLane was looking for a fight, and was going straight at it. We rode hard the rest of the morning, and after several hours of hard riding we stopped for a midday meal, as well as to rest the horses by a meandering stream. Captain McLane sent several riders in each direction to ensure our safety, and to look for the enemy.

A rider came by, and told us to check our flints and powder, as we were near some farms being occupied by the British. We had ridden south by east, and I figured we were somewhere below Philadelphia getting close to the Delaware River. We moved out in two groups shortly after one in the afternoon. Captain McLane led our unit, and a Lieutenant Biltmore from the 2nd Division led the other. We rounded a small hill, and came into sight of several farms in the valley, which had a large creek running through it. The head of the column lead by Captain McLane broke into a trot, then a gallop and then into a full run. We all followed down the road and headlong into the first farm.

As it was the middle of winter, the British soldiers stationed here didn't expect an attack. They scrambled out of the house and farm buildings in shock and disarray. Our men were firing as we rode in, and several of the British soldiers fell to the ground dead or wounded. The few that had tried to organize a defense fled in panic down the road to the next farm. The firing was sharp but brief, as the resistance at this farm crumbled. Several men dismounted and ran into the house, barns and outbuildings, securing them.

About half of our unit continued down the road after the retreating British soldiers, and towards the next farm. Off to my right and a half-mile away, lead by lieutenant Biltmore, our second unit, could be seen coming over a small rise, pushing the British from that side of the valley before them. They were also on a path to intersect our attack some distance down the road toward the farms down the valley. Seeing that this farm was secure, we followed the other charging men down the road.

Each farm we came to fell without much resistance, as the few defenders became overwhelmed by the speed of our assault. Finally, after ten farms were overrun and the British soldiers there were either killed or captured, we halted to take stock of where we were. Our lead forces were now down to thirty men. As the number of men left at each farm reduced our numbers, leaving our force dangerously low. Lieutenant Biltmore rode up with what remained of his command, fifteen men, and reported they had captured five farms.

As we looked down the road, the small farming community of Darby was a half-mile before us. As I looked past the town I could see the Delaware River, and the familiar sight of Mud Island, and what remained of Mud Island Fort. Dotting the Delaware River were the many ships of the British navy. I counted only seven men from my company that was still with me at this time.

Captain McLane looked at the men around him and stated, "The prize lies before us men. If we can capture Darby, if only for a short time, we can seize enough supplies to feed our army for a week, perhaps two. Let's ride," he stated wheeling his horse, and at a full gallop headed toward Darby with forty-five men riding hard behind him.

As we came within musket range of Darby, at a distance of one hundred yards, puffs of smoke could be seen coming from some of the windows of the numerous houses that comprised the town. It became apparent that the British had been preparing for our attack, as word of our push had long ago reached the town from British soldiers who had fled before our onslaught. The reports of the muskets were heard two or three seconds after the puffs of smoke appeared. Once, I even heard the whine of a bullet as a British soldier's fire almost hit its mark. As we rode into the town, the British soldiers ran from their hastily constructed barricades leaving us a clear path into the town. After several brief skirmishes, the few remaining British soldiers surrendered, and the town was ours. The barns in town were full of hay and other badly needed food stores for our army. Immediately, we began loading the wagons in town with as many of the supplies as they could carry, and the horses could pull. Captain McLane sent riders down the road toward Philadelphia to the northeast, as well as the town of Chester to the southwest, to warn us of any British counterattack.

We had loaded five wagons with hay, corn, potatoes, apples and several other kinds of vegetables, and were preparing to leave. Suddenly, the riders that Captain McLane had sent toward Philadelphia to scout the British, came galloping back into the town.

"Captain," the leading horseman, who was a corporal, stated as he reined his horse in. "British dragoons just crossed the bridge over the Schuylkill River, and are heading this way at a strong pace. We have no more than five minutes before they get here."

"You've done well," Captain McLane stated. "We've done our duty here, men. Let's not let the British catch us with our pants down."

With that, the wagons began to move out of town, and up the road we had just moments before, used to come down and attack this town. We waited until the wagons had a good start and then we followed, about a quarter of a mile behind.

We reached the first farm outside of town, and our men there had already started the wagons with their supplies back up the road, and to safety, with several British soldiers in tow as prisoners. This scene was repeated several times as we retraced our route away from Darby and the British lines. The British dragoons that had ridden out of Philadelphia never showed themselves, as they could not know our strength in numbers, and weren't spoiling for a fight.

Finally, we were back at the site of our midday camp, and stock was taken of our attack. Fifteen farms and one town were captured, even if it was only briefly, and a total of twenty wagons of badly needed supplies was confiscated.

All of the confiscated supplies were repacked onto fifteen wagons. Five of our men were assigned to escort the wagons to Valley Forge. We had several men wounded, two of them seriously and one dead, a corporal from a Massachusetts' company. All of my men were accounted for at camp that night.

The following morning we broke camp at nine. Captain McLane had sent out scouts an hour earlier, and several had reported back that there was no British activity in the immediate area. We moved out in two columns, traveling almost due south. We had traveled almost an hour when a halt was called, when one of the scouts returned to address Captain McLane at the head of our column. Word was passed down the line that we were within a mile or so of the town of Chester and that a large farm outside of town was our target. We had to ride over a small rise, and would then be within sight of the farm and town. Reportedly, a number of British warships were anchored in the Delaware River, and were close to the western shore.

We galloped over the rise, and down toward the large farm outside of Chester. As I viewed the farm, I thought it was the largest I had ever seen. It had cultivated fields for a mile in every direction and consisted of a large farmhouse, three large barns and numerous out buildings. As we drew nearer to the farm, we instinctively began to spread out in the fields as we advanced.

We were within a quarter-mile of the farm now, and there was no activity to be seen. It seemed unusually quiet. Suddenly, on the British warships anchored in the Delaware River, puffs of smoke could be seen coming from the sides of the ships, followed several seconds later by the report of the cannons. It was only a second or two later when the shells began exploding in the fields all around us. At the same time, scores of red coated British regulars could be seen flowing out of the farmhouse, as well as the three large barns. They were forming ranks quickly, and as I began to rein in my horse to stop my advance, I saw the front ranks kneel, and level their guns. The commander barked an order, and the thick smoke from the volley fired at us obscured the soldiers in their red uniforms. Several men were seen to fall from their horses across the fields. My mind was racing as I realized we had ridden into a British ambush.

It now appeared that several hundred British regulars had formed ranks, and were either preparing to fire on us again, or were advancing in long lines toward us, their weapons charged, bayonets gleaming in the sun. This, along with the continued bombardment from the ships halted our advance, and sent us on our heels to the small rise we had just come over.

I remembered the bombardment several years earlier by the British when we attacked their men just outside of Boston, and I knew we couldn't sustain our attack. Once I had stopped and turned to begin my retreat, my men instinctively followed. I was looking around to make sure all of my men were with me, when two hundred yards to my left, a shell exploded by a rider who was off by himself sending him sprawling to the ground.

I checked my retreat, and began to cross the open field toward him. The rider himself was not wounded, as he was up and reloading his musket almost as soon as he had hit the ground. His horse was struggling on the ground with her legs and head flailing in all directions. I didn't know this soldier, but I admired his courage even from this distance, as he calmly loaded his musket and fired a single shot at the advancing red line. One British soldier fell, as the entire line halted, leveled their guns and prepared to fire a volley at him. As the British were about to fire their volley, he took cover behind his now dead horse, to shelter himself from the coming onslaught.

As the red line fired, many shots hit the horse or the ground in the area of the horse, as dirt was kicked up before and around the animal, but he remained unscathed. I spurred my horse, as this was my chance to get to him while the British reloaded. He looked around for help and saw me coming to his aid. He ran to meet me, and as we met, I pulled my left foot out of my stirrup, as I offered him my free left hand. Placing his left foot in the stirrup and grabbing my left hand, he swung up onto the rump of my horse, and I spurred him back to a run. By the time the British had reloaded, we were out of range and heading back over the ridge, to safety. Several of my men provided covering fire for us.

We went another half-mile, and were catching up with the rear of our retreating forces when we stopped under a stand of oak trees alongside a small stream. My passenger slid off the back of my horse, and took account to see if he was injured. Finding that he was uninjured, and minus only a few of his belongings, as well as his horse, he looked up at me with a wide smile and bright blue eyes.

"I am Sergeant Keith Brown," he began, "and I am indebted to you my friend, for if you had not intervened, I fear the British would have assuredly captured or perhaps worse, killed me."

"I am glad to be of service, sir," I replied. "I was only doing my duty. When I saw you fall due to that shell exploding near you, I couldn't leave you to the hands of the British."

"As I said," Sergeant Brown stated, "I owe you a great debt," reaching out with his hand to shake mine.

Just then several men were seen riding up, led by Captain McLane. As they reigned in and dismounted, Sergeant Brown began almost immediately relating the story of being saved by me.

"We saw it all from just down the ridge," Captain McLane began. "Who is this young man who saved you from certain capture, Sergeant Brown?"

"I can't say, as he hasn't told me yet, sir," he replied.

"Sergeant Waterman, sir, of the 4th Connecticut," I began. "I was detailed to you last week, sir," I said looking at Captain McLane. "Also, Captain, I was detailed to you during the battle of Germantown last year," I related.

"Yes, now I remember you," Captain McLane said. "Let's be well rid of this place, and count our losses, before we are caught again by these devilish British."

We rode for several miles picking up several units as we went. That night we camped well away from the British lines, by a small town called Indian King Tavern. None of my men were wounded or missing, as they had all pulled up and began to retreat when I had. Word came later that night that we had lost ten men. Two were killed, five were wounded and three were missing, presumed now to be captives of the British army.

We licked our wounds for several days before we moved out again. It had been terribly cold, snowing on and off for several days. When we moved out, we went south by west and eventually turned due south, entering the colony of Delaware. Captain McLane seemed very familiar with this countryside, and moved freely about the land without worry. We found several farms that had been untouched by the war as of yet, still containing a bountiful supply of livestock and harvested stores of food.

All that we could take was confiscated with a promise that the Continental Congress would repay the farmers at a later time. None of them were happy with this confiscation of their property, and many threatened us with harm until we put up a strong show of force, and all backed down. We spent a week and a half in Delaware, and by the time we turned north to head back to Valley Forge, we had approximately fifteen hundred fatted hogs, 500 head of cattle, 200 hundred horses, as well as thirty wagons full of all types of fruits and vegetables.

The trip back was a long slow journey, as the livestock proved hard to control, as well as drive, and with the wagons continually breaking down. After a week of hardships and difficulties, we arrived at the outskirts of Valley Forge. We were the happiest soldiers in the army to turn our supplies over to the quartermaster.

Captain McLane dismissed each company of men under his command to return to their regiments. My men and I were all extremely tired as we made our way to the Rhode Island camp. Valley Forge seemed to be a different camp than it was in just the few weeks since we had left. The men seemed to be in worse condition than ever, with many walking around barely clothed. Some didn't have boots and were wearing cloth wrapped around their feet to try to keep them warm. On our way back to our camp, I saw several men warming themselves around small fires, and it seemed that they were so cold that they didn't realize they were burning their frozen hands.

As we arrived at our camp, several men were detailed to take our horses and see that they were picketed across the now frozen Schuylkill River. I was ready to go to my hut, and sleep for at least a day. I was just entering my hut when I heard my named called by a soldier coming from the area of our officer's hut.

"Sergeant Waterman," he began, "Captain Fitch has requested that you report to his hut as soon as you returned from your detail." The private said nothing more, and turned and walked away from me.

How could it be that after being away for over three weeks, Captain Fitch would need to see me right now? I needed sleep, hot food and a warm bed. That was all. I slowly made my way over to the officers' hut, and entered without being announced. I found both Captain Fitch and Colonel Durkee inside with very stern expressions on their faces.

"Sit down, Will," Captain Fitch said.

I thought to myself that I must be in some kind of trouble for Captain Fitch to address me by my first name, and not my rank.

"We have something to tell you and there is no easy way to do this," he said. "Eli Bingham died last week," he stated in a cold flat voice.

I sat there motionless for what seemed to be an eternity as the weight of what he said sank in. I couldn't move, as tears began to trickle down my cheeks, and my hands began to tremble as I clinched the chair's armrests.

Finally, after several more moments, I started with a whimpering voice, "You must be wrong, it wasn't Eli who died."

"Will," Colonel Durkee began, "we know how close you and Eli were, growing up together as boys back home and everything. The doctor did all that was humanly possible to help him. We all put in what money we had to try to buy him some medicine, but it didn't help," Colonel Durkee stated.

I was now bent over in the chair holding my head in my hands, trying to control my crying and emotions. "What happened?" I asked with a shaking voice through my sobbing.

"About a week after you left with Captain McLane, he took a turn for the worse," Captain Fitch stated in a low voice. "The doctor said the infection became too strong in his body, and that he wasn't fighting it any longer. Then, he was in what the doctor said was a coma like state, kind of a prolonged sleep, and then after about a week of that, he just passed," Captain Fitch concluded.

Colonel Durkee added after a moment of silence, "He wasn't suffering Will, and we checked on him several times a day. He just didn't wake up," Colonel Durkee said as he walked over, putting his hand on my shoulder.

"Where is he?" I asked after several minutes, when I could get my thoughts together.

"General Varnum had Chaplain David performed the ceremony, and the entire 4th Connecticut Regiment was called out, well, those who were able to stand and were fit for duty. We laid him to rest with full honors," Colonel Durkee stated, then hesitated for a moment before he began again. "We buried him down by the river under a large cottonwood tree," he stated. "It didn't seem right to bury him in a mass grave down the road somewhere, where they take all the other dead soldiers."

"I want to go see him," I stated as I stood up, looking from Colonel Durkee to Captain Fitch and back again. They could see that I wasn't going to take no for an answer. They gathered their coats and hats, and the three of us left the officers' hut.

When we walked out of the officers' hut, the wind had such a bite to it that I really hadn't noticed it before. But now, it seemed so cold and unforgiving. We walked past General Varnum's Headquarters without noticing the sentries that came to attention when Colonel Durkee and Captain Fitch passed. We went past redoubt number one and our fortification lines without talking to anyone who was on duty manning the lines. We began down the hill toward the river between the Flatland Ford and where the newly constructed bridge was located.

About halfway between the ford and the bridge were a couple of ancient cottonwood trees that were well over a hundred feet tall. Colonel Durkee and Captain Fitch walked over to the larger of the two trees. There, a few feet from its base was an area where the snow that covered the ground, rose a foot higher than in the rest of the area. It was an unmarked grave. I slowly walked over to where my friend was buried.

Dropping to my knees next to the grave, I began to cry. I briefly felt a hand on my shoulder, but I didn't even look to see if it was Captain Fitch, or Colonel Durkee. As I knelt there, I cried uncontrollably, for how long I didn't know. I couldn't control the sobbing, and as I rocked back and forth on my knees, a deep, guttural, uncontrollable moan came out of my body, as tears streamed down my face and froze as they landed in the snow. I had seen other men cry on the battlefield as I was now crying, as they found loved ones, a son, or brother, or father or a childhood friend dead on the battlefield. I never understood how they could cry so uncontrollably, for so long, with that deep moan coming out of their bodies. Now, I understood their pain and sorrow, so deep it was. How long I was there I didn't know, but I finally realized I was shivering violently from the cold and that it was getting dark. I was alone.

I had to go back to my hut, and as I began to walk back I couldn't control my shivering. It was now snowing hard. I didn't talk to anyone on my way to my hut, although several corporals and privates acknowledged my passing with salutes. I entered my hut, and although several of my men were there, no one said anything to me. I crawled into my bunk, pulled my blanket over me, turned my face toward the wall and cried myself to sleep.

The next morning came and although all of the soldiers in my hut were about their duties for the day, no one bothered to wake me. It was late morning by the time I finally awoke, and I had a terrible hurt in my stomach. I realized I hadn't eaten for over twenty-four hours. I rolled over and looked at the bunk above mine and just stared. Was I dreaming or did Colonel Durkee and Captain Fitch tell me that Eli was dead. It had to be true, but I just couldn't believe it.

I lay there for the longest time just staring, when I realized someone was looking at me from the door of the hut. I looked and saw Samuel Fuller gazing at me, with a forlorn look.

"Will," he began, "do you feel up to going out today?" he asked. "Some of the men were going to go around camp to see how the land lay now that we're back."

"No, I don't feel like it," I said. "I'm going to rest today."

Samuel turned and walked away without saying anything else. We were at the end of January now and the new division strength reports came out. All were seriously down in numbers. The 1st Division was down to seven hundred sixty-two men out of over seventeen hundred men under command. We had twenty-five deaths, fifteen desertions, and twelve were discharged due to their severe wounds or illness. The rest of the men, over eight hundred, were either sick in their huts or at the field hospital. It remained to be cold with heavy snow.

January turned to February and the situation for the army was critical. Not only was half of the army unfit for duty with various sicknesses and wounds, but men were deserting in droves, as others were being discharged because it was not believed that they would ever fully recover from their wounds or illness. There was never enough food now for everyone at camp. The clothing was literally falling off of some soldiers' backs due to rot and some men began to resemble scarecrows. Many soldiers began to refuse to leave their huts for days on end, electing to remain indoors, trying to get warm. Those in the huts began relying on healthy soldiers to bring them food, and clean their toiletries. The stench in many huts was unbearable as soldiers went days, or weeks without trying to bathe or clean themselves. It became a common sight to find soldiers dead, frozen stiff on their bunks.

I took my unit on several other patrols throughout February and into March, but my heart just wasn't in it anymore. I wasn't dealing with the death of Eli well, and we usually returned without any food stores or reports of enemy movements.

By the end of February our brigade was down to six hundred forty-seven men fit for duty. Men kept dying or deserting, and there were not enough men coming in to stem the flow of the men we were losing. The army was bleeding men, and unless something changed, it would die. To make matters worse for me, I now began to walk with a limp. My leg wound reopened and oozed blood and pus daily.

The only brightness for the army came in late February, when a Prussian officer arrived by the name of Baron von Steuben, to begin drilling the army and trying to turn us into a real fighting force.

A Pennsylvania Dutch officer had to be assigned to him to translate, as the Baron only spoke German. Only the Pennsylvania Dutch units were able to understand his commands, the rest of the army had to rely on the translation of the Dutch officer.

February turned to March, and some units in the army began to actually look like a fighting force, as results could be seen with their marching and firing drills.

The army was still in serious condition as the fitness for duty levels fell below a third of those under orders. The Rhode Island Brigade was down to just under four hundred fit for duty. This would be our low point in the winter and the war, for by the end of winter and coming of spring, those who were sick and still alive began to recover, along with the improving weather.

The Baron had such an impact on the army with his strict drilling, discipline, and shooting skills that the army, which would in a few weeks depart Valley Forge, in no way resembled the rag tag army that limped into Valley Forge in December of the previous year. It was felt by many, myself included, that the army leaving Valley Forge could stand up to the might of the British army.

With the warm weather came new recruits, and as well as old recruits who returned to the army after the winter. These were the darkest days the army and I had ever known, and as with the warmer weather, things were beginning to look up.

- CHAPTER 13 -

“Holding the Line at Philadelphia”

Spring 1778

Spring came quickly in southeastern Pennsylvania, as the winter’s cold grip finally gave way. The Continental army was beginning to resemble a real fighting force. With the warmer weather, many units began moving out of Valley Forge, although the official departure from the valley wouldn’t come until the middle of June.

To keep my spirits up with the loss of Eli, Captain Fitch allowed me to remain detailed to Captain McLane, and his unit of light infantrymen to provide information for Washington’s army. Although my leg wound was greatly aggravated by the constant pounding of riding on a horse, my spirits were greatly lifted by not being in the confines of Valley Forge. In addition to my twenty men, Captain McLane had thirty men of his own unit, and an additional ten Oneida Indians who hailed from the Northlands of New York colony, far above the New York Highlands, that I was familiar with.

March turned to April, and we were constantly harassing British patrols as well as the British lines. Captain McLane had more spies in and around Philadelphia than the British had ships anchored in the Delaware River. Captain McLane knew of many British movements before they left the British lines.

On May 6th, word was received that the French government had recognized the independence of the United States. The whole army celebrated in proper fashion and Baron von Steuben prepared a parade. A thirteen-gun salute was given amid the shouts of "Huzzah, long live the King of France," by all that remained in camp.

By the middle of May, the army numbered thirteen thousand men under arms. This was the largest number of men under arms since the campaign in New York, two years earlier.

By May 19th, the Marquis de Lafayette had moved out of Valley Forge with a force of two thousand two hundred men, and was encamped in the area of Barren Hill, just outside of Germantown.

Word reached General Howe, that morning, of the Marquis' position, along with the number of men in his force. Sensing that the Marquis was in an exposed position with a force too small for battle, Howe decided to try to capture the Marquis as a prize of war.

It took all day for General Howe to gather seven thousand men, almost his entire force, to send against the Marquis. As it turned out, on May 19th, my unit was riding with Captain McLane in the area of Germantown, when Captain McLane sensed that the British were up to something.

We rode hard to Three Mile Run, and there saw a massive movement of British soldiers in two columns. Captain McLane sensed that the Marquis was the prize for this evening, and sent his Oneida Indians at breakneck speed to warn the Marquis to make all haste for Maston's Ford over the Schuylkill River. This left us with fifty men to deal with what seemed to be the whole of General Howe's army.

When we caught up with the leading elements of Howe's army, it seemed that it might be too late for the Marquis, and his small Continental force. Sizing up the plans of Howe, Captain McLane looked at me and yelled, "See there, the Marquis is on the hill before the ford. I anticipate he'll feign an attack from the hill, and then fall back to the ford, while Howe is still forming his battle lines. Take your men and menace the lines of the right column closer to the ford, while I'll take my men and menace the left column. When you see the last of the Marquis' men go over the hill to the ford, make all speed along River Road, then turn inland, and we'll rendezvous on Skippack Road just outside of Whitemarsh," he instructed.

I wheeled my horse, riding hard to intercept the British column, followed by my meager unit of twenty men. I thought as we rode, what could we do against such a large force of British regulars. Crossing over several plowed fields, I could see the dust of the approaching column long before we encountered them. Suddenly, from our rear I heard firing, as Captain McLane's men engaged the left wing of the two columns.

Halting my men at a crossroads, I turned, and looked at my men stating, "When the lead element appears down the road, we'll fire one volley, and then reload. If they charge us, we'll retreat down the road, making all haste for Whitemarsh, as I don't want to be cut off by the other British column."

No sooner had I stopped speaking than Samuel Fuller pointed down the road, and yelled, "Dragoons!"

As I wheeled my horse and looked, about thirty dragoons came in sight around the bend in the road, one hundred yards from us, pulling up as they saw we blocked their passing.

"Take aim!" I yelled as the dragoons saw us raise our rifles, and they nervously wheeled their horses looking for the nearest cover.

"Fire!" I yelled as the rifles of my men went off almost in unison. Several dragoons fell from their horses, as others slouched in their saddles with our shots well told. Regaining control of their horses, the remaining dragoons charged us firing their pistols as they came. The whine of bullets passing close to us, let us know that the dragoons were decent marksmen, having almost hit their mark.

My men wheeled their horses, and we made for the River Road and safety. As we rode, I looked for the Marquis' men on the hill, but they were already gone. The firing by Captain McLane's men had already stopped, too. I prayed we weren't too late, and wouldn't be caught ourselves in between the two British columns. An hour later we were just outside of Whitemarsh meeting with Captain McLane, and his men.

"Well done, Sergeant," Captain McLane said. "One of the Oneidas brought me word that the Marquis, along with his men made their escape. The only soldiers the British columns encountered on Barren Hill were each other. I lost one man, killed." He continued, "Did you suffer any losses?"

"None, sir," I replied. "We were fortunate that the British dragoons were poor shots with their pistols from a hundred yards."

Falling back, we left the lines that day, knowing we had thwarted the British in capturing the Marquis de Lafayette, a prize truly coveted by General Howe.

For the rest of May and most of the first two weeks in June, Captain McLane, and his troop of mounted light infantry had been probing the perimeter around Philadelphia. Captain McLane was looking for any weaknesses to exploit, and gathered intelligence from captured British soldiers, as well as from any number of spies in the employ of General Washington, or himself.

Information was learned from captured British soldiers, that by late June, General Clinton, who had replaced General Howe as commander of the British forces in Philadelphia, would be evacuating the city, with the entire British army. While part of the army was to be transported by the British navy to New York City, the majority of the army was to march over land through the New Jersey colony countryside to New York City. Several spies confirmed this information. When General Washington was informed of the anticipated British move, he was said to have looked at his maps, and to order the army to prepare to move the moment the British began to evacuate Philadelphia, "We'll battle them in New Jersey," he declared.

On June 15th, a young woman had slipped through the British lines and found Captain McLane to deliver important information to him. We were at our forward camp enjoying a meager afternoon meal when the officer of the watch brought the girl to Captain McLane's tent. Samuel Fuller and I had the privilege of dining with Captain McLane on this day.

Upon dismissing the officer of the day, Captain McLane looked up from his meal and inquired, "What news do you bring from the enemy lines?"

The young lady was all of sixteen years old. She was wearing a housedress with an apron over the top of it, which was stained with a number of different colors from food being spilled on it. She was about five-feet-seven-inches tall with green eyes and with dark brown hair, which was pulled back tightly into a bun.

She curtsied before Captain McLane, and looked up as she did so to reveal that she was blushing deeply, as both of her cheeks were rosy red. She hesitated to speak as she looked from Captain McLane to Samuel and me, and back to Captain McLane.

Seeing the reason for the hesitation, Captain McLane became impatient and stated, "Come, come, girl, I have put my life in the hands of the men sitting here, you can give me your information before them."

"Yes, sir," she began looking back at Captain McLane. "My father has important intelligence to report to you." She continued, "He will meet you tomorrow morning at daybreak at the horse house near the Rising Sun Tavern," she concluded, again looking from the captain to Samuel and me.

Captain McLane seemed to digest this information without saying anything for several moments as he continued to chew a piece of meat.

Finally, he said, "Why did not your father bring this information himself?"

"My Da was entertaining several British officers when I left, and he said that if he disappeared, they may become suspicious of his absence," she answered.

"Good, good. Well, you've delivered your message," he stated. "Tell your father that I'll be at the tavern at daybreak."

"Sir," she replied as she curtsied and turned to leave without as much as a glance back.

We finished our meals without further talk of her, and then while we were enjoying some local rum after our meal, Captain McLane stated, "What are your plans on the morrow around daybreak, gentlemen?"

I looked at Samuel, who had a smirk on his face, as if he had been waiting for Captain McLane to bring up the subject.

"You know we are at your service, Captain," I said. "What do you propose?"

"Her father once before passed me information that turned out to be rather suspect in its accuracy, and cost me two wounded troopers," Captain McLane began. "I am beginning to think I smell a rat, and that the British want to take one more try at capturing me before they evacuate Philadelphia. If, in fact, the information we have received is true, that they are going to evacuate Philadelphia."

Pulling a map out from under several other charts on his table, he leaned over it, and began laying out a plan, "Here is what I propose….,

Forty-five minutes later, he had drawn up a plan in case this was, in fact, a trap being set by the British.

"Besides," he concluded, "many of my men are away on furlough until late in the day tomorrow, and I'll have need of all of your men."

On the morning of June 16th, at 3:00 am, Captain McLane led out of the camp. He had gathered twenty-five of his men, and along with the twenty under my command, he felt it was a sufficient force for whatever trickery the British may have up their sleeves, if, in fact, this was a trick.

Since the meeting place was outside the British lines, we weren't concerned with discovery until we drew closer. We had several miles to ride, and did so in silence with all of our weaponry wrapped in cloth to keep metal from clanking against metal, and alerting any British patrols that we were in the area.

We rode for forty-five minutes, and then came to a stop outside a small village. Word was passed that this was the town of the Rising Sun Tavern. We were going to wait until about 4:15 am, at which time Captain McLane, Samuel and I would slowly walk our horses into town. The remainder of our men would split into two units, covering the north and west sides of town, looking for any British patrols. Each unit was to conceal themselves as best they could behind the barns and scattered outbuildings on the outskirts of town.

As we came into town, all was quiet. We came to the intersection of the Old York and Frankfort Roads in the center of the small village. Here, Captain McLane left Samuel and me, with instructions to fire a shot if we saw any sign of a British patrol. Just in front of us, a few doors down was the Rising Sun Tavern, and behind that was located the horse house and the secretive meeting place.

Captain McLane began slowly down the road alone, as the clip clop of his mount's hooves on the cobblestone street seemed eerily loud at this hour of the morning. The sign that hung in front of the Rising Sun Tavern squeaked as the slight morning breeze blew against it. I looked around, and to the east; the gray signs of the sun's coming could be seen in the eastern sky. We were just in time. The only noise I heard other than the clip clop of Captain McLane's horse hooves on the cobblestone street, was the crow of a nearby rooster announcing the dawn of another day.

Captain McLane stopped as he reached the alleyway leading down the side of the tavern to the horse house. He looked around as if he expected to see the British upon him, then urged his mount down the alleyway, to his appointed meeting. He had not been out of our site for more than a few moments when Samuel and I were startled by the sound of horses, riding hard, as they were getting closer by the second. Suddenly, fifteen hard riding dragoons were seen riding down the Frankfort Road toward the Rising Sun Tavern.

Samuel and I had to rein in our mounts, as the sudden appearing of the horses and dragoons had unsettled them. Reining them in, I pulled my pistol from my belt, firing a shot at the oncoming dragoons. My shot obviously missed, as in the low sunlight I couldn't be sure of my aim. Samuel fired his pistol in turn, and we were readying our rifles for another shot just as the dragoons reached the alleyway that contained Captain McLane.

Just as the dragoons were about to enter the alleyway, and thus cornering Captain McLane at the horse house, Captain McLane came shooting out headlong into the lead dragoon, knocking him from his mount. With pistol in hand, Captain McLane fired in the face of the nearest dragoon sending him from his horse, sprawling to the ground. Spurring his horse to a full gallop, Captain McLane was heading toward us at full speed. The startled dragoons did not have time to gather themselves to give chase. As Captain McLane reached Samuel and me, he yelled, "To flight boys, or they may have us before we reach safety!"

Samuel and I spun our horses and were riding hard, hot on the heels of Captain McLane's horse, heading down the Old York Road out of town to the west. We cleared the town, and were about a hundred yards further down the road when the dragoons appeared at a full gait after us. The whine of their bullets, followed by the report of their weapons, affirmed that they had not given up the chase.

Suddenly, from a stand of trees next to the last barn outside of town, a volley was delivered into the dragoons that fell several from their saddles. Then the light infantry of Captain McLane's men appeared to further engage the enemy. The remaining dragoons, only a handful now, fled for cover of the town they had just come from. Seeing that Captain McLane, as well as Samuel and I were safe, the mounted light infantry let them go without further harassment.

My men met us, and shortly thereafter, when we were well out of range of the British lines, we rested by a stream to water our horses.

"It was as I suspected," Captain McLane began. "I met my contact but he was acting much too nervous even for him, and as the information he was spewing from his mouth was even dated a month ago, I suspected the British had a patrol in the area. Your warning shots came just in time," he said, looking at Samuel and me. "Another moment and I certainly now would be in the hands of the British. Well, that scoundrel won't ever again have the opportunity to hurt our cause," he related. "I just had time to slit his throat, before I mounted and fled the horse house."

With that, we rode back to camp to rest our tired mounts and our bodies.

The night of June 17th, arrived, and it seemed that the amount of activity going on in Philadelphia was much more than usual. With the last of the evening light fading, Captain McLane decided to gather together as many troopers for a morning patrol along the Schuylkill River, and to come in as close to Philadelphia as was practicable without drawing any enemy fire. We left camp at five in the morning of the eighteenth with almost one hundred twenty troopers. We traveled down to the middle ford, and about half of our force had crossed to the east side of the Schuylkill River, when a halt was called.

We were on the east side of the river with Captain McLane, and could see him talking to a man on a horse that I had not seen before. The man was talking frantically, and pointing toward Philadelphia. This man was apparently one of Captain McLane's many spies that lived in Philadelphia.

When the man was obviously finished providing his information to Captain McLane, he rode hard across the middle ford we had just crossed, heading northwest toward Valley Forge. Captain McLane pulled his spyglass from his inner coat pocket and began surveying Philadelphia in the early morning light. After several moments of survey, he slammed the spyglass closed, and began barking orders.

"All company sergeant's report to me immediately!" he called. "Bring the rest of the troopers across the ford, and make all ready for an attack!" With this said, he moved thirty yards to the left to a small rise that provided a slightly better view of the city. Again, he looked at the city with his spyglass for several more moments, as the company sergeants called for, assembled around him.

For my part, I told Samuel Fuller to remain with the men, and to prepare them for an attack. I rode over to Captain McLane's position, remaining at the back of the sergeants, as all the gathered men were handpicked by Captain McLane from around this very city to fight with him.

Putting away his spyglass, Captain McLane finally addressed the congregated men.

"I have received word from one of my spies that the British have been very busy last night!" he stated emphatically. "They have evacuated Philadelphia under the cover of darkness, and will be completely on the east side of the river shortly! I have sent my contact on to Valley Forge to alert General Washington, and the army of this development! We have before us, an opportunity to attack, and perhaps capture the rear guard that remains on this side of the Delaware River. Prepare your units for an immediate attack!" he shouted.

All of the sergeants began heading back to their companies to prepare. As I turned to go, I heard Captain McLane call for me. "Sergeant Waterman," he called, "I want you and your men up front with me. We've been through so much together these last few weeks, let's have another victory today, eh," he said.

"Sir," I responded as I wheeled my horse to return to my company. Within five minutes, the entire light infantry troop, all one hundred twenty, were moving out. We moved out in two columns, as half the troop commanded by Sergeant Brown, headed into Philadelphia along the Schuylkill River. Captain McLane, leading the other half of troopers, headed down the Skippack Road that led into the heart of Philadelphia.

We headed out at a gallop as Captain McLane felt that if we delayed any longer, we would not catch the rear guard on the west side of the Delaware River. We rode hard as we approached the outskirts of Germantown, and right on through as the British had pulled all of their outlying pickets into the city. Through Germantown and on toward Philadelphia, we rode as the horses began to show the strain of a prolonged hard ride, and my mount, Chester, was well-lathered. We rode hard until we reached the outskirts of Philadelphia, and then Captain McLane slowed our pace to a trot. I supposed that Captain McLane didn't want to run headlong into any British ambush that the rear guard may have planned. We continued unimpeded into the heart of Philadelphia, continuing on Second Street toward the riverfront. The citizens of the city drew toward the sides of the streets as we passed, all looking shocked to see an American patrol entering the city, even before the entire British army was evacuated.

We reached the riverfront and headed down the street toward the main harbor front where most of the commercial ships were docked and from where the British army had been ferrying men, along with supplies across the river. About two hundred yards in front of us were a cluster of fifty British soldiers in rank formation facing us. At the pier to the right of the British soldiers, were three long boats being loaded with the last of the British soldiers.

Captain McLane halted the advance for only a moment, as he surveyed the situation. Then he spurred his horse, followed by the sixty men under his command, as we charged the British rear guard. The loading of the soldiers on the pier renewed with earnest as they saw our charge begin. As for the British soldiers of the rear guard, they prepared to fire a volley at our advance. The front line kneeled as they presented their arms. As we closed to within a hundred yards of the British line the officer to the right of the line brought his sword down, and the front rank fired. Several men in our charge fell from their horses as the British soldiers' fire hit their mark. The smoke of their fire momentarily obscured the red scarlet of the British line. As the second line of British soldiers stepped forward to fire, out of a side street to the soldiers' left poured the second half of Captain McLane's troop, under the command of Sergeant Brown.

The attack from their rear was so unexpected by the British troops, that the entire formation was thrown into chaos, as Sergeant Brown's men began firing at close range into the British troops. Moments later Captain McLane and our command of troopers crashed into the faltering British line, crushing what remained of their resistance.

We then began to take fire from the British soldiers in the long boats at the pier, as the boat at the end of the pier had pulled away, and was making for the eastern shore. Our men along the waterfront dismounted their horses, and began to pour an accurate fire into the still docked long boats. Our fire hit several British soldiers as their resistance faded.

In addition to the remaining rear guard soldiers, we captured two of the long boats at the pier, each holding around twenty-five soldiers. Our cost was ten men killed and seven wounded. Samuel Abbe was the only soldier from my unit who was injured, receiving a shoulder wound that wasn't too serious, if he received proper medical attention. I found Captain McLane at the docks hastily writing a note to General Washington, advising him that Philadelphia was once again in American hands.

I heard someone call, "Will, Will Waterman," and I turned around in my saddle to see my Uncle Jeremiah walking up to me. I dismounted and turned to give my uncle a warm handshake. Looking at each other, I didn't know what to say. Uncle Jeremiah was first to speak.

"An impressive charge, indeed, Will," He said. "How is it that I find you back in Philadelphia," he said, adding, "you'll recall that I brought you to this very spot back in...," he hesitated trying to think what year it was when we had sailed to Philadelphia and met Mr. Franklin.

"It was '74," I said reminding him of the year my Da let me sail with Uncle Jeremiah for the summer. I then asked, "Why are you here?"

"I'm here delivering a load of supplies from the *Whisperer*, of course," he said and turning, looked back up the waterfront pointing, "She's docked right up there. I suppose you didn't have time to notice her in the middle of your charge."

"Yes, you are correct, Uncle," I said. "I have duties to take care of, but I will be by tonight for dinner, as long as Captain McLane doesn't have any special duties for me." I then remounted to help with the moving of prisoners to a safe location, and to await orders. I spoke with Captain McLane about seeing my uncle that night at the docks, and he was more than understanding. I released my men to Samuel Fuller, instructing them to be gathered in the morning, ready for orders.

I arrived at the docks at five in the afternoon to find the *Whisperer* being loaded with crates bound for the next port of call. As I walked up the plank, I saw the familiar faces of Jennings, Billings, Garden, Edwards and Boyle. The other hands, McKiernay and the cabin boy must have been below deck helping with the loading of the cargo. The crew who saw me, waved, and smiled, but they knew they couldn't stop with the work at hand of loading the cargo.

I found Uncle Jeremiah in his cabin looking over some charts. As I knocked on his cabin door, he yelled, "Come." Upon entering the cabin, Uncle Jeremiah was happy to see me, as if he hadn't seen me that morning. We sat down and had a long conversation about what had happened in our lives, as well as the war since we had last seen each other in Providence, when I had met the *Whisperer* to pick up Da.

For my part, I told Uncle Jeremiah of my duty along the Hudson River and in the New York Highlands. I then described my detail to General Washington's Continentals with our battles and skirmishes in and around Philadelphia, the latest of which he had witnessed firsthand that afternoon.

Uncle Jeremiah told me that in addition to delivering legitimate cargoes along the coast, he had also been a privateer along the coast of New Jersey, and around New York Harbor.

"Will," he began, "we've been fairly successful, as we have made a fair amount of money for ourselves in the process. You might want to think about sailing with us when your enlistment is up, and make some money for yourself to make a good start when the war is over. Besides," he continued, "I see that your leg is not healed yet. I'm sure that all of the riding that you've been doing, and lack of proper food has contributed to your wound not healing. Some rest and ocean breezes will do wonders for you."

"I will think on it, Uncle, I promise you," I said. "Now tell me of home," I continued, "is everyone well?"

Uncle Jeremiah couldn't tell me much about back home, as he had not been to his home port of Providence in over a year. He had been sailing in and around the coasts of New Jersey and New York, as a privateer, occasionally running legitimate cargoes to the Carolinas, and Savannah, Georgia.

In fact, this was his first stop in Philadelphia in some time, and he hoped that his ship wouldn't be recognized in these waters as a privateer. He said that when he had heard that the British would be evacuating Philadelphia, he wanted to see them go, so he came up the river to get a cargo, and watch the British depart. We talked late into the night as Jennings, Billing, and Edwards joined us. It was well after midnight when I fell asleep. In the morning, we had a hearty breakfast, and then I had to say my farewell.

As I walked down the plank and off the ship, Uncle Jeremiah called after me, "When your enlistment is up, come find me in Providence. We'll make you some money, so you can marry that sweet young girl that you always mention."

"I will think on it," I promised as I walked back up the waterfront and to my unit.

My unit remained detailed to Captain McLane and his men staying in and around Philadelphia for the next few weeks. General Washington, spoiling for a fight with the British army in retreat, moved his army out of Valley Forge in hopes of catching up with the British before they reached the safety of New York City.

As we patrolled Philadelphia, those loyal to the Crown stayed well clear of us, and at times yelled curses at us from a distance. It was reported that General Clinton evacuated up to three thousand civilians loyal to the Crown on the British navy ships that sailed to New York City.

Those loyal to the American cause were thankful to see us, as many of them had suffered at the hands of the British and those citizens loyal to the Crown while the British occupied the city.

Major General Benedict Arnold was placed in command of Philadelphia, and to the surprise of everyone, he became very friendly with a Miss Shippen. Her family was one of those prominent families of the city, who openly supported the Crown since the war's outbreak, and had entertained both Generals Howe and Clinton, while they occupied Philadelphia.

Captain McLane told me one night over a mug of rum in a local tavern, that he had sent a message to General Washington regarding General Benedict's strange associations in Philadelphia, and questioned his loyalty to our cause.

Captain McLane informed me, as he leaned forward so as to keep any unwanted ears from hearing, that General Washington had sent back, "A strong rebuke for suspecting disloyalty of one of his most trusted generals."

- CHAPTER 14 -

"Hudson River Detail and Winter Quarters at Redding, CT"

1778

We received word of the battle of Monmouth, New Jersey, several days after it took place. It was reported that General Washington himself saved the army from destruction, rallying it to victory, after General Lee had retreated shortly after the engagement with the enemy began. General Washington strongly rebuked General Lee for his actions. General Lee, for his part, protested the rebuke by Washington, demanding a court-martial. General Washington, a man who stood on his principles, obliged General Lee and had him placed under arrest. Six weeks later, a military court found General Lee guilty as charged, suspending him from service.

General Washington, wanting to keep the British army under his eye, sent a large portion of the army that defeated the British at Monmouth to the New York Highlands. General Washington and the Continentals occupied the same ground we had occupied the previous year.

My unit was still in Philadelphia detailed to Captain McLane's light infantry unit. I expected that any day, I would receive orders to head north with my detail to rejoin the Rhode Island Brigade under command of General Putnam, also in the New York Highlands.

I had to admit that my unit had spent so much of the winter, and almost all of the spring on detail to Captain McLane, and his mounted light infantry unit, that I'd lost contact with the 4th Connecticut Regiment.

I was looking forward to seeing both Colonel Durkee and Captain Fitch again.

I received the expected orders a few days later from a runner that General Varnum himself had dispatched. It read that Sergeant Waterman, with the men in his unit, and under his direct command, were to make all haste to rejoin the Rhode Island Brigade, now serving with the Continental army of General Washington in New York colony.

I found most of my men in a pub near our quarters, and directed them to gather their belongings. I informed them that we'd be departing Philadelphia as soon as the next morning. Afterwards, I found Samuel Fuller, now a trusted comrade and friend, directing him to locate the rest of the men and prepare them for travel. I also told him that I had to report to Captain McLane, that we had been ordered north, and were relieved of his command. I also told Samuel that I was going to see Eli one last time, before we traveled north to reunite with the army.

I found Captain McLane at his new headquarters requesting that additional men be assigned to his unit, so that he could continue his harassment of any Tories who were still looking for a fight. It didn't look like he was going to get them, as General Arnold got wind of Captain McLane's complaint against him to General Washington, which caused a significant rift between the two. Having to tell him that I was ordered north would not make his position any easier.

Getting the captain's attention, I handed him the orders I had received, and as he began to read them, I said, "Sir, my unit has been ordered north to rejoin our regiment in the New York Highlands. If you have no objection or immediate need of us, we'll depart in the morning."

Captain McLane looked up from the order, smiling as he stood, and grabbed my right hand, shaking it warmly, as he stated, "Sergeant Waterman, it has been my pleasure to serve with you and your men. If we are ever in the same theatre of war again, I will personally request of General Washington, that you be placed under my command."

"Thank you, sir," I replied. "I would gladly place myself, as well as my unit under your command." I then departed and went to find my men.

That night we were all gathered at an area pub for dinner and a mug of the local rum. As I looked over the faces of the men who had fought with me so admirably, I couldn't help but think of the men we'd lost, at Mud Island Fort, as well as the battle of Germantown. I could still see their faces. My thoughts turned to Eli and the loss of my best friend. Someday, if I survived the war, I would return home and face his family. What would

I say to them to make them understand the loss, and why he had died? I sat there thinking about Eli, as I listened to the men engaged in various conversations around the table. I had a great respect for all of them. The loss of just one of these men, would be a loss almost too great to bear. I made my pardons and went up to my room. I wanted to write to Diane of our movement to the north, and then, I needed to rest.

The next day, I found all of my men ready and waiting for me as I walked in front of our quarters with my horse. I mounted Chester and headed down the road, out of Philadelphia, west, toward Valley Forge.

It took all of the morning to ride to Valley Forge, as we were not hard pressed to get there, or even to New York colony for that matter. Valley Forge looked nothing like it had, just a few months earlier. Everything was green and alive. This was in stark contrast to the cold and death that pervaded the area this past winter. Gone now were most of the soldiers who had lived in such horrid conditions. There was a remnant of the army here, but the hundreds of huts, as well as defensive works and redoubts were largely and strangely empty of soldiers. We made our way into camp and walked our horses among the huts, as there was no one to challenge our passing. For the most part, it seemed eerily silent. We headed to the area of camp that had been designated for the Rhode Island Brigade. I passed my hut, which was now in disrepair and empty. I continued on, walking past the hospital and then redoubt number one. We then headed down to the large cottonwood trees, along the riverbank.

There under the ancient cottonwood tree was a grave with a marker on it. I was speechless as I walked to the grave. On the marker it read:

Eli Bingham
Died January 20, 1778,
Patriot
4th Connecticut Reg.

I didn't know who had placed the marker, but I was more than thankful that Eli was not going to be left in an unmarked grave. I knelt by his grave as my men filled in behind me. I prayed to God, that he welcomed a Christian and brave soldier home. I lingered for a few moments, and then I mounted without saying a word to my unit, crossed the Schuylkill River over Sullivan's Bridge and rode hard, north by east for an hour.

We crossed the Delaware River on Howell's Ferry, and continued northeast into the New Jersey colony. At some towns we passed the residents and kids came out to greet us and offered us food and rest. At others, the residents barely lifted their heads from their work to acknowledge our passing. Thus was the difference between passing through a patriot or Tory town. Such was the divide that remained in the colonies.

We made good time, not being burdened with wagons, baggage and cannons of the regular army. Within a few days we were in northern New Jersey colony, and began to encounter the outer pickets of our army. The pass that General Varnum had written weeks earlier, though faded and torn, gave unquestioned passage through our lines. Inquiries of the sentries we encountered revealed that the British seemed to be content with their quarters in New York City, and our army had just arrived at the New York Highlands.

We headed north, up the west side of the Hudson River, and arrived at the small garrison of Stony Point, just days after the army had arrived. The Rhode Island Brigade was again quartered in the area of Fort Independence, above Peekskill.

General Washington had established his headquarters at the now completed fortifications at West Point. General Knox and his artillery regiment were again headquartered just outside of Newburgh to the north, in New Windsor.

Upon crossing the King's Ferry, we located the Rhode Island Brigade and I dismissed my unit once we located the 4th Connecticut Regiment. I went to report to Captain Fitch.

I found Captain Fitch in his tent, and as usual, he was with Colonel Durkee. They were looking over maps of the area that seemed all too familiar from the preceding year. Standing to attention and saluting, I reported that my unit had returned to the 4th Connecticut as ordered.

"At ease, Sergeant," Captain Fitch stated. He pointed to a chair at the end of the table as he said, "Have a seat. We want to hear of your latest exploits."

I reported to Captain Fitch and Colonel Durkee all that I could remember about the various engagements that I was involved in with Captain McLane and his hard-riding, fast-hitting light infantry unit. Captain Fitch and Colonel Durkee were especially pleased that we were able to capture the rear guard in Philadelphia as the last of the British units were embarking for the east side of the Delaware River.

I then informed them that I had stopped by Valley Forge before heading north, "I saw the marker on Eli's grave," I said. "Who was kind enough to do that?" I inquired.

"That was General Varnum's idea," Colonel Durkee stated. "He knew that the regiment had taken significant losses from the various engagements in and around Philadelphia. He knew that Eli was well liked among the men and he hoped to lift the men's spirit somewhat," he said. "With the hard winter and all, it was something at least," he concluded.

"The general paid for it out of his own money, too," Captain Fitch added.

"If you would, sirs," I began, "please let General Varnum know how grateful I am that the general would be so generous at such a time of hardship to think of Eli and the men."

"We will pass on your sentiments, Sergeant," Colonel Durkee stated. "Now, here is the lay of the land," as he began explaining General Clinton's position in New York City and our positions to the north.

"It seems," he began, "at least for the time being that General Clinton is going to be content to sit in New York City and not come out to fight. General Washington has indicated that as long as we hold the countryside, and have the British bottled up, much like in Boston, eventually we will win without having to engage the enemy in an all out brawl. So it seems, we may have a quiet time of it ourselves," he concluded.

"Sergeant," Captain Fitch interjected, "I imagine that you have not had a real rest in some time. Go, find the 4th, and get some rest for let's say, a week, and then come and find us. We will have need of your dispatch skills again. I also heard tell that a dashing young captain whom General Washington favors has been ordered north, and I believe that your artillery friend…," Captain Fitch hesitated as he searched for Captain Doughty's name.

"Captain Doughty," I stated with a smile.

"Ah, yes, Captain Doughty is currently stationed at West Point. I'm sure you'll want to get reacquainted with him." he added.

"Yes, sir," I said as I was dismissed and found my way to the regiment. As I left, I could only think that Captain McLane had been ordered north. Perhaps this won't be as quiet a stay at the New York Highlands as everyone thinks.

By late July 1778, I began my duties as a dispatch rider for the regiment, and at times for General Putnam.

July quickly turned to August and August to September, as I remained riding dispatch for Colonel Durkee and General Putnam. I had seen or heard nothing of Captain McLane, and wondered if he had really been sent north as I had heard he was going to be.

Mail ran on a more regular basis now that we were in the New England area again, and the only stronghold for the British outside of New York was the city of Newport, on Rhode Island in Narragansett Bay. I wrote my family and Diane regularly now, receiving a letter almost weekly from one of them in return. All were in good spirits and healthy, and Da wrote that a bumper crop of corn and potatoes were expected this year. All was well with Diane and her family, and all asked when I would be on leave to return home again. It wasn't thought that leave would be granted until winter set in, and the Hudson River froze so that the British would not venture out of New York City.

Then, in early September, word came that we had attempted to take Newport, Rhode Island from the British. Major General Sullivan was in command, with a combined force of ten thousand men, consisting of three thousand Continentals and seven thousand militiamen. A French expeditionary force of soldiers and the French navy numbering four thousand were to coordinate an attack on the British garrison of three thousand men. The British garrison was under the command of Sir Robert Pigot, at Newport.

After embarking their French soldiers on Conanicut Island, across from Newport on Rhode Island, the French Admiral d'Estaing, upon sighting a fleet of English ships at the mouth of Narragansett Bay, sailed to attack the weaker English fleet. General Sullivan could only watch as the two fleets sailed over the horizon, and out of sight. Believing that Admiral d'Estaing would return in good order, General Sullivan began building siege trenches before the defenses of Newport.

When d'Estaing did return on August 20th, he reported that both fleets had been battered at sea by a storm before they could engage in a general action, and that he was sailing to Boston to refit his fleet. General Sullivan pleaded with him not to go, for without the fleet to bombard Newport from the water, he did not think he could take the city. Admiral d'Estaing sailed for Boston, taking with him the four thousand French soldiers.

When the French fleet sailed for Boston, most of the militia became disheartened with the thought of assaulting Newport without the French, and also left. Without the French to support him, and with his army down to around five thousand men, General Sullivan began to withdraw up Rhode Island, to the north, toward Howland's Ferry. Upon seeing the Americans withdraw, the British commander, Sir Pigot, came out of Newport and attacked General Sullivan's rear positions. Colonels John

Laurens and Henry Livingston were driven from their positions. The next day, the British were halted at Butts Hill, when General John Glover's Massachusetts' militia directed several heavy volleys at them. The rest of the day the Americans held off the British during several sharp engagements. That night, the army evacuated Rhode Island across Howland's Ferry to Tiverton, and safety.

As we heard of the reports, and details of the battle at Newport, it seemed to be another defeat for our army. No one said much about it. We weren't leaving the New York Highlands, and it seemed that the British were more than content for the time being, to remain in New York City.

Fall was coming on fast now, as the trees in the New York Highlands began to show the bright hues of red, yellow and auburn that marked the beginning of the change of seasons. Winter was just around the corner. I'm sure that more than a few commanders, as well as the men, were wondering if this winter would be as devastating as the previous one at Valley Forge.

In early October, I was called to Colonel Durkee's quarters, and ordered to see General Putnam at Peekskill for dispatches to be sent to General Washington at West Point. This was to be followed up with dispatches for General Knox at New Windsor.

I found Samuel Fuller at our camp with a number of men, who had been in our unit that had ridden together under Captain McLane. All seemed to be in good spirits, considering what we had been through in the last year. Most were jealous that Samuel and I were still riding dispatch, while they remained bored, and got fat on guard duty in and around Fort Independence. I wondered what was worse for an army. There was the boredom of camp and inactivity on one side, and the cold reality of battle and death with the enemy on the other.

As Samuel and I rode out of camp, I explained to him where our dispatch riding was going to take us. I told him that when we got to New Windsor, we needed to stop by a tavern there. I had someone to talk to about Eli.

We crossed the river at the King's Ferry after getting our dispatches from General Putnam's orderly, and headed north up the west side of the river. Nothing seemed to have changed from a year ago, when Eli and I were riding these very same roads delivering dispatches. It seemed almost eerie to me to be engaged again in dispatch riding on these very same routes.

We passed Forts Clinton and Montgomery without incident, approaching West Point by late afternoon. We passed the picket lines and the numerous sentries, who would only occasionally challenge us. We entered the works at West Point and headed towards General Washington's headquarters. As always, General Washington's aide-de-camp, Lieutenant Colonel Hamilton, greeted us and was as friendly as ever. Upon delivering our dispatches, I inquired if General Washington had any dispatches for General Knox, as we were heading to New Windsor in the morning.

"I will check and see if we have any dispatches for General Knox," he began. "But in the meantime, gentlemen, after you have fed and bedded your mounts, I request that you come to my tent for dinner tonight, as a special request of mine," the lieutenant colonel stated.

I was strangely tired this day, but thought the request by General Washington's aide-de-camp could not be ignored, and so stated that we would be there at seven.

The evening darkness fell early in late September in the New York Highlands, as the sun dipped below the high mountaintops, and the shadows quickly engulfed West Point. When we arrived at seven in the evening, it was already dark. As we approached Lieutenant Colonel Hamilton's large tent, we could hear the voices of men talking inside. Instead of just entering unannounced, Samuel and I stopped outside as I announced our arrival.

"Enter, gentlemen," responded Lieutenant Colonel Hamilton upon hearing my voice. I held the tent flap open for Samuel to enter, following after him. Upon entering, I found Lieutenant Colonel Hamilton seated at his dinner table with two familiar men. There, seated with Lieutenant Colonel Hamilton were Captains McLane and Doughty. Warm handshakes and greetings were exchanged by men who were not only friends, but had a deeper connection as comrades, who had fought, bled and shed tears on the same battlefields. The distinction of rank was almost totally forgotten during such times of gaiety. We were seated and provided with one of the best meals I had had since I had joined the army, of fresh venison, potatoes and carrots, all washed down with local rum that warmed the stomach.

After dinner we were enjoying a festive mug when I inquired of Lieutenant Colonel Hamilton as to our future.

"Colonel," I began, "we have been here for some time without engagement with the enemy. When will we again face the British?" I asked.

Lieutenant Colonel Hamilton looked at Captain McLane and stated, "Captain, you are correct that this young sergeant has a hunger for battle." Captain McLane lifted his mug of rum in a silent toast, and acknowledgement to Lieutenant Colonel Hamilton.

Then, looking at me, Lieutenant Colonel Hamilton stated, "I have it on good authority that we will begin winter quarters without seeing any British soldiers this far north. I also believe, that some of the units may be released to return home during the winter for a couple of months," he stated.

"Home!" I exclaimed in unbelief.

"Yes," Lieutenant Colonel Hamilton stated, and then added, "I believe for you it is a small town in eastern Connecticut, is it not, Sergeant Waterman?"

"It is, indeed, sir," I replied.

"And how long has it been since you've seen home, Sergeant?" Lieutenant Colonel Hamilton asked.

"I think it has been over a year," I said, and then thinking about it further, I stated, "maybe a year and a half."

"I believe," Lieutenant Colonel Hamilton began, "that the general wants to avoid another Valley Forge. That would be best served by sending a significant number of units home to spend the winter with their families. They could perhaps recruit some more men, while only retaining a small force here, sufficient to watch the British in New York City. At the very least, as I understand it, the 2nd and 4th Connecticut Regiments will be quartered in and around Redding, Connecticut, for most of the winter."

I didn't say anything at the end of this statement by Lieutenant Colonel Hamilton, but pondered the thought of going home and seeing Diane, as well as my family.

"Of course," Lieutenant Colonel Hamilton interjected, "talk of this will not leave this tent."

At this Captain McLane stated, "I'm sure that come spring, we'll have our fill of red coats again, Will."

"I hope so," I responded in a quiet tone.

Suddenly, without warning, as my back was to the tent flap, Lieutenant Colonel Hamilton stood and was saluting as he said, "Sir, you are welcome," he began, "I didn't know you would be calling on us this evening."

The commanding voice came from over my shoulder and stated, "Alex, I thought I would walk around in the cool fall air, hearing voices coming from your tent, I thought I'd investigate."

"You are welcome, sir," Lieutenant Colonel Hamilton stated again as I stood, turned and found myself standing before General Washington himself. Samuel, was now standing, as we were both stiff as a board and saluting, staring at the general. The general returned our salutes and asked, "Who have we here, gentlemen?" as his gaze fell upon Samuel and me.

"Sir," Lieutenant Colonel Hamilton stated, "this is Sergeant Waterman and Corporal Fuller, two of the 4th Connecticut, Rhode Island Brigade."

"You are stationed down by Peekskill and Fort Independence, are you not?" the general inquired, looking from Samuel to me. Neither of us spoke and Lieutenant Colonel Hamilton broke in.

"Sir, as you may recall, these two have been riding dispatch since we have been detailed here in the New York Highlands again," Lieutenant Colonel Hamilton interjected.

"And, if I may add," Captain McLane stated, "were detailed to me during the battle of Germantown, during our winter at Valley Forge, and during our siege of Philadelphia. They have distinguished themselves in several engagements, sir."

"Well," General Washington stated, again looking to Samuel and me.

"If I may be allowed to speak," Captain Doughty spoke up. "They were also engaged at the battle of Long Island, and were part of the heroic defense of Mud Island Fort in the Delaware River."

Looking at us, General Washington then stated, "Were you not also at the siege of Boston? I believe I recall your face," he said, looking at me.

"We were, sir," I stated flatly, still standing at attention.

"Well then, I must shake the hands of two patriots," he responded, holding out his hand toward us, "As I know, you have fought well, and suffered much if you have been so engaged the last few years. I hold it an honor to meet such fine young men as you, for it is truly men such as yourselves, who make up the core of this army, which will one day win this war."

"You are welcome to share our meager rum this evening, General, if you are so inclined," Lieutenant Colonel Hamilton added.

"Thank you, Alex, but I am so enjoying the cool evening air of the New England fall, that I believe I'll continue my rounds," the general replied.

General Washington made his excuses, and left us to our evening's enjoyments. I was stunned that General Washington would consider us heroes of the war.

As we resumed our conversation, I realized I could hear the raised voices of numerous gatherings such as ours in Lieutenant Colonel Hamilton's tent around the West Point camp, as the fair weather allowed the voices to carry great distances on this evening.

Somewhere out in a distant camp, perhaps on Constitution Island, I thought, a group of men began to sing a familiar old church hymn, by Wesley, as I recalled. Their voices were in unison, and their song resonated up and down the Hudson Valley, serenading all within its sound. How it reminded me of home!

The next morning, Samuel and I were up early and headed north to New Windsor and the headquarters of General Knox. We rode in silence as I pondered our previous night. "Patriots" the general had called us. What was a patriot? Was I a patriot? It read patriot on Eli's grave marker. General Washington referred to us as patriots, but was it true. What was I fighting for? Was I fighting for the cause of the American colonies - to be free of British rule? I had to admit to myself that I had grown to enjoy the thrill and dangers of battle, as well as being recognized by various officers of the army. Was I just in this war for what I could gain? I didn't mention any of my thoughts to Samuel as we continued on in silence.

We delivered our dispatches to General Knox without incident and began our return to Fort Independence. We left New Windsor by a different route, as I wanted to pass the Highland Inn and see Eli's friend, Rebecca.

It was the middle of the afternoon when we arrived, and since we hadn't had food since the morning meal, we stopped in. We found a corner table, seating ourselves without notice. Then, after several moments, the maid came out of the kitchen area with two mugs in her hand. She placed them on the table without looking at us as she said, "Will you be eating today, gentlemen?"

It was Rebecca, but she seemed older somehow.

"Rebecca," I said as she looked at me when I said her name, "it's me, Will Waterman, Eli's friend."

"Will," she replied, "I heard that the Rhode Island Brigade was back in the area. Is Eli with you?" she asked, looking from me to Samuel and back to me again.

I stood as I drew closer to her as I related, "I'm sorry I have to tell you this, but Eli died last winter at Valley Forge."

Rebecca just looked at me as the gravity of this news sank in. She didn't move and just stared, as I grabbed her arms to draw her to me to give her a hug, yet she tried to pull away. I held on and as I did, she began to cry. She sank into my arms as tears flowed down her face. I held her for several minutes as she sobbed, and then she took her apron, wiped her eyes and sat down at our table.

Finally, as she composed herself she revealed, "I knew something was wrong, when I stopped getting letters from him. He wrote me often, you know."

"No, I didn't know," I said, as I was surprised to hear that Eli had kept that from me.

"What happened?" she asked wiping fresh tears from her face.

I recounted to her what happened at Mud Island Fort and how during the siege, Eli developed a cough. Then, while in winter quarters at Valley Forge, without proper food or clothing, his body couldn't fight off the sickness and he died. Rebecca excused herself and disappeared into the kitchen.

Several minutes later Rebecca brought us our meal, which we ate in silence. It was apparent that she had continued to cry while she was in the kitchen, and out of our view. When our meal was over, we left our coin on the table for our meal. As we walked to the door, Rebecca was waiting on new customers who had come in. I stopped at the door, waiting for her to acknowledge me. She finally looked up from her customers, and I held my hand in the air, to say "goodbye." She looked at me, and then held her hand in the air towards mine for a moment, and dropped it. I bent my head to her in acknowledgement and left. I would see her no more.

With the turning of the earth, fall turned to winter and just as Lieutenant Colonel Hamilton had said, many of the units in the army were allowed extended leave to return home for the winter months. In part, to relieve the burden of supplies for the army during the cold months, and in part to avoid a second Valley Forge. This was a great relief to many of the men, as a large number of them had not seen their families in well over a year, in some cases more than two.

Orders were received that the 2nd and 4th Connecticut were two of the units that were going to winter quarters in Connecticut. I immediately posted a letter to Diane. In it, I told her to tell my folks, I'd be home, hopefully for Christmas. On December 11, 1778, the 4th Connecticut Regiment of the Rhode Island Brigade of the 1st Division headed to Redding, Connecticut, outside of Danbury. After several days' march we crossed the New York frontier and into Connecticut colony. Winter camp was quickly made.

In addition to the 2nd and 4th Connecticut, we found that several other units had already been ordered to this area for winter quarters. There was General Poor's 2nd New Hampshire Brigade, Colonel Moses Hazen's Infantry Corp, a rifle unit of two hundred Canadians and Major Elisha Sheldon's 5th Regiment of Connecticut Light Horse militia consisting of several hundred mounted troops. Major Sheldon's Cavalry Corps was used mainly to patrol the area from the British lines in New York, eastward along the sound. General Putnam chose for his headquarters, a farmhouse situated at the intersection of the Norwalk and Danbury Roads, about three miles west of the Redding Congregational Church.

I had an opportunity to take stock of the condition of the various units quartered in the Reading area, as compared to a year ago when we arrived at Valley Forge. It was clear to me that just as a year ago, the men were not fed and poorly clothed for a winter in New England. Worse yet, if any of them had been paid at all, it was in Continental bills, which, for the most part, weren't worth the paper they had been printed on. The Continental bills were worthless, as Congress had no money to back them with. The saying around the camp upon receiving a Continental bill for service in the army was that, "It's not worth a Continental."

Captain Fitch gave me orders to take my unit and return to Norwich, Connecticut, for a period of time not to exceed two months, from the day of our arrival. On December 14, 1778, my unit of twenty men headed for home. We arrived on the outskirts of town on December 18th, and there I gave orders that all were to reassemble on February 11th, of the next year, to return to duty with the Rhode Island Brigade. Having dismissed the men, each rode their own direction toward home. I rode to Diane's house in town, as I could not go home without first seeing her. As I turned the corner past Durkee's Tavern, I could see a group of people gathered in front of the Gallagher house. As I drew closer, I could see Diane and her family, as well as mine.

When they recognized that I was approaching, they all broke into a run toward me. I halted Chester, stepping from the saddle just as they got to me. I was overwhelmed with hugs, kisses, and slaps on my back from the two families. There wasn't a dry eye among us as we were all over taken with emotions and crying. Diane had tears flowing from her big brown eyes, as she kissed and hugged me. Finally, after several minutes of emotional elation, we all turned and headed for the Gallagher house. My brother, John, took Chester's reins from me, and said he'd take care of him. Rachel took my haversack and blanket, while Da took my gun and possible bag. Both John and Rachel had grown so since I'd seen them last. Ma was crying and holding my left hand, Diane had my right. Pastor and Mrs. Gallagher led the way to their house. A meal was already cooking and was almost done when we entered the Gallagher house. Mrs. Gallagher, my mother and Rachel brought the meal to the table in short order and then Pastor Gallagher prayed.

"Our father in heaven," he began, "we thank you, Lord, for bringing young Will home from the war to us. You know it is the answer to many of our prayers and a blessing beyond measure. We pray, father for your protection on his life and that you will keep him from harm. Now, father, we thank you for the food prepared, bless our bodies with it, in the name of the Son we pray, Amen."

Without question, I had the fullest meal I had had in a long, long time. Everyone had questions for me about where I'd been and what I'd seen. Then finally, my brother, John, asked, "Will, is war as bad as they say it is?"

The table became strangely silent. I paused as I looked from face to face, as each was looking at me, and finally I came to my Da. Looking into his deep blue eyes, I said, "It is as bad as they say it is, and all the more and worse, John." I looked away from Da as Mrs. Gallagher brought some tea from the kitchen for us and general conversation began to spring up around the table again.

We went home that night, and the farm I had grown up on had changed, and yet remained much the same. The next day, after breakfast, I asked Da to go with me to the Bingham's. Before we left, Da spoke to me about the letter Colonel Durkee had posted.

"Will," Da began, "the Bingham's took it hard when they received the letter from Colonel Durkee about Eli's death. The letter didn't say much, other than he'd been engaged in several battles and died as a result of them. I'm sure they will have some questions for you."

"I understand," I said as we headed for the Bingham farm.

We found the family gathered in the great room of their house having family devotions. All was silent as Da and I entered in the room, and were seated at the table.

Finally, Mr. Bingham stated, "Will, it is good to see you home and well. Tell us, what Colonel Durkee's letter didn't tell us, tell us how Eli died."

I began with the heroic defense of Mud Island Fort on Mud Island and how we all suffered greatly. I explained that we were fortunate that any of us survived the battle. I told the Bingham's how Eli had developed a cough during the siege. I described to them how we were then marched to Valley Forge for winter quarters, that the army had no winter clothes, and no food for such a large standing army. I told the Bingham's that I took Eli to the field hospital to be looked after, and that while I was out on patrol looking for food for the army, he died. I told them of the marker on Eli's grave. There wasn't a dry eye in the house as the Bingham's heard how their son had died alone, in a cold makeshift hospital in the Pennsylvania countryside. They thanked me and there wasn't any reason for us to stay longer, so Da and I left and began our walk home.

About halfway there, Da stopped and said to me, "Never tell your mother or Diane how bad it really is, Will. It would be the death of them if they truly understood the suffering you've been through," he said as we continued walking home.

Christmas came and went, and December turned to January. It was a cold, snowy winter and I was thankful not to be quartered at Valley Forge or the New York Highlands for that matter. During my time home, I rested and saw many residents of Norwich I had not seen in some time. Several times I had occasion to go and see Doctor Post. At first he seemed surprised to see me, as upon my entering his office, he looked up over his glasses and said, "Still alive are we, Will Waterman. What brings you to see me," he said as if he didn't know of my leg wound.

I told him that my leg wound still caused me great pain and if I rode for several days without much rest, the wound would reopen and ooze blood and pus as it had when I'd first seen him regarding the wound.

"Drop your pants," was his matter of fact response. I complied with his request as he had me lay down on his examination table. After several minutes of poking the leg muscle around the wound and looking at the wound with his magnifying glass, he went to his bag of doctoring tools and pulled out a small but very sharp knife, a scalpel he called it. He made a quick and small cut in my skin that hardly hurt, just where the bullet had entered my leg. It immediately began to bleed and ooze pus again.

"It is just as I said," he began. "The wound will not heal properly without proper food and rest. As long as you continue to ride about the countryside with that rebel army, this wound will not heal, and may yet be the cause of your death, young man." He seemed sincerely angry with me. "It may be best that you learn how to make a small cut just here," he said, pointing to the spot of his incision, "to allow the wound to bleed, drain and try to clean itself out and someday heal." Having finished his examination, Doctor Post quickly bandaged my leg.

I thanked Doctor Post and told him I would see him again before I returned to the army, to which he just shook his head.

In late January, an unexpected knock at our door, brought dispiriting news. Riders were sent throughout New England to recall the units that were on leave. The 2nd Connecticut Regiment and even parts of the 4th, were talking of mutiny and mass desertion, in order to march on Hartford, to demand of the Assembly, a redress of grievances. I instructed the dispatch rider to ride for Samuel Fuller's house and then on to Mark Fowler's. I charged him to direct Samuel and Mark to spread the word for all in my unit to gather west of town.

I began to gather equipment, as Da and John went to saddle Chester. Mother and Rachel hastily put together some food in a bag for me and within a half-hour, I was saying my goodbyes to my family and heading for town. I knew I had to stop and see Diane.

I told Diane the news I had received regarding the soldiers quartered in the Redding area, and that I was recalled along with my men to help quell the unrest. The Gallagher's understood and Diane cried as I kissed and hugged her and told her I'd write. I wheeled Chester and headed out of town. I crossed the bridge over the Thames River and there on the rise a half-mile away I could see a group of men. There, I found Samuel Fuller, Nathan Smith, William Bradford, Joseph and Dayton Birchard, John Fuller, Sean Reed, John Gallagher, John Edgerington, and John Lathrop.

"Samuel," I said, looking at my trusted friend, "you wait here for the rest of the men, and then ride hard for Redding. If everyone isn't here by late this afternoon, leave without them, and head for Redding at all speed. They'll have to figure we couldn't wait, and they'll have to come on their own."

Looking at the men before me, I stated, "I assume you've heard that there may be a rebellion at Redding with the 2nd Connecticut, and maybe even among the 4th. We are riding to help quell this discontent within our army. We'll ride hard until we reach Redding and see how the land lies once we get there."

With that said, I turn my horse to ride for Redding yelling over my shoulder to Samuel, "Come on hard when you've gathered the rest of our men."

We rode hard, only resting the horses for food and water. After two days we were approaching Redding. Not knowing what to expect, I rode to where I knew Captain Fitch's quarters to be. As we entered camp all seemed to be in order. I told my men to dismount and wait for me outside of Captain Fitch's tent.

"Sergeant Waterman," Captain Fitch began, "have a seat here and I'll give you the lay of the land. First, though, did all of your men return with you?" he asked.

"Only half, sir, as I wanted to get here as soon as possible. Samuel Fuller is to bring the rest and they will probably be here in the morning," I stated.

"That is well enough," Captain Fitch replied. "It seems that some men in the 2nd Connecticut who became discontented with camp life in the winter, and who probably remember all too well the miseries of Valley Forge, have sown discontent; not only in the 2nd Connecticut, but also in several companies in the 4th. General Putnam intends to address the troops within the next day or so, but he wanted to call in most of Sheldon's 5th Light Horse militia before doing so. In addition to the 4th Connecticut, and Hazen's militia, we can count on Poor's 2nd New Hampshire to quell any unrest. Go and make camp with your men, and be ready to move at a moment's notice if needed," he concluded.

"Yes, sir," I said and returned to my men, and our camp with the 4th Connecticut. The rest of that day, as well as the next, were mainly quiet, although I did hear men in the 4th, over the next day or two continue to grumble about the conditions in camp, including the lack of proper winter clothing and food. I mentioned this to Captain Fitch later that day when I saw him. Captain Fitch said he understood, and that special requests had been made to General Washington to address the problems at the Redding winter quarters.

As expected, Samuel Fuller arrived the next morning with the remainder of our unit. I took time that afternoon to bring my men the latest information regarding the discord with the 2nd Connecticut.

Two days after we had arrived back at camp, all men under arms were called to order and general assembly. The 2nd Connecticut was positioned at the center of the field, with Sheldon's Light Horse militia and Hazen's militia behind them and the 4th Connecticut on either flank. General Poor's 2nd New Hampshire was in front of the 2nd Connecticut, with General Putnam.

General Putnam spoke loudly and clearly. "My brave lads, where are you going? Do you intend to desert your officers, and invite the enemy to follow you into the country? For whose cause have you been fighting and suffering so long in? Is it not your own? Have you no property, no parents, wives, or children? You have behaved like men so far; the entire world is full of your praise, and posterity will stand astonished at your deeds, but not if you spoil it all at the last. Don't you consider how much the country is distressed by the war, and that your officers have not been better aided than yourselves? But we all expect better times, and that the country will do us ample justice. Let us all stand by one another, then, and fight it out like brave soldiers. Think what a shame it would be for Connecticut men to run away from their officers."[2]

---

2 Lossing, Benson J. "Lossing's Field Book of the Revolution, Vol 1., Chapter XVIII." Freepages.History.Rootsweb.Com. http://freepages.history.rootsweb.com/~wcarr1/lossing1/chap18.html (03-09-2008), page 9.

At the conclusion of General Putnam's speech, a loud cheer burst from the discontented regiments, and they returned to their quarters in good humor, resolved to suffer and fight still longer in the cause of liberty.

At the conclusion of this crisis, Captain Fitch ordered me to his tent. "Sergeant," he began, "since all is in order here again, Major Sheldon's Light Horse Infantry is short on men since several of his companies were dispersed to their homes and were not recalled in time to help quell the unrest with the 2nd. You will find Captain Watson at General Putnam's headquarters. Report to him with your company for a special assignment and detail," Captain Fitch stated.

"Yes, sir," I said and asked, "how long will this detail last, sir?"

"I would anticipate that you will be assigned to Major Sheldon's Light Horse Infantry until we return to the New York Highland, once spring comes upon us," he replied.

With these new orders, I left Captain Fitch's tent and returned to the 4th Connecticut camp, to prepare my unit to depart in the morning for General Putnam's headquarters.

In the morning, we reported to Captain Watson, who had on hand only ten men. Captain Watson stated that half of the 2nd Connecticut Light Horse was currently on leave at their homes, and the rest were already on detail patrolling the area between the British lines in New York colony all the way to West Greenwich.

January quickly turned to February, which found us on patrol with various elements of Major Sheldon's Light Horse. The winter was cold, snowy and hard now with supplies trickling in from the New York Highlands, as well as the surrounding Connecticut countryside. There was never enough food or warm clothing for the men relegated to remain at camp, and I pondered on how I could understand why the men would mutiny under such conditions. Surely, if they had, the officers would have had some understanding and compassion regarding their desperate state.

March came upon us and with it a touch of spring, and the anticipation of returning to the New York Highlands, along with better living and camp conditions.

By late March, with the warmer weather, General Putnam wished to check the area west of Norwalk toward the British lines and departed camp with Captain Watson's ten men, along with my twenty-man unit as protection and security against any British excursions out of their front line fortifications.

March 24th, 1779, found us in the area of West Greenwich, at the home of the late General Ebenezer Mead. General Putnam wanted to visit the late general's widow to see that all was well with her.

On the morning of March 26th, while shaving, General Putnam observed a column of redcoats marching up the road from the westward. Dropping his razor, General Putnam grabbed his sword, and ran from the house, shouting to us, "To arms, to arms, the redcoats are upon us." All mounted with their arms at the ready and moved forward to challenge the British column of fifteen hundred men.

It was now known that Governor Tryon, who commanded the British lines to the westward, in West Chester County, near Kings Bridge, had moved eastward the previous evening with British regulars, dragoons and Hessians. Governor Tyron was intent on surprising our troops, and destroying the salt works at Horse Neck Landing.

General Putnam ordered our thirty man scout unit under the command of Captain Watson, forward to check the enemies' forward movement, while other units in the area were called up. We engaged the enemy with several small skirmishes, before retreating to Sawpits on the Byram River, and then retreated further to Horse Neck Landing, being pursued hotly by the enemy.

Reinforcements of around one hundred fifty men, along with two cannons, moved forward and positioned themselves on the brow of a hill commanding the approach of the redcoats.

There was an exchange of volleys with the British, and General Putnam realized that several detachments of regulars were about to break off the column, in an attempt to gain our flanks. At the same time British dragoons were preparing to charge.

General Putnam ordered another volley to be fired at the still advancing British, along with a shot from the cannons, and then ordered a retreat. The British were now so close to our soldiers, that the front of the British column ran into our retreating men, and the retreat became a rout. Our men ran in every direction looking for safety and most found it in the nearby swamps. General Putnam spurred his horse and headed for Stamford with only three light horses with him, being pursued by fifteen dragoons.

Riding to Captain Watson's side, I pointed to the retreating general and yelled, "If those dragoons reach General Putnam, we'll all hang for his capture or death!"

"Bring your men!" Captain Watson shouted as he wheeled his horse, and spurring him to a full gallop, was promptly in pursuit of the dragoons, chasing General Putnam.

I still had half of my company with me and followed Captain Watson, as we pursued both General Putnam and the pursuing British dragoons. We rode at breakneck speed, as it was clearly seen that the British dragoons were closing the distance between themselves and their quarry. Seeing that the dragoons were catching him, General Putnam left the road and went down a steep embankment to safety. The dragoons did not follow down the steep embankment, but chose to fire several shots at the rapidly departing general. They didn't see us coming up upon them until it was too late. Closing the distance, several men fired their weapons, felling several dragoons from their mounts. The rest, seeing that they were in jeopardy of being cut off from the main column, beat a hasty retreat with us close behind them. Our men fired several more shots, and two more dragoons fell to the ground. We were now drawing uncomfortably close to the British column, and broke off our pursuit of the remaining dragoons.

"Sergeant," Captain Watson called to me, "gather up as many of our men as you can and head for Stamford. I'll try to catch the general, to let him know the danger has passed."

I did as Captain Watson had ordered, and soon had most of the men who were not killed, wounded or still hiding in the swamps, heading east to Stamford. I counted seventy-six men still able to bear arms. We found out later that we had sixteen killed, and twenty-five wounded. The rest of our men were either captured by the British, or were missing, and had not made it back to our lines yet. Among the dead was one of my men, Moses Rowley.

The British were content with their rout of us, and did not follow us in our retreat to Stamford, Connecticut colony.

Later that day, I found Captain Watson outside of a farmhouse that currently housed General Putnam. The general, for his part, was recomposing himself from such a near miss of being captured or killed by the British, before we headed north to our encampment.

Upon seeing me, Captain Watson stated, "Sergeant, we certainly earned our pay today. I wish to thank you for intervening for the general. Surely, the redcoats would have run him down had he not gone down that steep embankment, and had we not broken up the dragoons chasing him," he stated.

"We were only doing our duty, Captain," I replied. "If I have the captain's permission, I'd like to return to camp, as I have one dead from today's engagement. I wish to bury him properly and report to Captain Fitch."

"As you wish, Sergeant," he stated. "The general also sends his regards for your actions in today's battle. I hope we have occasion to ride and fight together again," Captain Watson added.

It was a silent ride back to camp, as everyone was dealing with yet another death in our company. I reported to Captain Fitch of the day's battle when we returned to camp and requested to bury Moses Rowley with full honors at dusk. Captain Fitch granted my request, as the entire 4th Connecticut Regiment was called out for the interment. At the conclusion, Captain Fitch requested I report to his tent the next morning.

Upon reporting, Captain Fitch had several items to address with me. "Sergeant," he began, "you will probably be glad to hear that by the first of April, we will break winter camp, as we have been ordered back to the New York Highlands. Word has reached us that the British column sacked the salt works at Horse Neck Landing, plundered most of the houses in town and surrounding area and burned most to the ground. They captured all of the residents of the town that are loyal to our cause, sailed them across the sound to Long Island and probably imprisoned them somewhere closer to New York City. And finally," he concluded, "I have read Captain Watson's report regarding this action and he, as well as General Putnam speaks highly of you and your men."

"Yes, sir. Thank you, sir," I said as I was dismissed. As I walked back to my camp, the only thing I could think of was that I had lost another man.

Before the week's end, we broke winter camp to begin our march back to the New York Highlands.

- CHAPTER 15 -

"Stony Point, Paulus Hook, Detachment of Horse and Winter Camp at Morristown"

Spring 1779 to Spring 1780

The army broke winter camp the first week in April. The 2nd and 4th Connecticut Regiments were the first units at the Redding camp to begin their march to the New York Frontier, and the New York Highlands. It seemed that, as during the previous year, the two armies were going to be content with staring at each other from their protected positions in the New York colony. The British remained in New York City, patrolling the land as far north as West Chester County, while our army settled into the comforts and familiar surroundings of the New York Highlands. The 4th Connecticut reoccupied the now very familiar surroundings of Peekskill and Fort Independence.

Spring in the New York Highlands had to be one of the most beautiful places on earth. The trees were alive with color as the leaves burst through the new buds, along with all of the flowers, and other plant life that exploded with new life. After the harsh, cold winter in Redding, Connecticut colony, the warm ocean air that spilled up the Hudson River Valley that warmed us was a welcome relief.

As we were to discover, the British Commander, Lieutenant General Sir Henry Clinton had other ideas. On the first of May, in a daring attack, the British with eight thousand men, stormed the rocky outcrop of Stony Point, taking our small outpost by surprise. Our army was taken aback with an attack so close to our stronghold in the highlands. With the taking of Stony Point, King's Ferry was in enemy hands, giving them access to Verplanck's Point, Peekskill, and the east side of the Hudson River.

At first, it seemed a forlorn hope to retake Stony Point, as the British left behind seven hundred men, which included elements of the 17th Regiment under Lieutenant Colonel Johnson. These units immediately began fortifying the area. A grenadier company of the 71st Highland Regiment, which also reportedly included nine cannons, four mortars and one howitzer, reinforced them. Stony Point was surrounded by water on three sides and at high tide the low area of land, connecting Stony Point to the mainland, flooded. The rocky outcrop of land rose sharply one hundred and fifty feet to a rocky crest where the British built several redoubts. Additionally, a Royal navy gunboat, the schooner HMS *Vulture,* now patrolled that part of the Hudson River, and was assigned to protect the river approaches to the fortifications.

General Washington himself reconnoitered the British position, devising a plan for the retaking of Stony Point. It was said that he personally gathered intelligence from local merchants to determine the strength of the British garrison, obtaining the types of passwords used, as well as the locations of the sentries. General Washington discovered a flaw in the defenses on the south side of the works. The British engineers had built abatis fifty yards out into the river, in order to prevent attack along a narrow beach at the base of the point, but it was discovered that during low tide, men could wade around the end of the abatis.[3]

General Washington's plan called for a relatively small, specially trained group of soldiers to storm Stony Point in a three prong attack at night, with bayonets only to avoid any possibility of an accidental discharge, thus alerting the enemy of the coming attack. General Washington put General Wayne in command of the attack. He changed Washington's plan only slightly. General Wayne wanted the middle attacking column under the command of Major Murfree to have loaded weapons, and once they reached the first defensive position of the British stronghold, to engage the British in a smart fire. This was to be a diversionary tactic, to draw the British defenders away from the two attacking columns on the British right and left.

Captain Fitch ordered me to gather my unit, and to report to Captain McLane at West Point for a special assignment.

There were many rocky outcrops and steep cliffs in the area of West Point that were similar to the rocky slopes of Stony Point. Gathered were one thousand men, who were selected from the brigades and regiments in the New York Highlands. We were to be the specially trained group to attack Stony Point.

Training began immediately and in earnest. It mostly consisted of finding the quickest way up steep, rocky outcrops, by following the man in front of you. Several routes were picked during each training session, and as when the real attack would come, we formed what resembled a human snake climbing up the rock face.

First, the climbing on the rock face was done without guns, possible bags, powder horns or rucksacks. After several days of climbing and innumerable scrapes, cuts and bruises on our extremities, which resulted in only two serious injuries consisting of a broken leg and collarbone, we began climbing the cliffs with our equipment. Besides falling and receiving a serious injury, falling rocks loosened by the men climbing above you as they scrambled up the rock face, were the biggest worry.

On June 30th, Captain McLane asked me to accompany him on a special assignment to Stony Point. Before we left West Point, Captain McLane produced some rough-looking backwoods attire of frayed hunting shirts and leggings. "Will," he said, "we need to change into these clothes as we need to be outside of Stony Point by midday."

---

3 Battle of Stony Point, Wikipedia, The free encyclopedia. http://en.wikipedia.org/wiki/battle_of_stony_point Pages 1 and 2.

We left West Point on horseback and rode the five miles or so to Stony Point with some speed, and without stopping. On the way, Captain McLane explained to me that we were going to enter Stony Point with a Mrs. Smith, whose sons as it turned out, were working inside the garrison at Stony Point. Just as we came through the Dunderberg Mountain Pass, we met an older lady who seemed quite familiar with Captain McLane.

"Mrs. Smith," he began, "how are you on this fine day?"

"Very well, Captain," she replied, "and who is this young lad you've brought with you?"

"Let me introduce you to my good friend and fellow soldier, Sergeant William Waterman of the 4th Connecticut, Continental Line of the American army."

Looking at me with an all-seeing eye, after several moments she stated, "That's an awful formal introduction for such a young man. He looks too young to be a sergeant."

"He has well earned his rank, I assure you, Mrs. Smith," Captain McLane replied.

"Well, let's get on with it," she stated, "it's all been arranged. I'm supposed to deliver some food to my sons, as I am escorted by their uncle." Looking at me she stated, "You'll have to be their cousin."

We wasted little time and went straight to it. Mrs. Smith continued on toward Stony Point on her wagon, as we followed close behind on our horses. We went down the road and crossed the low swampy area that flooded during high tide. We could see the fortifications now and there were several sentries outside the works where the road cut through them. As we approached, a sergeant stepped forward to challenge us. "What business do you have here," he demanded looking from Mrs. Smith to Captain McLane to me and back to Mrs. Smith.

"I'm here to visit my sons and give them some food for their midday meal, Captain, and these two are my escorts, don't you know," she stated.

"I'm am not an officer, Ma'am, and why do you need these two for escorts?" he inquired.

"Well, with all the Tories and rebels running about the countryside, these days, especially after you and your'n just took this rock by might the other week, well it just ain't safe for a lady to be about by herself," Mrs. Smith retorted.

"You'll find your sons up top working on the fortifications," the sergeant stated looking at Mrs. Smith. "You two can wait here for her, she'll be back shortly," the sergeant stated with a stern look at Captain McLane and me.

I had never been so nervous in all my life, as being so close to the enemy, and not planning on doing anything about it. Captain McLane was just himself as he stepped out of the saddle. He sat down next to the sentry post and pulled out his pipe, put some tobacco in it, and began to smoke. There were no less than ten British soldiers at this sentry post, all of whom would love to capture an officer as well known as Captain McLane. My heart was pounding in my chest, and I dared not look in the eyes of these soldiers, as I thought it would betray me as to who I truly was.

After several moments, a British captain who seemed to be preoccupied with inspecting the fortifications in the area of the sentry post, calmly walked over to Captain McLane, stating, "Well, Captain, what do you think of our fortress?" he asked. "Is it strong enough to keep Mister Washington out?"

Captain McLane, keeping his senses about him stated, "I know nothing of these matters. I am but a woodsman and can only use my rifle. But I would guess that General Washington, general, mind you, not mister, would be likely to think a bit before he would run his head against such works as these. Trust me; we are not such dolts as to attempt impossibilities."[4]

The British officer, puffed up by this response and superiority, resumed his inspection of the defenses. Mrs. Smith returned shortly from her visit with her sons, and thereafter we quit the fort.

Upon our return to West Point, Captain McLane reported to General Washington that the fort was not half as formidable as it looked, and that his keen eye noted that the entrenchments connecting the batteries hadn't been completed. Captain McLane had worked out an approach route by which an attacking force might come quite close without being observed.

Captain McLane's report brought General Washington to the scene for another personal reconnaissance, protected by the cavalry of Captain McLane and Major Lee.

After the reconnaissance by General Washington, the night of July 15th, was chosen for the attack. My unit was under the command of Captain McLane and we both were under the command of Colonel Richard Butler with three hundred men on the left flank. In the center was

4 Allen McLane, Unknown Hero of the American Revolution. American Heritage. Com, American Heritage Magazine. http://americanheritage.com/articles/magazine/ah1956/61956_6_74.shtml, page 4.

Major Hardy Murfree with one hundred and fifty men, as on the right in overall command was General Anthony Wayne with seven hundred men.

On July 14th, we left the safety of West Point and were marched down to Forts Montgomery and Clinton, just two miles above Stony Point. A restful day and night was spent on the 14th, at Fort Clinton. On the morning of July 15th, we were marched to Doodletown.

Although we were given the remainder of the day to rest, there was no rest to be gained; as we all knew that come evening we would engage the enemy in a daring night attack without our weapons loaded. While at Doodletown, and with much time on my hands and mind, the thought came to me that I hadn't been in a battle with the British in over six months. My heart was pounding like it was going to burst out of my chest at the idea of being in battle again. I briefly looked around at my men near me. The long look of coming battle was on everyone's face.

We were all ordered to gather by four in the afternoon. We formed columns for the march through the Dunderberg Mountain pass to our forward posts. All civilians encountered during our march were held to prevent them from warning the British. Our three columns rendezvoused at a farm just a mile from the fortifications. We were given a rum ration and our orders. All were given a white piece of paper to pin to our tri-corns in order to distinguish us from the British in the darkness. Our column under Colonel Butler was last in line, with Major Murfree in the middle and General Wayne's column leading, as they had to take up a position on the far right.

I went through my men's gear making sure all weapons were unloaded and all other equipment was properly wrapped in cloth to prevent unnecessary clanging of metal. As I looked about, I saw all the company commanders were busy doing the same. Captain McLane's men were before us in our column.

Even the night's weather was in our favor as the moon was obscured by a heavy cloud cover, and high winds forced the British ships at Haverstraw Bay to leave their posts off Stony Point, and move down river.

We moved out smartly and within the hour we were approaching our front lines. Care was taken to halt our advance in the woods before we reached our front lines as not to alert the British that our force was in the area. Word was passed to remain at the ready until dark, and then we'd move forward into our lines shortly after dark. All of us hated this kind of waiting the most. Down time before battle with nothing to occupy us, as the time past interminably slowly and our minds brought up what could happen in the coming engagement. Men checked and rechecked their equipment. Some lay down to rest while others played card games. All had a quiet meal of smoked meat with water to wash it down. Captain McLane came over to me several times to make small talk, and I believed him to be as nervous as a new recruit before an attack.

Captain McLane did pass along one piece of information to me, regarding latest intelligence on the defenses at Stony Point. "It appears," he stated, "that we will have to storm three defensive lines. There is an outer works that faces us directly. Once we get over that there will be a second defensive work, and finally, when we get past that, there are at least three redoubts and an inner fortification to be taken. We have our work cut out for us," he said as he shook my hand before returning to his men. Finally, as dusk began to overtake the area, we were ordered again to form columns. We moved forward and into our front lines as most of our defenders had been removed to make room for us. When it was totally dark, we moved forward from our lines in three columns.

Captain McLane found me again and pulled me aside, "Will," he began, "stay close to me, and I'll make sure our two units are in the same attacking group."

"Yes, Captain," I said.

"If this attack goes well, it will be a great success," he said. "But if it goes badly, and we don't make it up the steep hill to the top, it could cost us all our lives or certainly capture. At least we know we can count on each other during this attack."

We were all in place before midnight on July 15th, and moved forward. Before General Wayne's and our column, was a group of twenty ax men to chop holes in the British abatis.

The column of Major Murfree, along with our column under Colonel Butler made good progress without coming under fire from the British.

Major Murfree's men began their fire on the British center in hopes of drawing defenders to their diversionary tactic.

Our column reached the rocky slope leading up to the British stronghold. We began scurrying up the slope as quietly and quickly as we could, trying not to draw the attention of the British sentries, who had to be on high alert by now. I could hear chopping as our ax men were trying to punch holes in the abatis. This immediately drew British fire, and we all surged forward to reach the British lines.

The muzzle flash of the British cannons firing on Major Murfree's men lit up the night sky enough for the British to see General Wayne's column moving upon their defenses on the right, but it was too late to move the cannons.

The fire continued to our right as Major Murfree's men continued to draw British fire. The firing of the British before us lit up the dark night, as momentarily I could see where the enemy was, and how far I had to go. As the firing continued on us, I could see that some of our men had reached the top, and were fighting bayonet to bayonet and hand to hand with the enemy. As our men reached the top, they began yelling as they engaged the enemy; bringing yells from all of us, encouraging us forward. Finally, out of breath and bloodied by scrambling up the rock face in the dark, I reached the first defensive works. The British defenders were already being pushed back toward the second defensive line, by our men. There were a number of dead and wounded British soldiers littering the ground inside the first defensive line. To my right a group of twenty British soldiers was trying to surrender to the onslaught of attackers, who continued to swarm over the defensive works!

In the darkness we surged forward as one human mass, pushing the remaining defenders before us, towards the second defensive works. This defensive work was more heavily defended. A smart fire came from the works as the men at the front of our attack were beginning to reach this line. Several men were seen to fall, being shot at close range by the defenders; as yet others could be seen scrambling over the top, engaging the enemy.

I reached the second defensive works and scrambled to the top. Within the works there was a mêlée of men fighting for control of this ground. The defenders, who had time, reloaded their guns in an effort to fire point blank at their attackers. Our men fought for their lives with thrusts of their bayonets, the butts of their guns and with their hands. There were many more defenders here, but they too were overwhelmed by our attack, and they began to fall back to the inner fortifications and redoubts.

I came upon a British soldier on top of one of our men, trying to choke him with his rifle. I bayoneted him in the back and moved forward, as he screamed, rolling to the ground, writhing in pain.

To our right, two hundred yards away, the sky was lit up with the firing from the redoubt as the defenders tried to put up a defense, while being overwhelmed by General Wayne's surging forces.

In front of us, many defenders lay dead or wounded with scores surrendering before our charge. Only the inner fortification remained to be taken now. A glance to my right confirmed that the redoubt had fallen, and General Wayne's men were surging toward the inner fortifications from the south.

The leading men from Colonel Butler's attack had now reached the inner fortifications from the west, and the defenders' resistance was crumbling.

We stormed up the rocky slope and into the British works only moments after the right column. A wild melee ensued in which the British garrison was overwhelmed, forcing it to surrender. We had taken back Stony Point in only thirty minutes. The British lost sixty-three killed, seventy wounded and over five hundred captured. Our losses were fifteen killed, and eighty wounded, including General Wayne. After the attack, when the Stony Point perimeter was secure, we were relieved and returned to our forward lines.

I saw Captain McLane the next day after the attack, back at camp inside of our lines.

"Sergeant," he questioned, "how did you and your men fare during last night's attack?"

"Captain," I replied. "We were fortunate in that only one of my men received a slight wound to his arm during the attack. It seems," I continued, "that our attacking column met less resistance than the men under the command of General Wayne himself."

"Where are you off to now, Sergeant?" he asked.

"I return to my regiment on the morrow," I said. "And what of you Captain?" I questioned. "What of your next assignment?"

"My life is my with my general, and wherever he orders me to go, I'll go," Captain McLane stated.

"Well, until we meet, and fight together again," I said as I held out my hand, which he took warmly, with a broad smile on his face.

My departure from Captain McLane would be short-lived as the success of the night attack on Stony Point inspired Major Henry Lee to attempt a similar attack on Paulus Hook on the New Jersey colony shore of the Hudson River, across from New York City.

I was enjoying a quiet August afternoon at camp after spending the morning on guard duty at Fort Independence, when I saw a familiar face approaching me on horseback. I stood to meet the oncoming rider as he reached my tent.

"Captain McLane," I stated. "To what honor do I owe the pleasure of your presence in the camp of the 4th Connecticut?"

Captain McLane dismounted without answering my inquiry and only smiled, offering his hand to me, which I gladly took. He took a seat next to me by my tent and looked around without saying anything for a few moments.

"I have requested that you and your company of men accompany me on another venture to capture another British stronghold."

"I would have to be relieved of my duties here before I could be engaged in such a venture again, Captain," I stated flatly.

"I took the liberty of stopping by Captain Fitch's quarters before I came to see you," he replied. "It seems that Captain Fitch believes that you are quite bored on guard duty at Fort Independence, and thus has released you into my command, along with your company."

"I am indebted to you, Captain, as another week here on guard duty may be the death of me," I said with a wry smile on my face.

"Here is the lay of the land," Captain McLane stated, as he began to explain, in general terms, the plan of Major Lee to take the British fortifications at Paulus Hook. After half an hour of providing the detail of the plan, Captain McLane stated, "What do you think?"

"I think, Captain, that it sounds strangely similar to the attack on Stony Point from last month," I answered.

"Yes," Captain McLane said. "But even so, the British will never think that we will try the same basic attack plan twice, and particularly not so close to their stronghold of New York City. Besides," he continued, "Major Lee is using only three hundred handpicked men, most of whom took part in the attack on Stony Point. And I have already personally conducted a reconnaissance of the defensive works at Paulus Hook, and I can attest that with three hundred handpicked men, we will be successful. We also captured a deserter last week, and we have obtained from this British soldier, the precise information about the plan of the fort, as well as the strength of the garrison."

"This being the 13th of August," he continued, "I will meet you and your men in two days on the west side of the river at King's Ferry. That will give you time to get your men and equipment together for the ride south. We are to meet Major Lee and the rest of the men who will be in the attack with us at a town in New Jersey colony called Paramus. Once we're there, the final attack plans will be made, and the men will be divided into three companies. We will move immediately forward, and will attack on the night of the nineteenth." He added, "Of course you and your men will be in the same company as my men."

"I will see you on the morning of the fifteenth on the west side of the Hudson River at King's Ferry, Captain," I said, holding out my hand as Captain McLane shook it, and then returned to his mount.

"Till the fifteenth, then," he said as he turned and rode out of camp.

I met with Captain Fitch on the 14th, to confirm my detail with Captain McLane. Just as I was about to leave, Captain Fitch stopped me, to provide me with a list of the new soldiers that were assigned to my unit.

"Sergeant," Captain Fitch began, "since the death of Moses Rowley during your engagement with the enemy at Horse Neck Landing, I have had several requests from some soldiers to join your company of men. To give some men additional exposure to the special tactics you employ when engaged with the enemy, I am increasing your company command from twenty to a twenty-five man unit. Therefore, the following men, all of whom are from the Norwich area, will be assigned to your company. You will have Isaac Addison, William Bond, Isaac Bigalow, John Blakemore, Daniel Raymond and William Copp. They have all been given orders to report to you on the morrow. As I understand it, you will be crossing the King's Ferry to join Captain McLane's men, and then move into New Jersey colony for the attack on Paulus Hook."

"Yes, sir, I will," I replied.

"These men are inexperienced in the tactics that your company has become accustomed to employing. Take care to instruct them as much as you can, and for their safety, I would make sure they are at the back of the attacking column when you engage the enemy," he advised.

"Yes, I see the wisdom in your advice, sir, and will heed it," I replied.

"Then, Godspeed, Sergeant Waterman, and you can tell me about the success of the attack when you return," he said, saluting and dismissing me.

I returned to my tent to make all ready for the departure in the morning. The six new men assigned to my company met me outside my tent in the morning.

"You men are welcome, and as we have orders to be across the King's Ferry this morning, we will begin immediately," I said. "Once across the ferry, Corporal Fuller will be assigned to give you immediate instructions as to our orders and how we will be deployed. Follow Corporal Fuller's instructions to the letter, otherwise you will find yourself either being killed or captured by the enemy. Is that understood?" I asked.

A smattering of "Yes, sirs," came from the group, and I mounted my horse to lead out. We met the rest of my company of men at the King's Ferry. Once across, we found Captain McLane with one hundred mounted light infantry waiting for us on the west side of the Hudson River. We moved out immediately making good time, riding for most of the day to reach Paramus, New Jersey colony.

Camp was made and on the next day, Monday, the 16th, the men gathered were divided into three groups. Captain McLane and my company of men were under the command of Major Lee on the left wing of the attack. Captain Handy was to lead the center with another hundred men, while Lieutenant McCallister led the right with the final hundred men. On the sixteenth, patrols moved out toward Paulus Hook, capturing two more deserters from the British army, but they were unable to provide any additional information about the fort, than was already known.

On Tuesday, the 17th, two sergeants with twelve men each were sent to lie in the Bergen Woods, to report any movement by the British on Paulus Hook.

Wednesday, the 18th, Major Lee sent another sergeant and twelve men to an area near the Bergen Woods, to intercept any communications between Paulus Hook, and Fort Lee to the north. Our attack was to commence one half-hour after twelve o'clock in the morning on the 19th.

We moved forward, four hundred strong on the 18th, from Paramus to Hackensack, crossing the Hackensack River at New Bridge. Along our route of march, Major Lee dispatched patrols of horse to watch the communications with North River, and Fort Lee, as well as stationing parties of infantry at different roads leading to Paulus Hook. As in the attack on Stony Point, all civilians encountered along our route of march, as well as at the key intersections were detained until after the attack had begun.

At Union Hill, Major Lee led us into the woods where our guides became inexplicably lost, and our march was prolonged three hours until we regained the road. We didn't reach Prior's Mill before Paulus Hook until three in the morning. Due to the lateness of the hour, we all knew the tide would be on the rise. We still had the salt marsh and canals to ford before we could initiate the attack.

Finally, at four o'clock in the morning, three and one half-hours late, all were in place for the attack. We waded into the salt marsh and found the tide was still on the rise. We next encountered the canals, but found them still fordable, and we pushed forward.

As with our attack at Stony Point, the sloshing of three hundred men through the salt marsh alerted the sentries to the coming attack. Also, like Stony Point, the ax men were successful in chopping a path through the abatis. The firing of the British soldiers lit up the night sky, revealing to us the positions of the defenders. We stormed through the fortifications, yelling at the top of our lungs as we charged into the fort. We put fifty of the defenders to the bayonet. There was less resistance from the defenders at Paulus Hook than that which had been encountered at Stony Point.

The fighting was intense, but brief, as we overwhelmed the defenders in less than thirty minutes. We captured one blockhouse, two fortresses and the defenders' barracks, along with one hundred fifty British soldiers, including nine officers.

Our losses were limited to two killed, three wounded and several captured. The British Commander, Major Sutherland, and forty Hessians barricaded themselves in the remaining blockhouse at the southern end of the fortress and refused to surrender.

It was nearly daylight by the time the fortress was secure, and Major Lee found that he couldn't burn the barracks as he had intended, as sick British soldiers, along with sick women and children occupied them.

It was feared that the British in New York City, by now well aware of the attack on Paulus Hook, would have reinforcements in boats, and across the river in short order. The possibility of being cut off from our planned route of retreat became all too real.

We retreated out of Paulus Hook in good order with our one hundred fifty British prisoners in tow. We entered the Bergen Wood and waited as scouts went forward to the Hackensack River, to Dow's Ferry, to see if the boats Major Lee had arranged for, were in fact waiting. Major Lee had planned on crossing the Hackensack River at this point, and by way of the Belleville Turnpike, reaching the high ground east of the Paramus River, then returning to New Bridge. The scouts returned with a distressing report that the boats had been removed to Newark.

We now had to march the fourteen miles to New Bridge by the same route we had come, with ruined ammunition due to the dampness of the salt marsh, with tired men, and encumbered with one hundred fifty prisoners. We all expected to be intercepted, and overtaken by the British reinforcements sent out of New York City. Our brave troops started, undaunted and with the same courage it had taken to storm Paulus Hook, to march the fourteen miles to New Bridge.

At Wee Hock, we encountered Captain Catlett, who came up with fifty men and fresh ammunition to support us. Colonel Ball met us at the Fort Lee Road with another two hundred fresh men. With the help of Captain Catlett, Colonel Ball, as well as their men, we reached New Bridge. We then crossed the Hackensack River at one o'clock in the afternoon on the 19th of August, 1779. Never had rest been so welcome to the men involved in the Paulus Hook attack, as the next week was spent resting from the exertions of the night march, attack and retreat.

We received several reports over the next week that the British were much distressed, as well as annoyed over the attack on Paulus Hook. General Washington was much pleased, highly praising the commanders, and all of the men involved in the attack.

As for me and my men, we were not to return to the New York Highlands and the 4th Connecticut as expected. We remained on detail with Captain McLane and his men, patrolling the North River, an area from Fort Lee to Stony Point on the west side of the Hudson River. We patrolled this area for the next two months, and although we sparred with the British patrols and dragoons encountered, we were not involved in any general engagements with the British during this time. It seemed that they were smarting from our bold successes at taking back Stony Point, and stinging them at Paulus Hook. The intelligence circulating up and down the North River region, was that General Clinton wanted to move the war to the south. All believed that he would depart at some point during the fall, sailing from New York City with the bulk of his army.

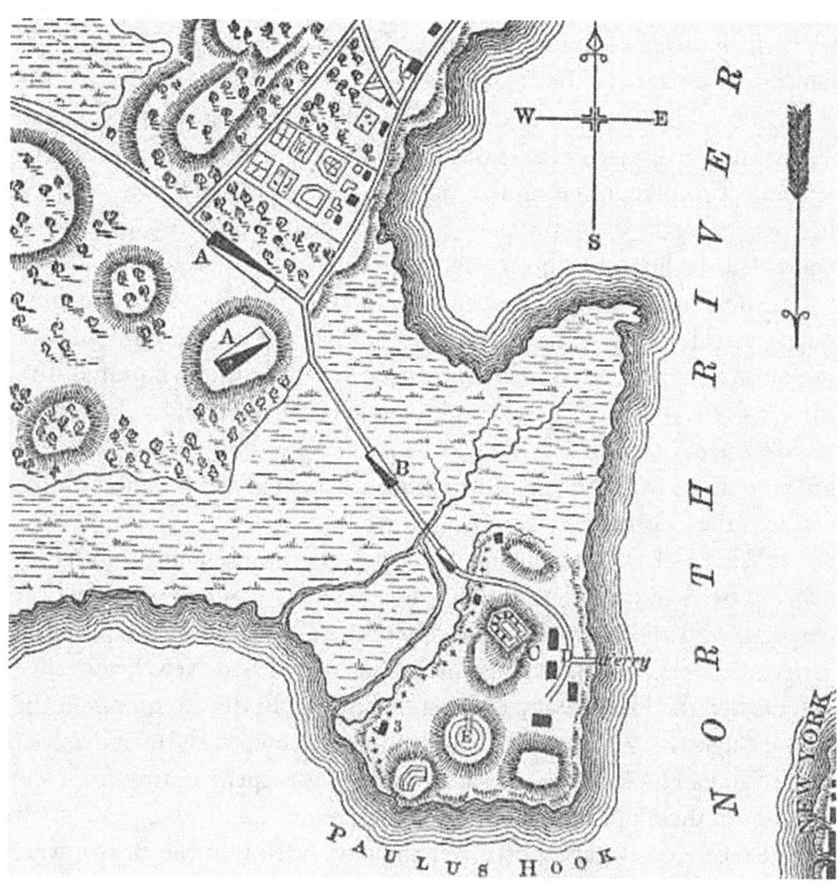

The summer months slipped away and fall was upon us with early cold weather. In early October, rumors circulated that our winter quarters were going to be at Morristown, New Jersey colony. General Washington chose Morristown due to several factors. First of all, was its proximity to New York City, being only a two-day march away, and it gave General Washington's army an eye on the British troops in New York, where we could respond to any British movements. There were a number of roads that intersected at Morristown, which gave our army the freedom to march in any number of directions to counter any British movements. Secondly, in between Morristown and New York City were the Watchung Mountains and the Great Swamp, which gave our army a great deal of security, as it was thought that a surprise attack on our winter camp was impossible. And thirdly, Morristown was also a military supply depot, and it was thought that our army would be able to receive both food and clothing in sufficient supply there.

What no one knew at the time was that the winter of 1779 – 1780, would later be considered the coldest winter in the last one hundred years. On October 17, 1779, the leading elements of our army began arriving and setting up winter quarters outside of the town of Morristown, New Jersey colony.

Immediately, the construction of huts to house all of the soldiers was begun. Those of us who still remained with the army from two years ago, and remembered the suffering of Valley Forge, felt the strange sensation that things were very much the same.

While elements of the army wintered in the New York Highlands to prevent the British army from making any excursions to the north, the main army wintered at Morristown. These units were comprised of the New Jersey Brigade, which included the 1st and 2nd New Jersey Regiments; the 2nd Maryland Brigade; and the 1st and 2nd Pennsylvania Brigades consisting of the 1st, 2nd, 7th and 10th Pennsylvania Regiments and the 3rd, 5th, 6th and 9th Pennsylvania Regiments respectively. Also quartering at Morristown was Brigadier General Edward Hand's Brigade, consisting of the 1st and 2nd Canadian Regiments along with the 4th and 11th Pennsylvania Regiments. Additionally, the 1st and 2nd Connecticut Brigades that included the 3rd, 4th, 6th and 8th Connecticut Regiments, along with the 1st, 2nd, 5th and 7th Connecticut Regiments were quartered at Morristown. Brigadier General Henry Knox arrived with his artillery brigade on November 10th, consisting of the 1st, 2nd, 3rd, and 4th Artillery Regiments and set up his winter quarters just outside of Morristown.

My unit, along with Captain McLane's, arrived at Morristown a week before the Connecticut Brigades and the 4th Connecticut Regiment. Once the 4th, did arrive, I was ordered to Captain Fitch's quarters. He was genuinely glad to see me, as it had been several months now that my unit had been detailed to Captain McLane, and away from the 4th, at the New York Highlands. I provided Captain Fitch with a detailed report of the attack on Paulus Hook, as well as the subsequent patrols in the North River area of the Hudson River. Upon the completion of my report, Captain Fitch stated, "Well, it seems that your unit has been extremely busy, and now it is time for you to rest."

"Sir?" I questioned, not sure what he meant by rest.

"You and your unit have seen more than their share of action during this war. It is my aim to see that, at least for these winter months, you and your men can rest. Besides, if the rumors prove to be true, the British, or at least the lion's share of them, should be sailing for parts south before too long."

"Sir," I explained, "I fear that a winter of inactivity may cause my men to become restless. At least at Valley Forge, we were kept busy, as that took our minds off of being cold and hungry. If we are left to sit around camp for most of the winter, if we lack winter clothing and proper food, I fear it may be too much to bear, sir. I fear another Valley Forge," I concluded, as I looked Captain Fitch in his eyes.

"We have been promised that there should not be a lack of clothing and food this winter, Sergeant," he cajoled. "But in any case, those are the orders for now. You're dismissed."

I walked slowly back to my camp not sure how I was going to tell the men that we were not to be used this winter, and I had to question the reality of receiving proper winter clothing and food.

Almost immediately cold weather set in and it began to snow heavily. If it wasn't snowing, the temperatures were bitterly cold. In addition to the cold, the promised cold weather clothing and sufficient food never materialized! October turned to November, and then to December. For the most part, the army had settled into its winter quarters, even if it were ever so precariously. Many units were already openly voicing their discontent with the lack of proper clothing and food.

Christmas came and everything at the camp appeared to be normal as most soldiers celebrated a quiet Christmas with the singing of songs and playing cards. Then, as the rumors had alluded to, several days after Christmas, dispatch riders brought news that on December 26, 1779, General Henry Clinton sailed out of New York Harbor with eight thousand five hundred men. To transport them, it was reported that it required fourteen warships and ninety transports. They were all destined for the invasion of Charleston, South Carolina colony.

The winter remained brutally cold in the north, with several feet of snow blanketing the ground. The Hudson River and New York Harbor were frozen solid, as supplies were routinely shipped to the British soldiers in New York City by way of sleighs over the ice. Several attempts to attack the remaining British soldiers in New York City were turned back due to the cold.

On January 15th, Major General Sterling, with three thousand men, attempted to attack the British commander in New York, General Wilhelm Von Knyphausen, on Staten Island, and they too were turned back due to the cold.

To make matters worse for the soldiers in camp, which began to sow the seeds of real discontent and eventually mutiny, was that the soldiers saw the officers were regularly well paid, fed and clothed. This, while most sergeants and privates were fed slop, marched in rags, and some without shoes, paid in virtually worthless Continental bills, or not paid at all for several months. Many soldiers were beaten and whipped by officers for the smallest breach of military discipline. What many of the men really wanted was out of the war, as many of the enlistments had expired and many of these soldiers were kept in the army by force, or, as in my case, were due to expire in the spring.

By the time spring began to make itself known, the army had lost one hundred and thirty men, due to illness and cold during the winter. The losses were minimized due to the fact that the army consisted mostly of veterans, many of whom had suffered through the Valley Forge winter quarters, and knew best how to survive the harsh winter conditions of Morristown.

By the spring of 1780, eleven deserters were captured and sentenced to death. At the last minute, a reprieve was given to ten of them, as the eleventh, the one who had forged discharge papers for over one hundred men, was hanged. The seeds of discontent still simmered and a few weeks later, a few hundred soldiers from the New Jersey Brigade mutinied. General Washington ordered the ringleaders shot. General Washington ordered a squad from a New Jersey Regiment to carry out the execution. The squad openly wept as they carried out the execution, and shot their comrades. Following the executions, the units gathered to witness the executions were dismissed. Most of these men were veterans who had fought in several, if not numerous campaigns. They had experienced some of the bitterest fighting of the war, and survived the harshest of winter conditions and suffering. They had survived the worst that the American army, as well as the British army could throw at them. As I watched these men stream by my position, I was stunned to see so many hardened veterans outright crying and sobbing as children. For the first time in almost six years of war, I thought the army was broken.

After the executions, I called my unit together, as I knew that several of them were openly advocating mutiny and desertion. We met around my campfire one evening after our meal. As the embers of my fire began to die down and the smoke from my fire streamed straight up into the cold evening sky, I looked around at the faces of the men looking back at me. Missing were Eli and the others who had lost their lives in places like Germantown, and Mud Island Fort and other battles from the Pennsylvania to New York colonies. They all looked tired and too thin for young men who should be in their prime of life.

"I know that it has been an extremely cold and hard winter," I began, "and that we were not given the food, clothing or pay that was promised to us at the beginning of this winter quarters. But I must ask all of you to remain in camp, even if the rest of the 4th deserts, as is rumored they are going to do. We have endured the hardships of battle, and the loss of friends, and the depravity of several winters on the campaign," I stated. "We are close to seeing this war to its end, and even some of you have remained through the term of your enlistment and have survived. Unbelievably, what most men cannot endure, we have endured and more remarkably, moved forward. To throw all that away now, to me, would make all of the sacrifices meaningless. I will not do that to the memory of Eli Bingham, and the others who have sacrificed all," I promised emphatically.

No one said anything when I was finished, but many of the men grumbled and all left my camp except Samuel Fuller, and returned to their camps.

"What do you think?" I asked Samuel, breaking the silence between us.

"I think some will remain loyal to the cause." He paused pensively and then began, "If the 4th rebels, at least half of them will go. They've already made up their minds, Will."

"Will," he continued after another moment, "they have been through so much and I don't really blame them," he stated. We sat there for almost an hour watching the fire die down, and then Samuel left without saying a word. I wondered how many would go with the 4th.

Then on May 25th, without warning the 4th and 6th Connecticut

Regiments conducted an armed march through the camp and demanded immediate payment of salary, which was overdue to some soldiers by five months, along with full rations. I watched them go and did not participate. I felt that they had legitimate grievances to state to their commanders, but they were going about it the wrong way.

The 1st and 2nd Pennsylvania Brigades were immediately called out to put down the rebellion. To quell the rebellion once and for all, General Washington ordered the two ringleaders hanged immediately. The entire Connecticut Brigades were called out to watch as the execution was performed. I didn't know the two men, as I later found out they were from the 2nd Brigade. The two Connecticut Regiments slowly made their way back to camp and walked as dead men with their shoulders hunched over. Even so, I still heard men grumbling with discontent.

With my leg wound still causing me great distress and my enlistment being almost fulfilled, I went to Captain Fitch's quarters to let him know that I was not going to reenlist. I found Captain Fitch having a midday meal with Colonel Durkee.

"Captain," I greeted, "may I enter your quarters?"

"Sergeant Waterman, you may enter," was Captain Fitch's reply.

"Please, sit down," Colonel Durkee directed as they watched me sit.

"Would you like some food?" Captain Fitch asked.

"No, thank you, sir," I answered, and then continuing said, "my enlistment is up next week. I have given this a lot of thought. I will not be reenlisting," I stated flatly, almost expecting them to be upset with me.

"Sergeant," Colonel Durkee began, "we have been going over the numbers of the men in the Connecticut regiments whose enlistments are up this spring. There will be several hundred men, leaving the 4th Connecticut alone with the expiration of their enlistments." He hesitated a few moments, and I thought this was where he was going to plead for me to stay, and reenlist in the army. To my surprise, Colonel Durkee stated "If anyone in the 4th, has done enough for the cause, for Connecticut and for our home town of Norwich, it has been you, Will. You need not explain anything to us. Everyone who has had the privilege of knowing you, and especially fighting with you has nothing but respect for you and your abilities," he complemented.

Captain Fitch then spoke up and added, "Will, we know most of the men haven't been paid in real currency in over a year. When we can, we will make sure the men in your unit are fairly compensated for all you and they have done. I just can't tell you right now when that will be."

"I understand, sir," I responded as Captain Fitch pulled a gallon jug of spirits from under his bunk.

We had a tot of rum together, and they drank several toasts to the army and me. I left Captain Fitch's quarters feeling much better than when I entered.

We were sent to Westfield, New Jersey colony, on June 5th, where the quartermaster general was currently stationed. There was a group of about fifty of us, who were given our discharge papers, effective in a week. Before departing the quartermaster general's office, we all posted letters home letting our loved ones know we'd be home within a month. I posted my letter to Diane, knowing that she or Pastor Gallagher would let my family know I would be home.

A week later, I was gathering my meager belongings with Samuel Fuller and several men from my unit whose enlistments were also up. It was a warm day for this spring, and we were slowly riding out of camp. As we passed the huts of many of the men we knew from the 4th, they came out and saluted or shook our hands as we passed by them.

And so it was, as Samuel Fuller and seven others from my unit rode out of camp, and out of the American army, twenty new recruits were marching in.

- CHAPTER 16 -

"Privateer"

1781

Along with Samuel Fuller, John Lathrop, John Edgerington, John Fuller, Dayton Birchard, William Bradford, Nathan Smith, and Joshua Calkins, I received my discharge papers.

When we left camp, it was decided that we would give the British army and New York City a wide berth. We decided to ride up to the New York Highlands to cross the Hudson River at King's Ferry, and head east for the Connecticut frontier from there.

We passed several checkpoints along the way, and for the most part the sentries allowed us passage upon seeing our discharge papers. We were still in the uniforms of the 4th Connecticut of the Continental Line and although no one recognized us on our way to the New York Highlands, they recognized the uniforms, which received immediate respect.

Several days after departing from Morristown, New Jersey colony, we were approaching the New York Highlands. It was only last year that we were detailed here for the defense of the highlands. But, this was a different year and it seemed that change had already come to the area. All of the units and men that were so familiar to us were gone. No one knew us as we made our way from town to town, and checkpoint to checkpoint.

Even when we reached the King's Ferry on the Hudson River, just above Stony Point, a gruff-looking, dirty and out-of-uniform sergeant from a New York regiment questioned us intolerably, as to who we were and where we were going.

"Who is in command at West Point now?" I asked the sergeant to engage him in conversation, hoping it would distract him from reviewing each discharge paper.

"General Benedict Arnold is in command now," he informed me. Looking up from reviewing Corporal Bradford's discharge papers, he inquired of me, "Why do you ask, Sergeant?"

"It was only last year, that we were here under the command of General Washington, and I was wondering who now commanded," I stated flatly. Inside I shuttered at the name of General Arnold, as chills went up my spine, knowing that Captain McLane was convinced the general was a traitor.

Satisfied that our discharge papers were in order, the New York sergeant allowed us to pass. We entered the ferry and began our crossing of the Hudson River. As we began, I looked back to the south at Stony Point, and thought that even that rock covered point of land jutting out into the Hudson River looked somehow different from what I remembered.

Samuel Fuller came to my side and was silent for a few moments as he looked at Stony Point.

"What are you thinking, Will?" he finally asked.

"Everything looks different now to me," I began. "Only a few months ago we were here storming those rocks with bayonets at the ready. Kill or be killed," I stated and then added. "And now here we are trying to get home, and we are challenged at every turn," I said and as I hesitated a few moments before I began again. "Nothing seems to be the same now, somehow," I concluded and was silent as I turned my gaze from Stony Point to Verplanck's Point ahead of us.

Samuel said nothing, and I was left to my thoughts. At Verplanck's Point, again a sergeant challenged us, and after reviewing our papers and deciding all was in order, we headed east for the New York frontier with the Connecticut colony.

Several days later, we crossed the frontier into Connecticut colony and rode past the towns of Danbury and Redding, where we had winter quartered two years ago now. Even here things had changed with the war moving to the southern colonies. Life in many New England towns had returned to normal. People watched us pass, but said nothing.

We stayed at taverns and ate our meals in quiet conversation, keeping to ourselves. We paid for our night's lodging with the meager coin we had in our pockets, as we had been paid mostly with the worthless Continentals.

We continued east, and went through the town of Hartford where we had enlisted three years earlier to fill the Connecticut levy. We all noted how much Hartford had grown in the past three years. A local tavern owner told us that most of the new people were moving in from Boston. A lot of them, he noted, wanted to move to the New York or Pennsylvania frontiers, now that the Indians had been pushed out.

Several days after departing from Hartford, we were again approaching Norwich and home. It was now late June, and it had been almost a year and a half since any of us had been home on winter leave, after being recalled to winter quarters to help put down the camp unrest.

On June 27th, we had ridden to within ten miles of Norwich on the Post Road from Hartford, and it was now in the twilight of the evening, as the darkness would soon be setting in. I called a halt to rest the horses and inquired of the men, whether they wished to continue on, and be home that night, or make camp and push on in the morning. Without exception, every man expressed the desire to reach their homes that night, even though everyone was experiencing extreme fatigue, since we had been traveling the better part of June to get home.

So, we pushed on that night toward Norwich, arriving well after dark. As we came to the roads leading to each man's home, we stopped and said our farewells as men broke off our group. Tears were shed partly for parting with men with whom we had shared so much suffering, and partly for being home and seeing our families. By the time we reached Norwich, the only ones left riding with me were Samuel and John Fuller, along with William Bradford. The Fullers lived on a farm to the south of Norwich and William lived on land farther to the east of Norwich, which had been owned by his family, since one of the Bradfords had left the Plymouth colony after the Pequot Indian War, one hundred years earlier.

As we reached the center of Norwich, by Durkee's Tavern, we shook hands and said our farewells, each going in his own direction.

It was now well on into the evening. I saw the light on in the Gallagher's house and decided to stop. I slowly walked Chester up to the front and dismounted, tying my reins to the horse rail out front. All was quiet and even though the lamp was lit in the window, I didn't think anyone was awake. I knocked lightly, not wanting to waken those who were asleep. Not hearing any stirring inside the house, I turned and grabbed the reins to remount Chester, when the door opened a crack.

"Will?" I heard Pastor Gallagher's voice whisper from behind the door.

"Yes, sir," I replied, in an equally low voice.

The door opened and Pastor Gallagher was standing there in his nightshirt, welcoming me in. It was dark in the house except for the lamp in the window. Pastor Gallagher walked over to the lamp, grasping it by the handle, then walked to the family table, and sat down, offering me a chair.

"Will," he said, continuing in a whispered voice, "Diane tried to stay up every night this week, hoping you'd be here, but she was so tired tonight that she fell asleep at the dinner table."

"I'll continue on home then, and see her in the morning," I stated as I stood up to leave.

"You'll do no such thing, Will," Pastor Gallagher stated in a strong whisper. "She'll be mad as a stirred up hornets hive if she finds out you were here, and I let you go home. There's a comforter and pillow on the deacon's bench in the family room. You can sleep there, and I'll go take your horse around back to bed him for the night."

I knew there was no use arguing with Pastor Gallagher about it, so I just shook my head and went to lie down on the bench. Pastor Gallagher went out the front door, and as I listened, I could hear him leading Chester around the house to the barn out back. As I took off my equipment and my jacket, I suddenly realized how tired I was. My back and shoulders ached from the long ride I had just endured. I must have fallen asleep before Pastor Gallagher came back, for the next memory I had was the beckoning smell of breakfast the next morning.

My back still ached when I woke up, this time from sleeping on the deacon's bench. I gathered my things, and made my way to the kitchen. Mrs. Gallagher was preparing some bacon and eggs for breakfast. Seeing me, she said I could wash up out back by the barn. I made my way out to the barn, stopping to see Chester on the way. He seemed content in his stall, munching on hay. I found the water pump and began pumping until it poured out into the bucket at the base of the pump. Once the bucket was full I scooped out water and began splashing my face with it. The water was ice cold and brought me fully awake. I removed my shirt, and began splashing my upper body, trying to get the dirt and smell of several weeks' travel off of me.

Suddenly, the back door to the house opened and outburst Diane, running to meet me, her brown hair blowing in the wind. Before I could gather myself she was upon me, hugging and kissing me. Finally, she took a step back and looking at me from head to toe and stated, "Will Waterman, aren't you a sore thing to look at. You look skinnier than the runt of the litter, and dirtier than a pig in slop. Didn't those soldier boys let you bath or anything?" she asked. Before I could answer she was pushing me and telling me to bend over, "Get your head under this water pump, and I'll give you a good washing," she said as she started pumping as hard as she could, sending cold water gushing over my head. I could only take a few moments of this as the water with each pump on the handle produced an even colder gush. I pulled my head out shaking from the cold. Diane ran inside to get a cloth to dry with. She returned, and before I was dry, her mother was at the door calling us for breakfast. We returned to the house, and found the breakfast table set with everyone waiting on us to eat.

Pastor Gallagher prayed, and we had a good breakfast together. Mrs. Gallagher was a fine cook and I complimented her on the food.

"How was this last winter for the army?" Pastor Gallagher finally asked.

"Well, sir," I began, "the winter at Morristown was very cold and snowy. In fact, it was much colder with much more snow at Morristown, than we had at Valley Forge two years ago or even Redding last year. I think we lost about a hundred and thirty men to the cold," I stated. I hesitated a few moments and then continued, "Most of the men were veterans of the previous winters and knew what to expect as far as dealing with the cold, and knew best how to survive those conditions. The problem became the men's treatment by some of the officers, coupled with the lack of food and pay," I said. "In various units there were several mutinies that had to be put down. Some of the instigators and ringleaders were shot or hanged," I concluded flatly, as all was quiet at the table. Then I added, "Even most of the 4th mutinied."

Pastor Gallagher found it hard to believe that the army could still be held together with so much discontent among the ranks. I assured him that now that the warmer weather was here again, the army would move forward until the next winter quarters, and then anything could happen again.

After breakfast, I made my pardons, as I told Diane that I had to go home to see my family. I was invited back anytime. I told Diane to come see me if I wasn't back in a day or two. I saddled Chester, and rode the remaining couple miles to our farm outside of town.

My ride home was uneventful, and when I arrived, it was late morning. Only my mother and Rachel were at home. Da and John were out in the fields working. Mother cried and hugged me while Rachel ran to the fields to tell Da and John I was home, returning with them several minutes later.

Da hugged me and shook my hand as John slapped my back, all happy to see me. Since it was so close to the midday meal, Da and John stayed home and we ate together.

I told my family of last winter's quartering problems, along with the various units that had mutinied. Da could only shake his head as he listened while I told him about the men they shot and hanged for being the leaders of the discontent at camp. Da and John went back to the fields for the remainder of the day, while I stayed at home taking care of Chester, and resting. I was amazed at the changes in John and Rachel. John was now almost as tall as me, and was filling out well with broad shoulders. Rachel, for her part, was becoming a young lady, looking every bit the part.

Much had changed in Norwich, as it had in much of the cities and towns in the colonies as the result of the war. People were more separated by their opinions than ever before. In those cities that had felt the brunt of the war, with battles that had raged in and around them, they struggled to recover. More and more people were moving into the area of Norwich. Many of them from Providence, but most were from Boston. Every time I was in town to see Diane, attend church, or conduct business for Da, I saw new people and faces. The summer passed quickly, finding that was September suddenly upon us.

During these months, the post rider continued to bring news about the war. For the most part, the war had moved to the southern colonies. It was difficult for me to hear the news from the war. I found that I was yearning to be with the army again, fighting our common enemy. Even with all of the hardships and struggles the army went through, I had to admit to myself, that I missed being in the army. This was something I could never admit to Diane.

Then, we received the disturbing news of treason beyond belief. The post rider brought the news that the commander of West Point had tried to turn the entire post over to the British. Upon hearing the news, I rode for Durkee's Tavern, and the board where the common posts was nailed. There, I found several men who had returned with me from my unit, including Samuel Fuller and William Bradford.

My heart pounded in my chest as I read the account of a British officer who was captured. A Major Andre, in civilian clothes, who was found to be with a pass signed by West Point commanding officer, General Benedict Arnold. The post went on to say that Major Andre was hanged, while General Arnold had escaped with his Tory wife to the British lines. Captain McLane had been right after all, in his suspicions about General Arnold. I wondered wherever Captain McLane was at this very moment, if he now felt vindicated, after General Washington had chastised him on the matter. I spoke briefly with Samuel and William on the subject and then rode home.

Harvest time came upon us and with it the colors of fall with all of the yellows, reds and auburn colors exploding into view. It took me back to the New York Highlands. I was out in the fields helping Da with gathering in the corn harvest. John was bringing the team and wagon out for another load, and I directed him to harvested and sheaved corn.

"John," I called from the far side of the field, "there are several sheaves of corn down this row!" I thought John was heading down the wrong row.

John glanced at me without replying, slapping the reins on the backs of the team, and getting them to respond to his urging. I continued cutting corn as Da and John continued loading the wagon, then taking the corn to the barn for storage. At day's end we had harvested over half of our fields, but still had the rest of the corn to finish, as well as over ten acres of potatoes.

That evening, as John and I were finishing up our chores in the barn, I suggested to John that perhaps if we stored the corn in the loft opposite the hay, we could get more potatoes in the storage bins beyond the horse stalls.

"I know where and how to store the corn and potatoes," John replied without looking at me, as he was putting up the horse tack.

"I just thought it would be easier," I began and before I got my whole sentence out, John turned and stated flatly to me.

"You may not have noticed but, Da and I have been taking care of this farm and getting in the harvest for more than five years while you've been off in the army," he retorted coldly. "I know where the corn and potatoes are stored for the winter, and I know how to store them," he argued with some degree of anger. "And I don't need you telling me where to drive the team or where to harvest and store the crops," then he turned and left the barn, going into the house. My chores took me several more minutes, and when I entered the house I found John seated at the table with Da, waiting for the evening meal to be served. John didn't look at me, or say anything during the entire meal. Da and Mother discussed the latest news on the war, along with how the harvest looked.

After the morning chores were completed on the morrow, I asked Da if it would be all right to drive a couple of goats into town. I stated that Doctor Post had need of them, and would pay a fair price. It was time for the doctor to look at my leg again, to determine the progress of my healing. Besides, I added at the end, I hadn't seen Diane yet this week and wished to see her.

Da looked at John and asked, "John, do you think we can finish a good portion of those corn fields without Will on the morrow?"

Without looking up from his plate of food, John stated coldly, "I suppose so, since we've been doing it for over five years now."

Da took notice of John's response, but didn't say anything as he asked Mother to pass more potatoes. Dinner was finished, and I went to John's and my room to spend some time alone. John didn't come up to bed for a couple of hours, and when he did, we didn't speak.

The next morning, I was up early to begin working on my chores. With all of the animals fed and watered, I saddled Chester and found two of the better looking goats of the fifteen or so that comprised our herd. As I was about to leave, Mother came out of the house, handing me a cloth containing some bread and cheese for me to eat on my trip to Norwich.

I made the trip thinking about John's attitude toward me the last few days, especially yesterday. I found Doctor Post at his house, which also doubled as his office. I sat down to wait for him, as he was just finishing up with another patient. As usual, he got right to the point, examining my leg. As he poked and prodded, I didn't even take notice of the pain it caused as I was thinking of home. When he had finished, he flatly stated, "Well, you are recovering now that you are home, and getting decent rest and proper food. You'll be fine now as long as you stay away from the army. Now, have you brought me something today?" he asked.

"Yes, sir," I stated. "There are two goats tied outside with my horse, if you are still interested in them."

"Let's see," he responded as he went outside to look.

Finding the goats to his liking, he paid my Da's asking price, placing the goats in his paddock area around back.

I rode over to Diane's house, thinking about John and home the whole time. I found Diane at home working with her mother, on some project in the kitchen. Diane said her father was at the church, preparing for the Sunday service. I excused myself, to go to the church to talk to Pastor Gallagher. I found him rearranging the pews in the church to fit more people. Offering to help, we continued moving pews for several minutes.

"Will," Pastor Gallagher finally stated, "is there something you want to talk about?"

I hesitated for several moments thinking in my mind how I wanted to tell Pastor Gallagher what was on my mind.

"I think my brother resents me being home from the army," I finally said looking at Pastor Gallagher.

Sitting down, Pastor Gallagher stated, "Tell me what has happened."

I explained to Pastor Gallagher what had happened the last week or so, with getting the harvest in and the anger directed toward me by my brother.

"Let me explain something to you, Will," Pastor Gallagher began. "I'm not saying that your brother is right, but let's look at it from his side of things. Everyone in the colonies has been suffering in one degree or another since this war started. Now, I understand that the suffering at the front lines, wherever that may be, and camp conditions are far worse than any of us will probably understand," he said. "But young boys like your brother John, and countless others, have had to grow up rather quickly since this war has started. Many of them had their fathers or brothers, like you, go off to war for years on end. These young boys are thrust into positions where they have to be father, farmer and everything else at home until those at war return, if they return at all. I believe that John probably feels that your coming back, in a large part, threatens all that he has worked for and become, even if he didn't want it thrust upon him," he concluded.

"I guess I can understand that, but I wasn't trying to boss him or take away anything he has earned," I said quietly under my breath.

"Perhaps you should let him know that, Will," Pastor Gallagher said.

We returned to the Gallagher house where we had dinner, as well as a quiet time with Diane the rest of the afternoon and into the evening.

I returned home late that night, and in the morning helped Da and John with the harvest. I was out in the field late that afternoon with Da, while John took a loaded wagon to the barn to store the harvest.

"Da, does Uncle Jeremiah still home port in Providence?" I asked.

"He does, Will, but why do you ask a question like that now that you're home?" he inquired.

"Da, I don't want to come between John and what he feels he rightly has earned," I stated. "It is clear to me that he is threatened by my return and feels I will take the farm away from him," I added.

Da just looked at me for a moment and then stated, "I have noticed a change in him since you've been home, and that there has been something between you two lately."

"I think when spring comes I will go to sea with Uncle Jeremiah to raid British shipping. If I get paid off well, I can buy my own land to farm, and marry Diane," I said flatly.

I left Da standing in the field, as I walked toward the barn to let John know he didn't have to worry about me interfering with the farm any longer. The hard part was telling Diane that I'd be leaving again, and how she would react.

With the crops in, winter was upon us quickly. Things at home were as normal as they could be. Only Da and John knew of my plans, as I had decided not to tell mother or Diane until I had to. With the coming of the New Year, I corresponded with Uncle Jeremiah by way of posting several letters to him. When I received Uncle Jeremiah's response, he said he would be glad to have me on board his ship. He did say that he planned on sailing in the middle of March for the Delaware, or Chesapeake capes, as spring came much earlier there, and he wanted to be active in those waters. This information only gave me a few weeks to prepare, and then I would have to ride to Providence.

February came upon me quickly, and I knew I had to give Mother, as well as Diane time to know I was leaving. When I told mother she cried as expected. She didn't understand why I was going to sea with Uncle Jeremiah again. Da, knowing the whole truth, did his best to console her. Diane as expected was in a state of shock when I told her. I knew she was beyond mad when she didn't cry, or ask me not to go. I guess I had gone enough times already, that if I said I was going to return to sea, I meant it.

The first week of March came and I began my final preparations to travel to Providence. Knowing I was going to sea again, I took my chest and began filling it with all of the things I thought I would need to keep warm on those cold days, and nights at sea. I included in my chest my 4th Connecticut uniform and my discharge papers. Da said he would hitch the team to the wagon, and ride over with me, as he had business to discuss with his brother. It was a cold morning when we left. There was no send off by Diane. Mother waved as we left, wiping her eyes with her apron.

Da and I had a couple of days to talk as we made our way to Providence. Da expressed his understanding on how John felt with me returning after being gone for several years. On the first day's travel we made for Waterman's Tavern, our usual stopping place, just outside of Scituate, Rhode Island colony. As always, Master Waterman treated us well. He seemed much older now, as it had been several years that I'd known him, since before the beginning of the war.

We arrived at Providence, finding the *Whisperer* docked as usual, and with the loading of supplies taking place. All of the hands seemed to be busy, as they were all at the yards swinging large cargo nets on deck, and into the hold. Even the cabin boy, Johnny, was helping, and he seemed much taller and older to me. While Uncle Jeremiah welcomed Da to his ship, Edwards yelled for me to come aboard, to stow my gear and chest.

Going below deck, I found the ship to be dark and damp. While I was with Edwards, Da accompanied Uncle Jeremiah to the captain's cabin, staying there for what seemed an unusually long time. I had stowed my gear and chest, and was up on deck helping with the final loading of the supplies, when Da and Uncle Jeremiah finally appeared.

Da shook hands with Uncle Jeremiah, as Uncle Jeremiah reassured Da that he would take care of me. Da turned and put his arm around my shoulder as we walked to the gangplank. We left the ship, and I walked with Da to the waiting team of horses.

"Your uncle assures me that you will be well taken care of, Will," he said as he climbed onto the wagon seat. Leaning over, he held out his hand for me to take. Taking it, I shook it warmly as he requested, "Write if you can, so that your mother and Diane know you are well. Godspeed to you and the *Whisperer*."

Da slapped the reins to the horses' backs and the wagon jumped forward, as the horses put their weight and strength to their yokes.

I returned to the ship. Since the cargo was loaded, and it was getting nigh unto dark, I went below decks to find the crew. The men of the crew were having a meal of stew and bread, and invited me to join them. We didn't see anything of Uncle Jeremiah that night, as he remained closed up in the captain's cabin.

In the morning, we were up with the sun on a cold March day. A tender pulled us away from the wharf. There was a light offshore breeze and Captain Waterman sent all hands to set all sails, and the *Whisperer* had little difficulty making headway down Narragansett Bay, toward the Atlantic Ocean. As I looked over the ship, the only difference I took notice of was the cannons, which were now located at the bow and stern of the ship with several swivel guns mounted along the port and starboard sides. It was obvious that these were used to hunt down, and stop any supply ships of the British that were encountered.

Several hours later we were approaching Newport, between the Connaicut and Rhode Islands. With the British evacuation of Newport, the French fleet now called Newport home, and numerous French frigates were seen at anchor. We continued sailing south and by early afternoon we had cleared Brenton Point, sailing into the Atlantic Ocean.

We sailed due south and then southwest. After several days of fair winds, during which time we did not see any other ships, we sighted land.

"Shorten sail!" the captain yelled to no one in particular, but to everyone who was on deck, which was all of the hands, save Johnny the cabin boy, who was below decks preparing a meal.

After shortening sail, I went back to the helm where Edwards was controlling the direction of the ship, with Captain Waterman watching every movement of the ship's sails and rigging.

"What coast is this, Captain?" I asked.

"We are at the New Jersey coast, about midway between New York City and Cape May, where the Delaware River meets the ocean," he explained. "We will sail along the coast from here, looking for any British supply ships groping along the coast, as they try to reach New York City to supply the soldiers still quartered there."

We continued to sail along the coast the rest of that day, but with our sails shortened, we barely made any headway. Captain Waterman kept his glass to the shore, scanning the coast for any ships sailing within the coastal waters.

Garden had scrambled up the ratlines, and was at the fighting top scanning the ocean in all directions for any sails to our seaward side.

We had sailed along in this state, practically remaining in place for about an hour, when Garden yelled from the fighting top, "Sail ho!"

Captain Waterman, looking up at Garden yelled "Where away?"

"Two points back the beam, Captain!" Garden yelled back.

Immediately, Captain Waterman turned and walked to the port side and then moved to the stern of the ship, looking back to the ocean with his spyglass. Following him, and looking in the same direction, I could see nothing of the ship just over the horizon bearing down on us. After several moments, Captain Waterman slammed the spyglass shut, turned, and finding me watching him, directed, "Will, take my glass up the ratlines to Garden, and report further what he sees," handing me the spyglass.

Immediately, I went to the port side of the ship and began climbing the ratlines to the fighting top. Handing Garden the spyglass, I wrapped my arm around the mast to stabilize my footing. Garden, with his long beard blowing in the breeze, leaned against the mast, and wrapping his arms around it as he extended the spyglass, putting it to his eye. After looking through the glass for several moments he said to me, "Looks like a frigate."

Looking down to the captain on the deck below, I yelled, "Looks like a frigate!"

Garden, still looking through the glass declared, "Three masts, thirtytwo guns, and she's flying British colors."

Looking back down to the captain on deck I repeated the vital information with vigor, "Three masts, thirty-two guns, and British colors!"

"All hands, all hands!" Captain Waterman barked, "Set all sail!"

The crew on deck instantaneously responded to the captain's orders, and began moving about the deck, pulling on ropes as the sails began to grow and catch the wind. I left Garden at the fighting top with the spyglass, and returned to the deck, to assist the crew with setting full sail.

"Mr. Edwards," the captain stated, "let's put some distance between us and this British frigate."

The captain again turned his attention to the sails and rigging, scrutinizing every movement of the ship. Garden remained at the fighting top for the better part of two hours, finally yelling down "Frigate is beyond the horizon, sir!"

Garden came down the ratlines, and returned the spyglass to the captain, who thanked Garden for his duty.

"Make for the Great Bay," the captain said to Edwards as he left and went below decks. We continued along the coast the rest of the day. As the day waned toward evening, Edwards called me to the helm and said, "Go below and tell the captain we are approaching the Little Egg Inlet, and the Great Bay, and request he come on deck."

"Yes, sir," I stated as I turned to go below deck. I knocked on the captain's cabin door and waited for a response.

After several moments, the captain called, "Enter."

I found the captain looking over charts of the coast of New Jersey.

As he looked up at me, I stated, "Edwards reports we are approaching the inlet, sir, and requests you come on deck."

"Very good," the captain replied, grabbing his hat, and departing the cabin immediately. I followed the captain on deck, and after scanning the approaching coast and inlet, as well as the sails and rigging, he called out to Jennings, "Get a lead out, Mr. Jennings, no sense running aground."

"Aye, sir," Jennings called out as he went forward.

"Will, go forward, and watch how Jennings checks our depth," the captain stated.

"Yes, sir," I stated, and went forward to watch Jennings. He pulled a lead ball out of a box which had a long line attached to it. Swinging the ball from that line, he threw it out in front of the ship and let the line run out until the lead ball hit bottom, and the line went slack. Then, based upon the knots in the rope, he knew the depth of the water under the ship.

"No bottom," was Jennings first reading, as the entire line was let out without the lead ball hitting bottom. Then repeating the process he called "Six fathoms," until the captain felt we were well within the bay and could not be challenged by any British frigate, which may be patrolling the area, as the water was too shallow for them to enter the inlet.

We dropped anchor, remaining in the Great Bay overnight. In the morning with an offshore breeze blowing strong, we set all sail and within an hour were out of the inlet and sailing south again toward Cape May.

Billings had climbed the ratlines and was on the fighting top keeping watch when, about halfway through the morning watch, he called out,

"Sail off the starboard bow!"

"Can you make her out, Mr. Billings?" the captain called out, while handing me his spyglass, pointing for me to go up the ratlines to Mr. Billings with it.

When I got up to Mr. Billings at the fighting top, I handed him the spyglass, and hung on to the rigging, while looking in the direction that Billings trained the glass. I could make out a white sail on the horizon, but could see no more. Billings closed the spyglass and looked down to the deck, and the captain.

Cupping his free hand to his mouth while holding to the rigging with the other, he shouted, "Two-masted schooner! Looks to be about twenty tons. Making out of Absecon Inlet, probably for New York City." He then added, "She's running heavy in the water and looks to be a British supply ship, Captain."

"Very good, Mr. Billings!" the captain called up. "Let us know any change in course, if you please."

Looking down at the captain, I could see him give instructions to Edwards at the helm and the *Whisperer* changed direction. With a strong northeast wind now blowing, the *Whisperer* began plowing through the water towards the British supply ship and her prey.

I was about to learn that action at sea was quite different than action on land. It would take us several hours to close the distance between us and the supply ship, so that we could see her from on deck. Then, it was more maneuvering between her, the *Whisperer* and the wind to close even further.

Finally, after what seemed all day, we were within a quarter-mile of our quarry. We could now see the ship clearly, and make out the men on her deck. She seemed to be about our equal in size, but not rigged as well, as her every move was countered by Captain Waterman. Finally, Captain Waterman called out to Jennings, Garden, and McKiernay to load the starboard bow chaser.

"Will," he added, "go forward and watch the hands load the gun.

Going forward, I tried to stay out of the way as McKiernay opened a box and removed a sack containing powder, while Jennings lighted the slow burn rope, placing it well away from the gun. Pulling the ropes, Garden and McKiernay pulled the gun away from the gun port. McKiernay put the powder in the end of the gun and rammed it home. Garden, then opened a second box, removing a six-pound, round, ball shot, and handing it to McKiernay who placed it in the end of the cannon, who rammed it home. Jennings then placed a pin in the priming hole, punching a hole in the powder bag in the cannon, and poured additional powder down the touch-hole. Then Garden and McKiernay grabbed the rope on each side of the gun and Garden called out, "Heave!" They pulled the gun so that it rammed forward and protruded out the gun port. Garden, McKiernay, and I stepped back. Jennings grabbed the linstock and blew on the slow match rope lightly, making the red hot embers at the end of the rope glow. He then looked back at Captain Waterman, waiting for orders. Looking around, Captain Waterman saw the cabin boy, Johnny, coming out the hatchway that led below decks. Calling to him, Captain Waterman then waited as Johnny ran over before calmly stating, "Run up the colors if you please, Johnny." Johnny opened a box at the stern of the ship where a rope led to a yardarm. He attached a flag from the box and began pulling. The colors unfurled as they went up, and it was the first time in over a year that I was fighting again under the American flag.

"Put a shot across her bow, if you will, Mr. Jennings!" Captain Waterman called out. Jennings leaned forward, looked down the length of the cannon to gage its aim and then, stepping back, put the linstock to the powder in the touch-hole. The cannon jumped back and was stopped by the ropes as it spewed forth its deadly shot. A spout of water rose in front of the supply ship where the shot entered the water. The supply ship showed no signs of lowering her sails, or submitting to our much faster, stronger ship.

"Mr. Waterman!" the captain called to me. "Go below with Johnny and secure from the arms locker two muskets and go up to the fighting top, if you please! It looks like we'll have to take her by force!"

Going below, Johnny and I found the arms locker unlocked and, securing two muskets along with powder and shot, made our way to the fighting top. Loading was most difficult as the ship rolled and swayed with the ocean waves.

"Reload!" the captain called to the gun crew of Jennings, Garden and McKiernay. Then, calling to Billings and Boyle, Captain Waterman ordered, "Load the two port swivel guns, if you please!" Billings and Boyle immediately went to work loading the two guns.

Jennings called out from the starboard bow chaser, "Loaded and awaiting orders, Captain!"

"Aim for her mast if you please, Mr. Jennings!" the captain called out.

Again, Jennings put the linstock, with the slow match glowing, to the touch-hole of the six pounder and again the gun jumped as fire spewed from the barrel, filling the air with smoke. Looking forward from the fighting top of our ship, we could see the forward mast splinter about halfway up. As the ropes and rigging could not support the weight, as the top half of the mast began to fall to the port side, giving way and crashing into the sea. The British supply ship was now crippled and at the mercy of our faster, more heavily armed ship.

"Master Will!" Captain Waterman called out. "You and Johnny be ready and fire at anyone on deck who brings a swivel, or any other gun to bear!"

"Yes, sir!" I called back, looking forward at the prey still before us. We were coming up on her now from her starboard quarter, less than a hundred yards away. I could see several men on her deck trying to clear the wreckage away with axes by chopping at the tangle of ropes and rigging dragging off their port side.

Several other men came to the starboard quarter and began loading a swivel gun. Their captain could be seen on the deck by the helm, giving orders.

I took aim at one of the men at the swivel gun, waited for us to roll up on a swell, and fired. The wood of the rail by the swivel gun splintered showing how close I had come with a musket at this distance. I began to reload as Johnny, following my example, fired his gun. Where the bullet went we could not tell, as it clearly missed its mark by some distance.

We had now closed to within fifty yards and Captain Waterman called to the captain of the supply ship.

"Do you yield and lower your colors?" he called.

There was no reply, only glances from the captain of the supply ship as he saw us bearing down on his wounded ship.

"Do you yield?" Captain Waterman again called, receiving no reply. "Mr. Billings," the captain called, "is your gun loaded and ready?"

"It is, sir!" Billings replied.

"Aim for the men at the swivel gun, if you please," Captain Waterman stated.

Billings and Boyle had loaded our port side swivel guns with grapeshot, which consisted of a small bag of round shot similar to that of a shotgun. Thus, the swivel guns became large shotguns, and when fired had the effect of clearing the decks of all the men on them.

Billings blew on his linstock slow match, while aiming at the opposing men on the supply ship, then fired his swivel gun. Again fire and smoke filled the air, as all three men at the opposing swivel gun fell to the deck either dead or wounded. Billings and Boyle moved to our second portside swivel gun, and prepared to fire. The British captain, realizing that further resistance to the onslaught would be futile, lowered his colors.

Johnny and I remained at the fighting top, as we drew alongside of the supply ship, covered the enemy ship's deck in case any of her crew decided on something other than surrender. Jennings, Garden, McKiernay, Billings and Boyle were all over the side and on the supply ship's deck in a moment.

Johnny and I returned to the deck of the *Whisperer* as Captain Waterman approached the British captain, who bowed his head, removing his sword from its scabbard in a show of submission.

"I am Captain Brown of the British supply ship *Sparrow*. To whom do I have the honor of surrendering my ship?" the British captain said flatly.

"Captain Waterman, of the ship *Whisperer*," Captain Waterman replied. "You and your crew, or those who remain, as well as your ship are prizes of war, Captain," Captain Waterman stated.

"Captain Waterman," Captain Brown began, "you have fought well and captured my ship. My crew and I pledge not to hinder your efforts any further." Then hesitating a moment, Captain Brown stated, "You have earned quite a name for yourself these last couple of years, Captain Waterman, with the taking of a number of our supply ships. You should be aware that the British navy is well aware of your exploits," Captain Brown warned.

"I endeavor to fight well for my cause," Captain Waterman retorted, as the conversation between the two antagonists concluded.

In a matter of minutes we had the wreckage of the *Sparrow* cleared away, and the two dead British sailors dumped over the side, into the ocean. One of the British sailors was wounded, but not severely, while three others along with the captain were herded onto the *Whisperer*, and placed below deck and locked in the hold.

Jennings, McKiernay and Boyle took command of the *Sparrow*, and escorted by the *Whisperer*, we made for Cape May and the mouth of the Delaware River Bay.

After several days of fair winds, we sailed up the Delaware River toward the city of Philadelphia. The last time I was there, I had been charging down 2nd street along the riverfront with Captain McLane and his men, capturing the British army's rear guard.

As we approached Mud Island, I saw the remnants of Mud Island Fort, now only a shambles of buildings and palisades that were pounded into mounds of debris by the British navy.

Passing the islands in the river, we continued on to Philadelphia where we docked. Captain Waterman went ashore to announce his arrival and the capture of another supply ship. The stores of the supply ship were still badly needed by the army, as well as the civilian population of the city. The captured ship would undoubtedly be put into service by an enterprising shipper, who would risk recapture by the British navy.

Captain Waterman was well paid off, receiving well over a hundred pounds for the supply ship, along with her cargo. We turned our prisoners over to the authorities and Captain Waterman, not wanting to waste time in port, obtained new supplies for our ship, then put to sea.

Over the next month we saw many supply ships sailing the coast or inner waterways along the coast of New Jersey colony, attempting to make New York City, to supply the British army there with badly needed provisions. We did not attempt to capture any number of these ships as they sailed with escorts, or were sailing in waters too shallow for the *Whisperer.* On other occasions we sighted British warships, putting as much distance between us and our pursuers, as to not allow them to even fire on us.

But there were two other British supply ships that fell into our hands, being captured without loss of life or injury to us. Again, we sailed the captured supply ships to Philadelphia, where Captain Waterman was well paid off. We now had more than three hundred pounds prize money on board, with my share being no less than thirty-five pounds. More money than I had ever owned before.

The middle of June found us again scouring the New Jersey coast in the area of Cape May, near the mouth of the Delaware River Bay when Billings, acting as look out at the fighting top called, "Sail Ho!"

Captain Waterman, who was by the helm with Boyle, taking in all the movements of the ship, called back, "Where away?"

Billings pointing straight off the bow, yelled, "Right off the bow about five miles out just clearing the cape, Captain!"

Captain Waterman had his glass to his eye, and was scanning the horizon for the ship. Speaking under his breath as he saw her, he said to no one in particular, "Ah, there she is, three masts, looks like a frigate, has to be an American." Closing his glass, the captain looked up at the sails and rigging and said to Boyle, "Bring her two points to port, if you please. Let's run down on her, and see who she may be."

After another hour of sailing we had closed considerably to the ship. Billings, who had been looking more to our stern and port for any enemy ships, now concentrated on the frigate, only a mile distant.

Looking down to Captain Waterman, Billings called out, "Looks like the *Congress*, Captain."

"The *Congress*," Captain Waterman confirmed, putting his glass to his eye again, "and Captain Geddis I believe. Keep our course, Mr. Boyle," the captain instructed. "Let's see what Captain Geddis is about."

Within the hour we were within several hundred yards of the *Congress*, as Edwards was running a flag up the yard, and according to Captain Waterman, requesting to come aboard. Captain Geddis replied that a council of war would be held at three that afternoon requesting Captain Waterman's attendance. The *Congress* reefed her sails, and we sailed to within a hundred yards of her.

Our sails were lowered, our boat was put over the side and we waited for Captain Waterman, who had gone below to gather some charts. Jennings, Boyle, McKiernay and Billings remained on board along with Johnny, as Edwards, Garden and I rowed the captain to the *Congress*. When we reached the *Congress*, we tied alongside while Captain Waterman went up and over the side and on deck. We stowed the oars and secured the boat to the side of the *Congress*, before going on deck. There we found Captain Waterman presenting himself to the officer of the watch, a Lieutenant Richard O'Brien, first lieutenant of the *Congress*.

I was standing on deck along with Edwards and Garden, talking to several hands, that were on duty and trying to keep out of the way, as Captain Waterman was escorted by Lieutenant O'Brien to Captain Geddis' cabin.

From behind me, I heard a familiar voice call out, "Sergeant Waterman, what are you doing on this ship!"

Turning away from the conversation that I was engaged in with Edwards and Garden, I found my old friend and comrade in arms, Captain McLane, coming toward me with a broad smile on his face, extending his big hand in friendship. Shaking my hand vigorously, he repeated, "What are you doing here?"

I briefly explained that the previous year my enlistment had been up, and that upon returning home had found that much had changed. I explained that I needed money to buy my own land to farm, since the Continental Congress had not met its obligation of payment to many soldiers who served in the Continental army. That being the case, I had put to sea with my uncle to make money as a privateer.

"A wise decision on your part, Sergeant," Captain McLane began, "but an equally dangerous one. You know that if captured as a privateer you are destined to a prison ship in New York Harbor, and the chances of a prisoner exchange are almost nonexistent."

"I understand, Captain," I said, turning, as I introduced both Edwards and Garden to Captain McLane.

"Gentlemen," Captain McLane stated as he directed his remarks toward Edwards and Garden, "I must borrow Sergeant Waterman for a while, as we have much to catch up on."

Excusing us, Captain McLane took me below deck to a small room near Captain Geddis' cabin. As we passed, I could hear Captain Waterman's voice in discussion with Captain Geddis from behind the closed door.

Entering a small room, that was just large enough to have a bunk and small table with two chairs, Captain McLane sat down, offering me the other chair. Pulling a jug of rum from behind a curtain, Captain McLane placed it on the table with two mugs, and began to pour generously, filling my mug.

"Captain," I began, "you shouldn't call me sergeant in front of the ship's company, and most certainly not in front of the men from my ship. I am the low hand on board, and have much to learn yet."

"I understand, Will," Captain McLane stated, "but old habits die hard. I, in fact, am no longer a captain," he stated. "General Washington saw fit to promote me to colonel, in part for smelling out that traitorous rat, Benedict Arnold, long before he tried to turn West Point over to the British. You did hear about it, didn't you?" he asked.

"I did," I replied as I took a large gulp of rum from my mug. Putting my mug down, I added, "Congratulations on your promotion."

"I, like you, have received the rank, but not the pay," Colonel McLane added. "But that is another matter," he concluded. "There is much afoot and that is what finds me on board this ship. General Washington himself has sent me on a mission as his special envoy to Count de Grasse, who as we speak, is anchored at Cape Francois, Martinique, in the Caribbean. General Washington has received intelligence that Lord Cornwallis will continue his march north out of the Carolinas and into

Virginia. As we speak, General Washington is making plans to slip away with the majority of his army from around New York City, to meet up with Lafayette. The plan is to try to trap Cornwallis on a peninsula in Virginia. The key will be, if we can get de Grasse, along with his fleet to sail from the Caribbean, to block the sea escape of Cornwallis, as well as to prevent the British fleet from coming to his aid. I have explicit dispatches in my possession, from General Washington to be delivered to de Grasse, outlining the significance to de Grasse, of his sailing north and supporting the armies in Virginia." Leaning forward, Colonel McLane conveyed emphatically, "If we can defeat Cornwallis in Virginia, we can end the war!"

"I hope so," I responded, for I was war-weary, as were many of the veterans with whom Colonel McLane and I had served. And so were the colonies, for the war had raged now for more than six years.

We remained in Colonel McLane's humble quarters for more than an hour recounting and reminiscing about old feats and victories won, as well as friends lost. Finally, there was a knock at the door and Lieutenant O'Brien presented himself, requesting Colonel McLane to join the senior officers along with both Captains Geddis and Waterman for the evening meal.

"It would be my pleasure," Colonel McLane replied, "but please, advise Captain Geddis, that one more will be joining us for our meal."

Colonel McLane and I entered the captain's cabin, and there, seated at the dining table, were all of the senior officers of the ship in their highly decorated uniforms. Only Captain Waterman, Colonel McLane and I were dressed in rather drab attire, with my clothing looking somewhat ragged next to the naval officers. Sheepishly, I followed Colonel McLane to the two open seats at the table, seating myself next to him being on my left, with Lieutenant O'Brien being on my right. Captain Waterman was seated to the left of Captain Geddis, who was at the head of the table.

"Gentlemen," Colonel McLane began as we sat down, "let me introduce to you, a young man, who has fought beside me in many a campaign and has proven his courage to be well in advance of his years. Although, he does not wear the splendid uniforms you wear at this table, he has well earned the respect of not only me, but indeed, even of the commander-in-chief of the Continental army, who has stated his praise toward this young man, in person, on more than one occasion. This is my comrade in arms, and more importantly my friend, Will Waterman."

I was indeed embarrassed by this formal introduction to the officers of the ship, as all the glasses were raised in a singular toast to me.

The conversation around the table was, as expected, of the war, our many losses, and of the several victories in the southern colonies.

The meal was served and to my surprise, it consisted of half a chicken, fresh vegetables and bread. Before all began to enjoy the meal, Captain Geddes led us in a prayer that asked for God's providence for our cause, our commander-in-chief, and our men at arms, along with the conclusion of hostilities between the colonies and the Crown.

Lieutenant O'Brien observed that I was more than enjoying the consumption of such a meal at sea and commented, "You will find, Mr. Waterman, that the longer we are at sea, the equally less desirous the meals become, as such meals as this may not be seen for months."

"I understand, as having spent three of the worst winters with the army, one being Valley Forge and another being Morristown, where mutinous rebellion in the army was put down with hangings and shootings. I well know the effect of prolonged starvation on men," I concluded.

"Come, come, Gentlemen," Colonel McLane broke in, "as I have already said, this young man has seen his share of suffering, and done more than his fair share of the fighting. Let us move on to more pleasant conversation."

And with that the conversation was turned to family and loved ones left at home. Captain Geddis turned to me and asked, "Tell us, Mr. Waterman, do you have a sweetheart at home?"

Looking up from my plate, I found all at the table looking at me waiting for my response. As I gazed upon Uncle Jeremiah, he had a particularly wide grin on his face.

"I do, sir," I said, putting down my fork and wiping my face, I searched my mind as to how much to say. "She is an uncommonly beautiful girl with long wavy brown hair and bright brown eyes," I stated waiting for a reply.

"Well, I hope when all this madness of war is completed, that you marry her and have a long, happy life with her," Captain Geddis stated.

There were "Here, here's," around the table from the officers, and especially from my friend Colonel McLane, who had a smile on his face, and a twinkle in his eye.

With the meal complete and Captains Geddis and Waterman having completed their business, we were excused to leave the ship.

Returning to the deck, we found Edwards and Garden involved in riotous conversation with several deck hands. Upon seeing the captains and several senior officers' return to the deck, the conversation was immediately quieted, with order being restored.

I thanked Captain Geddis and the officers for the dining privilege, along with the hospitality. Turning to Colonel McLane, I grabbed his already extended hand and shook it warmly.

"I hope," Colonel McLane hesitated a moment, and then stated, "that the blessing of God goes with you, Will, and that I may see you again when this war is over."

"Godspeed to you, too, Colonel," I responded. "It has meant more to me than you will ever know, to see you once again."

Edwards and Garden were already in the boat waiting for us to depart the ship. Once in the boat, we pulled hard for the *Whisperer*, as we still had several hours of light left, while Captain Waterman expressed his interest in sailing north in hopes of finding a supply ship to capture within the next few days.

As I rowed in rhythm with Edwards and Garden, I glanced up and saw my friend watching us go. When he saw me looking up, he waved, but I could only smile back, as a good friend was passing out of my life.

- CHAPTER 17 -

"Last Run of the *Whisperer*"

1781

An hour later we were well away from the *Congress*, and its sails were over the horizon, out of sight. We sailed north to the New Jersey coast, while they sailed for Cape Francois and history. The next morning found us well up the New Jersey coast, as Captain Waterman scanned the coastline for any slumbering supply ships. None were to be seen this day or the next, as we continued north. Once, as Garden took his turn as lookout on the fighting top, he reported several sails to seaward, but they quickly disappeared over the horizon, out to sea.

The following day, we saw two supply ships slowly lumbering up the coast, but they were in convoy with a frigate, so we sailed well clear of them.

Two days later, not sighting any supply ships that we could attack, we continued north, sailing closer to New York City and the British navy than we had ever done before. Captain Waterman said we were near the Manasquan Inlet, less than a day's sail from New York City.

By late June, the captain became very nervous about being so close to the main northern base of the enemy, and not sighting any supply ships, turned and sailed south, hoping to intercept any north sailing ships.

On the morning of June 22nd, with a light wind, we were met with a fog so thick that we could not get a fix on our location from the night before. Using his compass, Captain Waterman set a course due east to avoid any possibility of running aground on the New Jersey colony shore. By midday the fog began to burn off, and to our great distress, we found that we had sailed within sight of a British convoy of several frigates, along with transport ships sailing south from the New York Harbor, all of which were not more than a mile distant.

Our course was immediately changed to southwest to gain the safety of the fog bank, but our presence was greatly noted, with a flurry of flags that worked their way up and down on the frigates. Several were seen to change course in pursuit of us. The nearest frigate fired her bow chasers on us, and tore several holes in our canvas, but did no further damage.

"All hands, set all canvas," Captain Waterman barked as the stress of the moment weighed heavily upon him. Reaching for his sextant, the captain attempted to gain a reading of our longitude before we slipped back into the fog bank and safety. Quickly going below decks, the captain plotted what he thought our longitude to be and calculated the distance to the New Jersey colony shore.

Returning to the deck, he stated flatly to Jennings, who had the helm, "Keep us on a south, sou'west course the rest of the day, if you please."

Several other shots were heard to be fired from the frigates, but they were only shooting at shadows now, as their shot came nowhere near the *Whisperer,* as we hid in the fog.

By early afternoon the fog had entirely burned off, and the only sight we had of the frigates that had been chasing us, were the tops of their masts as seen from our fighting top.

A fairly strong north wind kept us well ahead of our pursuers, and as night fell we turned due south, paralleling the New Jersey coast which could be seen several miles distant.

"No lights tonight, Will," the captain stated to me, as I relieved Jennings, taking my shift at the helm. "I am unnerved by the unending pursuit of those frigates, and now am beginning to believe that a trap had been laid to draw us further north. We didn't see any supply ships these last couple of weeks," he said to himself as he looked to the north and east for any sign of our pursuers.

It was a long night, as each man took his turn at the helm, and we all tried to get some rest. Morning broke early with a red sun and bright blue skies. A due west wind kept us off the New Jersey coast and continued to push us southward at a strong eight knots. Garden had climbed the ratlines to the fighting top and reported that no ships could be seen to the north or nor' east.

Shortly after nine in the morning, Garden called out from the fighting top, "Sail ho!"

Captain Waterman stiffened at the call and replied, "Where away?"

"Two points off the starboard bow, heading almost straight for us, sir," Garden called. "She appears to be a frigate!" Garden yelled down.

"Do you see any ships to the stern or port, Mr. Garden!" the captain called back.

After several minutes of scanning the ocean to the north and east, Garden called down, "No sail in sight to the north or nor' east, Captain." The captain, mulling the developments over in his head, turned to Boyle, who was at the helm and stated, "Make our course east, sou' east, if you please, Mr. Boyle."

After half an hour on this course, Garden called out, "The frigate has changed course and now is running south along the coast."

Jennings, Billings and Edwards went below deck to rest. Garden, Boyle, McKiernay and I remained on watch. We sailed our new course for the remainder of the morning. All sail remained set. Later, Billings relieved Garden at the fighting top.

Shortly after midday was called, Billings called out, "Sails, sails ho."

The captain was obviously unnerved at this sighting called back, "Where away, Billings?"

"Two sails, Captain, off the port quarter!" Billings shouted.

The captain, taking his glass in his hand and eye, scanned the ocean off the port quarter. Slamming the glass closed in his hand, he looked from the deck to the sail and rigging. All sail was already set, and the damaged sail from the previous day's fire from the frigates had been repaired. Still, the look on the captain's face indicated that it might not be enough.

McKiernay had taken control of the helm with the midday being called, and the captain stated to him, "Keep our heading due south until further ordered."

Captain Waterman kept a wary eye to his glass, as he watched the three frigates pursue their quarry, the *Whisperer*. The captain knew that the *Whisperer* could easily outpace these frigates under any conditions, but what worried him was that the frigates seemed intent on chasing him, but did not seem interested in getting any closer, at least for now. What lay ahead on the bright blue ocean, was what concerned the captain. The rest of the day saw no change in the positions of our pursuers, now three frigates strong. The captain calculated that we were passing the Absecon Inlet. Another day, two at most, and we could reach Cape May and the relative safety of the Delaware River Bay.

The morning light brought a great distress to all on the *Whisperer*. Under the cover of darkness, the frigate running parallel to our course along the New Jersey coast had altered her course, and was now sailing southeast to our course, in an attempt to close the distance. To our stern, both pursuing frigates had gained on our port quarter, and any chance to escape to seaward seemed remote.

The captain kept looking at the ships through his glass, then took measurements of our position with the sextant. Looking forward and clasping his hands behind his back, he was heard to mutter, "I believe they've got us in a vice," as he stared straight ahead. "Run up the colors, Edwards," the captain stated, "let them know who they are chasing."

The rest of the day was spent tacking to starboard and then to port, in attempts to put greater distance between our pursuers and us. As evening fell on the third day of our pursuit, Captain Waterman seemed reassured that we had placed enough distance between us and our pursuers to reach the safety of Cape May and the Delaware River Bay.

On the morning of the fourth day, the captain's mood seemed remarkably upbeat as Jennings reported from the fighting top, that the sails remained to starboard along the coast, as well as on the port quarter. We had gained precious distance and thus time on them in the night.

Captain Waterman confirmed this with a thorough view through his glass, as he closed the piece stating, "It's well, very well."

We continued on our south course for the remainder of the morning, and the captain indicated that by early afternoon we would alter course to the west, sou'west, making for Cape May and the Delaware River Bay.

Just before the midday, Jennings, who remained at the fighting top called, "Another sail, Captain."

The captain reached for his glass, taking two steps forward, and called back, "Where now, Jennings?"

"I make her five miles distant off the port bow and she is making almost due west!" Jennings yelled. "On this tack we'll sail right to her, Captain," Jennings added.

The captain was already looking about him at the other ship just over the horizon. The two frigates off our port and stern seemed to be less of a concern now, than the closer frigate off our starboard stern, with the new threat off our port bow.

Looking to McKiernay, who was at the helm, Captain Waterman stated, "Change course to a south sou'west heading. I must go below to check the charts."

All hands remained on deck, as we were all nervous as to whether this might be the last run of the *Whisperer.*

The captain returned within the quarter-hour and called all hands, even Jennings, who was at the fighting top, to the quarterdeck. McKiernay remained at the helm. We all gathered in a semicircle around the helm as the captain had taken up a position behind the helm and McKiernay.

Everyone looked at the captain and the captain for his part, stared back for some time without speaking. Clearing his throat before he spoke, the captain clasped his hands behind his back and stated, "I have been a fool not to see this earlier, men. It seems that we have been chased like a fox, by the hounds to the hunters. The three frigates that have been chasing us for these past days probably were lightened of all of their cargo and most of their armaments, keeping their bow and stern chasers and perhaps some of their side guns. Lightening their ships has allowed them to keep within sight distance of our position, but not allowing them to actually catch us. Their game," he revealed as he hesitated for a moment, "is to push us to the hunters; one, is the ship now some distance off of our port bow. I believe there must be a second, as yet unseen frigate somewhere off Cape May guarding the Delaware River Bay mouth.

The situation is this," he continued, "if we alter course to the east and make for the open ocean, the two frigates off our port stern will have us by the hip, blowing us out of the water. If we continue south as had been our heading, we will continue to sail to the frigate now off our port bow and certain capture. The only option before us is to sail south, sou'west and make for Cape May, and pray to Providence that we can slip the frigate to our starboard stern, and the ship before us, to reach the safety of the Delaware River Bay.

I want Billings and McKiernay at the fighting top, telling me every change in the course of our antagonists. I want the rest of the hands at the rigging making adjustments to our sail as needed. Will, I want you at the helm with me," he commanded.

It was apparent that the captain was finished with his orders and all hands moved to their positions. There was no need to load the cannons or swivels as none of our guns could match the fire power of any of the frigates that now threatened our very existence, even if we survived to get within firing distance of our pursuers.

All sail had remained set and in the afternoon watch, the captain called for Edwards to check our knots, as the board and rope were thrown off the stern and the minute glass turned. As the retreating ocean pulled the rope to our stern, Edwards called out the knots as they passed through his hands. Finally, the sand had passed through the minute glass and the captain called "time."

"Twelve knots," Edwards called and then returned to the ropes and tackle to their box.

"Very good, very good indeed," the captain said. Then, stepping forward and standing next to me, he relayed, "If we can keep this speed, we might be able to outrun them still, Will."

"Are we going to make it?" I asked my uncle under my breath.

"I cannot lie to you, Will," he said softly so no one else could hear, "I don't think so."

With all sail set and running at about twelve knots, when the *Whisperer* dug into a larger swell, the spray of the ocean broke over our bow, soaking everyone and everything on deck in cold ocean water.

Turning and taking out his glass, and looking at the frigate running off our starboard stern, Captain Waterman said, "By changing our course to the south sou'west, we have already allowed them to significantly close the distance on us. The frigate off our bow can maintain her course, thus continuing to close with us. The two ships off our port stern are of no concern now, for they will only come into play, if we make for the open sea. What lies ahead, Will, what lies ahead, I don't know, and we could be sailing headlong to our destruction."

Billings called from the fighting top, "Ship to bow seems to be altering course toward us, as is the ship to our starboard stern. The ships to our port stern are fading."

"It is as I thought," the captain said, "they are pinch'n in on us, and once we are within range, they'll blow us out of the water. Come two points to starboard, if you please, Will," the captain said to me. Looking at the rigging and sail, he called to Edwards and Garden to take the slack out of the jib sail. Johnny was ordered below to heat some tea for everyone, while Jennings remained at the rigging, alert for orders.

"If only this was even a month from now, Will, and the sun set an hour earlier, I believe we could slip them in the darkness," he said. "As it is, everything is against us."

We changed course again. Now we were sailing more west, sou'west. The wind was still blowing hard from the north, helping us maintain our rapid passage through the seas. With each swell of the sea, the *Whisperer's* bow slammed into the seas, sending a large spray over our deck. The frigate to our starboard continued to close the distance on us, as our course now allowed them a great advantage over us. The frigate that had been on our port bow was now running parallel to us, and continued to nose toward us.

It was now late afternoon and the sun was before us, setting.

McKiernay called out from the fighting top, "Land ho, off the starboard beam."

The captain went to the starboard rail, putting his glass to his eye and surveyed the land for several moments. Then, he turned his attention to the frigate still closing off our starboard stern. Next, he looked at the frigate that was still running parallel to us. The captain then looked off the bow in search of any more enemy ships that may block our path to freedom.

Returning next to me at the helm, he stated, "Two more points to starboard, if you please, Will."

I looked at the compass before me. I turned the helm ever so slightly to the left as the needle on the compass responded, and moved to the right. We were now sailing a few points south of west, and making hard for the cape.

The captain again looked to the frigate to starboard, as she was closer than ever. She had closed to perhaps within a mile of us. I heard a rumble to my right, and I turned in time to see the smoke of her bow chasers, followed by a spout of water fifty yards to our starboard, as her shot fell just short.

The captain, seeing this turned to me and calmly stated, "Two points to port if you please, Will."

"Aye, Captain," I said, turning the helm as the ship responded.

Billings called out from the fighting top, "Sail, Captain, sail just coming off the cape!"

Captain Waterman immediately knew the ship Billings called out blocked our escape past the cape, into the Delaware River Bay and to safety. Stepping forward, he put his glass to his eye, viewing the ship coming from behind the cape at full sail.

The boom of cannon from our starboard broke his concentration as looking to our right; two spouts of water came from the ocean, now just twenty yards from our starboard beam.

"All hands," the captain called, "all hands prepare to haul sheets and tack!" Billings and McKiernay came scrambling down from the fighting top on the ratlines.

All hands gathered at the ropes on the port side of the *Whisperer.*

"Come about," Captain Waterman called, "make our course due east!"

"Aye, Captain!" I yelled as I spun the helm in my hands hard to the right, all the time watching the needle on the compass spin as it began to turn almost one hundred eighty degrees, to due east!

Jennings was heard calling, "Heave, heave," as he and the men at the stays pulled on the ropes tightening the sails as we turned to the east. Moving up the port side of the *Whisperer*, the crew repeated the process at the calling of Jennings, "Heave," from the mainsail to the foresail, then the jib. Then, repeating the process they moved to the ropes for the gaff-topsail and the main gaff-topsail. This process took only a few moments as the crew was well trained in the setting of the sails and rigging of the ship.

Captain Waterman put his glass to his eye and checked our closest pursuer now, the frigate that had been off our starboard beam, was now off our port beam and was now uncomfortably close. The frigate that had been paralleling us off our port was now tacking in response to our change in course, and was lumbering to do so, and for now was of no concern. Looking to our port bow, Captain Waterman could now just see the two frigates that had been pursuing us off our port stern, as they were now able to make up some closing distance.

The north wind changed to northwest, pushing us at a great rate as our bow slammed into the waves before us pushing them aside, as the spray of the ocean soaked our deck.

"We have a chance now, men!" Captain Waterman called to all on deck as the men hung on to the rigging and awaited orders.

The boom of the bow chasers of the frigate to our port reminded us we were not out of danger, as spouts of water emerged well to the starboard side of the *Whisperer.* We were within range of her bow chasers, and these were the critical moments. If they hit us with a crippling blow, all would be lost.

"Billings," Captain Waterman called, "tighten the jib and the fore gaff-sail, if you please!" Looking to me, he said calmly, "Bring us to a south sou'east heading, Will." Then he turned, glassing the frigate now on our port quarter.

The boom and splash of water off our starboard side again caused the captain to look up at the sails for damage. The main gaff-topsail had a hole torn through her, which caused her to spill all her wind. Still the damage to the sail wouldn't slow us enough for the frigate to catch us.

Splintering wood from our port side rail told that at least one of the next shots hit home, as gouges in the rails and deck told of where the shot had damaged our side. Edwards was on the deck holding his leg as splinters of wood protruded from his pants, his blood staining the deck. Jennings and Garden were at his side, tying a rope around his leg to help stem the flow of blood.

The captain's full attention was now directed to the frigate on our port quarter that was well within a half-mile of us, had found the range and was pounding us with shot from her bow chasers.

The next shots were high as she must have fired on the upward roll of a swell, sending the shots through our rigging, snapping several ropes, but otherwise causing no serious damage to the *Whisperer*, falling harmlessly into the ocean to our starboard.

We were making good headway still and putting enough distance between us and this frigate that the captain was heard to utter to himself, "Five more minutes and we are out to sea," as he scrutinized our pursuer's movements.

The next shot from our pursuers sealed our fate. One shot fell just off our bowsprit without causing any damage, but the other hit our foremast just below the fore gaff-topsail. It was not a glancing blow, but almost a direct hit on the wooden mast, which splintered greatly. The mast in the area of the damage began to lean to starboard, as the wind still blew hard out of the northwest.

"Hard to starboard," the captain called trying to relieve the stress off of the mast, but to no avail. The mast was too damaged and the wind blew too strong, as the ropes and rigging moaned as the mast leaned ever farther to starboard. Far past what could have been expected of the rigging and ropes to hold, they snapped with a loud release of energy, the top foremast and fore gaff-topsail crashed partly to the deck and partly into the ocean. Immediately, the debris began to act as a great anchor, having a twofold effect on the *Whisperer*. First, her forward speed was reduced to less than half; and secondly, it caused the ship to want to turn hard to starboard, as it was all I could handle to keep her on her current course.

Captain Waterman stepped forward and yelled, "Clear that wreckage away!" as the hands all moved forward, grabbing hatchets from the forward stowage box and began chopping away at the ropes and rigging holding the mast and sails to the ship!

The pursuing frigate, now within half a mile, fired again, with the shot passing through our main sail, but in no other way causing us damage. Before the frigate had time to reload and fire again, the wreckage was freed from the *Whisperer* and pushed into the ocean. The *Whisperer* responded immediately as she had enough remaining sail to escape our pursuer as she began to crash through the waves, pushing them aside again.

But our escape to the open ocean and safety was not to be. As another shot from the frigate hit our main mast half-way up from the deck and the main gaff-topsail. The main mast began to lean strongly to starboard and remained upright for only a few agonizing moments as it came crashing down, partly on the deck and partly into the ocean in a tangled mess of rope, rigging, tackle, block, masts and sails. The effect was much greater than that of the foremast and sails, as the mainsail and gaff-topsail along with all of the rigging almost stopped our forward momentum. To my great horror, the mast, when it crashed to the deck, crushed Edwards, killing him instantly.

Looking forward to the carnage on the deck, I saw Billings and McKiernay lay in their blood, as innumerable splinters from the second bow chaser shot had hit the deck, showering them in splinters. They were already dead. Jennings and Boyle, who had been swept overboard with the wreckage, were hanging onto it for their lives. Both showed signs of being severely injured, as their shirts showed signs of blood stains, even with grasping the wreckage in the ocean. A moment later, weakened by the loss of blood, they lost their grip on the wreckage and were lost to the ocean. Only Garden remained forward, as he had received serious injuries, showing signs of splinter wounds.

The captain, looking to the frigate now closing in on us from our port side, somehow looked ten years older as he stated to me, "Lower our colors, Will, I must go below deck and prepare to surrender my ship." Johnny, the cabin boy, had remained below deck during this entire scene of battle and carnage, as he had never been fired upon before.

Turning, I lowered the colors, draping them over the now useless helm.

The frigate, now within fifty yards, broke off her attack seeing that we were dead in the water, with our colors lowered. Sailors on the ship were hoisting a boat from the deck to be lowered into the water. I assumed a prize crew would be among the officers, marines and sailors who would be coming aboard.

I left the helm and made my way through the wreckage to Edwards. It was plain to see that he was crushed by the falling debris and was dead. I then made my way through the tangled mess and found Garden sitting on the deck, against the rail, trying to stop the bleeding in his left arm and upper chest. None of his wounds, at this time, seemed life-threatening. I sent Johnny below deck to find some clean cloth to dress Garden's wounds. With Johnny gone, I checked on Billings and McKiernay, finding that they were both dead, as they had long since bled out from the severe splinter wounds to their chest and abdomen areas. Johnny returned with some old sail cloth, and I turned to help Garden with his wounds. The British boat was now drawing alongside and I could see that over twenty men, including at least ten marines, were about to board our helpless ship.

The boat was now alongside, as several marines and sailors scurried over the side onto the deck of the *Whisperer*, securing the boat with several lines to our ship. Johnny, Garden and I just stood among the wreckage and debris, as we watched the British take our ship. The marines, when all were on board, formed a line five across and two deep, with their arms at the ready, bayonets affixed. The handful of sailors all congregated behind the marines and continued to secure the boat, then assisted the officers over the side. Three officers appeared last. It appeared to me to be two lieutenants, along with the captain of the frigate. The latter was first to speak.

He took several moments to survey the damage his ship's gunners had wreaked upon the *Whisperer*, and seemed satisfied with the job done. Looking at the three men before him amid the wreckage, in deep and resonating voice commanded, "Where is the captain?" Not waiting for a reply he continued, "Who is in command here?"

"The captain is below deck preparing to surrender his ship," I stated flatly, looking at the captain before me.

"Sergeant Herrington," the captain barked, "take four men and go below deck, bring this captain to me and see to it that there are no more crew lurking below!"

"Aye, Captain," the sergeant replied, pointing to the four nearest marines, directing them to follow him below deck.

The captain, looking at us with obvious disdain, turned to the remaining marines and stated, "Bring those three here, lets clap them in irons, so we don't have to worry about them."

The marines began moving forward toward our position, with some difficulty, having to climb over and through the debris of what remained of our rigging on deck, with their guns in hand.

We were obliged to follow them since we had nowhere to go, and nothing to fight with. All of our guns on deck remained unloaded through the whole desperate affair, and our pistols, along with our muskets were still stowed and locked below deck in the gun locker.

When we reached the stern of the *Whisperer*, two of the sailors scrambled back over the side, securing from the bottom of the jolly boat, several sets of ankle and hand irons. The sailors clapped us in irons and left us standing next to our marine guard, who relaxed their stance, now that any type of resistance would be utter suicide. The captain and lieutenants remained near the helm at the stern, still looking upon us with utter contempt.

Movement could now be heard in the hold, as those below were beginning to make their way out of the hold. I first heard the captain's voice as he was complaining to his captors about his treatment.

"I'm going, I'm going, you don't have to keep pointing that thing at me!" Captain Waterman was yelling to the marine that was menacing him with his bayonet.

As the captain emerged from below decks through the hatchway, he was wearing a blue uniform that I had never seen before, and obviously never knew he had. He looked the part of a real captain, as if wearing the uniform made him so. The sergeant and four marines followed him out of the hatchway. Captain Waterman walked over to the captain of the British frigate and stated before him, "I am Captain Jeremiah Waterman, Captain of the good ship, *Whisperer*."

The British captain ignored Captain Waterman's remarks and looking past him, directed his comments now to the marine sergeant.

"Report, Sergeant, if you please," the captain stated.

In his heavy British isle brogue, the sergeant replied, "No one below, sir, save the captain who we found in his cabin."

"Very well, Sergeant," the captain stated, "you and your men may fall in with the rest of your detachment."

With this said the five marines moved to position themselves behind us with the detail complement.

Now, turning his attention to Captain Waterman, the captain of the British ship surveyed his quarry that he had been chasing for so long, spending much energy and resources to catch. After thoroughly looking Captain Waterman over from head to toe, he proclaimed, "I am Captain Jonathon Bardwell. I am commander of the forces sent to destroy all privateers harassing His Majesty's commerce and operating in the theatre of the waters from New York City south along the New Jersey, Delaware, Maryland, and Virginia coasts to the North Carolina colony border. Furthermore, I have orders to find, capture or destroy the privateer, which sails from the port of Philadelphia identified as the *Whisperer.* Well, Captain, your days of privateering and raiding our commerce along these coasts have come to a decided and inglorious end. Additionally, I have in my possession, warrants from his lordship, General Sir Henry Clinton, commanding all British forces in His Majesty's colonies, issuing the death of all men, sailors and officers of the privateer known as the two-mast schooner *Whisperer.*"

"Death?" Captain Waterman uttered.

"Indeed, death," the captain repeated. "You and your men are to be hanged, from the yardarm, until dead," Captain Bardwell surmised with cold brown eyes staring at Captain Waterman.

"Captain," Captain Waterman pleaded, stepping forward as he spoke. This movement caused an immediate response from the marine guard, the forward two of whom forced their bayoneted guns between the two captains.

"I implore you," Captain Waterman stated earnestly as he pressed against the two guns stopping him from gaining another inch toward Captain Bardwell. "If I must die to satisfy the warrants of General Clinton and His Majesty in England, so be it, but these lads are just young men who are not responsible for my actions as captain of the *Whisperer.*"

"Lieutenant Cooper," Captain Bardwell barked half looking over his left shoulder for the young lieutenant he was addressing.

"Sir!" Lieutenant Cooper responded, as he was the nearer of the two lieutenants standing just behind the captain.

"Do you have the required length of rope to hang these traitorous rebels?" the captain demanded.

"I believe there is sufficient rope to do the job in the stern of the jolly boat, Captain," the lieutenant replied.

"If you please, Lieutenant, retrieve it and have four strong nooses slung," the captain ordered. "I don't want to have to hang any of these traitors more than once."

The lieutenant went to the side and directed two of the sailors to the stern of the jolly boat to retrieve the required rope.

Captain Waterman began to plead with Captain Bardwell to spare us as members of his crew, who only obeyed orders just as the men of his own crew were subjected to do. As the sailors came back over the side from the jolly boat, they were hauling the required length of rope, which took the two of them, as well as the three remaining sailors, to haul onto the deck of the *Whisperer.*

"Sergeant," Captain Bardwell called, "bind Captain Waterman's hands, if you please."

The sergeant, who was handed a length of rope by one of the sailors, walked behind Captain Waterman and grabbing both hands, which Captain Waterman willingly gave, bound his hands before him. Even as this was happening, Captain Waterman, going to his knees with tears flowing down his face, continued to plead with Captain Bardwell, to have mercy on his remaining crew.

"Sergeant, take two men and hang that rope over what remains of the foremast," the captain ordered in a cold voice.

The sergeant moved forward with two of his marines with a length of rope thirty feet long. The five sailors moved forward, on their own, with the marines, positioning themselves at the stay tackles on the port side of the ship. It took several repeated throws by the sergeant to get the rope to catch on the splintered remains of the foremast where it snapped off about ten feet above the deck, where the fore gaff-sail and boom had been. Once this was done, one end of the rope was looped around the stay tackle on the port side by two of the sailors, while the other sailors went to the end of the length hanging off the foremast and began working it into a noose. Once this was completed, the three sailors returned to the stay tackle, while the sergeant and two marines positioned themselves at the noose.

We all stood in silence as we watched the activity around the foremast and the completion of the noose, which was to be used to hang Captain Waterman. No one moved or spoke for a moment.

"Captain, if you please," Captain Bardwell spoke up suddenly, with a firm voice that was unwavering, indicating that he was fully prepared to go through with the execution of the captain of the *Whisperer.*

Captain Waterman, hesitating a moment, stated to Captain Bardwell, "Will you allow me two requests, Captain, before you go through with this outrageous act of barbarism?"

"Within reason, Captain," the British captain replied with a wry smirk on his face.

"First, I want your word as an officer and a gentleman that the three remaining members of my crew are not to be killed. That, if you must condemn them, that they be placed on a prison ship where they may have some chance of release or escape," Captain Waterman hesitated as Captain Bardwell mulled this request over in his mind, and finally acquiesced.

"I give you my word as a gentleman that I will deliver these three men alive, if it is possible and in their present condition to a prison ship in New York Harbor," Captain Bardwell conceded. "And your second request?" the captain asked.

"That you give me five minutes alone with my men to bid my farewells and to put what affairs I can, in order," Captain Waterman said.

"A most reasonable request, Captain," the British captain acknowledged, "you have your five minutes."

With that, Captain Waterman and the three of us made our way to the far corner of the stern where we could talk for a few brief moments out of the earshot of the British officers, marines and sailors. Once there, Captain Waterman began talking in earnest as he had much to tell us and only a few moments in which to do it.

"Listen carefully, as I want this to be my last wishes on earth and have to rely on you to carry them out," he said looking at all three of us. "First, Will, you are in charge of my matters and must look after Garden and Johnny, if any of you live."

"Yes," I said as a tear now streamed down my cheek.

"You must, absolutely must, take whatever steps necessary to escape from the prison ships you are now condemned to. Without parole or pardon, you will survive only a few months, at most, in such desperate conditions as those you will find in a stinking British prison hulk.

Next, if you are able to survive and escape, I have set aside a nice sum from the many prizes we have taken over the past two years as a privateer. Will," he said, looking at me, "do you remember the old man at the livery in Providence, Master Thomas?" he asked.

I squeaked out in a low voice as I held back my tears, "I do."

"Go and see him and tell him what has happened," my uncle stated. "Tell him that you are to receive all of my monies and property, and I will leave it up to you to disperse the monies between you and Garden here, and young Johnny."

I was crying now, as tears flowed freely down my face, and I could barely see my uncle standing before me, such was the flow of tears. Both Garden and Johnny were now crying, too.

"Will, tell your father what happened, and that I'm sorry it came to this for you and these good men. Now take my hand and shake it like men, and as hard as this is, as a follower of Christ, our Lord, I will see you again on the other side," Uncle Jeremiah finished, as he held out his hand. Now, for the first time he began to show emotion as tears welled up in his eyes.

Garden was the first to hold out his hand and Uncle Jeremiah shook it warmly. Next, was Johnny, who could barely hold his hand up to Uncle Jeremiah's. Finally, Uncle Jeremiah turned to me, and grabbing my hand, he took it, pulled me to him and he hugged me as I had never been hugged before. He held me tight as he whispered in my ear, "If ever I had a son, I'd want him to be you, Will," he said.

"It is time, Captain," Captain Bardwell stated coldly.

My uncle pulled away from me, and walked the dead man's walk to the foremast where his executioners awaited him. He turned as he got there and faced the stern of his ship, looking from face to face. Finally, his gaze remained fixed on me.

"Do your duty, Sergeant!" the British captain called out.

The sergeant of the marines moved forward, placing the noose over my uncle's head and tightened it so that it was now secured around his neck, and the knot was just behind his left ear. Stepping back, the sergeant looked at his commander.

The British captain just nodded his head toward the sergeant without saying a word. This being the signal to hang my uncle, the sergeant shouted out, "Heave, heave!"

The five sailors stationed at the stay tackle pulled with all their might as any slackness in the rope was taken away on the first pull. On the second pull my uncle was lifted off the deck, and he strained at the rope pulling his head, as the weight of his body pulled down. The five sailors at the stay tackle strained at the weight of my uncle as they pulled a third time, lifting him a little further off the deck. My uncle's face was now bright red, his eyes were bulging and his teeth were clenched together and sweat poured down his face, as with all of his strength he fought to breathe, as the pangs of death were at his door.

"Heave!" the sergeant called one more time.

For several agonizing moments he remained suspended between the heavens and earth. His body began to shake and moved with grotesque gestures as he struggled for air and life. This gross spectacle went on for what seemed several minutes, but in reality lasted less than a minute and as suddenly as he was lifted off the deck, his entire body went limp, as he was dead. I looked away, trying to stifle the sobbing, and shaking that now overtook my body.

Seeing that he was dead, the sergeant of the marines requested by the British captain, "Permission to remove the body and slip him overboard, sir."

"Leave him, and scuttle the ship," Captain Bardwell directed. "He'll go down with his ship."

The sergeant stared unbelieving that his captain would be so cold as not to allow for an honorable burial, even if this man was considered an enemy of the Crown.

"Scuttle the ship!" Captain Bardwell ordered sternly to the sergeant, "then prepare to move your prisoners to the *Wales*."

The sergeant ordered the two marines next to him down the hatch to scuttle the ship, presumably by knocking holes in the hull so that the ocean water would flood in, sinking the ship slowly, giving us time to evacuate to the British frigate.

The British sailors were quickly over the side and in the jolly boat making all preparations to depart to the frigate. After them went several of the marines who positioned themselves fore and aft in the jolly boat. Next, we were hurried to the side as well as could be done in shackles, and over we went into the boat. We were seated in the middle of the boat between the positions of the sailors who were to row. The only men remaining on the *Whisperer* were the captain, the two lieutenants, the sergeant of the marines, and the two marines who went below deck to scuttle the ship, along with the bodies of Billings, Edwards, McKiernay and my uncle.

Whisperer was already lower in the water when the captain appeared at the side of the ship. He came over smartly like he had done this all his life. The two lieutenants and the sergeant followed him. The two marines were last off the *Whisperer*. The captain positioned himself at the stern with one of his lieutenants, who took control of the tiller.

"Push off!" the captain called, as the sailors on the starboard side of the jolly boat used their oars to fend off the ship. The jolly boat bobbed across the water to the frigate, as I had to repress the urge to look behind me at the *Whisperer* before she went down. We were at the frigate in less than a quarter-hour and tied to her side. As prisoners, we went up the side and found ourselves on the deck of a British frigate, with the entire watch of the day staring at us. We huddled together as we were unsure of the next course of action.

The captain, lieutenants and marines all came over the side as the sailors remained in the jolly boat to prepare to hoist the boat on deck. Looking over at the *Whisperer*, she was up to her side rails in the water now, and it would only be a moment before the ocean would take her. I watched as the water suddenly flooded over the side rails, as the loose cargo and debris from below deck was pushed by the rushing water and blown by the air out of the open hatches and into the ocean. My uncle and his body slipped below the water line, as he remained attached to the rope, followed shortly by the remnants of the foremast. The *Whisperer* was gone. As I was pushed and prodded by the sergeant and his marines toward the open hatch that led below decks, the sun was setting in the western sky; I realized that I had lived to see the last run of the *Whisperer.*

- CHAPTER 18

"Prison Ship *Jersey*"

July - September 1781

I had seen many British warships since the start of the war. I counted many in Boston Harbor, at the island of Bermuda, Charleston, South Carolina colony, and Philadelphia when sailing with my uncle in 1774. I had seen many more in Boston Harbor during the siege of Boston in 1775. I had felt the full force of many British warships during the siege of Philadelphia and the reduction of Mud Island Fort on Mud Island, during the fall of 1777, but this was my first time on a ship of this size.

As we went down the hatchway below deck, I was taken aback by the stench and disorder. There were smells I had never smelled before nor thought I'd ever experience. On deck was the crew of the watch, but below deck there seemed to be double their numbers. Some were in their hammocks getting rest, some were at makeshift tables playing cards or other games of chance that they had thought up in their hours of boredom; as yet others were gathered in small groups on the middle deck engaged in all manner of conversation. There were a few lanterns scattered about, hanging by hooks from the bottom of the deck beams above, but the numbers were inadequate, as they left the middle deck a dark, dreary place.

I also took note of how cramped this deck was, as I had to bend over in order not to hit my head on the beams of the deck above. In addition to the men, hammocks and all of their belongings, there were at least fourteen cannons on this deck, which took up the lion's share of the remaining space.

As we followed our marine guard onto this deck, the sailors became silent watching us pass. Many of them cursed, and threw insults at us, as yet others spit upon us in our passing.

We went down another hatchway from this deck to an even darker, danker and more dimly lit deck. The marine guard led on, and I stumbled several times, as I could not see my footing on this deck, in the darkness. The lead marine did carry a lantern, but it only functioned to illuminate his path, and to outline his body. We were on the supply deck, the cargo hold, I supposed, as innumerable barrels and containers of supplies were passed, along with an occasional lantern that dimly lit the passageway. I thought that we now were below the water line as it was considerably cooler on this deck, and I could see my breath.

To my surprise we went down yet another hatchway, and we found ourselves in the bowels of the ship. This area of the ship was so small that I had to hunch over to get into the area. Garden and Johnny followed me, and we huddled in a corner next to each other. One marine followed us in, and taking a chain, ran it through our foot shackles. The marine then placed the chain through a ring attached to the hull of the ship, where a lock was located, and locked it. We were sitting on rocks, with water sloshing about our feet. There were no lanterns here, as our only light came from a lantern twenty feet away, on the deck above us in the cargo hold. It provided only indirect light, and it was nearly as dark as a night, without moonlight. Although the sun had just set when we were placed in the bottom of the ship, there was now no way of telling time or knowing if it was daytime or nighttime. Such was the darkness of our prison and current hell.

Before the marine departed with his comrades, he checked our lock and chains one last time, before returning to the upper decks. He only glanced once behind himself as he snickered at our cruel condition, then he left.

"Where are we?" I asked.

"We are below the cargo hold, in the ballast of the ship," Garden answered. He hesitated a moment and stated, "These rocks are the ballast. The water is entering the ship from a leaky seam. We are probably ten feet below the water line, and if the sailors of the watch don't work the pumps, to pump enough water out, we could drown here."

"If this ship is engaged in a battle, and is hit below the water line, we will drown for certain," I put in.

"Undoubtedly," Garden answered.

Johnny began to whimper, as he was already shivering from sitting on the cold ballast rocks, with his feet in a few inches of water. We huddled together as best we could, but we were all shivering within the hour from the cold, damp conditions of the ballast hold. We could tell when the ship was in high seas, as we could feel the rolling of the ship, with the sloshing of the water. After what seemed several hours of this rolling, we all became sick, and had no option, but to vomit where we were. The smell of our vomit made us even more nauseous, causing us to vomit again.

It was the same with relieving ourselves. With being chained to the hull in the ballast hold, we were reduced to relieving ourselves as needed. The smell in the ballast hold quickly became overwhelming, as we suffered in a hell of vomit, excrement and smells. I began to think that perhaps my uncle was the lucky one, as at least his suffering had come to an end.

It must have been several hours later when we heard a noise on the cargo deck above us, through the open hatchway, and a light began to show its illumination as it drew closer.

Suddenly, a British sailor appeared in the hatchway holding a lantern, looking down at us, and upon our poor miserable condition. Our eyes now accustomed to the darkness had to be shielded from the light of the lantern. Although we acknowledged he was there, none of us looked up after realizing that he was not there to change our condition.

"Will, is that you?" he asked after several moments of gazing upon us.

"My name is, Will, if that is what you are asking," I replied.

"It is me, Jones," he said, "don't you remember me? I thought that was you they brought on board."

"Jones," I mused a little bewildered.

"Don't you remember, Hotaling and I were pressed off the *Whisperer*, when we were off the island of Bermuda in '74," he recalled.

"Hotaling," I repeated as I searched my mind. "Yes, I remember now."

"This is the same ship that we were pressed on," Jones recollected, "do you remember now?"

Looking up at the sailor in the hatchway, I would never have known that it was Jones with whom I had sailed on the *Whisperer* in "74.

"I can't talk now," Jones said, "I am on watch. I knew the cook had some grub left from the evening meal. He let me bring it to you, well, with the permission of the officer of the watch," Jones detailed. "Here, take this," he said, handing me a plate with scraps of meat on it along with some gravy.

"I have to get back, but I'll see you on the morrow."

"Jones," I questioned as he turned to go, "what time of day is it now?"

"It's the evening watch," Jones said, "the sunset some time ago when you were brought on board. Look, I've got to go, but I'll see you on the morrow."

Jones left us in our murky darkness in the misery of our vomit and human waste. I was holding the plate, which held barely enough food for a child to eat as a meal, let alone three men chained in a hold that hadn't eaten for hours. We took turns using our fingers to scrape the morsels of food off the plate. We each had nothing more than half a mouthful before the food was gone. It was going to be a long, cold, and hungry night.

Garden developed a cough overnight as the cold, dark and wet conditions, in which we were imprisoned, weakened his condition from the wood splinter wounds he had suffered during the attack on the *Whisperer*. Most of his wounds had stopped bleeding, but many of them still contained the splinters. Undoubtedly, unless he received medical attention, they would fester, eventually causing his death.

Johnny and I seemed to be faring as well as possible under the conditions, other than being wet and cold all the time.

The following morning or at least I expected it to be morning, a gruff old sailor came to the hatchway of the ballast hold, throwing down some scraps of bread to us and departing without saying a word.

The time seemed to pass interminably slowly, for not knowing if it was day or night, left us confused and disoriented. We were all suffering greatly now as the cold and wetness was beginning to tell on us.

Jones appeared out of the darkness on what was our second day of captivity, and told us it was the change of the afternoon watch. He brought us our meager rations again.

"Jones," I pleaded, "is there a doctor on board?"

"Aye, there is, why do ye ask?" he replied.

"Garden here is in a bad way," I began. "He has splinters in many of his wounds still and needs attention."

"I'll mention it to the officer of the watch, but I don't think the captain will allow the doctor to give him any medical care. You know, Will, this captain is a plain nasty man, and when General Clinton gave him the warrants for the captain and crew of the *Whisperer*, it was his single mission in this war to find you. I am surprised that he let you live."

"Where are we Jones?" I asked.

"We sailed south after you were captured," Jones began. "I heard some of the lieutenants saying we were after the *Congress* out of Philadelphia.

Something about her sailing to the Caribbean on a secret mission," Jones said. "I heard one of the lieutenants tell that if we didn't sight anything today, we'd turn north, and head for New York City. Captain Bardwell wants to report to General Clinton that the *Whisperer* was captured, the captain killed, and the ship sunk. Will, half the British navy's been looking for the *Whisperer* for the better part of a year, they were."

"But why?" I wondered, speaking aloud.

"I suppose because of all the supply ships Captain Waterman took," Jones reasoned. "He put a hurtin' on the British sailors, and soldiers in New York City, denying all that food and supplies to 'em."

I mulled that over in my mind for a while. I had only been at sea with my uncle for a few months, and we had taken only a couple insignificant supply ships in that time. My uncle must have been a very busy privateer in the months and years prior to my sailing with him.

"Jones, where's Hotaling?" I asked.

"Don't ya know he died of scurvy, back three years ago now," Jones replied.

"Why didn't you escape when you had a chance?" I inquired.

"Me and Hotaling tried," Jones stated. "Many a time, and every time we were caught, they gave us two dozen at the grating, they did. Captain Buckham was bad enough, but when Captain Bardwell came aboard, well, he's just plain mean, giving us an extra twelve lashes the last time. Hotaling got sick after that one and he couldn't get better. We were low on proper food and water, and all the like. On half rations we were, and he couldn't fight anymore. Like I said, that was goin' on three years ago now, and I ain't tried since, not with this captain on board."

Jones hesitated for a moment, and I didn't know what to say. Garden was moaning now, and coughed once in a while. Johnny just sat there huddling next to me, listening to our conversation.

"Listen, Will," Jones warned as he began to go, "no one on board knows I know ye, and it is best kept that way. I'll help you best I can, but for now all I can do is bring you food."

Jones' face disappeared from the hatchway, and his light quickly faded as he walked down the cargo hold, to the decks above.

Nothing changed for the next several days. We would receive meager rations in the morning from a British sailor we didn't know. Then, during the afternoon watch Jones would bring us additional food, along with a little news. This was our existence for the first few days. Jones informed us that after the fourth day at sea, we had turned north to return to New York

City. A ship over the horizon had signaled that the *Congress* had slipped away, and was now believed to be well on its way to the Port of Francois, Martinique, in the Caribbean.

I calculated in my mind that if we had sailed south for almost four full days that we must be below the Carolinas. If we now headed north it would be another week or longer before we could expect to reach New York Harbor.

Our misery continued unabated during these days, as our living conditions never changed. It was on the third day north that Garden died. He stopped making his moaning, and coughing sounds, and I knew he must have passed. It was hard to tell by the touch if he was dead, because we were all so cold. I nudged him a couple of times, and got no response. I didn't tell Johnny, as I didn't want to cause him any more pain.

When Jones came down during the afternoon watch with our food, I told him.

"Jones," I said, "Garden here is dead. He died sometime this morning."

"Are you sure?" Jones questioned.

"I've been in this war now for six years, Jones, and I think I know a dead man when I see him, especially one right next to me," I retorted.

Johnny gasped as he realized that Garden was dead.

"I'll be back," Jones said, as he quickly disappeared.

He reappeared with an officer, and the two of them looked down into the ballast hold at us. The officer quickly pulled away as the stench from our condition overwhelmed him.

"It is as I said," Jones declared similarly. "The one is dead, and the other two will surely die if we don't get them out of there, Lieutenant."

"Go and get the marine guard, and have them report to me here," the lieutenant charged.

Jones was quickly gone, as the lieutenant remained at the hatchway holding a kerchief over his face to fend off the smells of squalor, coming up from the ballast hold.

After several moments, Jones returned with two marines in tow. One of the marines saluted, addressing the lieutenant.

"You called for us, sir," the marine stated smartly.

"Yes, escort these two prisoners," pointing to Johnny and me, "and secure them to the mast before the jolly boat."

Jones took a key from the lieutenant, and jumped down into the ballast hold. Within a moment he had us free, and was helping us to our feet. Both Johnny and I could hardly stand, as our feet were half frozen from being in cold water for a week. After several minutes we were able to stand on our own, and climbed up into the cargo hold. One marine remained in front of us, while one followed behind as our escorts. Jones, along with the lieutenant followed behind the second marine. I overheard the lieutenant order Jones to get a detail of men, remove the dead prisoner out of the ballast hold, and to get him over the side. The lieutenant was also going to report to the captain.

As we reached the gun deck where the crew was, the light streaming in from the hatchway from the main deck overwhelmed both Johnny and me, as I could not see. We each put our faces in the crook of our elbows to shield our eyes, holding our other hand out in front of us, to protect us from walking into the many objects on this deck. With all of the gear and belongings of the crew, along with the ship's supplies on this deck, we stumbled our way to the hatch. Once there, Jones grabbed my arm, to guide me, as Johnny held onto my shoulder to keep up. I knew we were on deck now as I could feel the warmth of the sun, accompanied with a strong, fresh breeze blowing. The putrid smells below deck were quickly forgotten.

We still couldn't see, as Jones told us to sit on the deck. Obeying quickly and quietly, we sat as we heard the chain that had bound us below deck, being wrapped around the mast and relocked.

The sounds of the ship were all too familiar to me, as I listened to the creak of the masts, and the ripple of the wind on the sails. I could imagine the men moving about doing their duties, as the officers shouted orders to them. It took the better part of half an hour before I could begin to see again. At first there were foggy images moving about. Then they became a little clearer, as I began to make out the bodies of men moving to and fro. I looked next to me, and saw Johnny sitting there still shielding his eyes.

"Johnny," I asked, "are you okay?"

Johnny could only nod as he was still regaining his senses. The fresh ocean air had brought me back to life. I was now looking around at the activity on the ship. It seemed that the British were so efficient in everything they did on board this ship. I surmised it was from centuries of perfecting the art of sailing.

Suddenly, out of the hatchway before us came four sailors, one of them being Jones. They were carrying the dead body of Garden. As unceremoniously as they could, they carried his lifeless body to the side of the ship, putting him over. I heard a splash as his body hit the water. Jones and his mates walked by us, none of them acknowledging our existence.

After leaving us at the mast for an hour, a marine guard came to escort us to the head, to properly relieve ourselves. There was also a bucket that was attached to a rope, and we were allowed to drop it into the ocean to douse ourselves with water, in an effort to clean ourselves. I almost began to feel like a person again.

We were then escorted by the marine guard below decks, but instead of being secured in the ballast hold; we were placed in a makeshift brig, in the cargo hold. Although we were well below deck, at least here there was a little light, and from time to time we would catch the smell of fresh air. We were also allowed regular trips above deck to the head. We were still given meager rations, and only an occasional drink of water, but our overall current conditions were a great improvement to being held in the ballast hold.

Two days later, Jones brought us our evening meal, if that is what it could be called. It consisted of two pieces of bread, and watery slop to dip the bread in.

"We'll be in New York Harbor by the morning, Will," he informed. "There are several prison ships in the harbor, and there is talk of separating you two."

"What are the prison ships like?" I asked.

"I've only seen them from a distance, but what they are, is different ships of the line that have been pulled out of commission, then stripped of everything of value, including all of the masts, sails, rigging and guns. They are anchored in Wallabout Bay off the Brooklyn shore of Long Island. There is a marine guard on each ship, and from what I hear they're not above brutalizing the prisoners. I've heard the food is probably worse than you got here, as the overall conditions are as bad as you've experience in the ballast hold. I was told that most of the prisoners held on these ships are dead within a few months, if they aren't paroled."

"It's all that bad is it?" I probed.

"It's all that and even worse from what I understand," Jones replied.

"How many prison ships are there in New York Harbor?" I questioned.

"Well, as best as I can recall, there must be fifteen or so," Jones calculated. "Pray you don't get the *Jersey*," he added. "Word is that's the worst of 'em with as many as ten dead men a day, taken off of her."

Jones left us, and we had the night to ponder what the next day would bring.

We must have reached the mouth of New York Harbor sometime in the night, for we bobbed about like a cork for most of the night. Morning came and the hands were called to set the headsails, as we were underway again, sailing into the harbor. Johnny and I were still below deck in the cargo hold, but we had enough sea experience to know what was happening up on deck. The anchor was let go, as we could hear the anchor chain run out. The normal ship's activity was underway with a ship that had just dropped anchor once it arrived in port. The captain had reports, along with dispatches to provide to the port admiral, as well as to his lordship, General Sir Henry Clinton.

With the captain over the side to provide his reports and dispatches to the British powers in New York City, we could hear the officer of the watch order another boat lowered.

A half-hour later, the sergeant of the marines, with a four-marine guard, appeared at our prison in the cargo hold. The door was unlocked. We remained in our shackles, shuffling our feet as we tried to keep up with the marines, as they made their way to the stairs of the hatchway, to the gun deck. We went up another set of stairs from the gun deck, and found ourselves on the main deck of the ship.

Although we had had a little indirect light in our makeshift prison on the cargo deck, it wasn't enough light to allow our eyes to adjust to the bright sun on deck. Once again we found ourselves blinded, relying on each other not to run into anything, or anyone until our eyes had adjusted.

After several minutes, with our eyes adjusted to the light, we were shuffled over to the side. There below us, was the jolly boat loaded with several seamen, along with four marines, all awaiting our disembarkation into the boat.

Johnny went over the side first, and had to make sure of every step, as not to slip, and fall into the jolly boat. As he was making his way down the side, I had time to look over the deck. Jones was twenty feet from me, watching all of the activities of our departure. When I put my gaze upon him, he looked away, not wanting to give any indication to his mates that he knew me, I supposed.

Looking out over the harbor, I had never seen so many ships. Most were British navy warships of every size and shape. All were flying the Union Jack off the jack staff. There were so many, I didn't even begin to count them. In addition to the warships, there were any number of merchant ships, whose flags I couldn't recognize. Assuredly, many nations from Europe, as well as the Far East were represented here. It looked to me as though we had anchored about a quarter-mile off of Staten Island. I could make out the lower tip of Manhattan, Nutten and Long Island, all off to the north and east side of the harbor.

I was actually lost in the view before me, when one of the marines to my side gave me a stern nudge with the butt of his musket, bringing me back to the reality of my captivity, and impending imprisonment.

As I began my descent into the jolly boat, I thought to myself that I hadn't taken notice of any ships in the harbor that appeared to be the dreaded prison ships.

Once in the jolly boat, I took my seat in front of Johnny and between the sailors who were to row the boat, with marine guards in front of, and behind us.

The sailors pushed off, as we began our trek across New York Harbor. I had no idea where these prison ships were located. As we pulled away from the frigate, I could see the sailors lining the starboard rail, to watch us go, among them was my old shipmate Jones.

We were crossed to the Brooklyn shore of Long Island, and then we rowed parallel to it. After a quarter-hour, we began to pass Gowanus Bay. I recognized the area where the Maryland Four Hundred had sacrificed themselves to help save the army during the battle of Long Island, several years earlier. We were then rowed between Nutten Island and Brooklyn Heights. I stared at Nutten Island, where the defensive works we had constructed could still be seen, for the defense of New York City. The British had strengthened, and expanded the works of the star fort we had built. An enormous tent city could be seen at the lower end of the island, which obviously supported the British soldiers detailed to defend the island now.

Off to my right on Brooklyn Heights, the British had built a large star fort, as well as redoubts that encircled the fort for an area that looked to be a mile square.

I tried to think back to the year I was here defending the area, and could not remember when it was now. I could only think how much everything had changed, since I had been here with the army.

We passed the island and began to enter the East River. The tide was with us; consequently the rowing of the seamen was aided by the flow of the tide.

The East River narrowed with Manhattan to our left side and Brooklyn on our right. I could now see along the Manhattan shoreline and to the hills overlooking the East River. The British had been busy indeed since their capture of New York City, as Brooklyn and Manhattan were now dotted with many impenetrable fortresses.

The East River made a sharp turn to the right. As we were rowed around the corner, a bay appeared that went several hundred yards inland, and was at least a half-mile across. As I gazed up the river still, where the East River narrowed, I could see the tip of Blackwell's Island several miles away.

Anchored before us were about fifteen ships in various states of disrepair, being stripped of their masts, rigging, sails, and armaments.

Standing on the decks of these ships were soldiers, and sailors in all manner of wretchedness. Some were half-clothed, as all were suffering from lack of food, or were in need of medical attention. Dotted among the masses on the decks of these ships were the British marine guards, dressed in their scarlet uniforms.

A gangplank came down the side of the ship, leading to a floating dock, which was tied alongside. Here our boat came to rest, as a sergeant of the marine guard on the floating prison came down with two additional marines, to meet our boat.

Looking in the boat, at the marines, the sergeant said, "What have we here, Corporal, two more for our complement of rebels?"

The corporal looking up from the boat stated, "Treat these two, well, Sergeant, as they are the only survivors of the privateer *Whisperer*, which we hunted down and sunk, some time ago."

"Surely, neither of these two are the captain," the sergeant stated. "What became of the captain?" he added.

"Hung from the mast and went down with his ship, he did," the corporal replied.

Standing, the corporal motioned for Johnny and me to stand, as he pulled a key from his pocket, which he used to unlock our hand and leg shackles.

"Up ye go," he ordered, indicating that Johnny and I were to exit the boat, by climbing up onto the floating dock. Once this was done the jolly boat of the *Wales* pushed off, and we were with our new captors.

The sergeant appeared to be in his middle forties and had long gangly hair protruding from under his tri-corn, along with two or three day beard. Several of his front teeth were missing, and I was so close to him that when he spoke, I could smell the odor of rum on his breath.

"Now, you two rebels aren't going to give me any trouble are ye," he stated with a challenging grin from ear to ear.

"No trouble, Sergeant," I returned as I moved toward the stairs that led to our new prison. One marine led the way, as the second marine, along with the sergeant followed behind us.

I considered jumping into the bay, but wondered where I would go. There were any number of boats being rowed about by British sailors and marines, as well as all of the ships in the harbor, and the entire city under British control. Even if I made it to shore alive, I would certainly be captured again, and would be on the wrong end of severe punishment. No, I reasoned, I'd have to find some other means of escape from the hell I was about to enter.

Johnny was ahead of me as we walked up the gangplank, and when he cleared the last step, and proceeded onto the deck of the *Jersey*, I heard a gasp come from him as he halted in his step, looking about him. I pushed past him as the marine, along with the sergeant behind me, kept coming up the gangplank.

I too paused, as I stepped past Johnny at the horror that greeted us. The marine behind us gave us a shove with the butt of his musket, ordering us to move on.

Johnny followed me, while I made my way among the scores of men who were on deck. Most of them looked so ill and sickly as to make me not want to touch, or be touched by any of them. Many couldn't stand and were sitting where they could find space. Many walked about, thin as scarecrows with their clothes hanging off them, in tattered rags. Some talked in a rambled delirium, speaking to no one in particular, with no one answering the unceasing ramblings. Many were crying where they sat, while others could be seen kneeling, praying to God for mercy or death, or perhaps both. Still others were cursing God; not believing that God could exist, and allow men to condone the unbelievable, unending suffering of others.

We made our way to the forecastle, where it seemed to be a little less crowded. As we were looking for an area where we could sit and take stock of ourselves, as well as our new surroundings, a middle-aged man sitting by himself, on the steps leading up to the forecastle spoke up.

"Where you boys from?" he asked. I looked at him and hesitated to answer, not knowing who this man may be.

He stood and held out his hand in friendship, introducing himself, "Captain Thomas Dring. Whom do I have the pleasure of addressing?"

I took his hand, shaking it wearily, still not trusting my new acquaintance, as I replied, "Will Waterman, of the privateer *Whisperer*." Then turning toward Johnny, I presented, "This is the cabin boy, Johnny." Not ever knowing Johnny's last name, I didn't know what to call him. Johnny stepped forward and added, "Johnny Jones, cabin boy of the *Whisperer*. I'm from Philadelphia."

"Well, welcome to our living hell, boys," Captain Dring greeted.

"You are on what remains of the ship-of-the-line, *HMS Jersey*. She was a seventy-four. There are around eight hundred fifty prisoners on board, give or take a few dead souls every day. We average eight dead souls each day. A month or so ago, we lost twenty-five in one day. That was the worst."

Motioning with his hand to follow him, Captain Dring walked, or more appropriately shuffled, over to the ship's side. Pointing to the shore some quarter of a mile distant, he illustrated "Do you see those men over there on the mud flats digging?"

"I see them," I responded.

"Every day it's the same," he explained. "They gather the dead from all of the prison ships here in Wallabout Bay each morning, take them ashore, to bury them in a common mass grave. It takes them all day to bury the dead."

Continuing, Captain Dring stated, "Every once in a while, we manage to have someone escape off of these ships, but there are really only two ways to freedom. One is if you are exchanged in a prisoner swap with the British, but that isn't likely to happen with you coming off a privateer. The British usually only do prisoner exchanges with regular soldiers or with officers of warships. The only other way off of these hell ships is death. It's a hard thing to say, but those poor beggars out there, they are burying, are better off than we are."

"Come, let me show you," Captain Dring guided as he began to shuffle across to the stairs leading up to the forecastle. Johnny and I followed warily at a respectable distance.

Upon climbing the stairs, we found seven bodies, laid out on the deck. Besides being dead, they were several of the worst looking corpses I had ever seen. That they were poorly treated before they died was obvious, as the beggarly clothes they had on, revealed their starved and diseased condition. There were several marine guards here, since when the captives are on deck, they are still obliged, to go the head to relieve themselves. Not wanting any prisoners to attempt escape by jumping into the bay while using the head, a marine guard is posted with orders to shoot anyone who attempts to escape in this manner.

"If we average five to ten dead off each prison ship, and there are fifteen ships at anchor here, you can see why seventy-five to one hundred fifty dead a day keeps those men busy burying our dead," Captain Dring stated.

"Is there nothing that can be done about this?" I implored.

Looking at me in disbelief, Captain Dring laughed heartily inquiring,

"What is your name again, Will," he reaffirmed as he beheld me with a face of bitter unbelief, that I would ask such a question? "You are in hell on earth and the men who put you here, along with the men guarding you, care not whether you live or die. To whom would you make an appeal?" he argued. "General Washington, and the whole Continental army are somewhere to the south trying to corner Lord Cornwallis. The Congress is afraid of their shadow, and presumably are somewhere in Pennsylvania or Virginia colony in hiding. King George is in England stuffing his face with chocolate truffles, probably laughing at us," Captain Dring concluded sarcastically.

We left the forecastle, returning to the main deck area, taking in all of the misery around us. It would be dark in an hour, and we hadn't had anything to eat all day.

Around half an hour before dark, three stoutly marines came on deck with a very large kettle, some bowls and several bags containing week old, stale and moldy bread. The scarecrow men began moving ever so slowly, to form a line in front of the enormous kettle out of habit. A marine with a ladle handed each man a bowl, as one scoop of the liquid from the pot was poured into it. The next marine handed each man a piece of bread as they passed. The liquid contained chunks of what would turn out to be spoiled meat. Johnny and I learned quickly to discard the meat and to dip the bread into the liquid, which made both the liquid and the bread easier to consume. All became quiet on the ship, as the prisoners consumed what meager rations were fed to us.

When the rations were eaten, the men began returning their bowls to the marines at the large kettle. Evening was coming upon us, and I noticed that ever so slowly, the skeletons on deck began to make their way to the hatchways leading below deck.

"Let's get below and find you a place to rest tonight," Captain Dring invited, as he turned, and customarily began to shuffle his feet toward the nearest hatchway.

If the conditions of the men and surroundings on deck were deplorable, what greeted us below decks could only be described as criminal. Men too weak to walk, or move were seen to be lying about the two lower decks. Most of them were almost completely unclothed with only the barest of rags covering them. They lay there in their waste, suffering from their lack of strength to do anything about it. Most of the prisoners that were found in these conditions were awaiting their death, and their release from this hellhole. As the number of men who came below deck began to grow, those who could move began to gather in-groups, being familiar with those with whom they gathered.

As we made our way through the first gun deck, Captain Dring began to point out the various groups of men we were passing. "The forward gun room is for captured officers. The rest of the American sailors and soldiers are expected to sleep where you can on this deck."

"The lower gun deck is where the Spaniards and the Dutch are expected to sleep," he explained as he pointed to a group of twenty men, in a corner of the gun deck by themselves, making their way to the hatchway leading to the lower gun deck. "I don't trust the Spaniards, as they only look out for themselves. Next," he continued as he pointed to a large group of men huddled in gun deck waiting to go to the lower gun deck, "are the Dutch. They are better than the Spaniards, and will help with the sick if asked. Most of them understand English, and some of them can speak it."

Stopping and pointing forward, Captain Dring remarked, "The blacks keep to themselves on the lower gun deck, up forward, as they don't trust us or the British. They think everyone is against them. The British won't do any prisoner exchanges with them, believing them all to be slaves still. They are indeed mostly runaway slaves, although, I hear there are a few freeborn among them."

"You'll be okay here tonight," Captain Dring assured, as he began to move forward. "I've got to go to the forward gun room for the night." As he was about to disappear from our view, he turned and remarked flatly, "Oh, by and by, you being new on board, you will be expected to help with the dead in the morning, having some strength still and all." Turning again to leave, he called over his shoulder, "The marines will be by on their evening rounds, before they close the hatches for the night."

The marine guard came by, covering their faces with kerchiefs, so as to not inhale the stench, or touch any of the sick. The hatchways were closed when the marine guard left. The pungency of dead and dying men along with the overwhelming odor of human waste, were almost more than I could bear. Looking at Johnny, I could see he was struggling with the same smells. Men were talking in low tones in various parts of the ship, but no one talked to us. It seemed everyone wanted to be left alone, to his own suffering. If someone did not know you, it was left that way. Then, if you died from starvation, disease or at the hands of our British captors, they wouldn't feel as sorrowful, as if they'd lost a friend or comrade.

All became quiet in the darkness of the gun deck, as only low tones of men talking could be heard in the recesses of the deck. I lay down next to Johnny on the cold hard wood of the deck, to try to get some sleep. I thought to myself how hungry and tired I was.

A restless night ended all too quickly, as the hatchways were opened by boisterous marine guards calling out, "Rebels, turn out your dead!" They made their way throughout the gun decks, rousing the prisoners who could walk and drag themselves to the top deck, for fresh air and sunshine, if there was any to be had.

Those too sick and weak to walk were left where they lay, until they recovered enough to walk, which almost never was the case, or until they died. At which time they were carried to the forecastle to await burial. At eight o'clock the following morning, all of the dead would be lowered from each prison ship, by ropes like cattle to an awaiting shore boat. Then they were rowed ashore to the mud flats where the mass burials for the day commenced. There were so many dead some days that not all the dead could be buried in one day, and they would have to be left until the next. To call it a gruesome sight was an understatement, for as we stared from the rail of the *Jersey*, we were keenly aware that eventually, one day, each of us was destined to be among the dead.

Johnny and I made our way up the hatchway to the deck immersing us in the warmth of a sunny, clear day. Fresh air was never more welcomed, as it was to me that morning. I looked about for Captain Dring, but didn't find him.

Within the half-hour, the morning meal was served, which was an almost identical recurrence of the evening meal. The huge kettle was found to contain some sort of liquid with chunks of rotten meat, along with stale bread. Johnny and I received our rations, eating in resigned silence. I was still as hungry as ever, as the meager rations did little to quench my hunger pains. I could fully understand how, consuming such food for weeks on end, left men with little or no strength, looking like scarecrows susceptible to all manner of crippling disease.

Captain Dring found us shortly after our meal, and we followed him to a marine detachment. A sergeant stood with three marines, and Captain Dring addressed the sergeant as, Sergeant Cook.

"Detail reporting to walk the gun decks for the day's dead, Sergeant Cook," Captain Dring declared smartly to the sergeant.

For his part the sergeant barely looked at Captain Dring, instructing, "Do your duty, Captain, and report to me upon conclusion, the number of dead on the forecastle."

"Yes, Sergeant," Captain Dring asserted as he turned and headed for the hatchway. We followed not knowing exactly what to expect. On the first gun deck, Captain Dring began checking all of the men who remained there, unable to gather enough strength to walk up the stairs to the hatchway. On our gun deck, we found twenty men in various stages of dying. Some were conscious and acknowledged our passing, by talking with us. Many were not conscious and Captain Dring commented that these would be dead within several days. Several dead were found on our deck, as we noted their locations upon our return, to drag their bodies to the forecastle.

On the lower gun deck, which was occupied mainly by the Spaniards, Dutch and blacks, we found two dead Spaniards. Making a mental note of them, we returned to the main deck, as Captain Dring petitioned the sergeant for two additional men to remove the bodies.

Two seamen named Smith and Johnson were gathered to help as they, too, were recent additions to the *Jersey*. The five of us returned to the first gun deck. The four of us, under the direction of Captain Dring, began to move one body at a time. I soon discovered that the dead weight of just an average man was difficult for the four of us to move. By the time we had the first body up the hatchway and onto the deck we were all sweating profusely, and panting like foxes, that had been chased by a pack of hounds. We repeated the process with the five dead men, laying them out on the forecastle deck.

Upon the completion of the removal of the dead bodies, Captain Dring asked Johnny and me to follow him down to the first gun deck again. When we were there and by ourselves, save for the sick and dying men, Captain Dring inquired of us both, "Have you two been exposed to the pox?" he asked.

"The pox," I questioned, "what is that?"

"It's a disease that causes red spots all over your body followed by fever, unconsciousness and delirium, and in the worst cases, death," Captain Dring described.

"What can be done on a ship of dying men to protect us from it?" I asked.

"Inoculation," Captain Dring answered solitarily.

"What by the heavens is that?" I inquired.

"You make a small wound on your hand, usually between the thumb and forefinger, and take some pus from an infected person, placing the pus in the wound," Captain Dring explained.

Johnny and I stared in disbelief that what he was telling us could be the truth.

Continuing Captain Dring resumed, "Then the disease enters your body and in most cases, if you come in contact with the disease from other infected prisoners, the disease won't hurt you."

"I don't know," I replied slowly in disbelief.

"Look here, man," Captain Dring demonstrated, showing Johnny and me a scar on his left hand between his thumb and forefinger. "I inoculated myself not long after I arrived on this ship, and I have not been affected at all by the disease. A good friend of mine, a doctor from Boston, told me about this inoculation process years ago, as he has used it on a number of patients with success."

"Has anyone ever contracted the disease from the inoculation and died?" I probed.

"Well," Captain Dring hesitated, "yes, I guess there have been a few of those. But by far, most are exposed to the disease, and never have to worry about suffering from the threat ever again in their lives, however long that may be."

I was reluctant, but after several moments of consideration, I held out my hand. Captain Dring pulled a small knife from under his shirt and the waist of his pants. A quick flick of the knife resulted in a small wound in between my thumb and forefinger on my left hand.

Walking along the gun deck, Captain Dring looked at several of the men lying about, too ill to go up on deck. After examining a number of them, he stopped at one poor looking fellow stating, "This is what I'm looking for."

Taking his knife, he scraped the scabs on the man's arm until a cream colored pus oozed from the sores. Scraping a small amount of the pus on the tip of his knife, Captain Dring turned to me to place it in the open wound on my hand.

"Wipe the blood away, Will," he said as I was still holding my hand out.

Complying with his request, I wiped the blood on the sleeve of my shirt and held out my hand again. Captain Dring wiped the tip of his knife in my wound, and then covered it with a small piece of cloth cut from the edge of his own shirt.

"Keep this on for as long as you can and you should be immune from the effects of the pox," Captain Dring instructed. Turning to Johnny he stated, "Now you, young man."

Johnny hesitated and then wavered, "I, I don't think I'm wanting to do that, sir."

"Don't you understand that this could mean the difference between life and death, son," Captain Dring encouraged strongly.

"I do, but even you admitted yourself that by receiving the inoculation, I could get sick and die," Johnny stated. "So, if it's all the same to you, I'll just take my chances."

"As you wish young man, as you wish," Captain Dring responded as he moved to return back on deck. Johnny and I followed at a distance.

I watched my inoculation site for the next few days as it festered and developed blisters on and around the area, and then cleared up. Captain Dring looked at it, grunting his consent as he felt I was now protected from the dreaded pox.

The next few weeks went by in the same manner as described above. We received our morning and evening meal of the watery soup with stale bread, and then we were locked below decks for our nights in our hellhole. Sleep, when it came, was always disturbed by the sounds of the hundreds of men confined in such a small space, or by the pains a body develops from sleeping on a hard, cold, wood deck. That I would occasionally stir because of the pains in my body, having to change my position, was putting it mildly. Men who were sick and could not move developed open sores that would not heal, helping to hasten their departure from this world. On rainy days, everyone who could, went above decks to wash in the rain, and to drink what fresh water they could gather.

Boredom overtook everyone, as our only duty, at least for Johnny and me, was to help with the removal of the dead each morning. Once we had the dead placed upon the forecastle, we had nothing to do but to watch the activities of the British army and navy in New York City, and throughout the harbor. That they held us in contempt was obvious, for the flow of fresh food and water into New York City was visible each day, yet we only received putrid water and stale bread for sustenance.

Johnny and I began to lose our weight and within a month I went from a healthy one hundred sixty pounds, down to around one hundred thirty-five. My clothes hung off my body and Johnny looked worse still.

I thought of escape, but so did everyone on this prison ship of living hell. How was I to accomplish my escape? As I stared at the activity of life on Manhattan Island to our west and Brooklyn all about us, I knew there had to be a way off this ship. Otherwise, like the men I carried each morning to the forecastle, I'd be buried in a shallow grave in the mud flats of Wallabout Bay.

Six weeks into our imprisonment on the *Jersey*, I woke to find Johnny unable to get up. He was shivering as he lay on the wood deck next to me, as a touch of his forehead confirmed that he was suffering from a severe fever. I pulled his shirt up and to my horror discovered that his body was covered with red sores the size of flea bites. Fearing the worst and knowing what it was, I left immediately to find Captain Dring. Captain Dring only confirmed my fears.

"It is the pox, all right, Will," Captain Dring confirmed sadly. "A bad case it is, too. The next few days will determine if he lives, or dies."

"What is to be done for him?" I asked.

"There is nothing we can do now. Get him extra water if you can and see if, or when, the fever breaks. If it doesn't, in two days, three at most, he'll be dead," Captain Dring determined, as he turned and went back on deck.

Captain Dring's words proved to be all too prophetic as within three days, Johnny died. Try as I may, there was nothing to do to ease his pain and suffering or to break the fever. On the morning of the second day, he passed into unconsciousness, and the next morning he was dead. Captain Dring and I carried him to the forecastle. I was not surprised at how easy he was to carry as he had lost over thirty pounds. As we laid him next to the other bodies, I hesitated, saying a prayer to God that he would receive Johnny into His arms; relieved I was that his suffering was ended.

I watched the next morning as his body was lowered to the shore boat for burial, and remained at the ship's rail while the boat was rowed to the mud flats, and the bodies removed. I remained there the rest of the day until I thought I saw them place Johnny in the grave. As I watched, I realized that I had seen everyone from the *Whisperer* either killed, or pressed into service, and I was now the lone survivor of the *Whisperer.*

Even now, at what I would consider the lowest point of the war for me, as I looked out over to the mud flats, I knew God was with me, even here.

Suddenly, I realized that Captain Dring was at my side. He placed his hand on my shoulder but said nothing. Our evening meal was soon to be served, and as I went below decks, I was determined to find a way off this morbid, death ship.

- CHAPTER 19 -

"Escape"

Fall 1781

Several days later Captain Dring came to me, as he seemed in an unusually good mood considering our state and condition.

"Will," he greeted as he approached me, "I've received good news. I'm to be paroled in two day's time. Seems a ship of ours had a great battle with a British frigate, besting her. A fair number of officers were captured, and I'm to be exchanged for one of them."

"That is very good news, indeed, Captain," I congratulated as I held out my hand for him to shake. I was, in all sincerity, glad for Captain Dring, and his good fortune to be released from this hellhole.

As he took my hand to shake it, he pledged, "I will not forget you are here, and will do what I can, once I've reached the commanding officers to advise them that you are here, imprisoned on this ship. I will see what can be done to secure your parole."

"I would be indebted to you, sir, if you did me such a service," I said gratefully. "For I fear, as all aboard this ship fear, that I shall never touch dry land again, or see the smiling faces of my family. If you would, sir, seek out Colonel McLane, who is well-favored by General Washington himself, and advise him of my situation. Surely he, if anyone can, will be able to secure my parole from this prison."

"I will do as you ask, Will," Captain Dring promised. "But for now, take my knife. I have no use for it now that I am to leave this place, and certainly you may find a good use for it," he urged. Lifting his shirt and looking about him to ensure none of our British sentries were looking; he pulled out the knife from his waist and placed it in my hand.

We shared our few remaining meals together, talking of better times when we were in the Continental army and fighting the British. We each had stories to tell, as we both commented on how we had not met years before, when we had fought in the same theatre of war, even during the same engagements.

It was a bright sunny day, when a large jolly boat pulled alongside the floating dock that was attached to the *Jersey*, not to deliver more prisoners, but to take several of the officers who were prisoners, including Captain Dring, to their freedom.

Five officers were marched under guard to the rail and then allowed one at a time to walk down the plank, to enter the jolly boat. In addition to the rowing crew of six British sailors, there was another marine guard of four in the boat, alongside a commanding officer, who was at the tiller.

Once the boat was loaded with our officers, it quickly shoved off and began to row around our prison ship, heading for the lower end of Manhattan Island. As the boat cleared our stern, Captain Dring waved. I returned the gesture, watching as the boat was rowed down the East River, and out of sight.

I felt alone on a ship of one thousand wretched souls. For the next two weeks, I was kept busy only by the removal of dead bodies from the various decks, and holds of the ship. The boredom of the rest of the day on the ship was interminable.

One day, two weeks after Captain Dring had left the *Jersey*; the sergeant of the marine guard came to me stating that he wanted me to make an additional search of the lower decks of the ship, for any dead prisoners. He informed me that several of the blacks, as well as two Spaniards were not accounted for. He instructed that I had an hour to search the requested areas before reporting back to him at the midday bell.

I shuffled my feet as I walked toward the hatchway, making my way to the lower bowels of the ship. The lower I got, the more the smell of death and human waste became unbearable, making it increasingly difficult to take a breath. I covered my face with the corner of my shirttail, as I continued to the lowest deck on the ship. I only came here when I had to, looking for the dead. The deck was illuminated by three lanterns only and so, was exceedingly dark. If I were to find any men down here I'd need a light, so I took the first lantern I came to, holding it before me, as I searched from the bow to the stern of the ship.

I performed my duty as best as I could, without finding any signs of any dead or missing blacks or Spaniards. As I was finishing looking around the lower gun deck in the stern area, I sensed an unusual aroma of fresh ocean air blow across my face. Since I had begun my inspection of the lower gun deck, I had smelled nothing but rotting and decaying human flesh mixed with human waste. Now, from an unseen space, a fresh ocean breeze had hit my face. Using the lantern, I began to inspect the lower gun deck more completely for the source of the fresh air. Holding the lantern farther out, as I inspected every area, I began to see spaces in the lower gun deck I had not seen before.

Here, in the stern, I found what seemed to be several old planks leaning up against the bulwark. That this corner of the ship had not been visited for some time was obvious, as the lack of human waste and the thickness of the cobweb's attested to. Looking more closely, during my more thorough inspection, I found that the planks covered an old porthole, which had two bars across it, to prevent anyone from escaping. As I moved several of the planks, I felt the fresh ocean air now blowing through the porthole. In addition to the fresh air, the light streaming in illuminated this corner of the stern gun deck.

I looked around quickly, to see if anyone had come down to this gun deck that might observe my new discovery, and thus give away this hidden treasure. Not seeing anyone, other than those who were too sick to go up on deck, I quickly turned my attention to the bars that were over the porthole. The top bar was securely in place and immovable. As I checked the lower bar, it moved readily and the nails on either side of the porthole, that held it in place, were quite loose as the wood around them had suffered a considerable degree of rot during years of neglect.

Looking out the porthole I found that I could see the ships to the north of us in Wallabout Bay, as well as a short distance up the East River. Realizing I had to be careful now, as not to alert the ship's sentries to the north of the newly discovered opening, I quickly and quietly returned the planks to their positions. As far as I knew, I was the only one on this ship that knew of the porthole, and the potential it possessed. Surely, even Captain Dring had not known of its existence. I now believed I had discovered my route of escape off the prison ship *Jersey*.

I returned up on deck and reported to the sergeant of the guard, that I had found several sick blacks, as well as a couple Spaniards on the lower gun deck, but that none of them were dead. I suggested that the missing men must have been included in the daily count of the prisoners on board, and that the count was done incorrectly.

The sergeant just grunted at my report, not wanting to acknowledge that his subordinates would provide an inaccurate count of the prisoners on board the *Jersey*. That the numbers fluctuated daily was indisputable, as the number of dead, along with the numbers of incoming prisoners changed each and every day.

As I turned to leave the presence of the sergeant, I relayed over my shoulder, "I will make myself available each day to check the lower decks for any presumed missing prisoners, to help give you an accurate count, Sergeant."

The sergeant spoke up immediately and ordered, "Come, see me each day after the morning meal, and I'll see if it will be needed."

I turned to the sergeant and responded, "Till the morrow, Sergeant." I then turned and walked to my corner of the deck to spend the rest of my day, as usual, watching the activity on the other prison ships in Wallabout Bay. I also noted the activity around the harbor, including that on Manhattan Island and Brooklyn.

I now knew that I had to formulate in my mind, what I would do if I were able to slip out of the porthole on the lower gun deck, and into the cold waters of the East River. That I had to wait for a cloudy, moonless night was without question, but a night that was also stormy would be almost a necessity, since the churning waters on a stormy night would cover the noise of my swimming to freedom.

I would also have to time the incoming tide to use it to help me swim up the East River a distance and then to shore. But on which side of the river was I to land? There were all types of activity by the British, and undoubtedly those loyal to the Crown along both shores. If I came ashore and was discovered by a loyalist, or yet worse a British patrol, the escape would be all for naught. I may have to leave that to chance, as the activity up the river out of Wallabout Bay may determine which side to eventually make for. Thinking about the weather, and the moon with the tide cycles, I realized that we were just approaching a new moon, as the high tide changed daily. Each day now, I would have to estimate when the morning high tide occurred, and then calculate out twelve hours to the evening or night high tide. I would then have to calculate when the next new moon was to occur, and those two factors, along with a stormy night, would determine when in the next few weeks, I could chance an escape from the *Jersey*. Of course, I thought, a stormy night with cloud cover that obscured the moon would do, as long as it was on an ebbing tide.

I began my calculations almost immediately. High tide came around six in the morning and was pushed back each day by forty minutes, coinciding with the pull of the moon's gravitation on the earth. Estimating out two or three weeks to the new moon, this would push the incoming high tide to well after dark each night, thus my escape would have to occur during one of the nights during the last two weeks of October.

If I missed those nights for whatever reason, I would have to wait almost a month for the next new moon. With each passing day, week and month, my state of health would decline until it would be impracticable to escape, as I would surely drown, lacking sufficient strength to swim to shore. In addition to this, my leg wound was beginning to hurt again, and I was afraid that in the coming days and weeks, it would reopen as my condition weakened, potentially causing my death.

Of course, there was then the threat of recapture if I made it to shore, if I chose my area of escape poorly. I could not chance swimming downstream as the entire British fleet was anchored in New York Harbor with innumerable support and supply ships. The likelihood of recapture was too great to go in that direction. Also, the incoming tide would dictate an escape up the East River.

Each day for the next week, I met the sergeant of the guard and asked him if I were needed to check the lower gun deck for any missing prisoners. Each day I made a quick and cursory search of the lower deck for any dead prisoners that had not been reported or removed by the dead detail.

After my quick check, I then made my way quietly to the stern of the ship, making sure that no one, either prisoners or any British guards who randomly patrolled the lower decks, saw me. I would then remove several of the planks, slipping in between the remaining planks. I used the knife given me by Captain Dring to begin to loosen the remaining rotten wood around the nails that held the lower bar over the porthole by chipping away at it. I only had a few minutes each day to accomplish my task, as the sergeant of the guard would expect a report from me. To my great relief, the wood around the nails was worse off than I had expected, and after several days of quick labor, the bar was well on the way of being removed.

A week later, I removed the right side nails and reaching through the porthole, grabbed the bar before it swung free. Then, I let it hang from its one remaining supporting nail. Looking out the porthole, as I did this, I took notice of the prison ships I could see, to determine if the movement of my arm out the porthole had been observed. To my great relief, none of the guards or prisoners on the ships in the area had observed the movement. I slowly returned my arm into the ship, observing the activity on the ships for a few more moments. No alarm was given, and I returned the planks to cover the porthole, before making my way on deck to make my report to the sergeant of the guard.

September was quickly upon us, and the temperatures at night quickly began to cool considerably. The thought occurred to me that by October the water of the East River may already be too cold for me to make my escape.

I waited and watched each day for a change in the weather when I could attempt my escape. I was determined to go on the first night that either had a storm at high tide or the new moon at high tide, as I was now convinced that I could not survive a winter on this ship. For the time being though, Indian summer came quickly upon us, as the weather warmed significantly, but there were still no storm clouds in sight.

When my long awaited storm came, it came quickly. It was now the third week of September and I had another week to wait for the new moon. It was shortly after our evening meal, and I was looking quietly over the rail at Manhattan Island, a half-mile away. I heard a far off noise that reminded me of distant cannon fire. It struck me a half-hour later, as I heard the noise again, that it was thunder from an approaching storm. It must still be over New Jersey somewhere I thought. We were losing our evening light quickly now that it was late September and I knew the marine guard would soon herd the prisoners remaining on deck to the hatchways, to our dark, dismal prison below.

I could hear the thunder as it approached and decided in my mind that if it began to rain hard, as it sounded like it would, that I would make my way down to the lower gun deck, then to the stern and quietly make my escape. I would have to wait until the midnight hour as most all of my fellow prisoners would be asleep, as the guards on the deck would undoubtedly be driven to their tents on the stern quarter deck, to avoid a soaking by the storm. A couple of the guards may even come below deck if the storm becomes bad enough, I thought.

The storms hit the *Jersey* two hours after we were herded below deck, and well after dark. The lightning flashes could be seen through the small holes in the side of the ship, as well as the small openings at the portholes. Save for the wind, rain and waves lashing at the ship, all was quiet below decks. When it stormed like this at night, it almost had a calming effect on the prisoners, helping most to sleep more easily. For me, I was lying down pretending to be asleep, but was listening to every sound to see if any prisoners were stirring. For the most part, the entire first gun deck was asleep. I could only pray that the lower gun deck with the blacks, Dutch and Spanish prisoners, was the same.

I waited as long as I could, as I was anxious to get to my escape hole before the storm passed over us, and moved down Long Island. My heart was pounding as I sat up, looking around. All seemed quiet, save the snoring of sleeping men, mingled with the coughing of sick ones. I saw no one else, who was stirring, as I was. I quietly began to move toward the hatchway leading to the lower gun deck. I was careful to step over the bodies of men who were lying about sleeping. At times, the boards creaked as I stepped over men, but no one stirred as the entire ship was creaking, as the storm continued to lash at it. I reached the hatchway, slowly stepping down the stairs. All was dark on the lower gun deck. As the lightning flashed outside, it gave me quick glimpses of where everyone lay about. There were two lanterns still lit, but they were woefully inadequate to light my way. As the lightning flashed and the light filtered in through the holes in the sides of the ship, it provided sufficient light to see what was before me. I then moved as far as I could, and then waited for another flash of lightning. Ever so slowly, I made my way along the lower gun deck toward my freedom. Once, I stepped on a man I hadn't seen in time, causing him to grunt, but he didn't stir awake. Finally, after what seemed an eternity, but was actually no more than half an hour, I was standing next to the planks in the stern of the lower gun deck of the *Jersey*. I remained there a few moments to see if any one stirred, but except for the storm, along with the sounds of men snoring or coughing, there was nothing to alert me to the fact that I had been watched, or discovered in my escape attempt.

I timed the moving of the planks away from the porthole with the rumbling of thunder. Slowly, I removed six or seven planks, more than I had ever removed before. As the lightning flashed now, it lit up the little room I was in at the stern of the ship. This helped me in seeing what was before me, but brought great consternation to me as I thought anyone, prisoner or guard, who saw the flash of light from the lightning, would come to investigate.

With enough of the planks removed I looked out the porthole, observing the sentry lights still glowing in the prisoner ships to my north. Even in this great thunderstorm, the British kept their lights lit. I could also see many of the lights of Manhattan Island.

I grabbed the remaining bar over the top of the porthole and using all of my strength, pulled my right leg up and into the porthole. Once my foot was securely out the porthole, I lifted my left leg, sticking my left foot out the porthole. I now began pulling with my arms and wiggling my legs out the porthole until my backside was up against the bottom of the porthole. With all my remaining strength, I continued wiggling until my bottom finally squeezed out the hole. With my legs and bottom out the hole and my upper body, arms and head still inside; it put a great stress on my lower back.

I began to sweat and grunt as I struggled to get the remainder of my body out of the porthole. Finally, after several more minutes of struggling, I was able to squeeze my upper body and head out of the porthole. Still hanging onto the bar, my back was against the *Jersey*, and I faced the prison ships to the North. I reversed my grip so that the front of my body and face was now against the ship, and I could fend off the ship with my legs.

I now held onto the top bar, as it held my weight. As I looked about, there was no alert on the *Jersey*, or any prison ship in the area as to my escape attempt. I extended my arms as far as they would go and my feet just touched the top of the water in Wallabout Bay. Pushing lightly off of the side of the ship with my legs, I let go of the bar and I slid silently into the water. I quickly found that the water in late September was extremely cold, taking my breath away. I began to wonder how long I could last in water this cold.

I began to swim ever so slowly out of the bay and into the East River. Even now with a severe thunderstorm pounding the area, with a torrential downpour of rain, I could feel the push of the incoming tide, and I was already drifting up the river, as I swam out, away from the *Jersey*.

I looked back and could see the sentry lights on the *Jersey*, as well as the other ships, but none of the guards on duty was alerted to my escape. The storm kept the guards in the relative dryness of their tents. As I continued to swim, I soon realized that I was much weaker than I had anticipated from my months of captivity, inactivity, and lack of food, as I was beginning to tire. Needing all of the strength I could muster, I stripped off my shirt and pants, which took a considerable weight off of me, as I continued to swim naked in the East River.

I was tiring quickly, even without my clothes and thought that I'd have to alter my course, to swim much closer to the shore than I had planned, and even put to shore much sooner. I was now two hundred yards out of Wallabout Bay, and to the north of the *Jersey*, when I was bumped by something hard in the water. I spun around in the water to see what it was, but couldn't see the object on account of the choppy water from the wind and rain, as well as the darkness. I put my hands out in front of me, feeling around for the object, yet it took me several seconds to find it again. Grabbing hold, I found that I had the good fortune to have been hit by several rather sturdy pieces of planks of wood held together by cross beams. They seemed to be the remnants of a dock broken by the storm, drifting with the wind and tide. I rested for several minutes, floating with my planks.

Once I was rested, I again began to make my way up the East River. Holding onto the planks with one arm, I kicked with my legs and pushed with my free arm. Even with the planks to keep me afloat, I tired quickly, having to rest several more times. Finally, after an hour of swimming in this manner, I was well away from Wallabout Bay and my prison hell of the *Jersey*. Now, I began to look for a place to put ashore. It was still raining hard, but most of the larger, more powerful thunderstorms had moved over Long Island to the east. I could see lights and several docks along the Brooklyn shore, as I slowly continued to make my way with the tide up stream.

Finally, I came to Blackwell's Island, in the middle of the East River, and going ashore on its tip, I rested. I remembered that there was a farm on this island when we occupied Manhattan Island several years earlier. I feared that the British now had a small garrison stationed here and that if I stayed I would be discovered. I knew I had to continue on. I rested until the next round of heavy rain and winds came in, and then resumed my escape.

I was shivering badly now from the cold water as I pushed off back into the channel as the rain torrents began again. After what seemed to be an hour more of swimming with my planks, I was at the north end of the island and saw what appeared to be a large inlet, in the area of an untended section along the Brooklyn shoreline, free of any lights or docks. I decided to swim for this area. As I approached the shore, I began instinctively reaching with my feet for the bottom, but didn't locate it, as the water remained deep until I was almost to the shoreline. Once I did, I was only a few feet from the shore. Using the planks to steady myself, I waded ashore in a small marshy area. As the high tide had not yet been reached, I found the going tough in the mucky bottom. I continued to use the planks to lean on, to maintain my balance, as I furthered my way inland among the marshy grasslands. As I went, I became extremely fatigued with each passing step, as the miry bottom pulled at my ever tiring legs. This strain, on top of my weakened state from captivity, combined with the cold water, sapped my strength, forcing me to look for an area where I could rest. After several more minutes of sloshing through the mud and water, I came upon a small sandy mound surrounded by tall marsh grass. I pulled my tired, cold and naked body up on the sandy mound amid this marshy haven, passing out from extreme exhaustion.

- CHAPTER 20 -

"Return to home"

1781 - 1782

I was brought out of my unconsciousness to a state of semi-awareness that someone was talking to me. I could not bring myself to total consciousness, as I could only remember an out-of-focus face before me. The next thing I remembered was a voice telling me to be quiet. As I was jostled about, I realized that I was in the back of a wagon, covered partly with hay and partly by several boxes and crates.

I heard voices engaged in a conversation, and again, I could not bring myself to total consciousness, but understood that the man driving the wagon must have been at a British checkpoint, as there were several voices heard with a heavy British brogue.

I passed out again, only awaking to find myself in the warm confines of a bed covered with a thick comforter in a small farmhouse, with a fire burning in the fireplace. As I lay there trying to take in the room, and its activity, I saw a young woman tending to food at the fireplace, as she then moved to setting the table. Two lanterns, in addition to the light sent out by the sparkling fire, dimly lighted the room.

The door suddenly opened, and an old man wearing an overcoat and hat entered. I noticed it was dark outside, as he shut the door. He walked over to the girl at the table, speaking to her in low tones. She nodded in affirmation, before walking to a back room. Looking at me, the old man realized that I was awake, while removing his hat and coat. After placing them on hooks by the door, he came over to my bed. Pulling a stool from the corner, he sat by my bed, placing his hand on my forehead.

"Aye, you still have a fever, lad," he said, pulling his hand away from my head and studying my face. "How do you feel?" he asked in a heavy Irish accent that reminded me of Mr. Waterman at Waterman's Tavern, after observing me for a few moments.

"I feel like I've been mostly dead," I responded slowly and faintly.

"Aye, that you have, that you have," the old man agreed, as he got up from the stool. "Maggie will feed you some broth, as I think you will eventually be as healthy as an ox, Lord willing," he concluded as he turned to go to the table.

"How long have I been lying here?" I inquired faintly.

"You've been lying there for the better part of a week, with my daughter Maggie tending to ye," the old man replied.

"How did I get here then?" I wondered, as the young woman made her way over to me, sitting on the stool the man had recently vacated. She waited patiently with a bowl and spoon in her hand to begin feeding me.

"You must have been worse off than I had expected when I found you, lad," the old man calculated. As he walked back over to the side of the bed, "I went down to the East River almost a week ago now, searching the mud flats for anything to eat. I mostly look for clams, or fish that have been trapped in pools of water when the tide has gone out," he added. "I got down there and was mucking about when, to my total surprise, I discovered you lying there completely and totally naked, and covered in mud. I thought you were a runaway black, when I first saw you, but upon closer inspection I discovered you were white.

Then I thought you were dead, and it wasn't until I pulled on your arm that you moaned painfully, that I realized you were still alive." Then continuing he recalled, "The devil of a time I had, pulling your limp body the thirty feet to my wagon. Good thing for you it was only that far. Any further and I'd have just left ye for dead. Then, there were the bloody British patrols, and checkpoints to get you through," he added. "If it weren't for the scars on your body, which shows you've been in many a battle, added to the fact that the prison ships are just down the East River in Wallabout Bay, I'd not have bothered with you. I figured you must be an escaped Continental soldier, so I decided to bring you home, and see if you'd live. It's been Maggie here that's done the most to keep you alive. Why she bathed, and cleaned ye up, and has been feeding you what she could since you've been mostly unconscious."

I glanced at Maggie who was still seated next to the bed, as she was waiting patiently to begin feeding me the hot broth she was holding. She stared down at the broth when I looked at her, in a shy manner, not wanting to look me in the face.

"You must be important too, as the British have had extra patrols out all week searching for someone," he added. "I believe it to be you. Enough talk for now, young lad, as Maggie has waited patiently to feed you, and your broth will grow cold if we continue," he said, concluding our conversation.

I sat up with great difficulty finding that I was still extremely weak from the cold water of the East River, along with my debilitated state from months of captivity on the *Jersey*. Maggie didn't speak as she fed me the bowl of broth. As I struggled to remain upright in my bed, I studied the young girl who was serving me my food. She appeared to be very gentle and dainty as she served me. Every movement of her arm seemed to be well-orchestrated. Her skin shone a smooth milky white in the low light of the house. She appeared to be wearing a laced white nightgown as the hour of the evening was growing late, with an overcoat to hide her bedwear. Her face was smooth and white, which was highlighted by her long, wavy red hair and piercing, bright blue eyes.

She smiled a couple of times as she served me, presumably at my lack of ability to keep all of the broth in my mouth, as it trickled several times down my face. She was quick to wipe my face with a cloth she maintained on her lap. With the nourishment consumed, Maggie got up from the stool, walking over to the hearth to dish up additional broth for herself, as well as her father, for their evening meal. As she walked over to the hearth, my eyes instinctively followed her, contemplating that this young woman could not be more than twenty. She was a striking young lady with amazing beauty and figure, which was obvious even with an overcoat covering her nightgown. She was seated next to her father after serving him his broth and bread for their meal, and as I continued to watch, they lowered their heads in prayer for their meal. While they dined, I lay back down in my bed, listening to the low tones of their conversation. Eventually, I closed my eyes to rest and must have fallen asleep, as I awoke the next morning to the smell and sound of breakfast cooking.

The old man was not in the room as I looked about, but only Maggie was to be seen, working at the hearth again, preparing the meal. There was sufficient light now in the room, as it was well into the morning hours.

I could now see that in addition to the family room I was in, there were several rooms off of the main room, with a small loft on the second floor.

After some time, the door opened and the old man entered. With the door opened for a moment, a cold wind blew in, reminding me of the harshness of the outside. I thought to myself that it must be into October, if I had been here for over a week now. The old man came over to my bed after removing his hat and coat, placing them on the hooks by the door. "Do you feel strong enough to eat at the table this morning, lad?" he asked.

"I will try," I returned, as I sat up in bed.

The old man held my arm and shoulder, as I removed my covers, swinging my feet to the side of the bed. Looking at my leg, it was freshly bandaged, with a small stain of blood soaked through the cloth. I now realized that I was only wearing a nightshirt. Trying to cover myself a little more, I stood to my feet with the help of the old man. I did the all too familiar shuffle walk that I remembered from the prison ship, as I made my way over to the table to sit down. There were four chairs at the table, and as I drew closer, I reached for the nearest chair for more support.

Sitting down, I grabbed the edge of the table to support myself. The old man sat in the chair at the head of the table, as he looked to the young woman preparing the meal.

"Maggie," he began, "how long until the breakfast is served, lass?"

"It will be coming right up, Da," she replied without looking at her father.

I said nothing, as I watched the activity of the young woman at the hearth as she placed some food on two plates, then delivered them to the table. As she did so, I thought to myself that I hadn't heard anyone call their father "Da" in such a long time; it reminded me of home. I thought to myself that this family must be from Ireland, or most certainly from the British Isles.

The plates that were placed before us contained eggs, several strips of meat, along with a piece of bread. There was also hot broth in a mug to drink with our meal. Maggie came over from the hearth with a plate of her own, sitting down opposite me at the table. She bowed her head, as did her father, and he said a prayer over our meal, thanking the Lord for the provisions He had provided, along with blessings on his family. With the prayer finished, the old man looked at me, stating simply, "Enjoy your meal, lad."

I began to eat, realizing that it had been so long since I had eaten proper food, that the taste of fresh eggs and meat in my mouth was almost overwhelming. The food tasted so good, and I consumed it so quickly that when I had finished, the old man and his daughter had barely eaten half of their meal.

Looking at me and seeing I was done already, the old man looked to Maggie declaring, "Our guest is getting his appetite back. I believe he is going to survive his ordeal. Perhaps he would like some more food."

"Perhaps a bit more," I responded, as I glanced from the old man to his daughter. Maggie got up from her seat and taking my plate, returned to the hearth to get some more food for me.

"What is your name, young man?" the old man inquired as he stopped his eating while Maggie got me more food.

"Will Waterman, of Norwich, Connecticut colony," I said, looking at the old man.

"And how is it, Will Waterman, that I found you on the mud flats of the East River?" he questioned.

Maggie had returned and placed my plate with fresh eggs and meat in front of me, as she seated herself across from me again.

I didn't know exactly where to begin with my story, as I had been fighting in the war for more than six years now, and the events that led up to my imprisonment on the prison ship *Jersey* were really, only recent events.

I explained briefly my sailing out of Providence, Rhode Island colony, with my uncle for the purpose of capturing British shipping for profit, privateering, as my uncle described it. I stated that we were captured off Cape May some months earlier, and, all save me were either killed as the result of our capture or died as the result of our imprisonment, and I alone was left from the ship *Whisperer*. I then told the old man and his daughter of my escape from the prison ship *Jersey* in Wallabout Bay. I then described how I swam up the East River with the help of the tide, and by the aid of some driftwood, coming ashore where I thought I would have a chance to further my escape.

The old man looked at me, and it seemed that he was somewhat puzzled at the explanation I had given. Looking at me he asserted, "But, surely you were at one time a soldier in the Continental army, as you have numerous scars on your body that appear to be battle wounds, and you are still suffering from a leg wound that hasn't healed."

"That I was, sir," I affirmed, as I began to give details of my service to the American cause. I started with the siege of Boston. I then told the old man, along with his daughter of the battle of Long Island, Manhattan

Island and White Plains, where I received my leg wound, which the old man had noted. I then spoke of the duty in the New York Highlands. I detailed how I was then moved with the army to the siege of Philadelphia, fighting in the defense of Mud Island Fort. I continued by describing how the army suffered at Valley Forge, including the information regarding the loss of my lifelong friend, Eli Bingham. I then described that I was then moved back to the New York Highlands, which resulted with the storming of Stony Point and Paulus Hook. Of being quartered at Redding, Connecticut and Morristown, New Jersey, and again of the suffering endured by the army due to lack of food, or winter clothing, which contributed to the mutiny by some of the units in the army. As I concluded, I stated that I had done and seen so much, that I was sure I had left out several engagements I had been in.

The old man looked at me and asked, "Did you ever meet a young man in the Continental army by the name of Ian Tracy?"

"I don't recall the name," I responded, and added, "why do you ask?"

"My son, who carried my name, was killed at the battle of Paoli, or at least that is what I am told," the old man conveyed, looking at me to see if he could see in my eyes that I had known or met his son.

"I am sorry, sir, but I do not recall ever meeting, or hearing of a soldier by that name," I reiterated.

"I was afraid that would be the case, you being from Connecticut and under the command of other officers during the war," he mused. "It has been a terrible burden to me that my son has been killed and can't be here to help with the farm. I am getting older by the day, and my wife died years ago. She passed long before the war even began. So, it has been me, along with poor Maggie here, all alone to take care of the farm, since my son's death."

"Da," Maggie finally spoke up, "you know everything will be okay here. I will stay on until we can sell the farm or someone wishes to settle down here with me, and take it on," she said, as she stood up to clear the table.

"You see how it is here, Will," Mr. Tracy explained dejectedly. "The British have a strangle hold on us, and if things don't change soon, I will have to sell the farm."

"But why?" I countered.

"With the army quartered here for so long, there hasn't been enough food for everyone in and around New York City," he stated. "I suppose," he said as he continued, "it would be due in part to the raids on British supplies by ships like the one you were on, and others that have caused the lack of food."

"I understand," I said, as I began to think about what he said.

"Mr. Tracy," I asked, "can you help me with two things?"

"Name them, lad, and if they are in my power to do, I will do all I can to see that they happen," he responded in earnest.

"First, I'd like to write letters to my family and my girl back in Connecticut and second, can you help me with getting back to Connecticut?" I asked.

"Your first request is accomplished easily enough, as we have pen, ink and paper on which you can pen any note you wish to your family and friends, and have it posted," Mr. Tracy stated. "The other matter you ask is much more difficult to do, Will, as it is October now, and the winter winds have begun to close in. More importantly, the British keep patrols year round on the length of the northern shore of Long Island. Attempting to get to a location where we can put to sea and get across the sound this time of year is nearly impossible. No, no, young man, we would be better served to wait until the spring and then, when many fishermen are out on the water, we can attempt to get you back to Connecticut. I know of several fishermen who owe me a favor or two, and will gladly accomplish the task, but not until the spring."

"Not till spring," I said out loud thinking in my mind of a long winter on Long Island, with nothing to do, and the British army afoot.

Late October was upon us, and at the urging of Mr. Tracy, I had to stay mostly in the house, as all of Mr. Tracy's neighbors knew of his son's death some years earlier during the war. Some neighbors were patriots and would not mention to the authorities that an unfamiliar man was seen on the Tracy farm. Yet, there were those in the area, and a great number of them, who were loyal to the Crown, and would for the pleasure of capturing an escaped rebel prisoner, contact the authorities, bringing the British regulars down upon the Tracy farm.

I could take care of myself, but the thought of the British arresting Mr. Tracy. Possibly taking his farm from him, along with taking poor Maggie for their own pleasures, was more than I could bear to think. I could not compromise the existence of the man who saved my life, or his daughter who was instrumental in nursing me back to health.

I was resigned to settle into my quiet life on the Tracy farm. By day I stayed mostly indoors, helping Maggie with the chores around the house, while Mr. Tracy would go tend to his farm. At night, I would slip out, to help Mr. Tracy in the barn with various tasks, along with the repair of wagons, planting equipment and horse tack.

A system was devised whereby Maggie could let us know if any British patrols or neighbors, loyal to the Crown were in the area or at the door to the house. A rope was run the thirty feet from the back of the house to the barn. At the barn end of the rope, a couple of cans were attached and Maggie, if she saw anyone approaching whose loyalties were questionable, or any British soldiers in the area, would tug on the rope from the kitchen end. The rattling of the two cans together in the barn would notify us of danger. A snug cubbyhole was made in the back of the hay stacked by the pig holding pen. If the alarm came, I immediately made my way there as quickly as possible, hiding until Mr. Tracy let me know the danger had passed.

By the end of October, I had written letters to my parents and Diane in Norwich, describing to them what I had been through. I reluctantly included to my father, the details of the circumstances of the death of his brother, my Uncle Jeremiah. I relayed the elements of our success in interrupting British shipping and supply ships, as well as the sea chase leading to our capture. I also mentioned the details of my imprisonment on the prison ship *Jersey*, but did not disclose all of the suffering, and horrors experienced while being imprisoned on such a ship. I felt confident that Da would understand, and that he wouldn't tell mother the gruesome reality of the situation.

Mr. Tracy departed early one morning to post the letters as he had other business in town, which he had been delaying and needed to address. The nearest town where the letters could be posted was Bedford, a distance of three miles away. While he attended to these matters, Maggie and I remained at the house alone.

Maggie was somewhat of a shy young woman. I, too, was shy for the most part. I was not a very talkative individual, but if I had something to say I said it, otherwise, I remained silent. As it was, not having much to say, most of the morning was spent in quietness as Maggie went about her business of keeping the house in order. For my part, I helped where I could, but stayed out of the way, as a woman has her own ways about her, particularly in the kitchen. Maggie took a rest about mid-morning, sitting with me at the table for a few moments.

Feeling uncomfortable, and not knowing exactly what to say, I inquired of Maggie as to how long the Tracy's had been farming on Long Island. "How long has your family had a farm here?" I asked in a quiet tone, watching Maggie, who had just seated herself.

"Da says that his Da came from outside of Dublin in the early seventeen forties when Da was just a wee lad," she stated. "I heard tell that he landed in Boston first and worked odd jobs. Then he continued to move across Connecticut and finally Long Island until he settled here and decided to stay. He liked being near the city of New York, but wanted to be far enough away to make a living farming. We've been here ever since, but when my mother died a few years ago, and then my brother was killed in the war, well, Da hasn't been the same. I think he wants to sell the farm and move on," she concluded.

"I understand how hard the loss of a friend or a loved one can be," I said. "This war has been difficult for everyone," I added.

"Well, it seems to me, Will Waterman, that you have seen more than your share of fighting and suffering if all that you say you've done is true," Maggie replied.

Looking at her and her big blue eyes, I flatly stated, "I assure you, Maggie, I've seen and done all I've said, and all the more that I can't even talk about these last five or six years. My Da warned me what it would be like, but I couldn't take his word for it. I had to see for myself," I concluded as I began to think back over the last few years of war.

"Well," Maggie stated as she stood to return to her work, "I can see that my Da has been a different man since he's had another man in the house to talk to, even helping with the work. He will be hard put indeed, when you return home," she said as she walked to the kitchen.

I said nothing in response to this as I watched her go, taking note of her figure as she walked away from me. Checking the area by looking out the windows, I found no one near the farm to concern myself with, so I quickly made my way to the barn to do some farm chores. I remained there the rest of the morning, and into the afternoon.

By the middle of the afternoon, Mr. Tracy had returned to the farm, almost running as he entered the barn, once Maggie had told him that was where I was. He found me cleaning out the pigpen when he entered, and he was so excited, he could barely contain himself.

"Will, Will," Mr. Tracy shouted breathlessly, "you must come to the house straight away, as I have the most astonishing news to relate, and I want to tell it to both you and Maggie at the same time. Put down the pitchfork, and come," he said, motioning to me with his hand from the barn door. Again, as I placed the pitchfork in the corner of the barn, he said, "Come, come," as he turned, making his way quickly from the barn to the house. I followed at a distance as he was almost running when he entered the house. When I entered, I found him standing at the head of the table with Maggie seated at her usual place. "Will, sit please, I want to tell you and Maggie the most wonderful news."

Seating myself in my usual place across from Maggie, I looked first at her, and as she had a bewildered expression on her face, then at her father. When I was seated, Mr. Tracy began to pull a piece of paper from his jacket pocket. He was so excited, that he fumbled several times with his fingers to obtain the note. Finally, securing it in one hand, he pulled his spectacles from another pocket, placing them on his nose.

Clearing his voice, he began to read without further delay, "News was received just this morning from a post rider from Philadelphia. General George Washington with the Continental army, supported by the Marquis de Lafayette and French land forces, along with the French navy under the command of Admiral Count de Grasse, surrounded the British army at Yorktown, Virginia colony. After several weeks' battle, General Washington secured the unconditional surrender of the entire army, which was under the command of Lord Cornwallis," Mr. Tracy read as he lowered the note, a tear streaming down his face. "Will, do you know what this means?" he said as both Maggie and I stood, and walked over to Mr. Tracy. We hugged each other in unison, crying together, "The war may soon be over!"

I mulled this over in my mind for a few moments, realizing that the war could actually be ending; it was almost inconceivable. I was only eighteen when I went to war during the siege of Boston in 1775. It was now 1781 and I had grown into a young man of twenty-four. I quickly related to Mr. Tracy and Maggie how months earlier when engaged on board the *Whisperer*, sailing just off of Cape May, we had contact with the *Congress*. Once on board the *Congress,* I met my old friend and comrade at arms, Captain McLane, now Colonel McLane, who was on a secret mission on behalf of General Washington himself. Colonel McLane was charged with sailing to the Port of Martinique in the Caribbean, in an effort persuade Count de Grasse to sail his fleet to the mouth of the Chesapeake Bay, in hopes of catching Lord Cornwallis in a trap on the Virginia peninsula. "Apparently, Colonel McLane was most successful in persuading Count de Grasse to sail north, to provide the invaluable assistance to General Washington," I stated.

"Let us pray to our good Lord, that this defeat of the British will signal the beginning of the end of this war," Mr. Tracy added.

Over the next few weeks, more news was received about the war. It seemed for the most part, that the British had finally realized that they were not to prevail in the Americas. With the entry of France and Spain into the war, the British had many more battles to fight in other areas of the world, than just North America. The drain on British resources and men became too great, and although the war would not end officially for another two years, hostilities had virtually ceased in the Americas, as a rather docile truce remained between the combatants of North America.

Several weeks then passed without any word from my family or from Diane. I remained close to the farm, since British soldiers would not be above seizing an escaped prisoner, if they happened to find out where I was. Mr. Tracy returned from Bedford one day, with a letter in his jacket pocket, addressed to me. As he handed it to me, I sat down at the dinner table to read. As I looked at the envelope, I noticed it was from Da. Looking up from the envelope, I asked Mr. Tracy, "There was no other post for me?"

Looking at me and sensing my disappointment, Mr. Tracy stated sincerely, "I'm sorry, Will. That's all there was, lad."

I nodded, as I looked back to my letter, opening the envelope. There was only one page in the post, and glancing at it before I started to read it, I could clearly see that it was written and signed by Da. He began by stating how relieved everyone, especially Ma, was to hear that I was indeed alive and safe. Having informed Da of the death of his brother, along with the sinking of the *Whisperer*, he expressed sorrow at the loss of his brother, and how he prayed for the end of this war. My brother John was well, Da wrote, and was courting a young lady from Norwich. It was anticipated that once John took over the farm, he would marry her. Rachel was now sixteen, being courted by a young man, who was the cousin of William Bradford.

Suddenly, the tone of the letter changed, and I could sense that Mr. Tracy, as well as Maggie, realized a change in my emotions. My hands began to shake, as tears streamed down my cheek. I crumpled the letter, storming out of the house, and running into the barn just a few yards away. I read and reread the lines that Da had written. It said that he was sorry that he was the one who had to bring me such dark news, but that I had to know before I came home. Diane had married a man from Boston several months ago, during the summer. His family was in the shipping business, and she was now living in Boston. I thought it was a bad dream, but there it was, and I knew Da wasn't the kind to write something like this unless it was brutally true.

As I sat there on a stool crying, I heard the creak of the barn door opening. I didn't look up as I was still crying, and didn't care who was there to see my emotional outburst. I felt a strong hand on my shoulder and realized it was Mr. Tracy.

After several moments of standing there next to me, and having his hand on my shoulder, Mr. Tracy quietly probed, "What is it, Will?"

I tried all I could to stifle my crying, but could only in the end, hand Mr. Tracy the letter. After several moments of reading the letter, Mr. Tracy whispered sympathetically, "I see," as he left the barn, leaving me to my pain and suffering. I could only think of all that I had been through over the last six years; of the battles fought, both won and lost, of enduring the suffering through three of the hardest winter quarters an army could see. I had experienced the loss of men in battle who were lifelong friends and companions, including my best friend, Eli Bingham. I remember thinking of the day the war would be over and returning home to loved ones. I dreamed of seeing my family and especially Diane with the hope that one day, I'd marry her, and live the rest of my life with her. Now that was gone, shattered by the realization that she had not waited for me and had married, most probably while I was suffering through my captivity on the prison ship *Jersey*.

The sting of the news about Diane took a long time to subside. I spent the winter months working on the Tracy farm on Long Island. November quickly slipped into December. I spent a quiet Christmas with the Tracy's and try as they may to lift my spirits, I remained in a state of denial into the New Year. Maggie had made me a shirt as a Christmas present. This did lift my spirits and as time went by, I came to treasure it. I found the winter on Long Island was not nearly as severe as it had been in New England, or for that matter, New Jersey, or a small town in Pennsylvania called Valley Forge.

Finally, spring was upon us. One day, as I was in the barn shoeing one of the horses, Mr. Tracy walked in and came over by my side. As he was watching what I was doing, I sensed he wanted to speak to me, so I stopped my work, waited for him to speak.

"I've posted letters to some fishermen I know, and they say next week, when there is a new moon, would be the best time to sail ye across the sound to Connecticut," he said.

Looking at him, I had mixed emotions about what he was telling me. I could return home to my family and friends, which included a life without Diane, I thought; or, I could remain with Mr. Tracy and Maggie, to begin a new life here with them. There was no denying it now, after I had recovered somewhat from the shock and hurt by the news of Diane's marriage, a true fondness had developed over the last few months between Maggie and me. That she was attractive was, without question, as she had long wavy red hair and bright blue eyes, but her countenance and how she held herself, were equally, if not more attractive than her physical beauty. She had a soft, sweet spirit about her that drew me to her continually. Whenever my chores were completed around the farm and Mr. Tracy was out on errands or completing his own business, I found myself in the Tracy home engaged in conversation with Maggie. I thought of these times, realizing that if I returned home, I would deeply miss being with her.

Recognizing I hadn't answered him, Mr. Tracy spoke up, "Of course, if you wish to remain here on the farm, I know that I, as well as Maggie, would be grateful to have you with us."

I looked at Mr. Tracy and asked, "If I decide to go, will it be as early as next week?"

"It will have to be, or wait another month if we miss the new moon," Mr. Tracy reasoned. "The British still patrol the waters, and are still looking for escaped rebels to capture and imprison," he warned.

"I will give you my answer on the morrow," I promised, as I returned to shoeing the horse.

The next morning, while we were at the breakfast table, I gave Mr. Tracy my decision on whether I was going to return home to Norwich, Connecticut. Maggie had just served us our breakfast of eggs and ham, seating herself.

"Mr. Tracy," I began, "I have come to the conclusion that I must return home, to visit my family to see what the future holds for me there."

There was silence at the table when I had stated this, as I looked from Mr. Tracy to Maggie. I could see a tear in Mr. Tracy's eye, and as I looked at Maggie, both her eyes were welling up with tears. She pushed her chair away from the table, as she half-ran to the kitchen. I could hear her crying in the kitchen, as she rattled dishes. I knew my decision would not be well received, but I didn't know that it would be as bad as it was. But even so, I knew I had to return home and see what, if anything, was left there for me.

The next week went quickly enough, as the work around the farm kept me busy. I hadn't much to pack, as all of the belongings I'd had in my chest, were at the bottom of the ocean with the *Whisperer*. We were to leave on a Tuesday afternoon, because Mr. Tracy wanted to reach our port of departure in the evening in two days' time, so that I could sail with a fisherman on an evening tide and under darkness.

Maggie cried as she hugged me the following day, kissing me on my cheek, and speaking ever so softly in my ear, "I will miss you, Will, and please don't forget me." She turned abruptly, entering the farmhouse.

Mr. Tracy was waiting for me on the seat of the wagon and as I climbed on board, he simply said, "Let's get on with it," as he gave the team a slap on their backs with the reins. Not much was said between us at the beginning of the ride. We headed east by north, and it took most of the two days' travel to reach the small fishing town of Port Washington. We encountered several British checkpoints along the way. We were allowed to pass thanks to the load of potatoes and corn we were hauling. As Mr. Tracy put it at each checkpoint, "For his majesty's servants out the island." It was long known that the vast majority of the residents in the scattered towns along the north shore of Long Island, held persuasion to the Crown. Several bushels were lost to British soldiers taking their price for our passing, as was the usual custom. Mr. Tracy didn't mind much as these crops were left over from the fall's harvest, and were not worth much this late in the spring season.

As we approached the town of my departure, Mr. Tracy became more talkative, providing me with more details about the man I would be sailing with.

"Will," he began, "the man to whom I will entrust you is a lifelong friend of mine. I first met him years ago during the French and Indian War up the Connecticut River at a small outpost called Fort Number Four. He is from a fine family from the Hartford area, and has been sailing these waters, on and off now for twenty years. His name is Master Ashbel Fox, and a fine seaman and sailor he is. Once you are on his boat, do as he says, and don't ask many questions, as it would be best to speak only when spoken to. He will give you the particulars of your departure from his boat once you are to sea."

I thought to myself as Mr. Tracy concluded, that he had never mentioned to me before, during the months I had been at his house that he had fought in the French and Indian War.

By now we were well into the small fishing town, and I was considering in my mind all that Mr. Tracy had related to me. The name of the man who was to sail me across the sound to Connecticut sounded so familiar, yet I could not place it. I mulled it over in my mind trying to recall how I knew this name.

Finally, I said, "I didn't know you fought in the French and Indian War."

"The heart of many a man hides the knowledge of a lifetime of struggles, lad," he replied.

"My Da fought in that war," I returned.

"This is a conversation for another time, Will," Mr. Tracy stated, "as we have arrived at our destination."

Looking about, I discovered that we had pulled up at a wharf that docked twenty small fishing vessels.

We stepped down from the wagon, and Mr. Tracy immediately began to walk down the wharf, as if he had been here a hundred times before. Most of the fishing vessels were unattended, and those that were occupied held men who were tending nets or securing rigging and rope.

About halfway down the pier, Mr. Tracy stopped abruptly, and I stared down into a boat, which was occupied by one man. The man in the boat had his back to us, as he was also engaged in tending his nets. He wore trousers, a shirt and an overcoat. On his head was a cap, similar to those worn by seamen who were accustomed to the changeable weather on the sea.

Clearing his throat, Mr. Tracy stated rather loudly to the man, "Master Fox is this boat seaworthy?"

Turning and looking up at us on the pier, Mr. Fox stood, offering his hand to Mr. Tracy, to assist him in disembarking the boat. Once on the pier, the master of the boat grabbed Mr. Tracy by the arms, giving him a genuine hug as pleasantries were exchanged between the two friends.

Finally, turning to me, Mr. Tracy stated matter-of-factly, "This is the young man of whom I wrote you, who wishes to go to sea, to learn your trade."

"Ashbel Fox, this is my nephew, Will," Mr. Tracy stated, as he presented me.

As Master Fox looked at me, his face became a picture of puzzlement, as he stared at me in wonderment. Nothing was said for several moments as we just looked at each other, struggling to recall how we knew each other.

Finally, Master Fox stated as he pointed a shaky crooked finger at me, "The Connecticut River, it was seventy-three, no, seventy-two," he stated as he continued, "your pa and you saved us from an Indian ambush."

"I thought I knew your name!" I replied, "When Mr. Tracy mentioned your name a few minutes ago."

As I stepped toward Master Fox, he gave me a big bear hug, slapping me on my back. Looking to Mr. Tracy he stated, "Have I got a story to tell you, Master Tracy, the next time I see you. Of how this young lad, and his family saved me and mine from certain death back in seventy-two. But that's for another day, as I want to be off before any British patrols come around," he added, and he began hurriedly to make preparations to depart.

I turned, as Master Fox returned to his boat to shove off, to say my farewell to Master Tracy.

I held out my hand, and as he took it, he stated, "Will, our paths must part ways here. I pray that it will only be for a short time. My Maggie has developed a warm place for you in her heart and I fear that it will break if she never sees you again. And, and this old man loves you as a son, and hopes that one day soon you will grace our door with your presence."

Mr. Tracy shook my hand warmly, and as he gave me a hug. "Be off with you now, lad, as Mr. Fox is prompt with his evening sail."

I turned and entered the boat. I looked to see Mr. Tracy had already regained the seat of the wagon, slapping the team with the reins as he yelled, "Get on," turning them for home. I sat in the middle of the boat as Mr. Fox shoved off. With an offshore breeze, we were under sail quickly and away from the shore. The boat was a fine craft of twenty feet. She drew a draft of at most of a foot or two, and could easily sail into any small inlet along the coast of Long Island or Connecticut. She had one mast, with one sail that was about thirty square feet. It was more than enough sail to propel her at a smart pace. I said nothing as we sailed out into the evening mist and setting sun.

We sailed all that night and I dozed off several times. As the morning sun began to lighten the eastern sky, Mr. Fox turned his little fishing vessel into an inlet.

"Where are we?" I asked as barely a word had been spoken between us all night.

"We are several miles to the east of Crane Neck Point, in an inlet that only a handful of trusted men know of, that is navigable to only vessels such as ours, and certainly is impossible for any British ships to enter," Mr. Fox replied.

Once in the inlet, the small harbor opened up to the east for about a mile, being dotted with several small islands. A sandy bluff ten feet in height, to the seaside obscured our presence from any passing vessel. To further hide our presence, Mr. Fox sailed to the south side of the largest of the islands in the inlet, anchoring on the south of it.

Any passing vessel could glass the inlet from the sea, and never be alerted to our presence. Once the sail and tackle were secure, Mr. Fox produced two oars, and with each of us pulling on one, we rowed until the small fishing vessel's bow nuzzled up on a sandy beach on the island. That Mr. Fox had been here before was never in doubt as once we were on the beach, he pointed to a small cabin hidden in the tree line. The only furniture in the cabin was three small beds, which were large enough for several men to sleep in comfortably, a table and two chairs. On the wall opposite the door, was a fireplace and chimney that would be used for cooking, or warmth, if needed. Just outside the cabin were the remains of a fire pit that showed that it had been used many times.

"Make yourself at home, Will," Mr. Fox welcomed, as he walked to the boat, returning with a satchel containing some smoked meat. Mr. Fox broke the meat up and, placing it in a pot, secured it in the fireplace and started a fire. A small stew for our meal seemed just the right thing for me, as I had not eaten but once in twenty-four hours.

As we sat down to eat, a prayer was said and the stew consumed. During the meal, Mr. Fox remarked, "I believe that we got away undetected, Master Will."

"Got away undetected?" I questioned.

"There were as many men loyal to the Crown in the port we sailed from as not," he revealed. "That we were under observation is without doubt," he stated. "That is why Mr. Tracy referred to you as his nephew, while not mentioning your surname. Any open ears that might hear the name, Will Waterman, American soldier and privateer, escaped from the prison ship *Jersey*, and reporting it to the authorities, would receive a fine reward for your recapture."

"You seem to know a great deal about me since our encounter back in 72'," I replied.

"If all that Mr. Tracy has written to me about you is true, then I am indebted to you, for the service and sacrifice you have given to our young nation and I count it an honor to assist you in returning home. As for me and my son, well we and others have silently been doing service for the cause, transporting such patriots as you safely home, while passing information to a network of spies, up and down the Connecticut and Long Island coasts. We will sail with the evening off shore breeze for the Connecticut coast, where my son, Ashbel the junior, will provide you a mount, to further assist you in your journey home. I know for certain that he will be as surprised as I was to see you again, Will," he concluded.

With our meal over, exhaustion overtook me and I lay down on one of the beds in the cabin, and although it was just a wood bed without any straw or hay for padding, I was fast asleep. I was awakened with a nudge to my shoulder to find Mr. Fox standing over me.

"Time to sail, Master Will," he said as he turned to walk outside. I followed as I rubbed my eyes to gain my senses. As I stumbled outside I found that it was late afternoon, with the sun well on its way to setting. We were underway quickly, and the small fishing vessel made good speed toward the outlet and the Long Island sound, just as the sun was setting.

There were no vessels to be seen in the evening twilight, as we slipped silently into the darkness. We sailed east by northeast most of the night and then, an hour before the sun began to once again gray the eastern sky, we sailed due north. Shortly after sunrise we sighted land.

"Where are we, sir?" I inquired.

"We are, if I'm any type of seaman, within sight of New London, Connecticut, and the mouth of the Thames River," Mr. Fox calculated. "Are you not from Norwich, Connecticut, being twenty miles up this very river?" he asked.

"That I am," I said as the thought of returning home, made my heart pound in my chest, and my stomach became unsettled. So many thoughts began to run through my mind, as I had only been home for short periods of time over the last six years, and I had not been home for over a year now, since I sailed from Providence with my uncle during March of the previous year.

"Once we are to shore, my son Ashbel, who already has secured you a mount, will assist in whatever way he may with advancing you toward your destination," Mr. Fox assured.

"Did your son serve in the war?" I asked abruptly, as Mr. Fox's comment had brought me back to the moment.

"He has served several times as armorer to the Continental army, in Colonel David Mosley's Regiment. He has seen none of the service, or hardship you have been through though, God be praised," Mr. Fox declared.

"Once you are ashore," Mr. Fox advised, "and young Ashbel has met you, be off quickly, as there are many Tories in New London, also."

We were smartly docked in New London, and departing the boat we found young Ashbel Fox, just down from the dock standing with two mounts. He looked much older to me than I remembered him from back in '72, but that was to be expected. He was now a fine looking young man of six feet, with shoulder length black hair and dark eyes. Looking about quickly, he spoke in a hushed tone to his father who looked about suspiciously.

Then, looking to me, Mr. Fox stated as he pulled me aside, "There seems to be treachery afoot, as it seems that the Tories know someone is to be delivered here today."

"But how could they?" I asked, searching the docks and surrounding buildings for anyone watching us.

"The enemy has many spies, perhaps even more than we do," Mr. Fox replied. "To your mounts," Mr. Fox earnestly stated, "it may yet not be too late."

Young Ashbel, who was not much younger than me, mounted immediately, as I followed him out of the small New England town of New London. We rode quickly, and as we crested the last hill outside of town, Ashbel hesitated to look behind us to see if anyone followed. Just then, we saw several mounted men departing town who appeared to be on a mission.

We spurred our mounts and were away. Another mile down the road, Ashbel leaned over as we slowed to a canter and shouted, "Around the next bend is a trail that will take you back down to the river. Follow the trail another mile. There is a crossing at a large island in the river. I'll continue on and lead our pursuers away!"

I stretched out my hand as we slowed to a trot and stated, "If you are ever in Norwich, Ashbel Fox, look me up, as I am indebted to you and your father."

We were now near the place where the trail split off into the woods, leading down to the river. As we parted ways, Ashbel shouted, "As we are indebted to you and yours for saving our lives so many years ago."

I slipped into the woods and onto the hidden trail, making my way the mile to where the trail entered the river at the crossing. Here, I stopped and listened for several minutes to see if I was followed. With no indication that I was, I eased my mount into the water and slowly crossed. I mulled over in my mind what Ashbel had said as we parted, and thought to myself, he had remembered me from all those years ago after all. Once across the river, I went up the east side of the Thames River and made my way slowly towards Norwich, and home.

EPILOGUE

"Return to the Green Mountains"

I entered Norwich late in the afternoon. It was true that hostilities for the most part had ceased in much of the Americas, but as I entered Norwich, I found a place that in no way indicated that it was a town that had been at war, or had sent many of her sons off to fight. Many of these same men, who had gone off to war to fight, including my friend Eli, never returned home. There were many new faces in town, much the same as there had been the last time I was home. Most were new immigrant families, migrating out of Boston or Providence. As I slowly approached, I led my horse through town, and past the Gallagher house, which seemed eerily silent. The realization that Diane was, in fact, now married, and living in Boston hit me hard. I could only continue on toward home with an ache in my heart and pain in the pit of my stomach.

All was as I thought it might be when I arrived home. Much had changed and the war was now so irrelevant to this area of New England, that my coming was hardly noted by most of the residents of Norwich. The only ones who actually took the time to come see me were the men from my unit during the war. Of course, Samuel Fuller and William Bradford greeted me warmly, inquiring as to what had happened since I sailed on the *Whisperer*. When I told them all of the details of the capture and sinking of the ship, followed by my eventual imprisonment on the *Jersey*, in New York Harbor, they expressed their amazement that I was alive. They also had long ago moved on with their lives, as they were looking to marry and start their own farms.

Da and Mother had moved out of the farmhouse, purchasing the Fowler house just down the road. The Fowlers, like many families, had moved west with the frontier in New York colony. It was believed that they moved above the New York Highlands to lands sold by the Indians, as part of the Fort Stanwix Treaty. My brother John had married while I was hiding on Long Island at the Tracy farm, and was running the family farm. Da still came to the farm almost every day to help John with the work. Rachel, just seventeen, was still being courted by young John Bradford, himself only twenty, and it was presumed by all parties that they would marry within the year.

Da pulled me aside shortly after I arrived home as we were working in the fields, and said he needed to talk to me.

"Will," he began, "I know that you've sacrificed and suffered greatly these past six years fighting in the war. John has set himself up pretty well with the farm and all. It is believed Rachel, in all likelihood, will be married by the New Year. Your mother and I are set in our new house, with a few pounds set aside, and should do well as long as the farm produces every year."

"I don't want your money, Da," I stated, as he hesitated.

Raising his hand and shaking his head to indicate I didn't understand, Da continued, "That's not what I'm thinking, Will," he said. "Do ye remember before you sailed with Jeremiah, I had a conversation with him below deck, while you were preparing to sail?" he asked.

"I do," I replied.

"I wanted assurances from your uncle that if things went badly for you on the ship, with no prize money to be gained during the voyage, that you wouldn't be left with nothing to start over with when you returned. Jeremiah told me that the old man at the livery, a Mr....," Da hesitated to find the man's name in his memory.

"Mr. Thomas," I stated, reminding him of the livery stable owner's name.

"Yes, Master Thomas," Da repeated, recalling the man's name. "Jeremiah had the foresight to leave with Mr. Thomas, a rather large portion of his prize money from raiding British commerce," Da stated. "When we received your post last winter that you had been captured and imprisoned in New York Harbor, with all lost on the *Whisperer*, including Jeremiah, when she was sunk, I traveled to Providence, informing Master Thomas of this unfortunate news. Master Thomas, after he was paid off what was owed him by Jeremiah, with a little extra added in for his troubles, turned over to me a sum of five hundred and fifty pounds."

"Five hundred and fifty pounds," I said under my breath, not believing my uncle could have owned such a large sum.

"Yes, Will, and most of it belongs to you," Da replied.

Looking at him with disbelief as to what he was saying, I didn't know how to reply.

"I took thirty pounds, to purchase the house your mother and I now live in," Da stated. "I took another thirty pounds, setting it aside for Rachel's dowry when she marries, as she and young Mr. Bradford will need something to help get them started. I gave fifty pounds to John to secure his start and future with the farm, in the event he has a crop failure or other unforeseen problems in the future," Da stated. "That leaves you with four hundred forty pounds with which to start your new life, Will," he concluded as he looked at me.

I didn't know what to say as tears of joy, intermingled with tears of six years of suffering, hardship, and sacrifice ran down my face. Da grabbed me by my shoulders to hug me, as I fell to my knees with my Da, crying like a baby. We remained there, both of us shedding tears of joy and, of suffering for what seemed to be an hour. Finally, as I could hear John approaching the far side of the field with a team, I began to pull myself together as we stood to our feet. We wiped our eyes, hugging each other once again.

"Only those who have taken your path, truly know the cost paid by you, son, along with countless others, to secure us the freedom we now have as a new country," Da stated. "I pray to our God, Jehovah, that cost was not too great, and that we have not, in the end, replaced one oppressive, tyrannical government, with another," Da concluded as we turned to leave the field and return home.

Over the next few weeks and months, I took a portion of the new found wealth I now had and paid off any remaining family debt for Da and mother. I then rode to Hartford, Connecticut, where in the land office I purchased a rather large portion, three hundred fifty acres of pristine land in a valley in the Green Mountains. This was the same land where Da and I, along with Eli and Mr. Bingham, as well as other families from Norwich, had hunted years earlier during more settled times. This was a place where we all had shared happier times.

I then took liberty of the farm, riding to New London, to secure passage on a boat that was sailing the sound of Long Island. I rode east to the Tracy farm, where I found Master Tracy and Maggie. I told them of my new found wealth, and after dinner that night, in the presence of Mr. Tracy, while he smoked his pipe by the fireplace, with his Bible in hand, I got on my knee, asking Maggie to marry me.

“Oh, Will, yes, a thousand times, yes!” she responded as tears streamed down her face.

As I stood to my feet, hugging Maggie, I looked to Mr. Tracy, who too, was wiping a tear from his face as he sat by the fire. Master Tracy knew of a couple of new immigrant families from the British Isles, who had shown interest in purchasing his farm. Over the next couple of weeks, arrangements for the sale were drawn up and quickly finalized. With all of their belongings loaded into their wagon, we headed for Norwich.

Maggie and I were married later that fall, as we spent most of the season trying to complete a log home on our land in the Green Mountains before winter set in. The following spring, along with Maggie’s father, we moved in, and began clearing the land.

Late in 1783, as a fresh blanket of snow cover the land, word reached us that the treaty ending the war had been signed. We celebrated Christmas, along with the New Year knowing the war was finally over. Maggie and I returned to Norwich at least once a year to see my family and old friends. Whenever there, I would ride into town and invariably would see men with whom I had fought. Regularly, I would see Samuel Fuller and William Bradford. One year, I found both Colonel Durkee and Captain Fitch, now advanced in years, at Durkee’s Tavern. Both were successful farmers and businessmen, and we would reminisce about our days during the war. These were always good times, as the bond that held us together, along with the memories we shared would forever cement our lives and friendships.

The years passed quickly for us in our new home. A daughter and a son were born to us in 1785 and 1787. Da passed quietly in 1788. Mother was at a loss with him gone, and it wasn’t a year later that she, too, passed. They were both buried in the family plot at the Norwich Cemetery.

My good friend Samuel Fuller moved to my valley in 1789, purchasing one hundred acres of land to farm a half-mile from Maggie and me. What a joy it was to have Samuel and his wife, Abigail, so close to us. Maggie and Abigail grew with time, to be as close friends as Samuel and I. Our children and families would invariably grow up together.

1790 entered with the death of Maggie’s father. The last few years of his life were filled with happiness as we worked the fields together, and he watched his grandchildren grow.

1791 saw some rather startling developments that reminded everyone who fought in the rebellion, of the similarities as to why we sought independence. The Congress, as urged by Alexander Hamilton, to pay down the debt incurred by the states during the rebellion, which was now assumed by the federal government, imposed a tax on distilled spirits and whiskey. The effect on small distillers from the frontier of Pennsylvania to Georgia was bitterly and fiercely opposed. The farmers in these outlying frontier areas considered the tax both unfair and discriminatory, as they, like us, converted our excess grain into liquor. Many small farms, like ours, were greatly affected as the spirits and whiskey were also used as a form of exchange or barter.

Protests were held throughout the states, which was reminiscent of the opposition to the Stamp Act of 1765, before the War of the Rebellion. The reaction in New England remained for the most part subdued, but in western Pennsylvania, as well as other areas in the more southern states, counties engaged in a campaign of harassment of the federal tax collectors.

In 1794, in western Pennsylvania, the civil protests turned to armed rebellion as shots were fired in a small town south of Pittsburgh. As word of the rebellion spread, loosely organized resistance to the tax was seen throughout the frontier. Armed mobs stopped the mail, interrupted court proceedings, and in some instances tarred and feathered federal tax collectors.

George Washington, along with Alexander Hamilton and General Lee, all of Revolutionary War fame, organized an army of twelve thousand men. With it, they sought to make Pennsylvania the testing ground for the new federal authority. Washington and his army marched to western Pennsylvania, and although no shots were fired, the Whiskey Rebellion, as it became known, was crushed with the death of only one person, a man who died accidentally in prison.

As I read the accounts of what happened leading up to the suppressing of the "Whiskey Rebellion," and its end, chills went up my spine as I thought to myself, what had we fought and suffered for all those years during the revolution? How could our new government, led by the very man who led us to victory over the British, now enforce oppressive taxes on the people of these new United States?

I thought of my Da's words so many years earlier as rumors of revolution were being spread throughout the colonies. That they now turned out to be eerily prophetic to me, as he had said, "I pray to our God, Jehovah, that the cost will not too great, and that we have not in the end, replaced one oppressive, tyrannical government, with another."

With the rebellion crushed, the years moved on. There were more children for Maggie and me, seven in all. 1799 saw the death of George Washington. Alexander Hamilton was killed in 1805 in a duel and 1812 saw another war with England. Being fifty-five and beyond my prime and fighting years, I did not volunteer or engage in any fighting.

In the year 1831, I now find that the winters in my Green Mountains are long and hard for a man of seventy-three years. With all of my papers, credentials, uniforms and arms long ago sunk with the *Whisperer*, nothing remains to mark the passing of that volatile time or to prove all that I have seen and done.

I grew to know and respect such men as General Washington, Lieutenant Colonel Hamilton, Captain McLane and Private Eli Bingham, all men that seemed larger than life to me, and with whom I had the privilege of serving honorably. These were the men who helped change our world and gave birth to a new nation.

So I have taken pen in hand to give an account of the details regarding my service in the late War of the Rebellion, in which I had the privilege to serve.

All that I have penned is a true and accurate account of my service. I first served in the militia from Connecticut, and then secondly in the Connecticut Line of the Continental army, under the command of General George Washington and finally on board the privateer, *Whisperer.*

With my children grown and all living within a day's ride, I now sit on the porch of my log home with Maggie at my side, looking out over my valley in the Green Mountains. A warm wind blows and lightly rustles the leaves on the trees, as a hawk just over the ridge cries out as it soars on the warm air currents.

I think back to the days of my youth and of growing up in Norwich with my family and friends, of the war we fought to have our freedom, from tyrannical rule. Was it, in the end worth the cost? I cannot say yes, or no, to that question any longer, for perhaps that question is better left for future generations to answer, for in the end, only they may be able answer it.

But sitting here with Maggie, even now, I often think of my childhood friend, Eli Bingham and the happy times we shared. I know that he has been with our God all these years, and is in heaven looking down on me and enjoying, as I am, the Green Mountain valley of our youth. And I now know that as I am nearing the end of my time, that I will be with him soon.

The End

BIBLIOGRAPHY

"Ashbel Fox." FamilySearch.Org. http://www.familysearch.org/eng/search/igi/individual_record.asp?recid=500099177410 (03-15-2008).

"Ashbel Fox born in Connecticut in 1755 – Massachusetts Soldiers and Sailors in the War." Ancestry.com. http://search.ancestry.com/cgibin/sse.dll?rank=1&gsfn=ashbel&gsln=fox&gsby=1755&g (03-15-2008).

"American Heritage Magazine – Allan McLane Unknown Hero of the Revolution." American Heritage.Com. http://www.americanheritage.com/articles/magazine/ah1956/56/1956_6_74.shtml (12-07-2007).

"American Prisoners of the Revolution: Names of 8000 Men." USMM.Net. http://www.usmm.net/revdead.html (04-24-2008).

"American Revolution Blog: Morristown: An Equal to Valley Forge." AmericanRevolutionblog.blogspot.com. http://americanrevolutionblog.blogspot.com/2007/11/morristown-equal-tovalley-forge.html (03-24-2008).

"Battle of Harlem Heights – Wikipedia, the free encyclopedia." Wikipedia.Org. http://enwikipedia.org/wiki/battle_of_harlem_heights (06-05-2008).

"Battle of Long Island." Wikipedia. http://en.wikipedia.org/wiki/Battle_of_Long_Island (06-05-2008).

"Battle of Long Island – American Revolution Battle of Long Island." MilitaryHistory.About.Com. http://militaryhistory.about.com/od/americanrevolution/p/longisland.html (06-05-2008).

"Battle of Long Island – Map." Upload.Wikipedia.Org. http://upload.wikipedia.org/wikipedia/commons/6/63/battle-of-long-island-mapsml.jpg (06-05-2008).

"Battle of New York 1776." Multied.Com. http://multied.com/revolt/ny2.html (06-05-2008).

"Battle of Paulus Hook." Wikipedia. http://en.wikipedia.org/wiki/battle_of_paulus_hook (03-20-2008).

"Battle of Rhode Island." Home.Comcast.Net. http://home.comcast.net/~fredra/rhodeisland.html (03-19-2008).

"Battle of Stony Point." Wikipedia. http://en.wikipedia.org/wiki/battle_of_stony_point (03-19-2008).

"Battle of White Plains – Wikipedia, the free encyclopedia." Wikipedia.Org. http://en.wikipedia.org/wiki/battle_of_white_plains (07-10-2008).

"Brigades." ValleyForgeMusterRoll.Org. http://www.valleyforgemusterroll.org/bios.html (12-14-2007).

"Connecticut Revolutionary War Military Lists, 1775-1783." Ancestry.com. http://search.ancestry.com/cgi-bin/sse.dll?rank=1&gsfn+ashbel&gsln=fox&=%2c%2c%2c (03-15-2008).

Cook, Fred. "Allan McLane, Unknown Hero of the Revolution." American Heritage.Com. http://www.americanheritage.com/articles/magazine/ah/1956/6/1956_6_74.shtml. (12-07-2007).

Deal, Cal. "American Troops Mutinied on Federal Hill in 1781." GraphicWitness.Com. http://www.graphicwitness.com/federalhill/mutiny.html (03-24-2008).

DeWan, George. "The Wretched Prison Ships." Newsday.Com. http://www.newsday.com/community/guide/lihistory/ny-historyhs425a,0,6698945.story?c (04-24-2008).

"Division/Brigade File." ValleyForgeMusterRoll.Org. http://www.valleyforgemusterroll.org/xdiv1main.html (12-14-2007).

"Divisions_Main." ValleyForgeMusterRoll.Org. http://www.valleyforgemusterroll.org/divisions_main.html (12-14-2007).

"Dragoon." Wikipedia. http://en.wikipedia.org/wiki/Dragoons (03-19-2008).

"Fort at Number 4." Wikipedia. http://en.wikipedia/org/wiki/fort_at_number_4 (10-04-2008).

"Fort Wentworth." Wikipedia. http://en.wikipedia.org/wiki/Fort_Wentworth (10-04-2008).

"Fourth Connecticut Regiment." MyRevolutionaryWar.Com. http://www.myrevolutionarywar.com/states/ct/ct-04a.html (12-14-2007).

"Hard Winter with Little Food Sows Mutiny among Rebels." ProJo.Com. http://www.projo.com/news/content/projo_20060628_nglive32.18f4538.html (03-24-2008).

Hickman, Kennedy. "American Revolution Battle of White Plains." http://militaryhistory.about.com/od/americanrevolution/p/whiteplains.html (07-10-2008).

Hickman, Kennedy. "American Revolution Winter at Valley Forge." MilitaryHistory.About.Com. http://militaryhistory.about.com/od/balteswars16011800/p/valleyforge.html (11-20-2008).

Higginbotham, Don. "The Continental Army." AmericanRevWar.Homestead.Com. http://americanrevwar.homestead.com/files/contar.html (11-20-2008).

"HMS Jersey (1736)." Wikipedia. http://enwikipedia.org/wiki/hms jersey %28british prison ship%29 (04-24-2009).

James, Terry. "Waterman's Tavern." TerryJamesArt.Com. http://www.terryjamesart.com/images/items/enlarge/267.jpg (03-31-2008).

"Jersey: The British Prison Ship." PublicBookshelf.Com. http://www.publicbookshelf.com/public html/our country vol 2/jerseybri jc.html (03-24-2008).

"Jockey Hollow." Wikipedia. http://en.wikipedia.org/wiki/jockey hollow (03-24-2008).

"Lists of Continental Army Units." Wikipedia. http://en.wikipedia.org/wiki/list of continental army units (03-19-2008).

Lossing, Benson J. "Lossing's Field Book of the Revolution, Vol. 1, Chapter XVIII." Freepages.History.Rootsweb.Com. http://freepages.history. rootsweb.ancestry.com/~wcarr1/Lossing1/Chap18.html (03-09-2008).

Marshall-Dutcher, Joan. "The Winter at Valley Forge." AmericanRevWar.Homestead.Com. http://americanrevwar.homestead.com/files/valley.html (11-20-2008).

"Maryland 400' helped turn the Revolution's early tide." http://www.somednews.com/stories/053106/entefea173542 32080.shtml (05-22-2009).

McDowell, Bart. "The American Revolution." National Geographic Society. Copyright Circa 1967 by the National Geographic Society.

"Morristown National Historic Park." NPS.Gov. http://www.nps.gov/history/history/online books/hh/7/hh/7fl .html (03-24-2008).

"Mud Island Fort – Wikipedia, the free encyclopedia." Wikipedia.Org. http://en.wikipedia.org/wiki/fort Mud Island Fort (10-18-2008).

"National Geographic Magazine/September 2009." Before New York, Rediscovering the Wilderness of 1609. By Peter Miller, Photographs by Robert Clark, Art by Markley Boyer and Philip Straub. (08-25-2009).

"New York Harbor." Celebrating200Years.NOAA.Gov. http://celebrating200years.noaa.gov/new york chars/ny harbor.html (04-24-2008).

"North River (New York-New Jersey." Wikipedia. http://en.wikipedia.org/wiki/north river (new york-new jersey) (03-09-2008).

"Nutten Island – Wikipedia, the free encyclopedia." Wikipedia.Org. http://en.wikipedia.org/wiki/governors island (06-05-2008).

"Olde Mud Island Fort Historical Society | Fort Mifflin." http://www.fortmifflin.com/group/olde-fort-mifflin-historical (10-04-2008).

"Order of Battle, Rhode Island, Aug. 29, 1778." Home.Comcast.Net. http://home.comcast.net/~fredra/orderbofri.html (03-19-2008).

"Park Map Viewer."NPS.Gov. http://www.nps.gov/pwr/customcf/apps/maps/showmap.cfm?alphacode=morr&parkname (03-24-2008).

"Person Query Results." ValleyForgeMusterRoll.Org. http://www.valleyforgemusterroll.org/detailmsaccess.asp?lname=ct03176 (12-14-2008).

"Pirates of the Caribbean Home page." Blindkat.Hegwisch.Net. http://blindkat.hegwisch.net/blindkat/pirates/merc.html (04-15-2008).

"Plan of the City of New York." SI.Umich.edu. http://www.si.umich.edu/spies/map-newyork.html (03-24-2008).

"Privateers and Mariners in the Revolutionary War." USMM.Org. http://www.usmm.org/revolution.html (04-24-2008).

"Quartering Act of 1774." http://www.ushistory.org/declaration/related/q74.html (03-07-2009).

"Rediscovering George Washington – Revolutionary War." PBS.Org. http://www.pbs.org/georgewashington/timeline/revolutionary_war.html (03-24-2008).

Reno, Linda. "Maryland 400 helped turn Revolution's early tide." SondNews.Com. Wednesday, May 31, 2006, 1. http://www.sondnews. com/stories/053106/entefea173542_32080.shtml (06-05-2008).

"Rogers' Rangers." Wikipedia. http://en.wikipedia.org/wiki/roger%27_rangers (10-04-2008).

"Schooner." Wikipedia. http://en.wikipedia.org/wiki/schooner (04-15-2008).

"Second Continental Light Dragoons." Answers.Com. http://www.answers.com/topic/2nd-continental-light-dragoons (03-19-2008).

"Second New Hampshire Regiment." Wikipedia.Org. http://en.wikipedia.org/wiki/2nd_new_hampshire_regiment (03-19-2008).

"Ship Specs." Washburn.k12.wi.us. http://www.washburn.k12.wi.us/denissullivanweb/ships%20specs/shipspecs.html (04-15-2008).

"Siege of Boston, 1775-1776." http://www.myrevolutionarywar.com/images/battles-maps/m750517.jpg (05-22-2009).

"St. Francis Raid – Wikipedia, the free encyclopedia." Wikipedia.org. http://en.wikipedia.org/wiki/St._Francis_Raid (08-25-2009).

Symonds, Craig L., Cartography by William J. Clipson, "A Battlefield Atlas of the American Revolution." Copyright circa 1986 by the Nautical & Aviation Publishing Company of America, Inc.

"The American Revolution in the Hudson Valley." HVNET.Com. http://www.hvnet.com (09-15-2008).

"The American Revolution – The Making of America and Her Independence." AmericanRevolution.com. http://www.americanrevolution.com/his_timeline.html (03-24-2008).

"The Battle/Siege of Boston." MyRevolutionaryWar.Com. http://www.myrevolutionarywar.com/battle/750517.html (04-25-2008).

"The Battle of Germantown." BritishBattles.Com. http://www.britishbattles.com/geramntown.html (09-30-2008).

"The Battle of White Plains – American Revolution." BritishBattles.Com. http://www.britishbattles.com/white-plains.html (07-10-2008).

"The Battle of White Plains." SonoftheSouth.Net. http://www.sonofthesouth.net/revolutionary-war/battle/white-plains.html (07-10-2008).

"The History Place – An Unlikely Victory 1777-1783." HistoryPlace.Com. http://www.historyplace.com/unitedstates/revolution/revwar-77.html (03-24-2008).

"The Maryland 400|Maryland Society Sons of the American Revolution." http://www.marylandsar.org/maryland_400 (05-22-2009).

"The Old Jersey" Prison Ship, 1782." Freepages.Genealogy.rootsbweb.ancestry.com. http://freepages.genealogy.rootsweb.ancestry.com/~anneryan/jerseyprisonship.jpg (04-24-2008).

"The Scarlet Standard #6 – Col. John Durkee, Norwichtown's Forgotten Hero." ConnecticutSar.Org. http://www.connecticutsar.org/articles/scarlet_no6.html (10-04-2008).

"Uniforms of the American Revolution-Fourth Connecticut Regiment of Infantry." Srcalifornia.com. http://www.srcalifornia.com/uniforms/p5.html (12-07-2007).

"United States Rangers." Wikipedia. http://en.wikipedia.org/wiki/United_States_Army_Rangers (10-04-2008).

"Untitled Document." NPS.Gov. http://www.nps.gov/archive/morr/morristown_primer.html (03-24-2008).

"Valley Forge Map." Reisenett.No. http://www.reisenett.no/map_collection/national_parks/valley_forge_map.jpg (11-20-2008).

"Valley Forge National Historical Park – Historical Park – History & Culture."
NPS.Gov. http://www.nps.gov/vafo/historyculture/index.html (11-20-2008).

"Weapons of the American Revolution-Artillery." American Revolution.Org-Artillery. http://www.americanrevolution.org/artillery.html (04-10-2008).

"Whiskey Rebellion." Wikipedia. http://en.wikipedia.or/wiki/whiskey_rebellion (06-24-2008).

"Why a Schooner." Jakatan.Com. http://jakatan.com/jakatan_003.html (04-15-2008).

"William Waterman." National Archives. National Archives and Records Administration, Textual Reference Branch (NWDT1), 7th and Pennsylvania Avenue, NW, Washington, DC 20408 (09-03-1999).

"Yorktown Battlefield – Brigadier General Moses Hazen." NPS.Gov. http://www.nps.gov/york/historyculture/hazenbio.html (03-19-2008).

Zinn, Howard. "A Campaign without Class." ThirdWorldTraveler.com. http://thirdworldtraveler.com/Zinn/Campaignwithoutclass.html (03-24-2008).